*Fei Xiaotong and
Sociology in Revolutionary China*

HARVARD EAST ASIAN MONOGRAPHS
98

Fei Xiaotong talking with foreign visitors, Central Institute of Nationalities, Peking, 1975. Photograph courtesy of Larry J. Shaw, California State University, San Diego.

FEI XIAOTONG
and Sociology
in Revolutionary China

R. DAVID ARKUSH

Published by COUNCIL ON EAST ASIAN STUDIES, HARVARD UNIVERSITY and distributed by HARVARD UNIVERSITY PRESS, Cambridge (Massachusetts) and London   1981

© Copyright 1981 by the President and Fellows of Harvard College

The Council on East Asian Studies at Harvard University publishes a monograph series and, through the Fairbank Center for East Asian Research and the Japan Institute, administers research projects designed to further scholarly understanding of China, Japan, Korea, Vietnam, Inner Asia, and adjacent areas.

Library of Congress Cataloging in Publication Data

Arkush, R. David, 1940–
Fei Xiaotong and sociology in revolutionary China.
(Harvard East Asian monographs; 98)
Bibliography: p.
Includes index.
1. Fei, Hsiao-t'ung. 2. Sociologists—China—Biography.
I. Title. II. Series.
HM22.C62F4329   301'.092'4 [B]   81–1801
ISBN 0-674-29815-2   AACR2

To the memory of my parents, Ralph Montgomery Arkush (1887–1965) and Inez Ferguson Arkush (1907–1972)

Contents

PREFACE   xi

1   FAMILY BACKGROUND AND EARLY SCHOOLING   1

     Family and Early Years in Wujiang and Suzhou   *2*
     Missionary Schools: Suzhou and Yanjing   *7*
     Fei Xiaotong as a Man   *14*

2   EDUCATION IN SOCIOLOGY AND ANTHROPOLOGY   23

     Sociology at Yanjing   *25*
     Park and Fei's Rejection of Library Research   *31*
     Anthropology at Qinghua: Shirokogoroff   *36*
     London and Malinowski   *40*
     Fei as a Functionalist: Basic Ideas about Society   *46*

3   FIELD STUDIES: GUANGXI, KAIXIANGONG, YUNNAN   57

     Marriage and Field Work in Guangxi, 1935   *60*
     Peasant Life in Kaixiangong, 1936   *68*
     Lu-cun, Yunnan, 1938–1939   *79*
     The Significance of Fei's Community Studies   *85*
     Fei as a Teacher: the Yunnan Research Station, 1939–1946   *97*

4 A CHINESE ANTHROPOLOGIST LOOKS AT THE UNITED
   STATES   105

   Visit to the United States, 1943–1944   *106*
   Changing Perceptions of American Culture   *112*
   Critic of American Policies, 1947–1948   *123*
   Urban Industry   *129*

5 PLAINTIFF FOR THE CHINESE PEASANTS   137

   Fei as a Popular Writer   *138*
   Rural China's Cultural Patterns   *142*
   The Gentry and Social Erosion   *152*
   Reform Proposals: Rural Industrialization   *160*

6 POLITICS, 1945–1948   175

   Kunming, 1945–1946   *176*
   Second Visit to England, 1946–1947   *193*
   Political Ideals: Democracy and Socialism   *198*
   Fei and the Communists Before 1949   *204*

7 THE BOURGEOIS INTELLECTUAL IN THE PEOPLE'S
   REPUBLIC   213

   Early Enthusiasm, 1949–1950   *214*
   National Minorities Work, 1950–1956   *225*

8 THE HUNDRED FLOWERS AND AFTER   239

   Intellectuals and Politics   *242*
   Return to Sociology and Kaixiangong   *249*
   The Anti-Rightist Movement, 1957–1958   *258*
   Epilogue: Return of the Hundred Flowers   *275*
   Postcript, March 1981   *282*

   NOTES   289

ANNOTATED BIBLIOGRAPHY OF THE WORKS OF FEI XIAOTONG   323

A. Books, Pamphlets, and Series of Five or More Articles   *325*
B. Articles in Chinese   *335*
C. Articles in English and Unpublished Materials   *361*

GLOSSARY   367

INDEX   377

Preface

Fei Xiaotong (sometimes written Fei Hsiao-tung*) can be thought of as playing three different kinds of roles in modern Chinese intellectual history. He was, first of all, a social scientist, indeed China's most prominent sociologist and anthropologist. His Chinese village field studies—among the earliest anthropological research on a civilized society—are important sources of information on the prerevolutionary Chinese peasantry; they and others of his works which have appeared in English are well known in the West to both anthropologists and students of China.[1] Then, he was what might be called a political journalist, publishing a dozen or more books and hundreds of magazine and newspaper articles on a wide range of topics of current interest. Particularly in the 1940s, at a critical moment in Chinese history, he was a popular and widely read essayist who influenced public opinion on issues of national concern. Finally, he also served as a cultural intermediary between China and the West (primarily the United States and England), traveling between them, writing about China in English and about the West in Chinese, making translations both ways, and, in general, explaining each culture to the other.

None of these activities—social science, journalism, cultural

---

*It is Fei Hsiao-t'ung in the older Wade-Giles system of romanization. In the Pinyin spelling used in this book, *x* stands for a sound akin to English "sh," *q* is like "ch," *zh* like "j," *c* like "ts," and *z* like "dz"; the *i* is silent in *zi, ci, si, zhi, chi, shi,* and *ri*.

exchange—had been important in China before the twentieth century. Though the Chinese had always been concerned with society—indeed, that vast body of writings from different ages that we call "Confucianism" was probably more than anything else concerned with improving the social order—the consciously "scientific" scholarly disciplines devoted to investigating and generalizing about society are modern innovations in China as in the west. Then, educated people have for centuries written and published books in China (where printing was, after all, invented), but the periodical press dates only from the foreign-dominated treaty ports of the late nineteenth century. Finally, Chinese have felt no great need for explaining cultures one to another (except perhaps for a while, centuries ago, when Buddhism first came from India) until they began to take Western culture seriously in the years around 1900.

The context for Fei's activities was the radically altered intellectual climate of the period of the Republic of China, from 1912 to 1949: the rise of a new intellectual class educated along modern lines, the proliferation of the periodical press and of publishing in the vernacular (as opposed to classical) language, and, above all, an extraordinary openness to Western intellectual influences. These changes had all been stimulated in one way or another by the presence and power of foreigners in China. The unequal treaties of the nineteenth century, secured by force of arms in the opium and later wars, made tens of thousands of Westerners (and Japanese) a privileged upper class in China, exempt from Chinese law. Governing miniature colonies in the coastal cities, traveling freely in the interior to trade or prosyletize on behalf of their religions, and running businesses, newspapers, hospitals, and schools, they were protected by gunboats which sailed along the coast and up inland waterways and by foreign troops stationed even in the capital city. It was in response to this threat to China's very survival as a nation that Chinese intellectuals, beginning in the 1890s, turned to Western learning in search of the means to strengthen the Chinese nation. China's inability to resist foreign encroachments led to the end of the old civil service examination system in 1905, the abandonment of the old Confucian curriculum on which the examinations had been based, and the beginning of a new educational system. Countless translations from foreign languages were made and published, and a bewildering variety of foreign ideas were introduced to China. Tens of thousands of Chinese went abroad to study, and more took up modern subjects in schools and colleges in China established on Western models and staffed with foreign-trained teachers.

The intellectuals, the educated people, of the Republican period were increasingly products of this modern education. In China's huge, predominantly peasant population they were a privileged elite—in the 1930s, China's higher education system was graduating fewer than 10,000 a year in a nation of 400 or 500 million[2] — and those who had returned from study abroad were the elite of this elite. Many, no doubt, were sons and (something new) daughters of the old Confucian-trained gentry, but quite different in ideas and style of life. They tended to live in modern cities, and to work as teachers, government officials, businessmen, engineers, lawyers, doctors, writers. They were the readers and writers of the new press, which in the first half of the twentieth century mushroomed to such a staggering extent that one is tempted to think of the Republican period as the time of the ten thousand periodicals. A list of Chinese library holdings of magazines published in China between 1903 and 1949 contains no fewer than 19,000 titles, and that does not include the thousands of newspapers.[3]

Fei Xiaotong was very much a Westernized intellectual. He was educated in China in missionary schools and then abroad. He read English, studied Western social science, traveled, had foreign friends and an international reputation, wrote at times for a foreign audience, and in China was considered an expert on Western ways. I had once thought he might be called a "marginal man," a term coined by the American sociologist Robert Park (with whom Fei studied), who wrote that the marginal man

> lives in two worlds, in both of which he is more or less a stranger . . . Inevitably he becomes, relatively to his cultural milieu, the individual with the wider horizon, the keener intelligence, the more detached and

rational viewpoint. The marginal man is always relatively the more civilized human being.⁴

Yet, though he participated in two cultures and was no doubt a more sensitive observer than most, Fei was not on the periphery of Chinese society. Rather he should be thought of as at the heart of its intellectual leadership at a time when this leadership was very foreign-oriented.

Meanwhile, in the countryside, rural poverty and distress seem to have been on the increase, at least in part as a consequence of unprecedented population growth in recent centuries, now exacerbated by bad government, warlordism, overtaxation, corruption, social dislocation, and the decay of old values. Some intellectuals became Communists and eventually found themselves in the countryside organizing peasants for revolution, and a few others engaged in rural reform of one sort or another. Fei studied Chinese peasant villages as a social scientist, and in his more journalistic writings in the 1940s, time of the Japanese invasion and the Civil War, he argued eloquently for proposals to alleviate the worsening rural situation. This led him inevitably towards the realm of politics. In the late 1940s, he came into conflict with the Nationalist Government and, though he was never a Marxist, he began to look to the Communists to bring China good government and leadership in rural reconstruction.

When the revolution came, however, led by Marxist intellectuals and peasants who had finally triumphed after years of bitter rural warfare, it was distrustful of foreign ways (except of course for Marxism), city values, and the elitism of the educated. After a hundred years of unhappy experiences with foreigners, China finally had a government strong enough to bring an end to foreign power, prestige, and influence in China. Urban, Westernized intellectuals, now seen as bourgeois, alienated from the masses, impractical in their bookishness, and selfishly individualistic, were subjected to thought reform. The press, education, and research were stringently controlled by this regime, which considered people's ideas and attitudes of utmost importance for achieving its goals. Social investigation, social theory, and social commentary, in particular, were too politically sensitive to be permitted outside party and government. In 1957, after he had briefly reassumed his old roles of social investigator and publicist during the moment of relaxation known as the Hundred Flowers period, Fei was made one of the principal targets of a vast national Anti-Rightist campaign. Hundreds of articles attacked all that he stood for: social science, independent political journalism, and international communication were thoroughly discredited in China. After that, his public voice was silenced for some two decades.

Now, however, since the late 1970s, Fei has unexpectedly returned to public prominence. He is taking on some of his old roles, first that of cultural intermediary—receiving foreign visitors, traveling abroad, writing in English for foreign consumption—and, more recently, that of leader in the now officially sanctioned attempt to develop some kind of social science in China again. As to his third role, discussing public issues in print, while the future is not clear, the press has already become much livelier than it was a few years ago, and his writing has once more begun to appear in the press. Just how far China should move towards the things Fei represents, however, seems certain to be a difficult issue (or issues, for they are separable) in the years immediately ahead. An understanding of the history of Fei Xiaotong will, I hope, throw light on what is involved in these issues.

Indeed, at a time when China is beginning once again to send large numbers of students abroad and to open up somewhat to foreign influences, the whole question of the success or failure of China's earlier experience with Westernized education takes on new interest. Fei himself thought that one of the reasons for the rural decline of the Republican period had been the leaching away of local leadership to the cities (he called it "social erosion"), in part the effect of modern education. Subsequently, a long study called *Chinese Intellectuals and the West* by Y.C. Wang has developed this argument, adding that Western education in China was harmful because it destroyed the Confucian ethic of social responsibility and replaced it largely with factual knowledge inappropriate to a China that was predominantly rural.

Foreign intellectual influences, Wang wrote, brought about

> the alienation of students from their native culture and surrounding life. There were almost no forces to counteract this tendency; even the strenuous promotion of science and technology served to reinforce it, for such knowledge had no immediate relevance to the Chinese rural scene. Consequently, there was a deep gulf between the higher intellectuals—the foreign-educated and the college graduates—and the mass of the Chinese people...
>
> [These intellectuals formed] an elite unconnected with the life surrounding them and who were not really aware of actual conditions in the country at large.
>
> ... there was a steady weakening of the moral sense and an increasing dedication to professional achievement. While the international standing of Chinese scientists rose perceptibly, their attachment to the masses became increasingly more remote... Thus, scholars became experts in their own fields but paid almost no attention to national needs.[5]

Yet, for all Fei's having made similar criticisms, an examination of his own case, I believe, will show that it was not necessary or inevitable that a Westernized education made one socially unconcerned or useless. Although intellectually Westernized, Fei was not deracinated or alienated from Chinese society; nor had he lost his moral sense. He felt keenly that China was in crisis and that it was the duty of educated people to take responsibility (was there a lingering Confucian sense of social responsibility here?). He was deeply concerned with rural China and with trying to overcome the gap between modern urban intellectuals and the peasant masses, and at a time of national crisis worked urgently to use his Western knowledge to benefit Chinese society. The pages that follow will, I hope, show that he made valuable contributions in all his three roles: as a social scientist pioneering empirical research on Chinese society (and training others to do the same); as a popular writer increasing public awareness of the problems and choices facing his country; and as an intermediary improving understanding between China and the West.

Yet, rather than argue the success of what Fei was trying to do too tendentiously, it has seemed to me more important to present his views and the facts of his life in sufficient detail to give the reader some feeling for this lively and prolific mind in an exciting age. Just as Fei thought Chinese society could be illuminated by microscopic studies of carefully chosen single communities, so too it is my hope that a study of a single influential example like him can contribute to an understanding of what it meant to be a Westernized intellectual at the time of one of the greatest revolutions in human history.

I have accumulated debts of gratitude to a large number of people, which I am now pleased to acknowledge. Chief among them are Benjamin Schwartz and John Fairbank, my principal mentors at Harvard. The Foreign Area Fellowship Program supported a generously long stay in Taiwan and Hong Kong, which included the early stages of research. In Hong Kong, I enjoyed office space and other services at the Universities Service Center and access to the unique clipping files of the Union Research Institute. I learned about Fei Xiaotong's family and early years by talking to several of his relatives, particularly his uncle, the late Yang Xiren of Taibei. A few dozen acquaintances of Fei in different parts of the world, from college friends of his to recent visitors to China, were kind enough to share with me their recollections of various periods of his life from the 1920s to the 1970s; I hope they will excuse me for not listing all their names. Maurice Freedman was most kind and helpful to me in London. Margaret Park Redfield and Wilma C. Fairbank generously let me see their files of correspondence with Fei, which I have made considerable use of. I am indebted to a number of librarians, particularly George Potter and Eugene Wu of the Harvard-Yenching Library. The Department of History and University Library of the University of Iowa helped in various ways. Sophia Lu-tao Kang Wang was, for a period, an ideal research assistant. A University of Iowa Faculty Developmental Assignment supported one semester of uninterrupted work in 1976. I have benefited from criticisms of earlier versions of this book made by John Fairbank, Wilma Fairbank, Paul Greenough, Jerome Grieder, Charles Hayford, Leo Lee,

Andrew Nathan, William Nelson, Don Price, Stephen Vlastos, Ezra Vogel, and James Watson. Debbie Slabaugh typed the whole thing twice, so accurately as to make proofreading unnecessary. Finally, it is my good fortune to be married to someone who not only is trained in a parallel field of Chinese studies but also has experience as a professional editor. Susan Nelson took many hours and days away from her own work to go through this study at various of its stages, and I doubt there is a page which has not been improved by her careful and intelligent suggestions. To all these, named and unnamed, I am grateful.

Kyoto, 1980

A Note on the Form of References Used in the Text This book is based primarily on the writings of Fei Xiaotong, which are cited by means of coded references in parentheses in the text. Five different kinds of abbreviations have been used to refer to different kinds of works, full citations for which will be found in the Bibliography, as follows:

XTZG	a book (or series of articles) in Chinese, referred to by the initials of the Chinese title; in Bibliography A.
Peasant Life	a book in English, indicated by a short title; also in Bibliography A.
1937Ap14	an article in Chinese; the symbol stands for the year, month, and day of publication (in this case April 14, 1937); in Bibliography B.
"Peasantry"	an article (or unpublished manuscript) in English; in Bibliography C.
9/4/46 to MPR	a letter, referred to by date and initials of recipient; in Bibliography C.

ONE

Family Background and Early Schooling

Fei Xiaotong, who is best known for his writings about the Chinese peasantry, was not of peasant background himself. He came from what is called a lower gentry family and was brought up not in a village but in small cities. His father was a school teacher who had studied briefly in Japan. Fei, born in 1910, just a year before the end of the last imperial dynasty and a few years after the abolition of the old examination system had destroyed the incentive for classical studies, was educated mostly in schools and colleges founded by American missionaries, before ultimately going abroad. It was a Western-oriented and non-traditional education.

He would later write about what he called "social erosion," the desertion in modern times of the landowning gentry-scholar elite from the countryside, which he thought drained rural society of its natural leaders. In the early decades of this century, his own parents, in fact, had moved from market town to county seat to Suzhou, and he and his brothers and cousins went on to live in Peking and Shanghai or abroad. Various members of the family moved away from rural China, sold their land, went to cities, studied abroad, adopted Western ideas, and took up modern occupations. In the details of his and his relatives' lives can be glimpsed a process of significance for China's modern history: the transformation of traditional local gentry into urban, Westernized, modern intellectuals, separated from the rural society which is most of China.

FAMILY AND EARLY YEARS IN WUJIANG AND SUZHOU

Just before the Yangzi River, after flowing across all of central China, meets the sea, it bisects Jiangsu province. The part of Jiangsu that is south of the river is a flat land, dotted with lakes and crisscrossed with canals. Much of the area is water, and boats are the chief means of transportation. It is a lush and densely populated region of paddy rice, silk, and fish, for centuries the richest and most commercially developed part of China, and the most culturally developed, too, famous for its scholars and poets and painters. In the late nineteenth century, it became one of the regions most affected by the Western intrusion; with the foreign-dominated metropolis of Shanghai flourishing at the juncture of river and ocean. A few miles west of Shanghai, on the Grand Canal, is the city of Suzhou and just south of Suzhou, next to Lake Tai, Wujiang county.

Fei's forbears[1] were men of education with a sense of being a social elite, though they included no noted writers or high officials.[2] They seem to have been modest landowners of local prominence. One of his maternal uncles thought the Fei family had owned a few hundred *mu* (a *mu* is about a sixth of an acre) of rice land in Wujiang county but had sold all of it by 1900. This would accord with a statement Fei made in the 1950s that "I was born of a landlord family, which declined in the hands of my grandfather" (1951D9).[3] His paternal grandfather, who died in the 1890s well before Fei was born, is said to have been a *shengyuan*, or first civil service degree holder, which would not have entitled him to an official post. He lived in Tongli-zhen, a small market town in Wujiang county, where there were only three or four other educated men, one of whom was his friend Yang Dunyi. After his death, his younger son (Xiaotong's father) was partly brought up in Yang's household and married his daughter.

Yang Dunyi,[4] Fei's maternal grandfather, had a more successful career. In 1885, he passed a special examination given for *shengyuan* every twelve years and became a *bagong,* almost equal to a *juren* and eligible for office. He served from 1890 to 1895 as a very minor official, the sub-director of schools (*xundao*) for Dantu county (Zhenjiang).[5] Later, he worked for the Commercial Press in Shanghai. He wrote a reading primer for primary school students and a set of poems in memory of his wife, and edited a collection of anti-Manchu revolutionary writings published in 1912.[6] He died in 1928 at about seventy, when Xiaotong was eighteen. In a late photograph, he appears a gentle and intelligent man with a long white beard.

The Yangs owned a rice mill and an oil press in Tongli as well as land in the district, which were sold before they moved to Shanghai in about 1905. They seem to have been well off; there were eleven children who were given good educations, and most went on to become professionals. The eldest son would achieve some prominence: Yang Tianji (Qianli) earned the degree of *yougong* in 1902, became a revolutionary journalist in Shanghai, and served in a series of government posts, including that of adviser at the Washington Conference in 1922, and district magistrate of his native Wujiang; he died in Hong Kong in 1958.[7] Another son, Yang Xiren (my source for much information about the family) took an MA at Columbia University and married the daughter of a member of that earliest group who had gone to study in the United States in the 1870s.[8] A third son was an architect in Peking. Another worked for Walt Disney and became an American citizen. One son and several of the daughters were Christians, including the eldest of the Yang children, Xiaotong's mother.

Fei Xiaotong's father, Fei Pu'an, had been born about 1879 and educated partly in the Yang household and partly in modern schools. He passed the examination for *shengyuan* sometime before going to Japan in about 1905 to study for a couple of years, at a time when Chinese were going there by the thousands in quest of the new learning from the West. After returning to China, he moved his family to Wujiang city, where he operated a middle school. His son later wrote admiringly of his efforts to serve his native place, which included a scheme to relieve the population pressure by reclaiming land from Lake Tai (1948Ja1a). At the time of the 1911 Revolution, he and some friends went from Shanghai to liberate Suzhou and then Wujiang, where he was elected chairman of the new county assembly they organized, but declined to serve as first head of the new government.[9] He went on to work for the Jiangsu provincial bureau of education in Nanjing as an inspector of schools, and then taught Chinese in a middle school in Suzhou. All the relatives I have talked to agree that Fei Pu'an had a considerable influence on the children. He was short and stout and very energetic, and is described as optimistic, cheerful, enthusiastic, extroverted, helpful. He is said to have been progressive and open-minded, and easygoing with his children, whom he sometimes taught himself, letting them study what they wanted. He was a friend to his sons rather than an authoritarian father, and this encouraged in them a spirit of independence and self-sufficiency. He was still alive in 1962, aged eighty-four, living in Suzhou, where Fei visited him and wrote of him in a short newspaper piece (1962Mr9), but he had died by 1972.

Pu'an married Yang Niulan (originally Xilun), in about 1900, and in the next decade they had a daughter and four sons, of whom Fei Xiaotong was the youngest. Yang was well educated for a woman of those times, and taught Chinese in a modern school started by her father; later, in Wujiang city, she opened and operated a kindergarten. Under the influence of one of her sisters, and perhaps in connection with J. R. Wilkinson, an American Presbyterian missionary doctor stationed in Suzhou and a friend of her father, she became a Christian. She died of an intestinal ailment in her late forties in 1927, when Xiaotong was sixteen.[10]

Of their children, all four sons went on to leave the region and become actors on a national or international stage, no fewer than three achieving sufficient fame to warrant entries in biographical dictionaries. The eldest, Fei Zhendong, born about 1904, went to college in Shanghai and then, apparently because he had been active in leftist politics, fled overseas. From 1927 to 1948, he lived in southeast Asia, working as a journalist and educator among Chinese communities in Indonesia. In China in the 1950s, he held various posts dealing with Overseas Chinese.[11] The second brother, Fei Qing, born about 1906, studied in Germany and became a professor of law at Peking University. He too held high posts in the 1950s, and was important enough to get a funeral notice in the official newspaper *Renmin ribao* when he died in 1957.[12] Fei Huo, the third, who alone remained obscure, seems to have been a civil engineer, worked for the Nationalist Government or Army during the Japanese War, and died in Shanghai in the 1960s.

Only the sister, Fei Dasheng, remained in the family's homeland. The second eldest, born about 1905, she went to a postprimary sericulture school near Suzhou and then, in the early 1920s, to one in Tokyo. She joined the staff of the Suzhou school (eventually she married the principal, in 1950) and has spent the rest of her life trying to improve silk production in her native area.[13] Her experiences reforming peasant industry greatly influenced Xiaotong, and more will be said about her later.

Fei Xiaotong was born on November 2, 1910, in the county seat of Wujiang, and there he spent the first ten years of his life. It was hardly a city; commerce was not as developed as in the market town of Tongli four miles east, which was a center of rice trade. The population was estimated a few years later at only 10,000 (the county had perhaps half a million); the wall was not two miles in circumference, and there were fields inside.[14] The family lived on a pine-covered hill in a big house that had a court with flowers. They owned a little land with mulberry trees within the city walls, and they used to raise silkworms on the leaves and then sell the cocoons. A cousin remembers going boating with Xiaotong on Lake Tai to see the lotuses and getting caught in a big storm. It was a time of fighting among warlord armies, and once or twice the family had to flee and hide in the countryside. Two parents, five children, the paternal grandmother, and the widow of an uncle made a large and lively household. They were not rich, but they could afford servants and were comfortable enough. Fei Pu'an was working at the time in Nanjing in the provincial department of education, where he may have been a section chief.¹⁵

Xiaotong went to the local public primary school for four years. That he went to school at all made him one of a privileged minority; in the whole district, of his age-mates only seventy-eight boys and thirty-five girls graduated from primary school in 1922.¹⁶ The primary school curriculum, as set by the national government in 1916, included eight to fourteen hours a week of Chinese reading, composition, and calligraphy; four to six hours of arithmetic (including use of the abacus); and two to three hours of ethics (self-cultivation). In addition, there were Chinese history and geography, science, physical education, singing, handicrafts, drawing, and, in the sixth and seventh grades, a foreign language (presumably English).¹⁷ Fei's favorite was a course on the local area, in which he learned the history and lore of familiar places such as a certain pavilion where he and his classmates used to go after school to play. This course made a great impression on him, and he later wrote that it was perhaps because its teacher directed his attention to the local countryside that in the 1930s he went back to his native place for the detailed investigation that became his first book (1948Ja1a:30).¹⁸

When Fei was ten years old, his family left Wujiang and moved to the small city of Suzhou, ten miles north on the Grand Canal (*XTZG*:78). Suzhou is an old place (Marco Polo wrote of it), long famous as a center of culture and for its beautiful women and luxury-loving people. It is a scenic city of picturesque (if smelly) canals, arched stone bridges, and streets too narrow for anything but sedan chairs and donkeys; a city noted for its historical sites, lovely gardens, and teahouses. By 1920, Suzhou had a population of about 300,000 and was beginning to be affected by Western contact. A treaty port opened to foreign trade in 1896, it was connected by steamers with Shanghai, Wuxi, Hangzhou, and elsewhere, and by a railroad built in the first decade of the century with Nanjing and Shanghai, the latter just fifty miles away. The city had electricity, telephones, four movie houses (by 1930), and a foreign population of a couple of hundred, including several dozen American missionaries.¹⁹

In Suzhou, Fei attended the nearby Zhenhua Girls' School for the upper primary grades. The school was run by Wang Jiyu, a Christian who had been graduated from Mount Holyoke in 1916 and then took a BS in botany from the University of Illinois; her sister Wang Jizhao, who also worked in the school, was a 1915 Pomona graduate.[20] Years later Fei wrote of Headmistress Wang's devotion to her students: although with her foreign degrees she could have had a better job in Shanghai, she stayed on, writing on the blackboard with swollen hands on cold Suzhou winter mornings (1946N1). The Wang sisters were friends of Fei's mother and the Yang family—Yang Dunyi had donated his library of old books to the school after he moved from Tongli to Shanghai—which is why Xiaotong was sent to this girls' school. He was not the only boy there apparently,[21] but that he had been "a girl student" would be the source of a good bit of joking and, for a while, he was quite sensitive about it. When his mother died, a few years later, a favorite teacher of his from Zhenhua, who had been one of her friends, came to comfort him at his middle school; but Fei, sixteen and embarrassed to be seen with a girls' school teacher, ran inside without even a good-bye (1946My1).

MISSIONARY SCHOOLS: SUZHOU AND YANJING

The next dozen years Fei spent at educational institutions that had been founded and were to some extent run by American Protestant missionaries. From 1922 to 1928, he attended a middle school attached to Suzhou University ("Soochow" in the old spelling; the Chinese name was Dongwu Daxue), one of the sixteen Christian colleges—thirteen Protestant and three Roman Catholic—in China at that time. He then spent two years at the college itself before transferring to another missionary school, Yanjing University in Peking, which graduated him in 1933. Fei was not sent to a missionary school for religious reasons; neither he nor his father were Christian, and in fact less than half the students at Suzhou were Christian. These schools had originally been founded for religious ends of course but, by the 1920s, their emphasis was on a general education in Western subjects of the sort that had become a means of advancement in China. This, including the stress on English in the curriculum, attracted young people from urban scholarly or commercial backgrounds who were interested in studying abroad later.[22]

Most of the colleges had their own feeder schools, and formed what was in effect a separate educational system, distinct from that of the government. Suzhou University's first middle school, which Fei attended, seems to have been located right on the university campus, which was inside the city walls and looked very much like that of a small American college, with grass and trees, athletic grounds, and Western-style classroom and dormitory buildings.[23] Available data, for 1929-1930, show the middle school's faculty of eighteen to have been all Chinese; in addition a dozen university faculty members taught there part time. To judge from the number of teachers for each subject, the curriculum appears to have stressed written Chinese, English, and mathematics, in that order. Then would come science, history and geography (Chinese and Western), Mandarin, Chinese painting, religion, and physical education.[24] Traditional Confucian texts were certainly read in the Chinese language courses, but, all in all, perhaps more time was spent on modern Western subjects. In the mid-1920s, when Fei was a middle school student, there was doubtless more emphasis on religion, including services and religious classes for which attendance was required.

These religious requirements, and indeed the whole system of foreign-controlled education, came increasingly under attack in the 1920s as a result of a growing Chinese nationalism that must have touched Fei's life at several points. He had been just an eight-year-old primary student at the time of the patriotic and anti-traditional May Fourth Movement in 1919. But, as a middle school pupil in a missionary school at a time of anti-Christian student agitation for the "recovery of educational rights" (1922–1924), he must have heard charges that schools like his were training grounds for the running dogs of capitalism. Patriotic feelings rose again in the May Thirtieth Movement of 1925 in sympathy with labor demonstrators shot by police commanded by British officers in foreign-controlled Shanghai. At Suzhou University there was no student strike, but a group of young Chinese teachers issued a manifesto calling on the Western faculty members to take a strong pro-Chinese stand. During the Nationalists' Northern Expedition, at the time of the March 1927 Nanjing Incident, in which foreigners were attacked and the American vice-president of the missionary University of Nanjing was killed, only a little more than a hundred miles from Suzhou, most foreign missionaries left China, and the foreign staff of Suzhou University fled to the safety of Shanghai. They later returned, only to flee again in the face of student radicalism; eventually the students backed down under administration threats to suspend classes, and the foreign faculty returned for commencement at the end of June, but the school had carried on without them for three months.[25]

There is no evidence that Fei was one of the student activists, though his two eldest brothers were apparently involved in radical politics. In general, student activism tended to be less intense in missionary schools than in government schools, and one of the complaints of the activists was that the Christian school students often remained aloof from student demonstrations. Yet Fei could hardly have been unaffected by the strong nationalism that was in the air at that time, especially among students. Nor could he fail to have been upset by the political chaos in China, which touched him at least twice, in 1924 and in 1925, when nearby fighting between warlord armies caused Suzhou University, and presumably the middle school, to be a month late in opening.

In 1928, Fei had completed his six years of middle school and entered the college. Chartered by the state of Tennessee in 1900, Suzhou University had grown out of schools founded by Southern Methodist missionaries in the late nineteenth century. By the 1920s (the statistics we have are for 1925–1926), it had a faculty of thirty-six, of whom three had PhDs and fifteen MAs, and twenty-two were Chinese, six of whom had studied abroad. There were only 341 students, and classes were small. The students were almost all from Jiangsu, Zhejiang, and Guangdong, three coastal provinces which had most been affected by Western contact. All but 14 percent of the students had come from Christian middle schools, and over a third came from Suzhou University's own three middle schools.[26] Women were first admitted in 1928. The boys lived in dormitories. They wore long gowns and sometimes Western suits.[27]

It is not clear what courses Fei concentrated on; one cousin thinks he was originally enrolled in a pre-med program, but couldn't bear the dissections—this would fit in with a later friend's assertion that Fei had had "several years' training in biology."[28] At any rate, he was a good student; in the spring of his first year he was one of ten students in his class of 127 to make honors, and the next fall was one of six in the class to make highest honors. He began to get interested in girls and would later laugh to think of "my college years standing in the northwest wind outside the gate of the girls' dormitory" (1943F22). Among the other honor students was the girl he is said to have been in love with, Yang Jikang, who was later to marry the essayist Qian Zhongshu, and to write under the name Yang Jiang. Fei anglicized his name as S.T. Vee, presumably reflecting his native Wu dialect, and in a photograph in the Suzhou yearbook—a perfect replica of its American prototype, with its pictures of seniors, faculty, clubs, athletic teams, and so on—he can be recognized, wearing eyeglasses and Western tie and jacket.[29] He was corresponding secretary for this yearbook in his sophomore year (Yang Jikang was also on the board, and one of the faculty advisers was the well-known writer Su Xuelin), and contributed to it his first published piece, a semi-humorous recounting in classical Chinese of experiences attending a Christian college summer school in Shanghai (1930).

After two years at Suzhou University, Fei transferred to Yanjing University in Peking (called Beiping from 1928 to 1949, while the national capital was elsewhere), and began his study of sociology. Yanjing had been formed in 1916 by the merger of Methodist, Congregational, and Presbyterian schools dating from the late 1880s. The campus was (and is—it is now part of Peking University) beautiful: classroom and dormitory buildings in a neo-Chinese style, including a water tower in the form of a pagoda, set around a lake on what had once been the country estate of the notoriously rich eighteenth-century official Ho Shen, five miles or so northwest of the dirt and bustle of the city. The president from 1919 until 1941 was John Leighton Stuart, a Presbyterian minister and one-time teacher of Greek, later American Ambassador to China. He had built the school up in the 1920s by getting rid of the weaker missionary teachers and hiring first-rate young Chinese scholars.[30] By 1930, when Fei came, Yanjing was probably the best of the missionary colleges and on a par with the better government universities, such as Peking University and Qinghua University. Like them, it had less than a thousand students, a faculty-student ratio of around one to four, and a library of about 250,000 volumes.[31]

The patriotic protests against missionary schools in the 1920s had brought government regulations prohibiting compulsory religion courses and services, and requiring that the schools be controlled by Chinese rather than foreigners. The former regulation was more effectively implemented than the latter. By the time Fei was at Yanjing, religion was no longer central to the purpose or life of the college. In 1930, only 37 percent of the students and 53 percent of the faculty were Christians. In effect, the religious courses and services had been replaced by political indoctrination: a required course on "Party Principles" (of the ruling Guomindang), military training, and a Monday morning memorial service for Sun Yat-sen. Control still rested largely in foreign hands, however; Stuart was indispensable, for he was a great fund-raiser, and three-quarters of the budget came from the United States. Student fees paid for less than 20 percent of this expensive, high-quality education.[32]

Yanjing was in many ways very American. The Chinese-looking campus buildings had been designed by a New York architect, and most were named after American donors. A sizeable minority of the faculty were Americans, many of them missionaries whose salaries, paid by mission boards, were higher than those of the Chinese on the faculty. Of the Chinese faculty, most had been

American-educated. English was the language of instruction in many courses, especially in the sciences. Traditional Chinese education had no place for either women or physical exercise; but at Yanjing about 30 percent of the students were women, and athletics were encouraged for both sexes. As in the American colleges Yanjing was modeled on, classes were fifty minutes long, the academic year began in September, and commencement was in June.[33] After four years and a certain number of course credits, two diplomas were conferred, one under authority of the Chinese government, the other authorized by the state of New York.

Yanjing's students came from relatively wealthy and Westernized backgrounds. As at Suzhou, the majority, 74 percent in 1931, were graduates of Christian middle schools, favored by a perferential admissions policy (a good number of graduates went on to become teachers or principals in Christian schools).[34] Yanjing's reputation of being a school for the wealthy must have been partly deserved, for, despite the generous amounts of foreign funding, it was costly to send a son or daughter there; in 1928, tuition and room and board were said to exceed considerably a year's pay for a full-time laborer. A third of the students had financial aid, but mostly in the form of jobs and small loans; there were only twelve scholarships.[35] Geographically, the students tended to come from the more Western-affected littoral rather than from the hinterland. The largest number in 1930 were from faraway Guangdong (23 percent, while inland Sichuan, the most populous province, supplied only 2 percent), followed by Hobei, Fujian, Zhejiang, Jiangsu, and Shandong—the six coastal provinces together accounting for over three-quarters of the student body. Of those who gave their fathers' occupations on a student questionnaire, 38 percent specified commerce and another 9 percent banking, transportation, industry, or engineering; 15 percent were in education, 14 percent in the government (plus 1 percent in the army), 12 percent in medicine, religion, or social work. Most of these were urban occupations requiring some modern education; agriculture, the occupation of the great majority of the Chinese people, was given as the father's occupation by only 11 percent of the Yanjing students, and some of these fathers may have been landlords.[36]

All in all, Yanjing was a tiny island, very different from the surrounding society: a lovely campus, well-equipped laboratories, a good library, athletics, a small number of upper-class Westernized students receiving an excellent education with Western or Western-trained professors. At the same time, the university was pervaded by a spirit of service for the nation, a spirit fed both by Yanjing's Christian social gospel traditions and also by the students' awareness of being an elite, of receiving rare and valuable training in a nation of poverty and social problems.

One form that this spirit of social responsibility took was patriotic activism. In the 1920s students in missionary schools had been on the defensive, under attack by radicals as running dogs of imperialism. But in the 1930s, after Japanese aggression, starting in Manchuria in 1931, had become the object of nationalistic hatred, students in American-run schools could participate in patriotic activities. Yanjing's students were particularly active; they organized demonstrations, went to Inner Mongolia to fight the Japanese, and to the countryside to arouse the peasants. In 1935, the anti-Japanese December Ninth Movement was organized primarily by Yanjing students. These activities, in part dominated by leftists, were in fact largely directed against the Nationalist Government, which refused to take a strong stand against the Japanese.[37] Fei had left Yanjing and Peking by the time of the December Ninth Movement, but earlier, at the time of the Japanese invasion of Manchuria, he and his brother Fei Qing had made a translation of an English sailor's eye-witness account of the 1894 Sino-Japanese War, to which they appended an emotional preface denouncing Chinese cowardice and incompetence in that conflict, and declaring that the only way to achieve peace was to fight bravely for one's country (1932).

On the whole, however, Fei seems not to have become involved in student activities, political, religious, athletic, or other. His senior year roommate at Yanjing, C. K. Yang (Yang Qingkun), went off to fight the Japanese in Inner Mongolia, but not Fei, of whom Yang says (and others who were at Yanjing at the time agree): "In those times he was the most politically inert animal who ever lived." He liked to talk, and spent hours trying out ideas and theories about society on his friends and fellow sociology students like Yang and Lin Yaohua. Most of all, he devoted himself to his studies. As he later put it, he did not worry about the future, but worked hard in every course, studying for the sake of knowledge (1947My3), and taking examinations so seriously that for years he had nightmares about them (*MGRXG:*26).

Urban and foreign-oriented as Fei's education was, however, it was almost all in China. Not until he was twenty-six, had an MA, been married, and done field research in China, did he go abroad for the first time, and then only for two years. He was unlike those hundreds of Chinese—Hu Shi is one—who left China as adolescents to spend many years in college, graduate school, sometimes preceded by preparatory school too, before returning to China, uncomfortable, estranged, occasionally half unable to speak Chinese. Fei was never deracinated in that way, never more at home abroad than in China. Intellectually distant from the traditional culture, he nonetheless never thought of himself as anything other than part of Chinese society.

Fei Xiaotong as a Man

In this background and training we can see the source of many aspects of Fei's mature personality. He was, of course, intellectually Westernized. He could read English easily and did so frequently. His spoken English is accented and ungrammatical, but fluent; his letters to American friends have some awkwardnesses, many of which I have retained in quotations, but are clear and expressive. His marvelously clear and graceful Chinese essays contain an occasional sentence that seems more English than Chinese and foreign phrases like "ivory tower," "vicious circle," or "new wine in old bottles" (though some of his contemporaries were even more prone to this than he). His missionary schooling is revealed in a tendency to use Biblical or Christian language from time to time: "our ancestors in the garden of Eden" (1943Mr20), "which of us dares throw the first stone?" (*SYZD:* 47), "God is giving mankind a serious test" (1945N?), "when I go to Heaven" (12/12/45 to MPR), and so on. Perhaps we should not be surprised to read that, "as for the theatre, up to the present still no one can claim he excels Shakespeare" (1946Jl25:37), but it is startling to be told by someone from China, where grapes are not native and adults abhor milk, that "everyone's idea of paradise is more or less the same: trees [*sic*] full of grapes and rivers flowing with milk" (*XTCJ:* 168).

More significant, I believe that Fei looked for inspiration and ideas not to the Chinese tradition but to modern Western social science. The precise nature of these intellectual influences will be made clearer below, but an indication may be found by a glance at the only one of Fei's works that is heavily footnoted, his 1947 book on the functions of family and kinship patterns in China and elsewhere (*Shengyu zhidu*), which offers an opportunity to see what kinds of things he read, at least on this one topic.

No fewer than forty-three western authors are quoted or referred to (a few in Chinese translation). Five works of Malinowski's are quoted, and his theories and his Trobriand Islanders much discussed. Among other anthropologists, the names Lowie, Firth, W.R.H. Rivers, Kroeber, and Radcliffe-Brown are mentioned frequently and others occasionally, as well as older theorists like Morgan, Maine, Bachofen, Frazer, and Westermarck. A few sociologists are cited, including Giddings, Hobhouse, Park, and T.N. Whitehead (whom he came to know in the United States). Fei reveals that he is conversant with Freud's theories, which Malinowski had tested among primitives. He makes considerable use of Havelock Ellis's book on the *Psychology of Sex,* in his friend Pan Guangdan's Chinese translation, and of some other works on biology. There are passing references to Margaret Sanger, Bertrand Russell, Nietzsche, Schopenhauer, Kant, Leibniz, Darwin, Malthus, Tolstoy (*Anna Karenina* quoted), Turgenev, the Bible, and Aristotle. He is not likely to have know all of these at first hand, but the number of Western books actually quoted is twenty-seven. On the Chinese side, the list is much shorter. There are isolated references to modern social scientists such as Pan Guangdan, Wu Wenzao, Chen Da, Li Ji, Li Anzhe, the philosophers Liang Shuming and Feng Youlan, and writers Ba Jin and Bing Xin. There are occasional mentions of a range of older Chinese legends, novels, poems, and so forth, but only one Chinese work is cited more than once or twice, the eighteenth-century novel *Story of the Stone* (*Dream of the Red Chamber*).

His classical Chinese education I think was not very profound. He must have read a certain amount of old Chinese in his school years, but, in modern and missionary schools several years after the end of the old examination system, this was far short of the rigorous classical training given earlier generations. He did research using historical documents while he was in college but not thereafter. He never wrote classical Chinese after college, and seems only occasionally to have tried his hand at poetry, one pastime of the traditionally educated (*JZS* #5; *RQ&BJ:* 41, 43). His later writings mention Confucius and Lao-zi, an occasional Tang or Song dynasty poem, a few famous historical figures, the familiar traditional novels; only rarely is there any indication of a deeper knowledge of the enormous universe of premodern Chinese culture, although this is also explained by the fact that he was more concerned with making his articles accessible to a wide public than with displaying his erudition. He later wrote that he remembered little of the Chinese history he had studied in school and college, that most of what he knew on the subject was from historical novels he had read surreptitiously as a boy, and that even these he did not read anymore (1945F). One of the few times we find him reading traditional literature after leaving school is in the late 1940s when a perusal of such basics as the *Analects* of Confucius seems to have given him a great sense of discovery. This accords with a recent statement that he learned little Confucianism in school and read the Classics only later (1974My).

Yet, unlike so many early twentieth-century intellectuals, Fei went through no emotional rejection of Chinese culture. He came by his Western learning easily, without having to turn his back on years of earlier schooling in the tradition. That his father had studied in Japan meant that the father and not his sons represented the generation that made the transition from traditional to modern education, and thus Fei Xiaotong was spared the emotional stress experienced by so many others struggling against old-fashioned parents. He was not really of the May Fourth generation, but rather heir to its new culture movement, accepting its anti-traditionalism (and much else, too) naturally and without rancor or turmoil. The issue of Chinese culture versus Western culture, which so exercised a slightly older generation of intellectuals, did not trouble him.

He was capable of a statement like "Chinese tradition is rotten" (1947Je14), sometimes thought of the older scholars as antiquarian fogeys, and could not understand why an American student would want to study Chinese Classics (9/3/45 to MPR:4). At other times, however, he could utter quite kind, in a bland sort of way, words about Confucianism or traditional scholars. He could praise the Confucian spirit of social responsibility (which he saw in his father; 1948Ja1a), or the traditional "scholarly habit of paying attention to local conditions and to human feelings and customs" (1935N15). But mostly he was simply not very interested in the traditional culture. For Fei it was Chinese society of the present that was important.

Sometimes the Chinese tradition seemed to be associated in Fei's mind with childhood memories, pleasant memories to be sure, but far away and of things with which he was no longer concerned. His attitude to Buddhism, for example, is summed up in the following anecdote:

> My relationship with Buddhism began in early childhood. After my grandmother died, there was a monk in every day in front of the death bed . . . chanting sutras and beating time on a wooden fish. When I was the only one in the room, he would stop his chanting and beating to play with me, and as time went on he became very familiar. I was only ten and he seemed like an ordinary person who enjoyed children and eating, and so I treated him as an ordinary person with whom one

could be close. Apart from his clothing, which I didn't particularly like, I didn't see anything peculiar about him. At the time my head was also shaved and as shiny as his. Perhaps it was because this monk seemed so close and ordinary that Buddhism did not stimulate my curiosity. Even today I remain ignorant about this religion and philosophy. Kasyapa, Ananda, Maitreya and so on are unfamiliar names to me. I don't know many Buddhist stories, but there is one which I often recall. (*JZS* 20:4)

He then goes on to recount a Buddhist legend connected with a mountaintop temple in western Yunnan he visited in 1943. It is the only time he ever showed any interest in Buddhism.

His image of the traditional gentry and their old-fashioned lifestyle was also mixed up with agreeable childhood memories, particularly of teahouses of his native Wujiang and Suzhou:

> The town in which I was born, and which I know very well, mainly consists of residences of the gentry, rice stores, pawnshops, tea houses, and private gardens . . . Tea houses, big gardens, and magnificent residences are . . . the paraphernalia of the gentry. From morning until nightfall, the leisured gentlemen gather in the tea houses to amuse themselves in sipping tea, in listening to the storytellers, in talking nonsense, in gambling, and in smoking opium. . . Such towns do not lack their charm. If one is prepared to amuse one's self in an artistic expression of life, there are hundreds of small attractions here that win his admiration. I myself have often missed much of the delicious food of my native town. ("Peasantry":7)

The warm associations of these childhood places have perhaps also been connected with an idealized view of rural peacefulness. He was not really of rural background, but Suzhou and Wujiang were very small cities with gardens and fields inside the walls and countryside close by, and most of the rest of his life has been spent in the suburbs, outside of Kunming during World War II and, for most of the years before and since, on college campuses a few miles from Peking: Yanjing, Qinghua, and, since 1952, the Central Institute of Nationalities. Although cultured, gregarious, and cosmopolitan, Fei did not feel at home in really big cities. He called himself "an unsuccessful city-dweller" (5/17/44 to

MPR), and complained of the confusion of Hong Kong and Shanghai, of the hurry of New York and of loneliness in London (*CFMG:*7). Once in Hong Kong, after ending up in a police station when he could not make himself understood to a rickshaw puller with what he called his Suzhou accent and poor English, he confined himself to his hotel room for several days, looking out the window—a strange imprisonment for an anthropologist (11/11/46 to WCF). He sometimes spoke of yearning for the peacefulness of the countryside, and in the 1940s began to enjoy puttering in a garden, which he found mentally settling. "A happy family, a small garden, a sense of confidence in one's own value, an easy association with neighbors . . . The wise way of living is the same everywhere" (6/16/44 to MPR).

A happy and secure childhood, we may speculate, has had something to do with Fei's cheerful and exuberant personality. Short in stature, slight (until the 1950s when he became rather chubby), prone to asthma, cigarette-smoking, he has liked to talk and joke, and his conversation has always been animated, wide-ranging, and stimulating, full of excitement and enthusiasm. It would seem he has been well-liked and self-confident. Although occasionally subject to fits of depression, he was usually happily active and energetic, at times even impetuous and childlike—he once said he was like Monkey in the novel *Journey to the West* and had not yet learned to "behave like a professor" (11/22/43 to WCF). Intellectually, too, he was exuberant, energetic, and active, carrying on several projects at the same time, finishing things very rapidly, and writing an enormous amount, particularly in the 1940s. In his haste he could be careless and superficial; as a primary school student, he had always been the first to turn in his arithmetic assignment, full of careless errors (1946My1). As a mature scholar, he had no patience for the slow, methodical, painstaking accumulation of data: "I am a man who seeks quick results, impatient, unable to grind away for days and months" (*JZS* 20:4).

Happy and optimistic like his father, he has tended to see the bright side of things, to be an easygoing reformer rather than a crusader against evil ("soft-hearted" he called himself: "Soft-hearted people are willing to see the hopeful side in others" [*CFYL:*81]). Perhaps because he never had to revolt against and do battle with a tyrannical father, he does not seem to have had a strong sense of evil. He has tended to think of the world as basically good rather than as an arena for conflict between good and bad; it is hard to find villains in his writings.

Like most educated Chinese, Fei has never felt attracted to religion. In spite of his upbringing by a Christian mother and his years in missionary schools (he later wrote that all the foreigners he met as a young man were missionaries, so that he was very surprised when he later visited the United States and found people there who didn't go to church [*CFMG:*128]), he was "an irreligious man" (2/9/44 to MPR): "I am not a Christian, and my eyes are not turned to God" (*CFMG:*137). When his Christian sister wrote a newspaper column asserting that China's problem was a lack of religious spirit to motivate people to work unselfishly for the good of society, Fei replied that, yes, social construction and even family cohesion depend on forgetting self-interest in a kind of religious faith, but God and an afterlife were illusions which would sooner or later be dispelled. Much better, he said, was the humanistic Confucian impulse to perfect the objects of the Chinese faith, man and society (1934My16).

For Fei, the meaning of life was to come from a sense of belonging to a group, sharing values and interests, and working for the common good: ". . . the joy of life must be derived from group life . . . through . . . consensus" (2/5/47 to MPR). He has always had a moral concern for the well-being of society, his society, China. Though not traditionally educated, he no doubt inherited from his gentry family a Confucian sense of the social responsibility of the elite, a feeling that those few who have had long years of education have an obligation to look after the welfare of those who labor in the fields. Such a feeling may well have been reinforced by the moral education of his missionary schools. Certainly it was strengthened by the nationalism and sense that China was in crisis which was pervasive among young intellectuals at the time and which surely affected Fei in spite of his holding back from political activities in college. Thus, I believe, it was a moral and nationalistic impulse, a concern for Chinese society and a desire to alleviate the suffering of its people, that lay behind Fei's attraction to sociology. And his study of China's peasantry was, in a sense, an attempt to bridge the gulf that had been opened up between himself and the majority of Chinese by his urban, Westernized education.

TWO

Education in Sociology and Anthropology

> . . . my three esteemed masters, Professors S.M. Shirokogoroff, R.E. Park, and B. Malinowski. From them I inherited most of my ideas.
> —*Earthbound*:xiv

> We learned from books about Chicago gangs and Russian immigrants in America, but we knew very little or nothing about the Chinese gentry in the town and the peasants in the village, because these were not in books.
> —*Earthbound*:viii

It is easy to guess why Fei took up the study of sociology, which was a popular college major in those years. He later wrote that, in the late 1920s, China seemed to be entering a period of stability and reconstruction, and that students were turning away from political enthusiasm to fundamental and practical study of social realities (*Earthbound*:ix). Sociology and anthropology were sciences, from the West, when Western science had great appeal; they were concerned with society at a time when China's social ills were crying for attention. Fei got a solid training in this field. He first studied sociology at Yanjing University, working with American-trained teachers and the eminent Chicago sociologist Robert Park, who was there for a semester. He then took an MA in anthropology at Qinghua University, also in Peking, under the Russian anthropologist S.M. Shirokogoroff. Finally he spent two years at the London School of Economics, studying largely with the great Bronislaw Malinowski.

His training was thus Western, though he was actually in the West for only two years of it, but it must be emphasized that it was in only one of the many diverse strands of Western culture. His Western education was largely in English; he was not directly influenced by French or German or Soviet Russian writers, or by their Japanese interpreters, and when he wrote of the social theories of "Weibo" he meant not Max Weber but Sidney and Beatrice Webb (1933D27). He was not educated in Western literary and classical traditions, as was such a one as Gu Hongming, who loved to quote French and German and Latin. Nor was he much affected by Marxism, though Marxism was popular among more than a few Chinese intellectuals of his generation. His education rather was in an Anglo-American social-scientific tradition which stemmed from Comte and Spencer and emphasized social reform rather than revolution.

Post-World War I social science was in a process of reaction against what were felt to be the errors of its predecessors. Late nineteenth-century sociology and anthropology had been concerned with theories of human evolution and social progress. Comte and Spencer and their followers had, like Marx, created grand theories of how society had changed from its ancient or medieval past to its modern European and American present. The early anthropologists, too, had used what was known about primitive societies to construct unilinear theories of social evolution. They thought all societies sooner or later went through the same series of stages in a single universal pattern of development. This progress was conceived of as, on the whole, for the good; society was in general improving, and the industrialized nations of the nineteenth-century West represented the most advanced stage realized so far. This confidence in human progress was shattered by World War I in Europe, whose terrible destructiveness cast doubt on the notion that society was getting better in any simple or clear-cut way. The post-war generation of social scientists turned away from grand historical generalizations to more careful empirical studies, to patiently gathering data and only cautiously generalizing. Rather than speculating about the past, they concentrated on describing present social reality. Such tendencies in Anglo-American social science widened the gap between it and the Marxist tradition, which was still largely historical and theoretical.

SOCIOLOGY AT YANJING

Chinese scholars ever since Confucius had been interested in society and social problems, and considerable data about society, on local customs and population, for example, were collected in local gazetteers and other works both official and private. Aside from information gathered for use in the administration of government, however, Chinese social thought had tended to be more normative than descriptive, concerned with how people ought to act rather than how things actually were. In Fei's view, a real science of society—a science in the sense of having explanatory power—had never developed, because of this importance attached to the proprieties of human relations; the critical spirit necessary for science would have questioned and threatened these social values (1947O15:8; also 1935N15:37).

The early history of sociology in China is very much a story of foreign influences; the very term which came to be used for "sociology," *shehuixue,* was taken from Japanese. The first decade of the twentieth century saw a few translations of Western and Japanese works, such as Yan Fu's famous rendering of Herbert Spencer's *Study of Sociology.* There were perhaps fifteen such translations in all in the first two decades of the century, and then, in the 1920s and 1930s, over fifty foreign works on sociological subjects were published in Chinese.[1] The teaching of sociology was led by American Protestant missionary colleges. St. John's in Shanghai offered the first courses in 1905, and Shanghai Baptist College established the first sociology department in China in 1913. By 1925-1926, fourteen out of the sixteen Christian colleges offered sociology; government universities offered fewer courses in the subject, and several, including the most prestigious, Peking University, never set up sociology departments at all. At first, instruction was given mainly by American teachers, who were gradually joined by Chinese sociologists trained in the West, beginning with Y. Y. Tsu (Zhu Youyu) who earned a PhD in sociology from Columbia in 1912 (he later became an Episcopal bishop). Chinese sociology was to remain American-oriented. In 1947, of 143 university faculty members teaching sociology in all of China, 71 had studied in the United States, 27 in western Europe, and 12 were Americans.[2]

There was apparently some confusion in the popular mind, or at least among the authorities, in the 1920s between sociology (*shehuixue*) and socialism (*shehui zhuyi*), and there are stories of books being suppressed and scholars harassed and even arrested because of this misunderstanding.[3] This confusion was exacerbated after 1927 by the now anti-Communist Nationalist Government's restrictions on publication, which obliged Marxists (doubtless rendered pensive by the failure of their revolution in 1927) to write, instead of openly revolutionary works, theoretical analyses of Chinese society. Their "new social sciences movement" consisted mostly of disputes on the nature of Chinese society and on Chinese social history, carried on within a Marxist theoretical framework.[4] The titles of the books it produced are indistinguishable from those of academic sociology, and the two are intermixed in bibliographies of the period and surely in many people's minds. But, in fact, the academic sociologists, typically American-trained and often teaching in missionary colleges, had nothing to do with the Marxists and their controversies. Fei Xiaotong, for one, seems to have been unaffected by these leftist writings, to which he never referred except to dismiss the Marxist view of unilinear social change as dogmatic and simplistic (1947O15; *LCNT*: 189-190).

By 1930, there were enough Chinese sociologists to form a Chinese Sociological Society, which held annual meetings and published a quarterly journal called *Shehuixue kan;* about seventy-five original Chinese books on sociological topics were published each decade in the 1920s and 1930s.[5] The quality of these works was not always impressive. As one critic has complained:

> During the earlier periods every beginner began his sociological career by writing an introduction to sociology or anthropology. For a long time "Principles" and "Outlines" based upon fragments of Giddings, Ross or Park flooded the sociological market. One "social anthropologist" wrote as his first work *Introduction to Social Anthropology,* as his second work *Races of Mankind,* and as his third work *History of the Chinese People.*[6]

Professors who had written their PhD theses in American libraries had no experience doing research on Chinese society, and found their teaching loads too heavy to allow for much research anyway.[7] There was little real research on China, and much of that was done by foreigners. John Stewart Burgess of the Y.M.C.A., a Columbia sociology MA (who later founded the Yanjing sociology department), made a modest survey of Peking rickshaw coolies in 1914-1915, and then with Sidney Gamble produced the substantial *Peking: A Social Survey* (1921).[8] Rural studies were done in the 1920s by J.S. Bucklin and D.H. Kulp of Shanghai Baptist College, C.B. Malone and J.B. Taylor, and the agricultural economist John L. Buck at the missionary University of Nanjing. Only a handful of Chinese were publishing studies on Chinese society in the 1920s. Tao Menghe (L.K. Tao), an early London School of Economics graduate who had been involved in the 1914 Y.M.C.A. survey, wrote in the 1920s on Peking household budgets. Pan Guangdan, trained in biology, published a work on the Chinese family system. H.D. Fong (Fang Xianting), D.K. Lieu (Liu Dajun), and others did economic surveys. Qiao Qiming, an associate of Buck's at Nanjing, studied rural problems. Chen Da, a 1923 Columbia PhD in sociology, did research on labor and other subjects. Li Jinghan, who had worked with Gamble on Peking rickshaw pullers in 1924-1925, published in 1929 a slim book of four rural surveys done outside Peking (he went on to work on a large survey of Ding county).[9]

Courses taught by Americans or American-trained Chinese were naturally more apt to deal with American labor legislation than with Chinese villages. Fei later wrote that, at the time he went north to enter Yanjing, "sociology in China was still in its infancy. It contained more vacuous arguing than careful reporting, and evidence for social facts was mostly taken from imported materials" (*WHL*:i). In 1936, he could write of the failure of "American-style" sociology in China: "In the past few decades 'sociology' has made no apparent contribution to understanding or reforming Chinese society" (1936Ag12). It was a failure he was to set out to correct.

For studying American sociology, however, Yanjing was probably a good place. When Fei entered in 1930, its sociology department was the best in China, thanks in large part to generous Rockefeller funding. Yanjing had been founded by liberal, social gospel missionaries who believed that the study of sociology and social problems should be included as part of seminary training, and the department was first organized in the School of Religion, in 1919, by J.S. Burgess, who had close Y.M.C.A. ties.[10] Burgess was succeeded as chairman by Leonard Hsu (Xu Shilian), Stanford BA, 1923 Iowa PhD, who was married to an American and is said to have lectured in English. He was the author of books in English on Confucianism and on Sun Yat-sen, and later left Yanjing to take a position in the Nationalist Government. In 1930, the department had a full-time teaching staff of six or seven, mostly young Chinese, who together with others from outside gave about twenty-five courses a semester, of which a third or a half related to social work. Sociology was, in 1930, the third most popular major, after economics and political science, with seventy-three students, including a few graduate students; from 1928 on, the department graduated ten or twelve bachelors and a couple of masters every year. Its graduates went to work primarily in social and religious organizations or as teachers in middle schools and universities, often after advanced study abroad.[11]

Beginning in 1927, the department published a thick (over 300 pages) annual journal called *Shehuixue jie* (Sociological world), full of articles mostly by Yanjing faculty and students. The articles, which fall into three categories, no doubt give a good idea of what the concerns of the department were at that time. Some, on such topics as Han dynasty social life or Xun-zi's theory of social education, were based on Chinese historical materials. Other articles were summaries of modern Western sociological theories, such as Leonard Hsu's article in Volume 4 on "The Psychological Basis of Social Life," the footnotes to which refer to four Chinese books (two by Sun Yat-sen) and thirty-two works in English. Finally, there were reports of research, generally by questionnaire survey, on topics like rickshaw pullers, crime and prisons, household budgets, student opinions on marriage, and village demographic patterns.

We have some idea of the courses Fei must have taken. He entered as a sophomore, presumably satisfying in some way the requirements for freshman courses in English, Chinese, biology, political science, economics, and "social problems." (There were also requirements in physical education, military training, and Guomindang Party principles.) Then, as a sociology major, he would have had to take courses on the principles of sociology, human origins and cultural evolution, the history of Western social thought, social psychology, contemporary social theories, social research methods, and a number of electives in sociology and other social sciences.[12] The department library received over twenty English language sociological journals, seventy Chinese journals and government report series, and had two thousand books.[13] Fei later remembered terribly heavy reading assignments, and his roommate, C.K. Yang, says that they read mostly in English. He seems to have studied partly under Yang Kaidao (Cato Young), a recent PhD from Michigan State College, who taught research methods and rural sociology. If we are to judge from Yang's books, which are based more on the works of American rural sociologists than field work in China,[14] his courses must have been largely in the vein of American sociological writing.

Fei's principal mentor at Yanjing was Wu Wenzao, husband of the well-known author (and Wellesley graduate) Xie Wanying, who wrote popular poetry and short stories under the pen name Bing Xin. Wu had gone to Dartmouth and then Columbia, where he studied with Giddings, Ogburn, and others, and wrote a library PhD thesis, using British government and missionary publications, on *The Chinese Opium Question in British Opinion and Action* (New York, 1928). He came to Yanjing in 1929, where he taught the required courses on principles of sociology, evolution, and social theory, and also a course on the family, all of which Fei probably took. Wu was only nine years older than Fei, like him from southern Jiangsu province, and the two formed a close bond which was to continue into the 1970s. Wu wrote very little; he was clearly not much of a social researcher, but Fei found him an inspiring teacher. According to Fei's later testimony, because "the grand planner must nurture talent, Professor Wu untiringly spent ten years among young students as if it were a day, for he looked to sociology's coming of age" (*WHL*:i). Wu's few articles were largely introductions to Western social theory with titles like "The Sociological Theories of F.H. Giddings,"[15] and it is reasonable to suppose that from this teacher Fei gained not only a sense of commitment to the development of Chinese sociology but also solid grounding in Western sociological theory.

In 1933, the year he was graduated from Yanjing, Fei began publishing regularly, and from these early articles his familiarity with certain American and English sociologists is clear. He published a translation of an American article summarizing the sociological theories of Franklin Henry Giddings, who had been Wu's teacher at Columbia (1933Jl). He then did a long and rather academic piece comparing Giddings's ideas with those of Robert Park (of whom we shall have more to say in a moment); this article, full of extended translations from English, indicates that Fei had read widely in the original works of both men, and was able to understand the philosophical differences between them (1933D).

Several other such pieces are about human progress and the role of social reform. A translation (1933D27) of the last chapter of the Fabians Sidney and Beatrice Webb's *Methods of Social Study* (1922) emphasized the usefulness of sociology to social reform: "The twentieth century is not, in any civilized country, as was the eighteenth [they had written]; and no small part of the change is due directly to improvements in social institutions which have been, in fact, though often unconsciously so, the outcome of the study of society" (p. 249). Fei also wrote a long two-part summary and analysis of the English sociologist and moral philosopher L.T. Hobhouse's theories of how society develops. Hobhouse used ethnographic data about primitive people for statistical comparisons (here Fei expressed reservations) which he claimed demonstrated progress, though not in a straight line, toward the good, harmonious society. This progress, he said, came from people's purposeful efforts, for human behavior is goal-directed, and thus (this is the point Fei emphasized) Hobhouse rejected Spencer's laissez-faire views and established a theoretical basis for social reform (1934Ag8). In about 1935, Fei published as his first book a translation (*SHBQ*) of *Social Change* (1922) by William Fielding Ogburn, who had been another of Wu Wenzao's teachers at Columbia before going on to a long career at Chicago. Ogburn's thesis was that social change is not, as Spencer and Giddings claimed, caused by human biological evolution, but rather by cultural accumulation, particularly of technology (reflected in the increasing number of patents granted each year in the United States). Progress is largely determined by material culture, he said, but people can and should deliberately influence it to some extent.

PARK AND FEI'S REJECTION OF LIBRARY RESEARCH

Besides Wu, the other great influence on Fei while he was at Yanjing was the eminent American sociologist Robert Ezra Park, who was visiting professor at Yanjing from September to December 1932, in the fall of Fei's senior year. Then sixty-eight years old, he had recently retired from the University of Chicago where he had led that famous sociology department in developing studies of urban communities. He had had a varied career, beginning with over ten years as a newspaper reporter, then studying philosophy at Harvard with William James and sociology in Germany with Georg Simmel and Wilhelm Windelband, and working on race relations in the American south with Booker T. Washington, before going to Chicago at the age of fifty. His *Introduction to the Science of Sociology* (Chicago, 1921), a thousand-page textbook and source book written with his student E.W. Burgess (not Yanjing's Burgess), was widely used for many years in China as well as in the United States. He was also interested in immigrants in the United States, and originated the concept of the "marginal man" who lives in two cultural worlds but is entirely at home in neither, a description that might be thought appropriate for Westernized Chinese intellectuals, but that made no impression on Fei.

Park was an inspiring teacher who stimulated much important research among his students at Chicago. At Yanjing, he taught a course on collective behavior and a seminar on social research. Fei was greatly impressed by his industry and spirit of responsibility in spending hours standing in the library stacks preparing for class, correcting twenty- to thirty-page essays in bad English from each student every week, and apologizing profusely when once he was late for class (1933O1:7). Fei later wrote that he worshipped Park and never missed his class, even though it met early in the morning, and that it determined his later career (*CFMG:*106). In many of his early articles the influence of Park is clear. A 1933 article on studying cities, for example, follows Park closely in describing urban "natural communities" whose concentric patterns can be plotted on demographic maps and studied through the residents' life histories. In striking contrast to his later interest in the peasantry, here Fei, reflecting Park the urban sociologist's interest in the city as a sociological laboratory, argues that, to understand social change, one should study the cities and not the countryside, for rural change would come from the natural and inevitable pattern of villagers going to the city for a while and then returning home with new ideas and attitudes (1933N15).

From Park, too, came the notion of "social roles" (*mingfen*), which was so important in several of Fei's 1930s articles, perhaps in part because of a certain resemblance to Confucian ideas of social morality. Embodied in custom and social morality, learned effortlessly and unconsciously, social roles are fixed not by the individual but by tradition, by the society's common history and accumulated experience. It is necessary, Fei argued, that we know what others will do and how to fulfill their expectations of us: "Because we cannot for a moment live apart from others, we must always control the set form of each person's behavior." Social roles are like parts in a play, prescribing how we should act in various circumstances. That we should act according to our roles, Fei said, is just what Confucius meant by "A ruler should be a ruler, a minister a minister, a father a father, and a son a son" (1934F7).

Park's greatest influence on Fei, however, was in turning him away from the kind of library historical research he seems to have concentrated on in college. Fei's two major pieces of research during his college years had both been about the history of Chinese marriage customs. The first, written in 1932 (and published in 1934), was on the marriage system of the Zhou people in ancient China. Fei examined the definitions of relationship terms in the late Zhou and Han dynasty dictionaries *Er-ya* and *Shuo-wen* and found that one's mother's brother and one's wife's father (and certain other relatives, too) were called by the same term (*jiu*); three other sets of multiple relationships were similarly denoted by single terms. He reasoned that relatives called by the same name must normally have been the same person; that is, in the Zhou, a man could only marry what anthropologists call a cross-cousin, the daughter of his mother's brother (or father's sister), which would not violate the prohibition against marrying someone of the same surname (1934My7). This type of argument, deducing ancient kinship structure from its terminology, had been common among anthropologists since L.H. Morgan in the 1870s, and indeed Marcel Granet had made the same deduction about the Chinese from the same *Er-ya* definitions in 1929, although he did not discuss the sources in as great detail.[16]

The other article is his Yanjing BA thesis, also based on "old books." It is an extensive examination of the custom of *qinying*, or "going in person to meet [the bride]," which can be found described in the ancient *Yi-li* as well as in modern materials from Ding county.[17] On the day of the wedding, the groom goes in a procession to the bride's house and ceremoniously escorts her, in carriage or sedan chair, back to his house, where the wedding takes place. Fei wrote that he spent two years in the Yanjing library going through a vast number of local gazetteers and found that this custom was practiced in some places and not in others. He made a map of the geographical distribution of *qin-ying,* showing that it was practiced universally in an area of the north China plain roughly encompassing Hubei, Henan, Shandong, and the southern parts of Hebei and Shanxi, as well as in scattered areas elsewhere. He attempted to explain how this geographical distribution came about historically, giving lengthy consideration to Han population densities, geography, and migration routes, Shirokogoroff's theories of Chinese racial types and ideas about how customs change, or rather resist change. He concluded with the hypothesis that the custom was a survival of matriarchal society (1934Je).

This short summary does not convey how exhaustive and meticulous Fei was in his research. Besides modern anthropological works, he made use of the Classics, dynastic histories and legal codes, local gazetteers, and modern secondary works on Chinese history. Clearly he had considerable control over the apparatus of historical, Sinological scholarship; even if he was not deeply learned in classical studies, he could use historical texts. The list of teachers whose guidance he acknowledges gives an idea of where he got this training in Chinese studies. He names (in addition to Wu Wenzao, Park, and Shirokogoroff) Gu Jiegang, a leading Chinese historian who taught at Yanjing and whose courses Fei may have taken; Wang Peizheng, who taught Chinese literature at Suzhou University; and Pan Guangdan, a Qinghua sociologist specializing in eugenics and the family, who had done some Chinese historical studies (and who was to become a colleague and good friend in the 1940s).

Historical scholarship of the kind displayed in Fei's thesis was, however, beginning to fall out of fashion among Western sociologists and anthropologists. His suggestion that *qin-ying* may represent a survival of matrilocal marriage was in the nineteenth-century evolutionary tradition of assigning various social phenomena to different stages in a unilinear pattern of social development. It was based on the theory that traces of ancient customs survive in later times and on the theory of a universal progression from matrilineal to patrilineal family systems—theories propounded by Edward Tylor (*Primitive Culture,* 1871) and Lewis Henry Morgan (*Ancient Society,* 1877). Later scholars like Park, however, were more empirical and less confident about theories of the evolution of human society. Already, in his thesis, Fei expressed regret at having had to rely on unscientific gazetteers instead of carrying out a survey of all of China. And in a postscript to the other article, he apologized for using the old-fashioned method of textual research (*kaoju*); he now felt that social history should be based on actual anthropological and archaeological materials and not on "old books."

Fei subsequently wrote on kinship from time to time, but he was never again to do this kind of historical research. A book on the family written several years later (*SYZD*) was a theoretical discussion of its functions based largely on the observations of anthropologists, including his own. In *Peasant Life in China,* he discussed the family, including a preference he found for matrilateral cross-cousin marriage, but his description of *qin-ying* there made no mention of survivals (pp. 44–45), a concept that was anathema to Malinowski, under whom this book was written as a doctoral thesis. A 1936 article on relationship terms relied not on literary sources, but on native informants, himself one. Indeed, his new attitude was clearly revealed in the sharp criticism he made of scholars who use written materials, which preserve dead terms no longer in spoken use and ignore regional diversity ("Relationship System"). Fei came to feel that the Chinese tradition of scholarship was too bookish, too apt to believe "that all wisdom could be found in books" (*Earthbound:* viii), and too concerned with ideal instead of actual behavior.

The idea that truth was to be found by getting out of the

library and into the field was one of the major lessons Fei gained from Western social science in these years; he said he had learned it from Robert Park, when Park was at Yanjing. Park, Fei wrote, insisted that society is a living organism, constantly changing in response to the environment, and that, instead of reading textbooks, students would do better to learn about human nature from novels and from concrete experience of different kinds of life. He "had the power to liberate students from books and lead them into a living world to understand what human life is really like" (1933O1:6). Yanjing sociology students were greatly inspired that a man of his age and status should personally visit Peking's prisons and red-light district (*Earthbound*:ix). To be sure, this was not as unprecedented in China as Fei's later account makes it sound—Peking prisons and prostitution, for example, had both previously been studied by Yanjing students.[18] But the idea of field studies was still new enough to seem exciting.

Park was urging not just empirical study of living society but a particular kind of social study. He did not care for quantitative social surveys; Fei quoted him as saying that living society should not be described by dead numbers, just as a man with a headache is better understood by listening to what he says than by reading a thermometer (1933O1:7–8). He called for intensive studies of small (urban) communities, stressing attitudes and communicated experience, using life histories and the techniques of direct observation and participation that had been developed by anthropologists. Wu Wenzao, too, began urging his students to make community studies using the field research methods of anthropologists.[19] It was to learn these anthropological techniques that Fei went to Qinghua.

ANTHROPOLOGY AT QINGHUA: SHIROKOGOROFF

After graduating from Yanjing in 1933, Fei was invited by Liang Shuming to go to Zouping in Shandong to take part in rural reconstruction work there.[20] But, under Park's influence, he was more interested in the study of cities and, in an article written about this time, we find an aloof and slightly contemptuous attitude to rural reconstruction in his reference to "intellectuals going down to the countryside to propagandize, calling for the reform of this and that" (1933N15). A few years later, he was even more explicit: "The various social movements of today," he said, because of their ignorance of the functions and the interconnections of the various parts of the culture, were more destructive than constructive. Slow, careful research was the only method that would succeed in helping Chinese society (*HLY:* 49-50). And so Fei chose to continue his academic study, switching to the discipline of anthropology.

Anthropology, traditionally concerned with primitive peoples, seemed to most people to have little relevance to civilized China except for the study of her tribal minorities. At that time, there was not a single anthropology department in any Chinese university, with the sole partial exception of Qinghua University, which had a joint department of sociology and anthropology.[21] Qinghua was located near Yanjing, in the suburbs northwest of Peking. It had begun in the 1910s as a training school for students going to college in the United States, and was supported by Boxer Indemnity Funds remitted by the United States. By the 1930s, it had become one of the major national universities in China, perhaps second only to Peking University. Here Fei was admitted to the graduate school after passing a competitive examination. Chen Da and Pan Guangdan taught sociology in the department, but Fei studied primarily with the anthropologist Shirokogoroff.

Sergei Mikhailovich Shirokogoroff had been trained in anthropology at St. Petersburg and then, from 1912 to 1917, made several trips to Siberia, Mongolia, and Manchuria lasting a total of two and a half years. He did field work among the Tungus people in Siberia and the closely related Manchus to the south. After the 1917 Revolution, he left Russia for good and settled in China where the results of his research were published in English in the 1920s.[22] At Qinghua, he lectured in English; apparently he knew little Chinese.[23] Shirokogoroff must have been able to teach Fei much about anthropological field work techniques. His books on the social organization of the Tungus and Manchus are competent ethnographic accounts, based on theoretical training, firsthand investigation, and some knowledge of the Tungus and Manchu languages. He gives detailed accounts of social customs, marriage, the family, inheritance, and the clan, devoting less attention to economic activities and religious beliefs.

Shirokogoroff thought of the organization of society as a complex and delicate equilibrium, resulting from adaptation to the environment in the struggle for survival. Ideas, social organization, and the economic system "form a complex, possessing a certain equilibrium," so that a partial change of the complex will produce "a harmful effect on the whole," resulting "very often if not always" in the extinction of the ethnic unit. As an example, he described how Christian ideas had tended to supplant the Tungus' religious restraints on over-hunting and thus upset their whole economy. He refused to use words like "progress" and "evolution," he wrote, for they imply value judgments; various elements are always changing, and institutions and habits must also change or equilibrium will be lost.[24]

Such ideas can be found in articles Fei wrote for a Peking newspaper supplement during the time he was studying with Shirokogoroff at Qinghua, and it is interesting to note that long before going to London and Malinowski he was turning away from the older sociological concern with social evolution found in such theorists as Giddings, Hobhouse, the Webbs, and Ogburn, and embraced the basic notions of anthropological functionalism. A 1934 article, for example, asserted approvingly that "equilibrium" (a word Park used also) was replacing "social progress" as the dominant concept in sociology. He conceded that the idea of progress, associated with Marx and Spencer, gives people faith that their lives have meaning, and that in general it is true that society is moving from simple to complex. But Fei felt it would be more useful in understanding social change to look at the equilibrium between population, land (environment), and culture. Culture is man's tool for adapting to the environment, and cultural change is generated by men trying to maintain the equilibrium when one element has altered. All the various parts of a culture function toward maintaining the social equilibrium and thus maintaining life, but their functions can only be understood in the context of the whole. Thus, it is more useful to study a concrete group with a uniform way of life to see how it manages to maintain itself than it is to study the "evolution" of abstract institutions like the family or government (1934Mr7).

At the same time, Shirokogoroff turned Fei (temporarily) in quite another direction from the study of culture; it was toward that other anthropological tradition, the study of race, or physical anthropology. Among the civilized Chinese, Shirokogoroff did not continue his ethnographic work, but turned instead to anthropometrics. This science did not require a knowledge of Chinese, but rather callipers and an "anthropometer," with which he would measure the bodies of Chinese in jails or hospitals or wherever subjects could be found. He would first record twenty-three absolute measurements, going from height to "greatest breadth of the ear." Later he would derive from these a further eighteen relative measurements, such as cephalic index, for each subject, and then he would calculate means and modes and correlations and interserial differences, filling books with hundreds of pages of charts and graphs. The object was to identify the basic East Asian ethnic groups by physical type, because "language is not a stable characteristic for ethnical units." As far as I can see, he reached no conclusions of any great interest.[25]

Nonetheless, Fei became much interested in anthropometrics and Shirokogoroff's theories of Chinese racial types, and laboriously measured criminals in Peking prisons (for his MA thesis, according to a cousin). In a brief article, he said he found that most grave robbers were what Shirokogoroff called "delta types"; his explanation for this was that delta types included Manchus who were the people most familiar with Qing tombs (1935Je19). In the late spring of 1935, he measured troops of the 32nd Army at its invitation (*GTBR*, #3:38). The importance of this kind of physical anthropology, which Chinese scholars have neglected, Fei wrote, is that it alone could distinguish races. Much remained to be done; rather than spin empty theories, scholars ought to get out and do field work (1934O17). In a later article, he was concerned less with identifying races than with relating physical types to the division of labor. Eugenicists were wrong, he argued, to speak of racial progress or decline; fitness was not absolute but relative to occupation, and the problem was to get the right type in the right job. For instance, if the army would accept only "muscular" types, it would avoid the current expensive high turnover of "respiratory'" "digestive," and "cerebral" types. Relying on natural process of selection was inefficient; artificial selection was better, but required knowledge. Thus, he said, the importance of research on physical types was obvious (1935Je19).

Fei received his MA in social anthropology in 1935, the first awarded by Qinghua's sociology department.[26] and at the same time won through competitive examination a British Boxer Indemnity Fund scholarship for advanced study overseas (no Chinese university awarded the doctorate). The provisions of his scholarship required that he do a year of field research before going abroad. He was married in the summer of 1935 and immediately set out with his new bride to do field work studying Yao aborigines (and their physical measurements) in the distant mountains of Guangxi province, in the far south of China. This experience, which will be described in the next chapter, came to a sudden and tragic end in an accident in which she was killed and he badly injured. He spent the following winter and spring recovering, and in the summer went to the village of Kaixiangong in his native Wujiang county for his second field experience (which formed the basis of his London PhD thesis and the book *Peasant Life in China*). Then, in the fall of 1936, he went to England.

LONDON AND MALINOWSKI

Fei chose to use his two-year Boxer fellowship to go to the London School of Economics and Political Science (L.S.E.), part of the University of London, to study anthropology under Malinowski. This decision was doubtless due to the influence of Wu Wenzao who, although trained in American sociology, had recently become an advocate of the British school of functionalist anthropology. Wu had been responsible for getting Radcliffe-Brown, one of the two pillars of that school, then teaching at the University of Chicago, to come to lecture at Yanjing, as he had done with Park previously; that was in the fall of 1935 when Fei was in Guangxi. The other pillar, Malinowski, Wu visited in England in late 1936, after they had met as delegates to the Harvard Tercentenary.

We do not know much of Fei's personal life during those two years in London. He later wrote of reading the Parliamentary debates in the *Times* for half an hour every morning in order to improve his English, of taking long walks along the Thames in the evening, feeling lonely in the midst of the urban bustle, and of thinking constantly of China (*GDYN*:iii; *CFMG*:7; *RQ&BJ*:69). He was not the only Chinese at L.S.E., for Chinese had been going there at least since before World War I when L. K. Tao and Y. K. Leong, authors of *Village and Town Life in China,* had studied with Hobhouse. In 1936–1937, of the 717 foreign students, no fewer than 104 were from China, more than from any other nation.[27] But, aside from Francis L.K. Hsu, also a student of Malinowski, it is not clear who Fei's friends were. In the winter of 1936–1937, he spent his vacation in Berlin visiting his brother Fei Qing, who was there studying law (*MZ,XF,RQ*:44). It was there that he translated into Chinese the revision of Malinowski's long article on "Culture" from the *Encyclopedia of the Social Sciences,* the original manuscript of which, intended for publication as a book, Malinowski had entrusted to Wu Wenzao, who gave it to Fei (*WHL*:i).

Fei was formally registered at L.S.E. from October 1936 to June 1938, when he was awarded the PhD. The school records show that he signed up for a number of courses, each really a series of six to ten lectures, in the Department of Anthropology and Colonial Studies. They were given by just three people: Malinowski, Raymond Firth, and Audrey I. Richards.[28] It is possible, although there is no indication of it in the records, that Fei heard some of the great scholars in other departments, such as

R.H. Tawney, Harold Laski, or Karl Mannheim, for these names occur in his later essays; he reviewed a book of Mannheim's (1937Ap28) and once referred to Mannheim as "a former teacher of mine" (11/27/43 to WLH, in IPR 68). But it seems most of his time was spent on rather specialized, professional—and no doubt first-rate—training in social anthropology, and in writing his dissertation about the Kaixiangong village economy. There is some reason to think he got to know Firth fairly well, and he translated an article (1938Je) and a book (*RWLX*) of his, but there are no indications that Firth made an intellectual impression on Fei comparable to Malinowski's.

Fei's principal inspiration during these two years was, like his earlier teacher Shirokogoroff, an east European exile who wrote and taught anthropology in English. Bronislaw Malinowski had been born in Poland and educated there in the natural sciences, taking a PhD in physics and mathematics at a university in Cracow in 1908. After reading Frazer's *The Golden Bough* he became interested in anthropology, studied in England for a few years, and did field work in and near Australia during the long years of World War I. He made three trips to the Trobriand Islands off the coast of New Guinea, living with the natives for about two years in all, and learning a great deal about them. In the 1920s and 1930s he was the first professor of anthropology at the London School of Economics, and wrote a whole series of books (some with racy titles like *The Sexual Life of Savages*), rich in detail about various facets of the lives of his Trobriand Islanders.

Malinowski was a superb teacher. His lectures, enthusiastic, stimulating, on the frontiers of the field, were very popular. In his famous seminar, he took great pains with and made great demands on his students, whom he attracted from all over the world and from various branches of knowledge. Here is how Raymond Firth remembers Malinowski in seminar discussion:

> Bending over his sheaf of notes at the head of the table or sunk in his deep armchair, nothing would escape him—no loose phrase, no shoddy thinking, no subtle point of emphasis. With a suave question, a caustic word, or a flash of wit, he would expose a fallacy, probe for further

explanation, or throw new light on something said. At the end, after inviting opinion from all sides, he would draw together the threads in a masterly way, lifting the whole discussion to a higher theoretical level, and putting it in a perspective of still wider problems.[29]

With Fei he developed a warm avuncular relationship, styling himself in letters "your affectionate uncle," and admonishing his pupil to "be a good boy; think it out; carefully; write it down . . ." Fei in return spoke of his "filial affection" to "my dear Master," and asked for "your orders to your young children" (9/6/38 from BM; 9/10/38 to BM).

Fei was greatly impressed with Malinowski's seminar and intellectual style and wrote for a newspaper at home that China needed more frank and open discussion among scholars. "In the last half year the thing which has made the deepest impression on me is the lively spirit in 'seminar'" (1937Mr17):

> The progress of foreign scholarship is fast not because they have more native ability than we, but because they are intellectually socialized. Who says Chinese individualism is weak?—at least in academic circles we are a long way from being socialized . . . The atmosphere we should promote is of discussion, not controversy. Controversy means covering up oneself while exposing others, whereas the important thing in discussion is exposing oneself for the benefit of others. The only results of the controversies we had on "science and metaphysics" and "social history" were that, as [Zhang] Junmai said, "Everyone dried himself out and then stopped." (1937Ap14)

As a field worker Malinowski was unsurpassed. He and his generation of anthropologists set new standards of scientific rigor that were an enormous advance over the earlier generation of armchair theorizers, like Tylor or Frazer, who never saw a native but relied on reports of travelers and missionaries. Malinowski learned the language of the Trobrianders, lived with them, participated in their affairs, checked the statements of his informants with careful concrete observations, and kept detailed records, including photographs and voluminous notes in their language of what he heard. Always he had hypotheses in mind which he was testing, scientific generalizations he was refining, going from theory to observation and back as all true scientists are supposed to do. The books that resulted are admired even by those who disagree with his theories; a recent critic concedes his Trobriand Island monographs "still constitute the greatest ethnographic description ever achieved."[30]

Malinowski's theoretical contribution, "functionalism," the basic exposition of which Fei thought important enough to translate into Chinese (*WHL*), was essentially a theory of culture stressing its integral wholeness and the usefulness of all its elements. According to Malinowski, culture is people's social heritage, encompassing material artifacts, techniques, language, ideas, values, customs, social institutions, and more, all of which are complexly interconnected. It is a tool enabling people to survive in their environment, and all its elements must fill, directly or indirectly, some basic physical need. These elements can be understood only by examining, not their forms, but how they function in the context of the whole culture. Culture conditions and transforms the individual to make cooperation possible; it influences him in everything he does; it is much more important than race in explaining human differences.

Much of this was directed against what Malinowski saw as the mistakes of previous anthropologists. In particular, he castigated the concept of "survival," curious customs explained as left over from previous stages of evolution, such as peculiarities of kinship terminology or strange marriage ceremonies, taken as remains of earlier forms of the family and thus evidence of how it evolved. This concept Malinowski saw as lending itself to the facile explaining away of insufficiently understood facts instead of leading to further investigation. Functionalist theory denied the existence of survivals by teaching that all elements of a culture must perform some function, although the function may change. Malinowski criticized as premature speculation attempts at reconstructing historical stages of evolution. He was also contemptuous of comparative studies that brought together institutions or even material objects taken out of their cultural contexts. A stick cannot be understood apart from how it is used; even as broad a sector as economics cannot be isolated without distortion, for economic activities are shaped by complex traditional and social factors, not just utilitarian self-interest. In short, the anthropologist should study culture, in the here and now, and in the round, intensively, thoroughly, in all its aspects, from a multi-disciplinary point of view. While open to argument as theory, functionalism doubtless served to stimulate better field work.

More broadly, the thrust of all of Malinowski's work was that primitive non-Western people should be regarded more seriously and respectfully than they had been previously. He urged that they be studied for what they are, and not as supposed glimpses of what the civilized used to be like. He showed that primitive people do not live in a state of nature, but have complex, functioning cultures. He saw their customs not as quaint exotica or senseless antics, but as useful, rational, appropriate behavior, filling universal needs. He argued that magic, for example, was not, as Frazer claimed, a primitive form of science, and thus backward and eventually to be discarded. Rather it met a real physiological need by giving men courage in those enterprises, such as ocean sailing, over which they lack total control. He saw it as quite separate from science, which primitive cultures have also, in the form of practical knowledge based on experience of how to make a fire and so on. The need for magic is universal, and even modern men use it when it comes to matters such as war, love, gambling, or health; indeed "the savage is not . . . more superstitious" than "modern man."[31]

Malinowski spoke of culture change as merely the product of the pressure of one group on another.[32] He doubtless believed in some sort of progress, and that European civilization was higher than primitive culture, but the emphasis in his work is all the other way, away from the theories of progress of the evolutionary anthropologists. He wrote of "European stupidity and prejudice," and was angered by the missionary who called his natives "lawless, inhuman, and savage."[33] His explanation of the ultimate goal of his research indicates a profound sense of his subjects' humanity and basic similarity to civilized people: "In grasping the essential outlook of others, with the reverence and real understanding due even to savages, we cannot help widening our own."[34]

Fei was moved by the contrast between Malinowski's attitude and that of earlier anthropologists, in whose works, he said, "an arrogant attitude toward the cultures of non-white races, criticizing them as semi-civilized if not castigating them as barbarous, overflows from between the lines" (*WHL*:i). He was greatly influenced by Malinowski, coming away more than ever convinced of the importance of field research, although not of the sort he had done under Shirokogoroff—Malinowski had no use for physical anthropology,[35] and after Fei had gone to London he never measured heads and bodies again. More important, he accepted much of Malinowski's understanding of culture (indeed an excerpt from Fei's translation of his "Theory of Culture" once appeared under Fei's name [1946Ag1]), and sometimes called himself a functionalist.

FEI AS A FUNCTIONALIST: BASIC IDEAS ABOUT SOCIETY

Before an examination of Fei's studies of Chinese society, it may be useful to try to summarize his fundamental notions about society—the ideas that he took from his study of Western social science and which he would carry with him to the field in China. One basic idea was a belief that individuals are shaped to a considerable extent by culture—that which they inherit as members of society, and which, in Firth's uncompromising image, hammers them into social implements the way a factory beats pieces of metal into shape.[36] Fei had early leaned in this direction, favoring, for example, Park's understanding of the person as a social product over Giddings's Spencerian view that the biological individual is basic (Fei attributed Park's insistence on the primacy of society to his German training; 1933D). As he would later put it (talking about national character), "Society, to make the individual able to live together with others, forces him to take a common form; it prepares a model . . . Individuals shaped by the same model are on the whole all alike" (*MGRXG*:83). Another basic idea was that culture is useful, and specifically that it functions to meet various needs of society.

These ideas about society and the individual are most apparent in the book he would later write about the family and kinship, *Shengyu zhidu* (*SYZD*). Although not published until 1947, it was based on a course he had first taught several years earlier, and substantial parts of it had appeared as articles in 1941 (1941Ag30; 1941O15; 1941O30). Fei's longest and most theoretical book—Wu Jingchao, Qinghua sociologist, thought it for that reason "without doubt the best of all Mr. Fei's works"[37]—it is also his most functionalist; the influence of Malinowski, whose Trobriand Islanders turn up on almost every page, is pronounced. Although Fei used illustrations from his own field work in China as well as from Malinowski and other anthropologists,[38] he was less interested in reporting on social reality in China or anywhere else than in *explaining* customs. These explanations are worth looking at, not because we need be concerned specifically with his views about courtship, marriage, family structure, child-rearing, kinship, and so on, but because they show us his general view of how culture and society work; they also show how speculative this kind of functionalist reasoning could be.

Fei rejected, of course, the idea that the family develops through a succession of patterns according to an evolutionary dynamic of its own. At various places he argued against the theories of Lewis Henry Morgan (which Engels followed) that there is a fixed progression of stages from free sex to monogamy which all societies go through. Culture does not have its own will or objectives, Fei said; it is a tool of men. The basic patterns, such as the family triangle of mother, father, and child, are found in all societies. Free sex, matriarchy, and group marriage were just hypothesized by Morgan on the basis of kinship terminology and have never actually been found to exist; polygamous or polyandrous families take the form of multiple triangles (pp. 73–78). Some form of exogamy and endogamy are practiced by all societies, as are marriage ceremonies, kinship classification systems, and so on. It is also universal that descent be through one sex or the other; unlike the basic family triangle, larger kinship structures are always matrilineal or patrilineal.

Biological explanations of social facts he rejected time and again, too. If the family and its customs were physiological or instinctive, Fei said, there would not be so many cultural rules to regulate courtship, marriage, and child-rearing—culture is necessary only to meet needs not satisfied by natural bio-mechanisms. Human, unlike animal, reproduction is not guaranteed by the sex instinct, for people can and do practice contraception, abortion, and infanticide (pp. 6–13). The need for two parents has nothing to do with the physiology of bisexual reproduction, for social fatherhood is separable from biological fatherhood (pp. 21–23). The incest prohibition is not for the sake of biologically superior offspring, but to avoid upsetting the social relationships in the family. Unilateral kinship structures are obviously socially determined, as people have biological relatives equally on both sides (p. 154). The age at which one enters and retires from society is determined not wholly by biology but partly by culture (p. 148).

Nor, Fei argued, are social institutions to be explained by reference to cultural traditions or ethical values. That Chinese villagers have many children is due to the high death rate and not ultimately to the high value placed on continuing the family line (p. 142). The Chinese joint family is not to be explained by Confucian ideals, for peasants share the ideal but do not practice it, but by economic utility: the connections of a big family are useful to the wealthy in market towns, not to farmers using simple tools (pp. 89–91). The Chinese bias against females is not the cause of the patrilineal kinship structure, but its result. It is a cultural device to make people accept unilateral inheritance, which is socially necessary but goes against the natural tendency to love sons and daughters equally (p. 160).

It is rather in terms of filling some social need that Fei explained custom after custom. The basic function of the family is to provide successors to fill the social structure. Two parents are needed because male and female children need male and female adults to teach them their social roles, for the basic divisions of labor, at least at present, are along sex lines. To be sure, he made verbal obeisance to Malinowski's dictum that culture functions to satisfy only *individual* biological needs. But he got around it by arguing that people are dependent on society's division of labor to live, and thus it is essential to the individual that society's needs be met. Thereafter he felt free to deny the importance of individual needs. The family cannot be for the purpose of individual sex, for it restricts sexual activity. The public nature of wedding ceremonies shows that marriage is not a private affair but done for the good of society (pp. 34–38). Child-rearing is, in fact, a burden entailing personal sacrifice, and, to induce individuals to make this sacrifice for the good of society, various cultural devices are necessary, such as Chinese religious beliefs about the importance of having descendants in order to provide food for ancestral ghosts (pp. 172–173). The family does not result from individuals' feelings of love; just the converse, sentiments of affection within the basic family come from living and working (for the family often has secondary economic functions) together over a period of time. It is to overcome these natural sentiments and get the grown child to leave and take his place in society that puberty rites have been instituted.

At times Fei's explanations seemed to justify all kinds of customs. Unilateral descent, the cause of the inferior position of women in China, was universal and necessitated by the requirements of inheritance (inherited items like land and status, he argued, cannot conveniently be divided between sons and daughters to be recombined by each with the inheritance of his or her spouse). Even for arranged marriages, a burning issue among Chinese of his generation, Fei had some good words. Yet he also emphasized that, in a changed environment, such customs can become inappropriate. When parents and children come to have different values and not understand each other, it is intolerable to have one's spouse chosen by one's parents, and Fei at one point called arranged marriages "a moral teaching that devours people" (*chi ren de lijiao,* an echo of Lu Xun's anti-traditional story, "A Madman's Diary"). As the family loses other functions, for example joint economic production, it becomes possible for it to be given over more and more to emotional life (Chapter 5). Indeed, Fei was so unconservative as to be willing to contemplate the end of the family altogether, although he did not seem to consider this likely. If the division of labor were no longer primarily along sex lines, upbringing by two parents would no longer be necessary. In the future, even childbirth might be replaced with artificial conception and machine gestation ("Mankind has a responsibility to get rid of this pain for women"; p. 20). Education could be carried out entirely by institutions (pp. 28-29). So far, the family has been the most efficient way of rearing children but, in the future, this need might better be satisfied in other ways (Chapter 6). Clearly, if social institutions like the family are not biological or instinctual, nor their evolution fixed, then traditional ways are not the only valid ones.

The necessity of subordinating personal wants to social needs Fei recognized as the cause of much suffering. Society's need for children is in conflict with individual self-interest in avoiding such burdens. Social stability requires that sexual activities be regulated and restrained, for sex is potentially disruptive to society (pp. 47-50). Personal desire for divorce must be discouraged by group pressure, law, and religious sanctions, for society's interest is in long-term marriage (pp. 37-38). Exogamy, marrying outside some basic group, serves society by forging wider ties of cooperation and cultural diffusion among families, even though it makes for unhappy marriages in which partners lack the shared background and experiences necessary for deep communication and friendship (pp. 51-52). Society's need that children be socialized requires parents to be dictators—this, Fei asserted, and not, as Freud thought, sexual jealousy, is the origin of Oedipal conflict. Oedipal feelings are an expression of the basic conflict between the child and the father who is deputed by society to discipline him, between individual instincts and the needs of collective life (pp. 98-111).

Yet, for all this talk about the conflict between the individual and society and the unhappiness it causes, Fei's was not (like

Freud's) a tragic view. Culture is man-made and thus imperfect, he admitted; indeed, it is precisely because the institution of the family is basically cultural and not biological that it does not operate more smoothly (pp. 97–98). Yet ways have been found to mitigate these pains, and on the whole, he seemed to feel, cultural mechanisms work fairly well. In China, for instance, the problems caused by exogamy and patrilocal marriage, thrusting a bride into a family of strangers, were mitigated by customs such as cross-cousin marriage, early marriage, the practice of *tongyangxi* (bringing girls up in the families of their future husbands—less sanguine scholars have seen it as a kind of slavery), and the Chinese convention that husband and wife do not spend much time together or make emotional demands on each other (pp. 54–60). Fei's tendency to look on the bright side and feel confidence in the self-regulatory power of society is clear, too, in his rejection of Malthus's pessimistic theory that population growth is checked only by starvation or disaster. People do not reproduce like flies to the limits of the food supply, Fei said, or else the population of twentieth-century Europe would not be declining in spite of increased food production. Rather, human reproduction is controlled by cultural mechanisms to fill vacancies in the social structure. A given social structure has a certain optimum capacity, and population tends to grow or decline accordingly; attempts by governments to change it artificially will probably be ineffective (pp. 138–141).

In various of Fei's 1930s writings he suggested ways in which these sociological theories helped illuminate China's present distressing situation. The question of how and why society changes could hardly fail to have been pressing to one living in China then, and presumably for that reason he had made his translation of Ogburn's *Social Change*. Ogburn's thesis, that change is generated internally by the accumulation of culture, particularly technical knowledge, however, seemed less convincing to one not living in twentieth-century America, and Fei seems not to have accepted it—he published a brief critique of Ogburn's theory after getting to London (1937Ap14). He leaned rather to the functionalist view that, unless disturbed from the outside, society tends toward stability and equilibrium. Without contact with other social groups, the only innovation is from invention and is apt to be very slow, he said.

Social change Fei thought of as a disruption of social harmony. It comes from outside, when the "environment," broadly conceived, changes. For example, the climate may alter, population may grow, new products be introduced, or strong neighbors appear; the most important cause of social change is population movement which causes contact with other groups with different lifestyles (1934F7). It is destabilizing; he quoted Park: "Every now and then something occurs . . . to disturb . . . the social equilibrium, thus tending to undermine the existing social order . . . Under these circumstances, forces and tendencies formerly held in check are released, and a period of intense activity and rapid change ensues . . ." (1937Ap21). Various problems then arise because some parts of culture change more quickly than others (this is Ogburn's theory of "cultural lag," which Fei did find helpful). Social change is thus a cause of conflict and unhappiness.

A happy society to live in, Fei thought, was a stable, unchanging or slowly changing one. When change is slow, people all share the same experience, knowledge, activities, and standards; they all know their roles and can live un-self-consciously in undisturbed contentment. He quoted Park on how, in relatively traditional Peking, everyone acted according to his role and the roles all meshed smoothly (for the elements of Chinese civilization had become harmonized and adjusted over a long time) while, in more Westernized Shanghai, people's behavior seemed chaotic, individualistic, unregulated by custom. Happiness, Fei said, came from living in a society such as Lao-zi described where, "though its chickens and dogs can be heard, people grow old and die without visiting the neighboring country." He did not draw the conclusion that China's tradition-bound peasants in the comparatively static countryside were happier than city people. But Fei did look enviously on the happiness of those who had lived in the past, in the more harmonious, traditional society (1933O1:3–4).

These ideas seemed to Fei to explain the pain he saw around him in twentieth-century China. The environment had been changed by the Western intrusion, he said; the old culture was no longer well adapted, and thus the present was a painful period to live in. The old Confucian morality was no longer in the common interest, which is why some could come to see it as "cannibalistic." Some people had changed their behavior patterns while others had not, causing conflict and revolution. Without clear social roles, people do not know how to act or how others are going to act; they feel self-conscious, as if in a foreign country. This is emotionally upsetting, causing the suicide rate to rise. Thus, our dependence on common life becomes a source of great anxiety and distress. Fei's resigned advice, which indicates poignantly his attitude to past and present, was that we who live in a period of change should just accept our fate; it is useless to complain that we are paying for the happiness of a previous age of stability (1933N15; 1934F7; 1934My16; 1934Je6).

Yet, for all this nostalgia for the past, Fei's functionalism could make him quite ruthless about China's traditional culture. The notion that all cultural elements have functions would seem to lead to a justification of traditional ways against the attacks of iconoclastic radicals. Fei certainly followed Malinowski in insisting that culture was useful, but he did not agree that it was impossible for a custom that is still observed to be useless. Malinowski took the position that even a horse-drawn hansom cab in twentieth-century London or New York had a real function ("retrospective sentiment"), albeit a different one from what it had in the past, or else it would not have survived.[39] Fei, however, who once called Malinowski one "able to find a reason for any custom" (*NDNC:* 58) and said that only to middle-aged eyes would the world seem rational and even magic have functions (1937My5), was more willing to talk of customs becoming useless. For him, part of the point of the dictum that culture was a tool was, I believe, the implication that it was *only* a tool, that it had no other value and was not worth preserving for other than instrumental reasons. Culture is not (he wrote), as many claimed, fixed by Heaven, or the evolution of highest perfection, or an expression of the national essence (1937Mr17). Culture is useful in adapting to a particular environment, and it follows from this that, if the environment should change, the culture would become no longer useful, in which case it should be discarded. That, Fei thought, was just what had happened in China.

That did not, however, mean he agreed with those who in the 1930s argued for "wholesale Westernization." Fei's Western-derived social views led him to oppose Westernization for China. We have seen how he favored the idea of social equilibrium over theories of progress and evolution which, whether Spencer's or Hobhouse's or Marx's, suggested that the only route forward was that which the West was traveling. The idea that the parts of culture are closely interrelated might seem to suggest that, together with modern technology, China must adopt the rest of Western culture to go with it; but, in fact, Fei drew another conclusion. If culture is to be adaptive to the environment, China needs a culture appropriate to its own environment and not an alien culture transplanted from abroad. Furthermore, since new cultural elements must inevitably be introduced piecemeal, they have to be compatible with the old elements or they will ultimately be rejected. In other words, reform should build on existing institutions rather than court failure by inserting inappropriate foreign ones. Fei was no traditionalist, but he was impatient with those of his countrymen who could think of nothing to do but

> . . . transplant Western institutions, trying this one and then that one without finding out about national conditions and customs—trying this and that and causing more and more disorder. Blind and reckless action—how can that create a culture which can adapt to the new environment! (1933N15)

China needed "a solid, deep new sociology which can help understand Chinese society and provide a foundation for reforming it" (1936Ag12). A correct understanding of the functions of customs and institutions, Fei believed, would make it possible to introduce new elements so as best to fit with existing conditions and so make social change less painful, and to this he dedicated himself.

Here lay Fei's greatest difference from Malinowski. The Western anthropological tradition had always been concerned with the foreign and exotic, and had leaned towards conserving rather than changing native cultures. There is in Malinowski's portrayal of functional Trobriand society with its useful culture at times the hint of an idyllic tropical paradise, suggesting a romantic yearning to be away from the stress and conflict of modern Europe. In the Preface he wrote to Fei's book, he confessed that "anthropology, to me at least, was a romantic escape from our over-standardized culture" (*Peasant Life*:xxi). Fei's perspective was different. He never showed the slightest interest in South Sea Islands natives; his focus was always on China and how to understand his own society with a view to improving it. Compared with Malinowski (who seemed to be having an afterthought when in his later years, around the time Fei studied with him, he called for the development of an applied anthropology on the grounds that the basic characteristic of science was an orientation to practical application[40]), Fei's studies seem very practical in orientation, and Malinowski said Fei's book made him feel impatient with the "remoteness, exoticism, and irrelevance" of his own work.

On the eve of the war with Japan, Fei wrote in response to those who said they did sociology because it was "interesting":

> As for myself, I have no interests, or perhaps my interest would be in tilling a field. But I recognize my responsibility because I know that the work I do has a function. The larger community needs this work of ours; it is directly or indirectly related to the welfare of others. For better or for worse, I have received this training and now must bear the responsibility. If one has a taste for it, fine; if not, it still must be done—that is discipline... A soldier halfway into battle cannot simply put down his arms and return home because he suddenly decides he doesn't care for fighting.
>
> What is the function of "social research"? My answer is that it

provides a practical means for controlling social change. I believe that the society of China, no matter how you feel about it, will continue to change. There is no going back, but there is the possibility of controlling where and how we go, for we are human beings. The basis for this control, however, is not "isms" but factual knowledge.

We should be conscious of the function of sociology itself, in order to control its development so that we don't go off into thin air or get off the track. We can write hundreds of essays discussing whether or not there were "cannabilistic" customs in the Zhou dynasty, but I ask what use this kind of information has for real life? "Research for research's sake" is the defense of parasitic scholars; I have no sympathy with "respect for scholarship." I only know that "true scholarship" is useful knowledge. Scholarship can be decoration (which has a function) or it can be food (also functional). If you ask me to choose, I will take food. (1937Mr24)

THREE

Field Studies: Guangxi, Kaixiangong, Yunnan

> An inaccurate definition of situation . . . is dangerous for the group because it may lead to an undesired future. . .
>
> An adequate definition of situation, if it is to organize successful actions and attain the desired end, must be reached through a careful analysis of the functions of the social institutions . . . This is the work of a social scientist. Social science therefore should play an important role in directing cultural change.
>
> The need of such knowledge has become more and more urgent in China.
>
> —*Peasant Life:* 3–4

China urgently needed social research, Fei thought, but so far little of value had been done. While Marxists were engaged in sterile dispute about whether Chinese society was feudal or semi-feudal (1937Mr10), China's fledgling sociology movement had not accomplished much either—in 1936 Fei spoke of the failure of American-style sociology in China (1936Ag12). One can put together from remarks made here and there in pieces he wrote in London what he thought was wrong with it. It was too concerned with past history or foreign theory; the value of Malinowski's theory of culture, he said, lay in the fact that it was based not on meditation or on the synthesis of a lot of foreign volumes, but on many years of firsthand research (1937F24). Fei was harsh with scholars who used written materials to study Chinese society

("Relationship System"; "Review of Feng"). Historical materials on China, though abundant, represented the views of the upper class, were more normative than descriptive, and did not reflect the great local variations in Chinese culture: "The real life of the common people has never been fully described" ("K'aihsienkung": 1–5).

Of those Chinese social scientists who avoided the pitfall of library research, most, Fei thought, made the mistake of relying on social surveys. Surveys produced isolated facts, schematic statistical information, and missed the complexity of social relations; Li Jinghan's Ding county survey, for example, was "unable to represent the actual life of the people" ("K'aihsienkung":1–5). Secondhand collection of data, using questionnaires wielded by uninterested and unreliable assistants, made for errors. Far from the field, the scholar could not choose the best categories for his questionnaire, alter them when they proved unsuitable, understand the significance of the facts he gathered, or pursue explanations to unexpected observations. Local customs varied considerably in China, but surveys tended to lump them together in rigid categories. Later, in Yunnan, Fei would criticize two major social surveys, J.L. Buck's monumental work on Chinese agriculture, *Land Utilization in China* (Shanghai, 1937) and the government Rural Reconstruction Commission survey of rural Yunnan, *Yunnan-sheng nongcun diaocha* (Shanghai, 1935). They used rigid land tenure categories which misleadingly classed as "owner-cultivators" Yunnan owner-managers who hired labor and did not till the land themselves. It was absurd, he said, to compare tenancy rates in Yunnan with coastal areas, where the situation was quite different, or with the United States. He also questioned as impossibly high Buck's yield-per-acre figures for both Jiangsu and Yunnan, and wondered if ignorant data-collectors had not mistaken unhusked for husked quantities. The Yunnan survey he declared so full of errors as to be useless (*LCNT*:100–107; *Earthbound*:1–5).

What Fei advocated was the method of the "community study" (*shequ yanjiu*), the firsthand field investigation of a relatively small social group, and in a number of articles sent back from

England he described what he had in mind. A "community" is "a place where people live with culture," such as a village or a county. It is better not to study single aspects of society, like education or kinship or customs, but to study the whole, for the parts are all interrelated. The strong point of community studies is that they clarify the relationships of various aspects of human life, but this comprehensiveness requires comparatively long residence and intimate knowledge of a small area (1937F10). Fei advised a friend about to set off to study a rural community: that he start by explaining to the local leaders what he was doing; then take a family-by-family census, which would get his foot in the door of every house and start conversation, suggesting avenues for further research; and so on (1937Mr10). Research should not be too problem-oriented, for that implied condemnation from the start; rather the social scientist, at least while in the field, should put aside his values in order to try to understand the reasons for social customs (1936Je24). In writing up one's research reports, one should provide richly detailed descriptions of social life, not unlike those of a good novel (1937Jl7). Ultimately, however, monographic studies are for the purpose of comparisons and generalizations.

Fei was not the only one to become interested in "community research" at that time. Wu Wenzao, perhaps stimulated by Park's ideas about studying Chicago, had pushed the idea in the mid-1930s, and a few of his students had made beginning studies; C.K. Yang, for instance, did a brief study of a Shandong rural marketing area and Lin Yaohua one of a lineage village in Fujian. It was a tiny minority, however, who were interested in this kind of research in China, and Fei's own field studies are close to being both the earliest and the most important.

In a sense, Fei's rural studies were part of a widespread turning of attention to the countryside by scholars, novelists, reformers, and political activists in China in the late 1920s and 1930s. In the first two and a half decades of this century, there had been little interest in rural China in the writings of those intoxicated with new ideas from the West, ideas about science and democracy, evolution, nationalism, and literary revolution. Then, beginning slowly in the 1920s, certain Communist intellectuals—Peng Pai was the first—began to get interested in organizing peasants, and others—the Y.M.C.A. literacy campaigner Yan Yangchu and the philosopher Liang Shuming are the most famous—began going to villages to organize "rural reconstruction" projects. This shift of interest is clearly visible in the writings of that period. The old and important magazine *Dongfang zazhi,* for example, had only about one article a year on rural matters in the 1920s (with the exception of a special issue on peasant conditions in 1927), but, in the 1930s, the number increased to reach a high of about eighty in 1935. A Yanjing colleague of Fei's made a tally of 9,025 social survey reports from the period 1927 to 1935, and figured that rural surveys outnumbered urban ones from 1933 on.[1] This turn to the countryside was no doubt partly due to the apparently worsening rural economy, but it was also a part of adapting to China, a predominantly peasant society, knowledge learned from the West. Whether that knowledge was of Marxism with its analysis of advanced capitalism and the role of the industrial proletariat, Y.M.C.A. techniques developed in American cities, or Park's sociological ideas based on research on the city of Chicago (and studied by Fei in an imitation-American university), applying them to China meant going to the peasantry.

No matter that Fei's first field study was not really with Chinese peasants, but with a small group of non-Han (that is, not ethnic Chinese) aborigines—as China's equivalent of America's Indians, a more traditionally appropriate object of anthropological study. Apart from the fact that such people are part of China and have influenced and been influenced by ethnic Chinese, Fei explained, this study of a less complex border tribe was intended to give him experience and a comparative point of view; it was to be the first step in a long-term study of Chinese society (*HLY:*50; 1936F12).

Marriage and Field Work in Guangxi, 1935

In the summer of 1935, after receiving his MA from Qinghua, Fei was married. The ceremony was held on the lovely Yanjing campus, next to the lake, and Yanjing's President, Leighton Stuart, was there. That was August 1; four days later the newlyweds left for the mountains of Guangxi to do field work among aborigines; four and half months later Fei's young bride was dead.

Her name was Wang Tonghui and, in 1935, she had finished her third year in sociology at Yanjing, three years behind Fei. She came from a relatively upper-class, Christian family in Feixiang county in southern Hebei province. Her father had gone to a missionary middle school run by Oberlin College in Shanxi and then to a university; he later became a provincial assemblyman and a county magistrate.[2] Tonghui, an only child whose mother died when she was four, had been brought up by her maternal grandmother until she went away to boarding school at ten. She attended Duzhi Middle School, an English-run girls' school in Peking, before going on to Yanjing.

At Yanjing she impressed other students as being serious, straightforward, determined. She wore simple clothes, generally a plain blue gown, little make-up and no jewelry, and did not curl her hair like many upper-class city girls. A roommate said she was ardently religious, read the Bible, sang hymns morning and night, and prayed next to her bed. She liked serious conversation and would argue earnestly and persistently. Her frequent questions in class made some classmates think her a show-off; people did not take to her immediately, but many came in time to respect her intelligence and vigor. Her mind was quick, but she worked hastily and left careless mistakes. Eventually, she became fascinated by sociology, and threw herself into it under Wu Wenzao.[3] Fei too had a quick mind, a gift for talk, and an energetic devotion to sociology. When she was a junior, and he a second-year graduate student, she collaborated with him on the translation of Ogburn's *Social Change*. When that was finished she went on, at Wenzao's urging, though she had had only two years of French, to translate a book by a Belgian missionary about marriage among a small ethnic group in Gansu. Fei wrote a preface (1935N15) to her translation, which was perhaps never published. When he was invited to Guangxi, Wang Tonghui determined to go with him as an assistant and return for her senior year at Yanjing a semester later. She would not be dissuaded by friends anxious about the dangers of going to such a wild area; she said a woman could go anywhere a man could.

The Guangxi project came about through Zhang Junmai (Carsun Chang).[4] Zhang had lectured at Yanjing in 1931–1932 and while in Peking formed an anti-Guomindang group which was to become the Nationalist Socialist Party, later the Democratic Socialist Party, consisting largely of college professors, and publishing the monthly *Zaisheng*. Fei's brother Qing was a frequent contributor and presumably active in this group. In 1934, Zhang went to Canton where he was given certain educational posts, and the next year was an adviser to the Guangxi government, which was then virtually independent of the Guomindang Central Government in Nanjing. Fei probably had access to Zhang through his brother, and Zhang recommended him to the Guangxi government. In appreciation, the book that emerged was dedicated to Zhang "who took scholarship to be the foundation of the nation" (*HLY*).

Fei was hired by the education department of the Guangxi provincial government to study ethnically non-Chinese peoples, of which that province has a large number (Fei gave a figure of 700,000 [*GTBR* #4], but the 1953 census found some ten times that many). In particular, he was to travel to non-Chinese areas in several counties to make physical measurements of people. It was thought this would be helpful in developing minority educational programs. Here is how he explained the research he was going to do:

> The aim of anthropological research, besides establishing correctly and quantitatively differences in racial physical characteristics, is also to clarify trends of expansion and movement of the Chinese people and the distribution, mixing, and assimilation of various peoples. The method is anthropometrics—measuring the height, breadth, circumference, color, and shape of various parts of the body, and then analyzing these statistically to get conclusions. (*GTBR* #3:37–38)

His findings were never published in detail, but in various places in the reports he sent back he gives height and cephalic index figures for small groups of Yaos he measured. At one point, he declared these showed the Yao people were very close to Shirokogoroff's type B (Koreans and east Chinese), and that this was very significant (GTBR #4); but he did not explain why.

He and Wang Tonghui were also to make a quick survey of the social organization of various minorities, apparently with a view to helping govern them (here is grist for the argument that anthropology is the handmaiden of imperialism). Only three years before, there had been a large-scale uprising, bloodily surpressed by the army. To prevent a repetition of this, Fei suggested that, "only if we understand these people's psychology, religious beliefs, and social organization, can we know why they 'rebel'." Anthropology could further aid in integrating them into the provincial economy and bringing them the benefits of economic cooperation, such as had been enjoyed by natives in English colonies, who are protected by the British because they produce materials for British industry (GTBR #5:25).

It was a long way from student life in northern Peking to the wild mountains of southern Guangxi. On their six-week honeymoon trip south by train and steamship via Wuxi, Shanghai, Hong Kong, and Canton, Fei and his wife worked in spare moments checking her translation of Schram's book. In Fei's preface, he stressed the importance of learning about non-Han border people if government policies were not to oppress them (1935N15). At last in Guangxi, in the provincial capital of Nanning, they had meetings with education officials and were assigned a section chief from the provincial education department to travel with them in the hinterland. They decided to begin in the Dacheng Yao mountains in Xiang county east of Liuzhou. After travel by car and steamer and then a two-day sedan chair ride to a village at the foot of the mountains, they finally entered the mountains, on foot, on October 21. It was a terribly isolated area, without roads or waterways, electricity, or telephones, a hundred miles from the nearest post office, and far from the kind of life they had known in the city.

The country was too rugged and steep for sedan chairs, and, although they hired porters to carry their luggage, they found it rough going. Traveling between isolated villages, they sometimes had to go on all fours climbing up hill and slipped and slid going down. They complained of sore legs and bruised feet, and more than once regretted they had come at all. But they also found the scenery breathtakingly beautiful. Coming from the plain, they had never seen such views or felt so close to nature. They frequently fell behind their porters and the education official, and sometimes lost their way. One time, with a dizzying gorge below, Miss Wang wrote, "We didn't know the way and were afraid of getting lost and dying in the mountains, and no one would know" (*GTBR* #10:30). In the tiny villages, their boots were stared at by people who walked the mountains barefoot. Although, they were surprised to find, bamboo pipes brought running water, the crude, windowless earth houses were dirty. They were bothered by mosquitoes and bedbugs, and had trouble lighting a fire. Since the Yaos' plank beds were uncomfortable, they were glad to have brought canvas cots.

Fei wrote of practicing the techniques that Shirokogoroff had taught him, such as winning people's trust by painting watercolors instead of using a mysterious, frightening camera. He smoked with the Yao men and drank their homemade rice wine ("Those who do ethnological research must be able to drink. Shirokogoroff repeatedly urged me to practice" [*GTBR* #9:28]), but got drunk after three cups and had to quit. He overcame their fear that his physical measuring would lead to conscription by telling them the lie, perhaps at the education official's instigation, that the purpose was to diagnose diseases in order to be able to bring medicines next time.

Fei and his wife were probably not very well prepared for this kind of difficult field work. Ethnographic studies had been done on the Yaos, for instance by students from Sun Yat-sen University in Canton,[5] but they seemed not to know all of them. They did not speak the Yao language, nor Cantonese, the dialect of many Chinese in that region, and indeed even had difficulty with Guangxi

Mandarin, although Miss Wang was proud of picking up a little of it. During one period of three weeks, while Fei traveled about making his measurements, she stayed in one village waiting every day for her sole informant to come home from the fields in the evening; the local chieftain's somewhat Sinicized son, a Christian who had traveled outside the area and knew Mandarin, was the only person in the village she could converse with.

In spite of these problems, they managed to learn much that was new, albeit about a tiny group of people. The Yaos are primitive mountain tribesmen, numbering in 1953 some 600,000, of which two-thirds are in Guangxi. In Xiang county in the 1930s there were, according to Fei, only a few thousand, divided into six groups. The group they found out most about were called Hualan (Flower Basket) Yaos, and numbered less than a thousand in five villages. This group they considered to be what Shirokogoroff called an "ethnical unit" by virtue of being an endogamous marriage unit with a common culture, language, and group consciousness (*HYL*:42). They sent back descriptions of the Hualan Yaos' customs and ceremonies regarding birth, marriage, and death; their elaborate initiation rite and its religious significance; their gods (derived from the Chinese) and magical practices; their houses, relationship system, internal conflicts, and laws; and their economy of irrigated rice culture, other crops (such as vegetables, cotton, tea, and tobacco), fishing, hunting with rifles they made themselves, and trade with Chinese merchants to whom they sold mostly lumber.

Miss Wang was particularly interested in their practice of strictly limiting births. Families had almost always only two children, practicing, if necessary, abortion or even infanticide. Family property was never divided and would all be inherited by one of the two children; the other would marry someone who was inheriting from his own family. Thus there was no population growth and no fragmentation of land, which could not be bought or sold. She also spoke at length, without hint of disapproval, of the Yaos' sexual freedom. Lovers, both before and after marriage, were socially tolerated if not too flagrant, and the opportunities were apparently many and used—one of Fei's porters claimed to have had fifty lovers. Miss Wang wrote that this gave great scope to natural selection, for not everyone could attract a lover, and furthermore probably made marriages more stable and less likely to break up for emotional dissatisfaction; divorce was rare and generally for the economic reason of the partner's inability to work (*HLY*:6–8).

Fei was not so busy measuring heads that he entirely neglected more political information. While Miss Wang stayed in one village, he traveled among other Yao groups and learned about relations among them. Some of these groups, such as the Ban Yaos and Shanzi, were exceedingly poor, owning no land themselves and eking out a precarious existence tilling scattered non-paddy patches rented from the better-off, landowning Hualan and other Yao groups, known together as "long-haired" Yaos. All the groups had long suffered from Chinese oppression, Fei considered, and now were being subjected to a cultural invasion as the provincial government spread administration and education into these areas. The less-advantaged Ban Yaos looked to the Chinese for support against the other groups. They had become more Sinicized and welcomed Chinese schools; the long-hairs had on occasion used violence to try and stop them from attending. In time, the ideas they were receiving from their Chinese teachers, ideas of equality and of giving land to the tiller, would bring more conflict with the long-haired Yaos (*GTBR* #15 & 16; *HLY*:43–48).

Then, on December 16, the accident occurred. After finishing with the Hualan Yaos, the Feis had started on another long-haired group. They planned to finish all the long-haired Yaos in the Dacheng Yao mountains by February, when Miss Wang was to return to finish her undergraduate studies at Yanjing. They were traveling on a mountain path between two villages, as usual fell behind their companions, and then got onto the wrong path. The account given by an American missionary who talked with Fei shortly after the accident is so vivid as to warrant quoting at length:

> Pathways in the Yao Mountains are often small and indistinct and Mr. and Mrs. Fei did not realize they were on the wrong trail, and being

unconscious of their danger, tramped on. For hours they had followed the winding pathway in and out among the hills without meeting anyone or coming in sight of any human habitation. Late in the afternoon they approached a crude bamboo fence leading to a sort of gateway and thinking they were nearing a mountaineer's home, they eagerly stepped forward. The innocent looking gateway proved to be a "dead fall" tiger trap and as Mr. Fei, who was in the lead, stepped through, his foot released the trigger and at once huge quantities of stone and timber came crashing down upon him. He was injured badly. The right leg was partly paralyzed; several joints in the left foot were crushed out of place and he was pinned beneath a mass of debris. Mrs. Fei was not hurt. She worked heroically pulling the stones off her prostrate husband until she had released him. But Mr. Fei was so badly injured that he could not walk, and night was coming on. They had no food or bedding, and Mr. Fei was suffering dreadfully. Finally, his devoted wife determined to go in search of help, and comforting her husband with a few cheering words, she started off down the mountain trail. She did not return that evening, and Mr. Fei lay on the cold ground, chilled to the bone by the cool mountain atmosphere, hungry, thirsty and in great pain. In this condition the long awful night was passed. The following morning as Mrs. Fei had not returned, Mr. Fei started to slowly crawl along the narrow pathway. He crawled all day until four o'clock in the afternoon when he was found by tribesmen—members of his party, who, having missed them the night before, had started out to search for them. Mr. Fei asked about his wife, but no one had seen her. Mr. Fei was then carried to the nearest Yao village and a general alarm call was sent out. The tribesmen from the various villages responded to the call, and for several days they followed the mountain trails searching the wooded hills in a vain attempt to find the lost woman. On the seventh day one of the companies of searchers found the body floating in a mountain stream.[6]

In Peking their friends were stunned, and spoke of Miss Wang's great promise and of her courage in giving her life to scholarship. Wu Wenzao wrote, "We childish people are struggling in various ways to save a declining nation. These fresh troops on the social anthropology front were just nearing battle when they met disaster—how can we not be disheartened for our work and for the nation?" (*HLY*:v). Arrangements were eventually made for her to be buried on the Guangxi University campus, where the provincial government erected a stele with an inscription by Fei.[7] Fei meanwhile lay badly hurt in a hospital in Wuzhou, Guangxi, and then in Canton. He had to have a couple of operations on his leg; years later he still walked with a limp. Lying in hospital rooms for months and months in south China where he had no friends, lonely, depressed, bereft of his young bride after only a few months of marriage, feeling like a "boat without a compass," going over and over the accident in his mind as though it were "a nightmare from which I cannot awaken myself," blaming himself for her death—he several times thought of suicide.[8]

Eventually he pulled himself out of this depression with work:

> That I did not die in Guangxi has made life a heavy burden for me. I feel that, apart from work, I can take no pleasure in life. Tonghui died for me, I can never forget. That I reluctantly presume to enter the world once more is because I believe that in work I can atone for my sin, so that if we meet again I can tell her at length of what has happened since we parted. (*JCTX* #1)

In Shanghai and Peking in the spring of 1936, he edited their notes on the Hualan Yao into a book. In May, he gave a talk about his findings in Guangxi to the inaugural meeting of the Yu Gong Society on the Yanjing campus.[9] He finished the book in June, publishing it (*HLY*) under Wang Tonghui's name. A photograph taken in the summer shows Fei holding a cane and looking much thinner and weaker than before the accident.[10]

PEASANT LIFE IN KAIXIANGONG, 1936

In the summer of 1936, still recovering, Fei went to stay with his older sister in a village called Kaixiangong in their native Wujiang county. There is every reason to think he was very close to Fei Dasheng, who was five or six years older than he; perhaps he looked to her to fill some of the void left by the death of their mother when he was sixteen. She was an extension worker from a sericulture school outside Suzhou, and had gone to the village to try to introduce more modern techniques and cooperative organization to the local silk-producing industry. Her "devotion to the rehabilitation of the livelihood of the villagers . . . inspired me to take up this investigation," and she "introduced me to the village and financed my work" (*Peasant Life:*xi). Perhaps it was she who turned his attention away from aborigines and measuring heads to Chinese villagers and their economic welfare, and it was certainly her work that inspired his ideas about rural industry. In Fei Dasheng he came into contact with a tradition of gentry rural reformism which had nothing to do with Malinowski or Western sociology and which antedated the 1930s rural reconstruction movement. It is worth taking a moment to examine this tradition.

The idea that people of education and high social position, officials and gentry, had a responsibility as community leaders to promote the economic welfare of the peasants was not a new one in China. It is stressed in the Classic *Mencius*, one of the cornerstones of a Confucian education, and indeed one of Mencius's recommendations was to encourage the planting of mulberry trees, the leaves of which are fed to silkworms. In the Ming and Qing dynasties certainly, if not before, one of the ways it was felt this duty should be discharged was by spreading knowledge about the best methods of sericulture. The "Sacred Instructions" of the various Qing emperors included sections on promoting agriculture and sericulture, and similar proposals can be found in the writings of the "statecraft" *(jing-shi)* school of politics. Evelyn Rawski has described how early Qing officials went about bringing experts on sericulture technology from more advanced areas to other parts of China. In the Tongzhi period, the promotion of new methods in sericulture was part of the program for recovery from the devastation of the rebellions; Zuo Zongtang, for example, set up a sericulture bureau in Fuzhou.[11]

The late Qing effort to modernize China's silk industry involved importing technology from abroad for what had once been a Chinese monopoly. This effort was motivated by the realization that Chinese silk exports, though growing, were being overtaken in international markets by more efficient competition. As Zhang Zhidong wrote in his enormously influential *Quan xue pian,* published in 1898, China had supplied 60 percent of the demand of

Western nations ten years earlier, but this had been reduced to 10 percent by Japan and Italy, whose production costs were lower because they knew how to winnow out the eggs of diseased silkworms. He recommended specialized schools to teach scientific methods. Similar proposals could be found in *Nongxue bao,* an agricultural journal published in Shanghai beginning in 1897, from reformers like Liang Qichao, Zhang Jian, Luo Zhenyu, together with articles and translations on Japanese silk technology. A sericulture academy (Canxue Guan) was founded in Hangzhou by the prefect in 1897, using Japanese instructors and sending some students to Japan. Similar schools were subsequently established elsewhere.[12]

The school that Fei's older sister Fei Dasheng went to and then spent most of her life working for was one of the few such schools for girls. It was founded in 1911 at Hushuguan, a few miles northwest of Suzhou, as the Suzhou Sericulture Technical Girls' School.[13] By 1917, there were over two hundred students taught by more than ten teachers, all of whom, including the principal Zheng Bijiang (whom Fei Dasheng married much later in about 1950), had been trained in Japan. Fei Dasheng was graduated from this school, which was equivalent to a high school, in 1922 when she was about eighteen, and then with a scholarship from the school went to Japan for a one-year practical course for girls on silk reeling at the Tōkyō Kōtō Sanshi Gakkō.[14]

Returning to China in 1923, she went to work for the Hushuguan school's extension division, going to villages to give lectures on better techniques of raising silkworms. That winter, the principal Zheng, Miss Fei, and another young woman went to lecture in the little village of Kaixiangong, on the shore of Lake Tai in Wujiang county, about four miles north of the market town of Zhenze. There the local leader, a holder of the lowest old civil service degree *(shengyuan),* was sufficiently impressed with the possibilities for strengthening the shaky silk industry that a project was initiated, with the help of some money from the Zhenze town government. At first the emphasis was on technical improvement in growing silkworms: classes for village girls, breeding and

Peasant Life in Kaixiangong, 1936

selecting eggs by outside experts. In 1926, they started cooperatively raising worms in the early stages in common rooms, where temperature and humidity could be controlled and contact with diseased worms prevented; in later stages of growth, the worms were removed to individual homes, which had been sanitized and were under the supervision of people from the school. These efforts had considerable success, and the income from silkworm raising of those villagers who participated was significantly increased.

But these improvements still did not produce silk thread of sufficient uniformity for export for machine weaving. For that, better reeling techniques were required and, after some attempts with home equipment, it was finally decided that the only solution would be steam-driven machinery. That meant a factory. Miss Fei and her co-workers were strongly of the view that, insofar as possible, the silk industry should be kept in the village; indeed that was the whole object of their efforts. They also felt strongly that a capitalist enterprise would benefit the few, and that their aim should be to bring the benefits of modern technology to all. Thus, in 1929, the Kaixiangong Silk Manufacturing and Selling Cooperative Limited (Kaixiangong Shengsi Jingzhi Yunxiao Youxian Hezuoshe) was started, buying cocoons from members, reeling the silk in a small factory in the village with village girls hired as workers, selling the raw silk in Shanghai, and distributing profits to the members. The cooperative was, in theory, owned and operated by the participating villagers but, in fact, the amount raised by selling shares to villagers was not nearly enough to buy the necessary equipment, so it was dependent on large loans from the provincial government's Farmers' Bank (Jiangsu-sheng Nongmin Yinhang); moreover, it was run by the local literate elite and outside experts (Miss Fei), who felt the peasants needed their guidance. Silk of a higher quality was produced, but the steady fall in price and in demand for silk on the international market because of the world depression brought financial problems. Chinese silk exports fell off rapidly after 1929 from 11,500 metric tons to 3,300 in 1934, while the price per pound on the U.S. market dropped from $5.24 in 1927 to $1.21 in 1934.[15]

Nonetheless, the experiment seemed a success, and Miss Fei wrote articles expounding the advantages of this kind of small village cooperative industry using modern technology. A village cooperative was in a position to oversee and direct the raising of silkworms, and thus could get better and standardized raw materials. A village factory had smaller expenses than a city one—raw materials did not need to be transported, land was cheaper, and so was labor because of the cheaper living costs. Most important, it was operated not for the gain of capitalists but to give villagers work without treating them as mere economic units and without separating them from their friends and families and the happiness of a full social life. The peasants in much of south Jiangsu and north Zhejiang, she argued, depended on their income from silk to make ends meet; if the village silk industry were not revived they would be impoverished.[16] This experience and this line of reasoning made a great impression on her brother Fei Xiaotong, for whom his sister's silk cooperative was the model in his later advocacy of developing village industry.

One of the themes in certain of Fei Dasheng's articles was the need for greater knowledge about society, a need she demonstrated with examples from her own experience. Some of the reforms she and the sericulture school had introduced had had unforeseen and undesired side effects. The girl workers hired by the factory were paid a wage they were apt to see as their own money and not family property; the independence this gave them upset their relationships with their husbands and mothers-in-law. "The seriousness of this can often make a young lady who has gone to the village full of benevolent aims doubt the value of her work."[17] Another example: electric pumps for irrigation work were rented to the farmers at a low rate by the government, effecting a great saving of labor; but this left the farmers idle and inclined to gamble, losing money and driving their wives to grief.[18] In short, Fei Dasheng had become convinced that, if the kind of reform efforts she was engaged in were to be successful, they must be based on better understanding of society and how its parts—

customs, institutions, methods of production—were interrelated. Notions of this sort we may assume she learned from her brother, whose influence on her is clear from her references to Park, for example.

It was just such understanding that her brother set out to gain. He stayed with her in the village for a month of very hard work in July 1936, returning for a few more days in August to clear up some further points (*JCTX* #7). He published some preliminary findings in a series of articles in a newspaper that summer (*JCTX*), and then, in the fall, took the materials he had collected to London, where he used them to write, under Malinowski's direction, his 1938 PhD thesis, published the next year. It was one of Fei's most important books.

The aim of *Peasant Life in China: A Field Study of Country Life in the Yangtze Valley,* Fei said, was to show "the relation of this economic system to a specific geographical setting and the social structure of the community" (p. 1). Kaixiangong (which he calls "Jiang-cun"—Yangzi village—in his Chinese work, transcribed "Kiangts'un" in *Earthbound*) is in southern Jiangsu province, in the lower Yangzi delta, an area of water transport on a maze of streams, canals, and lakes, and of fertile irrigated rice paddies. At the time of Fei's stay, 1,458 people lived in the village, some three-quarters of the families engaged mainly in agriculture on only 461 acres. They grew rice in the summer; in the winter, wheat and rapeseed (for oil) were cultivated on only a small part of the land (much more of the land is double-and even triple-cropped in that area now). The remaining quarter of the population was engaged in fishing or other occupations; the majority of farmers were also dependent on supplementary income from silk, sheep raising, or inter-village transport and trading. In Kaixiangong and in China as a whole, Fei thought, there was not enough land to support the large rural population on agriculture alone.

Sericulture was of major importance in the village economy. Women, who did not work in the fields in this village, raised silkworms on mulberry leaves and then reeled raw silk from the cocoons. In the past, this had all been done at home and had been a source of considerable income but, in the 1920s and 1930s, the competition of Japanese and European silk, the development of artificial fibers, and the Depression caused a decline in the price the villagers received for this silk. As a result, the village was much worse off than it had been a decade before. Fei described at some length his sister's efforts, only partly successful, to alleviate this situation by modernizing the silk technology in the village. The domestic weaving industry also had been practically ruined (p. 124). Kaixiangong was a case of rural suffering caused by "the industrial expansion of the West" (p. 285).

Another cause of hardship in the village was the fact that about two-thirds of the land was owned by absentee landlords living totally apart from the village, some of whom, relying on agents to collect their rent, did not even know where their land was located. The rent amounted to about 40 percent of the tenants' rice crop, a great economic burden. As long as they paid rent, the position of the tenants was not precarious, however, for they had permanent tenancy rights, thought of as ownership of the surface of the land, and could not be evicted. Even a tenant who could not pay his rent was, in effect, secure because of the impossibility of finding a replacement: villagers would not take advantage of the misfortune of one of their number and would not tolerate an outsider coming in. Apart from the burden of rent, there were also usurious interest payments, as high as 53 percent a month, on loans from urban moneylenders (p. 278). Defaulting on such loans was how peasants lost their land to absentee landlords, Fei thought, although they were hardly aware of the difference in paying rent instead of interest. In other words, he thought villagers had once owned the land and lost it because of the decline in the silk industry.

The basic social and economic unit was the family (*jia*), living together and collectively producing, consuming, and owning. The larger kinship organization, the lineage or clan (*zu*), was unimportant in this village. Families were small, four persons on the average, tending to break up when friction developed between, for example, two married brothers. Land would be divided equally among sons except that a slightly larger portion would be given to the son who supported his parents in their old age. To avoid the further division of already small holdings, families tended to restrict births by abortion and infanticide, averaging only 1.3 children per family. Describing marriage and child-rearing customs, Fei found that ceremonies for marriage, funerals, and births were very expensive and a common cause for borrowing, and that, as anthropologists have often found in patrilineal societies, there was a specially close warm relationship between a child and its mother's brother.

The book is largely descriptive, but the facts Fei chose to collect and the interpretations he put on them were informed by his picture of society and the way it works, of a harmonious and smoothly functioning culture, in which environment, technology, economy, social institutions, customs, and beliefs were all well adapted to each other. Just as Malinowski had done in his Trobriand monographs, Fei brought out the close connections between the economy and other parts of the culture. On almost every page, he showed economic aspects of various kinds of customs or beliefs, or conversely how in order to understand an economic institution one had to consider other things like religious values (attached to the land) or kinship relations (in the case of financial-aid societies).

The land and labor were "well-adjusted," in that the average area of land per adult male was just about the maximum that could be cultivated with the existing technology (pp. 170–171). The tendency for large landowners to have more children, resulting in the division of their holdings, and poor ones fewer was the means by which this "ratio between land and population is adjusted" (p. 196). Cultivation of farms by small households was appropriate to an agricultural technology based on the hoe. The cultural value attached to contentment with a moderate standard of living, which allowed people to save instead of spending the surplus in good years, was necessary in a place subject to natural disasters from time to time.

In his examination of marriage and the family, he found for

various customs hidden functions which were not understood by the participants. In arranging a marriage, for example, the use of a fortuneteller, whose prognosis actually expressed the desires of the parents, meant that the declining of a proposal, or later a failed marriage, could be blamed on fate. The belief that a marriage was held together by the man in the moon made a young bride accept her helpless position in her new family. The preference for matrilateral cross-cousin marriage (that is, marriage with the daughter of one's mother's brother) lessened the friction between mother-in-law and daughter-in-law, for they would at the same time be aunt and niece.[19] Marriage gifts from the groom's to the bride's family really became part of her dowry and helped provide the material basis for the new household. The marriage feast served to reinforce ties of the larger kinship group. The birth of children, encouraged by religious and ethical beliefs, functioned to consolidate the marriage and to provide economic support for parents in their old age. A kind of mock adoption, rationalized by the belief that children might be protected from malevolent spirits by powerful adoptive parents, served to provide the child with wider social connections, particularly with people of wealth and influence (pp. 41–51, 30–31, 88). One less imbued with functionalist ideas might have viewed as dysfunctional, for instance, customs requiring peasants to go into debt and impoverish themselves for lavish funeral, wedding, and birth ceremonies. But Fei drew no such conclusions.

Not only was the culture well adapted and smoothly functioning, but the social relations within the village he perceived as generally harmonious. Fei wrote that, within the family (generally portrayed as an arena of great conflict by Chinese of his generation), although there was commonly some friction between mother-in-law and daughter-in-law, nonetheless "disharmony . . . should not be exaggerated. In the group, co-operation is essential . . . The economic value of a daughter-in-law, and the common interest in the child, make for a harmonious give and take" (pp. 49–50). Friction between a married son and his parents was resolved by the division of property. As to larger groups,

Fei cited instances of neighborhood and village cooperation.

Fei did not mention class conflict within the village, although there must have been great differences in status between the ordinary illiterate villagers, and the village headman and others who had had advanced education outside and wore long gowns, or, in the case of the younger generation, European trousers and shirts. Instead he stressed that "there are no essential differences in housing and food" among the villagers, and that "the amount of land cultivated by each [family] is much the same" in spite of wide differences in the amount of land owned (pp. 120, 192). The village headman used his literacy to perform valuable functions and introduce beneficial measures without direct economic reward; "Headmanship is not connected with any privileged 'class'" (pp. 106-109). That relatively wealthy landowners, assigned to collect land tax, were free to assess as they saw fit, collecting even from tenants who did not own land and should not have had to pay, did not strike him as outrageous. "The collector is able to use common sense in distributing the burden according to the ability of people. Honesty and the sense of equality checks the abuses possible under such an informal practice" (p. 193).

Conflict and trouble came from outside the village, upsetting its well-adapted system. It was outsiders, not villagers, who practiced usury. The result was that villagers lost their land, and 70 percent of them had to pay an onerous rent, totaling a quarter of the village's entire rice production, to absentee landlords who lived as "parasites." This was what caused differences in wealth among villagers—the different amounts of rent paid. New radical ideas, such as Sun Yat-sen's slogan of "land to the tillers," had begun to erode the old feeling that paying rent was a moral duty, resulting in "an intensification of conflict between tenants and landlords" (pp. 183-191). But, although they use illegitimate means to take from the peasants more than is their due, "it is incorrect to condemn landowners and even usurers as wicked persons." They too have a function—extending credit to the peasants; for, without sources of credit, the peasants would be even worse off. The real cause of the economic crisis was the decline in domestic industry due again to outside forces, "the force of international capitalist economy." Fei thought land reform would help, but the basic solution had to involve the recovery of rural industry; and he regretted that the Nationalist Government was spending most of its revenue on fighting Communists instead of taking practical measures to alleviate the agrarian problem (pp. 282–285).

In Kaixiangong, such actions as had been taken by the government tended to be ineffective because they were not based on an understanding of the actual needs of the village. Existing side by side with village custom was outside-imposed law which, because of its artificiality, did not take hold. The new political subdivisions, for example, were rigid, of uniform size, without economic basis, in contrast to functional units like the village or the marketing area. The *baojia* units (government-imposed security groups) Fei called "very artificial"; *bao* areas were divided by streams, when in fact the streams were means of communication. As a result, the de jure administration head was less important than the de facto village headman (pp. 110–116). The public school, run according to Ministry of Education rules, taught a literary curriculum not useful to peasants, and its terms coincided with busy agricultural periods; the result was very small attendance, except when the inspector came around (pp. 38–40). A new law requiring equal inheritance for sons and daughters had become ineffective after seven years, for it did not take into account the true function of inheritance, to reciprocate the support a son provides his old parents, support to which a daughter, who leaves the family when she marries, does not contribute (pp. 4, 79–82). The annual calendar booklet, banned because it contained superstitious material, continued to be found in every house for it was necessary for agriculture; and the government's prohibition of magic failed too, for, as Malinowski said, even magic had practical functions (pp. 150, 168–169).[20]

Peasant Life in China was published with a long and laudatory preface by Malinowski, expressing "genuine admiration" for Fei's "vivid and well-documented accounts" and "clear and convincing arguments." A contemporary Chinese sociologist called it "the most profound and detailed description of peasant life in one community so far in English or Chinese,"[21] and it has been well received by Western scholars, too. In a recent volume of summaries of ethnographic classics, for example, it is called "one of the earliest and best known of the attempts anthropologists have made to analyze the communities of the great civilized nations," and a chapter on Fei's Kaixiangong stands alongside Malinowski's Trobriand Islanders, Radcliffe-Brown's Andaman Islanders, Redfield's Yucatan village, Shirokogoroff's Siberian Tungus, and others.[22]

Shirokogoroff himself, however, was not so well disposed toward Fei's work. Beginners should not hurry to publish, he wrote in an article from Japanese-occupied Peking just before his death in 1939; books like *Peasant Life*, which imply little is known about Chinese society, ignore the large corpus of existing writings. Rather than the village, the "ethnical unit" (a regional, linguistic, cultural group) should be the unit of investigation. A critical-bibliographic history of Chinese ethnography, surveying works in all languages including Russian and Chinese, he said, would be "more useful than the description of a dozen of villages taken at random."[23] It is a criticism we shall return to.

LU-CUN, YUNNAN, 1938–1939

When Fei returned from England, it was to a China at war. The long-expected conflict with Japan had finally broken out in the summer of 1937, and Japan had quickly occupied north China and the coastal cities, including Peking and Fei's native region in southern Jiangsu. He sailed from France on September 30, 1938, traveling fourth class on a French ship, disembarking at Hanoi, still French-controlled, and proceeding overland to Yunnan in China's unoccupied far southwest.[24] Yunnan was, like Guangxi, a remote mountainous area, sparsely populated by aborigines in the hills and by more recently arrived Chinese settlers in the fertile valleys. He went to Kunming, the capital city of Yunnan, which was to become a great intellectual center of free China during the war, to join his old teacher, Wu Wenzao. Now that Yanjing University was under Japanese control in occupied Peking, Wu had recently come to set up (with Rockefeller funds) a sociological research center, attached to Yunnan National University, called the Yanjing-Yunnan Station for Sociological Research, bringing with him a few young Yanjing sociologists. Fei joined this group, becoming both an associate at the Station and faculty member in the sociology department at Yunnan University.

Two weeks after arriving in Yunnan, he set off to do field work in an isolated village in Lufeng county, sixty miles to the west of Kunming, which he called by the fictional name Lu-cun. He was introduced to the villagers by a maiden aunt on his mother's side, Yang Jiwei, who had been there for a year as a Christian missionary, and by a Yanjing classmate, Wang Wuke, who was a native of the village. His first visit was from November 15 to December 23, 1938, and he was assisted by another Yanjing sociology graduate, Li Youyi. In the first half of 1939, he returned to Kunming to teach, and then, during summer vacation, went back to Lu-cun, where he stayed from August 3 to October 15, 1939, this time assisted by Zhang Ziyi and Zhang Zhongjiong (*LCNT*:3-4; the dates in *Earthbound*:12 are off by a year). His work was supported by grants from the British Boxer Indemnity Fund and from the Chinese Farmers' Bank. The book about Lu-cun was finished in January 1940 and published under the title *Lu-cun nongtian* (Paddy fields of Lu-cun; *LCNT*); it won a prize from the Ministry of Education. Fei's English translation of it and of two village studies by Zhang Ziyi were later published as *Earthbound China.*

This second village study was even more exclusively concerned with economic conditions. Unlike Kaixiangong, Lu-cun had no household industries at all but was entirely dependent on agriculture, although, with 611 people cultivating about 165 acres of land, it was even more crowded. Paddy rice was grown in the summer, and on about 70 percent of the land a second crop of broad beans was produced in the winter. Fei studied the agricultural calendar and the labor requirements in some detail, finding that long periods of idleness, during the winter, alternated with periods of intense activity, at the fall harvest or in the spring when the picking of beans had to be immediately followed with plowing and the transplanting of rice seedlings. Taking into account how much or little leeway was possible with these activities, he calculated that a man and a woman by themselves could handle no more than about three-fifths of an acre, which was not enough for a family to live on; this had created the necessity for staggering the dates of planting in order to exchange labor. Even so, during busy seasons, it was necessary to hire people from other villages.

Rather than tenancy, the typical pattern in Lu-cun was for petty landowners to hire laborers and manage the land themselves, overseeing the work and setting the schedule, supplying seed, tools, and money for wages. This required being on the spot, living in the village rather than away in a town like the owners of most of the land in Kaixiangong, and, according to Fei's calculations, brought a somewhat higher return than renting the land out. Lu-cun's rented land usually had collective owners, such as clans or temples or other associations, which together owned a quarter of the land in the village. Renting from such an organization, especially from one's own clan, was generally at fairly favorable terms, and many such tenants were quite well off, better off than the hired laborers.

The typical self-managing landowner had only one or two acres; the largest had less than four acres. Fei speculated on the absence of concentrated landownership such as he had seen in the east. He noted that there was not much of a market in land, very little buying and selling, because of people's extreme reluctance to part with the family heritage. It was impossible to accumulate very much money in agriculture and, without industry in the village, the only way to get rich was on the outside, as an official in the government for instance; but few could afford the education for this. And those who did get rich and so were able to accumulate land tended to have many sons, with the result that the land would be divided and return to petty plots again.

But, although the rich were not very rich, Fei was much more struck than he had been in Kaixiangong with inequities and with the basic class difference between those who worked and those who enjoyed their leisure. He gave figures showing that the eighteen largest landowners, representing 15 percent of the 122 families in the village, owned 41 percent of the privately owned land, and three-quarters of the privately owned land was in the hands of one-third of the families, while 31 percent of the families were landless. He studied the family budgets for five households, finding enormous differences in living standards. He described how clan and temple lands were administered by wealthier villagers to their corrupt profit (*Earthbound:* 55–56, 78), and how the lack of economic opportunity in Lu-cun forced people to seek wealth through exploitation of political power, as army officers, local government leaders, or tax collectors (pp. 129–131).

It was not only the poor who were wronged. Seeing women with bound feet at work in the fields even women from families that included leisured males, moved Fei to speak of the "exploitation" of women. He attributed this situation to the unilateral system of inheritance; it was the men who inherited and hence owned the land (pp. 110–111). No longer did he think as he had in *Peasant Life* of the family owning its property collectively. But, though unilateral inheritance was responsible for the low position of women, he felt bilateral inheritance would be impractical. For the husband and wife to inherit land from two sources would not change the amount they controlled, on the average, but, unless people married only their next-door neighbors, it would result in further fragmented and scattered holdings, impairing efficiency (*NDNC:* 22–23).

One-third of the families in Lu-cun had men who did not work, ever, not even in the busiest periods, not even those who were strong and healthy, not even though the family women labored in the fields. They were not rich—not on the income from one or two acres—but were able to enjoy the prestige of not working because of the low wages (ten cents a day, Chinese currency) paid laborers, who were in oversupply. They spent their days and years in idleness, talking in teashops, gambling or smoking opium, the better-educated painting pictures or practicing calligraphy. Fei felt both attracted and repelled by this leisure class, who were the people he lived with and talked to most. "For a time we were very much prejudiced against them . . . but as we became familiar with their life, we came to appreciate, if not admire, them" (*3 Types:*16). When the wartime draft reduced the available labor and a few of these gentlemen were forced to doff their long gowns and take part in farm work, Fei felt pleased. But mostly he was intrigued that they should be content with a meager income when by working they could have been better off. It seemed a different kind of economic calculus than that of the modern West; avoiding pain—and in Lu-cun farm work was indeed painful—restricting desires, contentment. Was this really less rational than the insatiable striving for more production and more goods which is the basis for modern capitalism? "In our villages people . . . know how to get pleasure without paying in pain. This is what is called relaxation (*xiaoqian*) . . . not necessarily spending anything but spare time" (*LCNT:*108-14).

Fei had come to Lu-cun with a question about Kaixiangong: how to explain Kaixiangong's very high rate of tenancy and absentee landlordism—70 percent of the farmers were tenants and half the land was owned by a landlord in Suzhou. R. H. Tawney, in *Land and Labour in China* (pp. 36-37), had speculated that absentee ownership represented investment of urban capital in the village, and was thus to be found in villages near cities in areas where the soil was fertile enough to make it worth investing in, for example, in the vicinity of southern coastal cities rather than in north China. Fei interpreted Tawney as stressing high agricultural productivity rather than the proximity of urban centers, and claimed that the case of Lu-cun disproved this theory, for there was little tenancy but high fertility; indeed, the average yield of about sixty-six bushels (of sixty-seven pounds each) of husked rice per acre was much more than the forty bushels an acre he had determined for Kaixiangong. Furthermore, he argued, Tawney was wrong in suggesting urban capitalists would want to buy land as an investment, for the annual return from renting out land was only about 15 percent of cost (*NDNC:*10; in 1940My19, he says less than 10 percent) compared with 30 percent or more to be made from moneylending (Fei ignored the factor of risk). He felt a more likely explanation for "the loss of land ownership" from a village—he silently assumed that peasants must have owned their own land until recently—was that it resulted from peasants defaulting on their loans. Peasant loans were made for purposes of consumption, not production, and were a result of financial distress; the likeliest hypothesis of why this would be most apt to occur near cities was that rural industries had been destroyed by competition with machine industries. This, Fei concluded, was the cause of high tenancy rates near modern cities; it had nothing to do with fertility of the land (*LCNT*:186-189; *NDNC*:1-11).

Lu-cun had no handicraft industry. To study further the relationship between rural industry and tenancy, Fei then encouraged one of his associates at the Yunnan Research Station, Zhang Ziyi, to make a study of a village that did have such industries, Yi-cun. Here too there was very little tenancy, but one kind of industry, papermaking, produced high profits for those few rich enough to make the necessary capital investment; they then used the profits to buy land in other villages, thus becoming absentee landlords. Yi-cun was a very isolated village, so Zhang next chose to study one, called Yu-cun, located near a town, and here there was a certain amount of tenancy, though less than in Kaixiangong: 28 percent of the land was rented from outside owners. Fei suggested, in the conclusion to *Earthbound China* in which the three Yunnan studies were translated, that these three villages, Lu-cun, Yi-cun, and Yu-cun, plus Kaixiangong, showed the process by which extensive tenancy and absentee landlordism came about. The process was really in two parts. First commerce and industry (certain kinds of industry, not handicrafts) permitted the accumulation of wealth—for one could not get rich tilling the land in China, Fei showed that convincingly—and this led to the concentration of landownership. In other words, "the development of industry and commerce brings . . . disastrous consequences" for, "where commerce is developed in China, tenancy follows suit" (p. 303). The second stage came when the intrusion of foreign goods destroyed the market for handicrafts, which led to further impoverishment and loss of land. This conclusion took for granted an association of low tenancy rates with general peasant welfare, but, strangely, Fei's own studies might be used to question this—it is not at all clear that the many tenant farmers in Kaixiangong, who had a considerable degree of security of tenure, were necessarily worse off than the numerous hired laborers of Lu-cun.

THE SIGNIFICANCE OF FEI'S COMMUNITY STUDIES

A number of questions can be raised about the value of Fei's field studies, about their empirical accuracy, their political bias, and their theoretical significance. As for accuracy, it must be noted that they were hastily done. His field work was brief; in contrast to Malinowski's years in the Trobriand Islands, Fei spent less than two months in Kaixiangong, less than four in Lu-cun. Not much of his important analyses of the agricultural year and its seasonal labor requirements could have been based on firsthand observation. In neither village did he take a census of the population, but made calculations on the basis of local government figures he knew to be inaccurate (*Peasant Life*:21: *Earthbound*:37); in several places, he admitted that more direct observation would have been desirable (for example, *Earthbound*:25, 32).

A number of errors are apparent (some no doubt misprints) regarding equivalences, addition, percentages, dates, and so on. In the book on Lu-cun, for example, he calculated that, if the profit is $5.93 (misprinted $5.73) from managing land worth $80 in 1938 and $100 in 1939, then the rate of return is 13 percent (*LCNT*:179); and he continued to use this figure elsewhere (*LCNT*:187; *NDNC*:7, 98) before correcting it to 7 percent in *Earthbound* (p. 127). Although his studies focused on economic life, he was not well trained in economics, and some of his arguments are very curious. "Hoarding" money had an inflationary effect, he insisted in one article (*NDNC*:85–86); or, a tenant would not be better off owning the land he tilled because the rate of return from farming was too low—a rate Fei calculated assuming

86   *Field Studies*

that the farmer did not work but hired labor (*NDNC:*98). He himself admitted his calculations on Lu-cun pig-raising, which indicated it was unprofitable, must have been in error (*Earthbound:* 49-50).

As an example of the problems with Fei's quantitative data, following are the passages in *Peasant Life* in which he calculates the average family's income from the land, a calculation that formed the backbone of his thesis that income from supplementary industry such as silk was absolutely necessary for peasant livelihood. My comments appear in brackets:

> The total area of cultivated land is 3,065 *mow* [*mu*] or 461 acres [elsewhere this figure is given as "a rough estimate" of the *total* land in the village, only 90 percent of which is cultivated (pp. 17-18, 170, 236)]. If this area were equally allotted to 360 households [the total number in the village; but it would seem more reasonable to count only the 274 households engaged in farming (p. 139)], it would mean that each household could only occupy a piece of land about 9.5 *mow* [a misprint for 8.5] or 1.2 acres [really closer to 1.3] in size. Each *mow* of land can produce in a normal year six bushels of rice [presumably a rough estimate from an informant; but how much is a bushel and is this polished or unhusked?[25]]
>
> The total produce will then be 51 bushels for that average holding of land [but shouldn't something be added for other crops besides rice? in *Earthbound:*298, he suggested these were worth about 10 bushels of rice]. The amount of rice needed for direct consumption by members of the household is 42 bushels [miscopied from the 32 on p. 126, which in turn was faulty addition of his own figures which come to 33; later (perhaps converting to polished rice?) he used the figure of 20.3 bushels as the requirement of an average Kaixiangong family (*Earthbound:*298; *Gentry:*111; in 1957Je1 #1:12, he suggested 1,500 catties, or about 25 bushels]. Therefore there is a surplus of 9 bushels . . . If the surplus is sold the return will be about 22 dollars. But for current expenses alone a [family] needs at least 200 [Chinese] dollars [This estimate, taken from his calculations on p. 137, includes an allowance for periodic ceremonial expenses—weddings, funerals, and so on—and thus does not represent only current costs]. It is thus evident that life cannot be supported by agriculture alone. (pp. 33, 201-202)

If this calculation, which is most important to Fei's argument, is redone with some of the corrections suggested above, one can come up with a surplus of over 122 dollars instead of 22—a big difference, although, when land rent paid by the majority who were tenants is taken into account, I think Fei's conclusion still stands. I would conclude from this that Fei's quantitative data should be handled with caution. It seems very risky, for instance, to calculate, as a recent scholar has done, the size of the surplus going to cities and towns on the basis of the figures Fei gives for annual production and consumption in Lu-cun.[26]

In the 1957 attacks on Fei and his work, it was mostly another kind of issue that was raised, and this was what might be called the problem of class bias. Due to his own class stand, because these studies were not made from the peasant point of view, it was said, they could not serve peasant interests. Rather than getting information from the less well off, as Communist investigators did, he had, for example, lived with the village head in Kaixiangong, an evil landlord named Zhou Baoshan, and relied on him, *baojia* heads (police agents in a way), and Guomindang underlings.[27] He did not use Marxist class analysis. He wrote for foreign consumption, asking about subjects of interest to the imperialists rather than about matters of concern to the peasants themselves. His view was shaped by functionalist anthropology, which was anti-Marxist and had a long history of serving colonialism. As Fei himself put it in 1972:

> I can't even read the works I've written on the Chinese peasant in the past... I lacked their class viewpoint. My ideas and feelings were different from the labouring people. The problems I wanted to solve, the questions I wanted to answer were not those that the peasants wanted solved and answered. My viewpoint didn't correspond with that of the broad masses of peasants. At that time, I looked down on them as inferior, as illiterate country bumpkins. Because of this, the works I wrote did not serve the peasants, but rather those who ruled over them. ("Interview")

Or, as he is reported to have remarked to a foreign visitor in 1976, Malinowski should have helped the Trobrianders to write their own studies.

Though it should be kept in mind that such criticisms were

made for political reasons, there is some truth to them. It is true that he wore a long gown in Kaixiangong (see the photograph opposite the title page of *Peasant Life*), and no doubt he depended on upper-class informants for much information about the villages he studied. He spoke of getting data from an "ex-magistrate" (*Peasant Life*:192), and the people his sister introduced him to in the village were, we may suppose, more apt to be village leaders than poor peasants. In Lu-cun, he tells us, he quickly became good friends with his landlord, with the village head, and with another man "of the old Chinese gentry class, with his amiable personality and hospitable spirit" (*Earthbound*:12-13).

His view of village life was certainly colored by his functionalist ideas about society. That he thought in these rather than in Marxist categories surely inhibited his awareness, for example, of class conflict and exploitation within the villages. He did often talk about an average village family rather than emphasize the differences between better and worse off. It is probably true that Fei was not as sensitive to the possibility of conceptual bias or the difficulty of value neutrality as many would wish today—nor were most social scientists at that time. He felt it important to be objective, but he seems to have thought objectivity was assured by not letting emotions becloud his view—that emotions should be avoided, at any rate, is suggested by his remark that on a certain occasion the sight of the cruel treatment accorded horses "made us forget our role as investigators and feel sympathy for them" (*LCNT*:53-54).

As for the argument that anthropology, and Fei's studies, served imperialism, it is true that the discipline grew with the spread of white domination over much of the globe, and that Malinowski and others were wont sometimes to justify their work in terms of its usefulness to colonial administrators, although it seems overly harsh to blame anthropologists for the sins of imperialism.[28] It is true, too, that Fei's field studies seem to have been more widely read abroad than in China. The Guangxi Yao report was privately printed in an edition of 500.[29] The Lu-cun study, widely read in English, exists in Chinese only in a poorly printed wartime edition which was so rare that even Harvard's Chinese library lacked a copy when I began my research. Except for a very preliminary series of articles in the *Yi-shi bao* in 1936 (*JCTX*), *Peasant Life in China* never appeared in a Chinese version, but has been often reprinted in English and was translated into Japanese twice within a year of its original publication—at a time when Japan had just occupied the area.

A third kind of problem concerns the theoretical significance of Fei's work. He said when he went to Kaixiangong that he wanted to lay to rest the idea that the ethnographic method was suitable only for culturally simple "savages" (*JCTX* #1). Yet these techniques had been developed for studying societies without written records, societies which were sufficiently simple and so remote that it made sense for one person to try to see and hear "everything" in a year or two, societies which were so totally strange and foreign that it was reasonable to fear the significance of their customs would be misunderstood apart from the full cultural context. The strategy of studying all aspects of culture and their interrelations by means of firsthand observation, however, necessarily limits the size of the group that can be studied. With Malinowski's Trobrianders the whole society numbered only 8,000 or so, and Radcliffe-Brown's Andaman Islanders were even fewer, but in the case of China any "community" of that size would be but an infinitesimal part of the whole.

Fei was not guilty, it deserves to be said right off, of portraying the Chinese village as a society in itself, cut off from the outside like isolated primitive islanders. He made it quite clear that his villagers shared in a larger Chinese culture with its ideas, values, and traditions. He showed outsiders coming in and villagers going outside, for work, trade, recreation, education. He stressed the non-self-sufficient aspects of the village economy and its dependence on trade with the outside. In the case of Kaixiangong, he showed how villagers went outside to sell their rice and silk and bought even such necessities as vegetables; they went to towns for recreation in teashops, for certain religious ceremonies, to get priests for funerals or craftsmen to build houses; some worked in factories outside, many engaged in inter-village trade by boat, the leaders were educated outside. Most of the village was owned by city-dwellers, to whom rent was paid. The village was affected by government actions, by the ideas of reformers such as Fei Dasheng, and even by other nations and the international demand for silk. Nor was Fei wedded to the idea of studying just villages. He also spoke of the need for studying larger communities, such as towns or marketing areas. He supervised students in Yunnan in such studies, as well as in factory studies, and later planned to do a marketing community himself (*XTCJ*:152).

Still the problem remains. What is the value of studies of small communities, no matter how reliable, for a complex society such as China's? Fei's answer was that community studies should be designed to test theories of larger significance. Social research should start with a theory, which is then tested and modified in the course of the research, to produce a new theory to be tested in further research in a process producing a progressively more refined theory of Chinese society without the need to study every village. As he states it one time, there are a limited number of *types* of villages and one can study one of each type, just as a biologist studies a frog as a species-type without studying all frogs. Deciding what constitutes a type and choosing which villages to study depends on having a theory. If one's theory, generated from previous studies, suggests that factor A is the cause of factor B, one next finds a village in which factor A is lacking and looks to see if B obtains; according to what one finds, one modifies the theory and comes up with a new question to be tested by a study of a different type of village ("Chicago Talk"). As to why intensive comprehensive anthropological studies are necessary if the object is merely to test the correlation of a few factors at a time, Fei maintained that only a field worker in close contact with his subject in its full context could understand the relationship between factors and alter the theory to fit new facts (*LCNT*:105-106).

In Guangxi, Fei later wrote, he had done his best to avoid theory, thinking that "the field worker needs only facts not theory"; theory was useful only for arranging the facts in logical order in the write-up. And in Kaixiangong he still believed that the investigator "should not carry any theory to the countryside, but rather let himself be a roll of film automatically photographing the facts of the outside world." Later in London, Malinowski, who had emphasized that anthropology should be a science in the sense of developing universal laws and not just a hodgepodge of unrelated data, and that to this end field workers should go out with theoretical constructs to be tested, had made him feel his previous view was in error. While writing *Peasant Life,* he felt very unhappy that the field work had not been guided by theory and that the materials gathered were unconnected and meaningless (*LCNT:*4-5). Thus, it was only in Yunnan that he began to work towards testing and refining theoretical propositions.

Yet the theories he seemed most interested in had to do with historical trends, and it is not at all easy to prove them with studies made at a single point in time. His attempt to get around this by claiming that Kaixiangong and the three Yunnan villages represented different points along a temporal continuum of change and that the "four types, put together, show the process of economic development going on in the rural China today" (*Earthbound:* 206) seems to extrapolate too far on the basis of a few village studies. Such an approach assumes there was only one type of Chinese village with differences being simply a matter of time—that Kaixiangong had once been like Lu-cun and Lu-cun would become like Kaixiangong—which is to deny the importance of regional and other differences which, in other contexts, Fei frequently emphasized. Furthermore, without historical data, there is no way to know the direction of change; why could not the general tendency be away from a past pattern of high tenancy and towards Lu-cun and occupying ownership. In a way Fei's approach, which was similar to one used by Redfield for four Yucatan villages, was like the theories of nineteenth-century evolutionists—arranging co-existing data in a putative historical order to show a unilinear pattern of social development—whose speculative character Malinowski (dead by the time *Earthbound* was written) so abhorred.[30]

Similarly, without historical evidence, Fei's isolated village studies are not enough on which to rest his claim that "the intrusion of foreign goods . . . [is] gradually wiping out traditional industry" in China (*Earthbound*:304). The decline of Kaixiangong's silk industry had been caused by competition with superior Japanese and Western products on the world market and by the shrinking American demand due to the Depression. It was not a problem of imports, nor was it caused by foreign trade, for foriegn trade was what had previously brought the village industry the prosperity which was now being lost. (To be sure, getting involved in foreign trade makes a village vulnerable to fluctuations in world markets; but that is not the argument Fei made.)

Interestingly enough, the weakness of Fei's generalizations I think stemmed from his commitment to field work instead of long hours in the library. He did not use historical materials, such as local gazetteers, for the areas he studied. He did not take seriously the massive literature on rural conditions accumulated in the 1930s, except occasionally to refer to Chen Hansheng's work or a current article. He once said that his intensive investigations of a small field were intended to "supplement" broader surveys of problems (*Peasant Life:*1; "Chicago Talk":3–4), but he himself never used them that way. He cited J. L. Buck or the Rural Reconstruction Commission surveys almost always to criticize them, not to draw on information in them. Probably more than anything else on rural China, he quoted Tawney's *Land and Labour in China,* a work based on secondhand information; and once he even cited Pearl Buck's *The Good Earth* to show how peasants feel about land (1940My19).

On the whole his social analyses were based almost exclusively on his own field work or observations, supplemented by the studies done by his own students at the Yunnan Research Station. For example, a discussion of the technology of husking grain involved comparing: the village he was living in outside of Kunming, where a man lifts a stone mortar with his back and shoulder muscles; his Guangxi Yao tribesmen, who used their feet to pump on a lever; Lu-cun, where a stream worked while people watched; and his native area of south Jiangsu, where mill boats with diesel-operated machines could husk a whole village's rice in a day or two (*NDNC*:54–55). During the war, this was no doubt partly due to the unavailability of books and libraries; "Literary research becomes impossible," he said. "This encourages field study" ("Chicago Talk":10). But even after the war, back in Peking, he was still more inclined to get information from personal observation or from talking to people than from books. A 1948 article on rural industry, for instance, draws all its examples of Chinese rural industry from Zhang Ziyi's studies of the two villages of Yi-cun and Yu-cun, ignoring all that had been written about rural industry elsewhere in China. Then, talking about cooperative organization, Fei cites nothing from the enormous literature produced since the early 1920s on this subject, but confines himself to describing only his sister's silk cooperative in Kaixiangong. Finally, discussing extension education to bring technical knowledge to rural areas, he simple repeats what he had been told in visits to the University of Wisconsin and Oxford (*XTCJ*:118–24).

Yet, when all these criticisms have been made, Fei's work still stands. If he did not solve all the problems of using studies of small communities to draw generalizations about China, it must still be granted that he was a pioneer in the application of anthropological field techniques to complex societies. Anthropological studies of communities within complex societies—common now—were almost unheard of before World War II. Indeed Fei's *Peasant Life in China,* published in 1939, was one of the very first. An earlier book about a Chinese village, *Country Life in South China* (1925), by D. H. Kulp, an American sociologist teaching at a missionary college in China, was apparently based largely on second-hand information from his students. American sociologists had begun to make a few intensive studies of American communities (the Lynds' famous *Middletown* of 1929 was one of the first), but the only earlier anthropological peasant studies were 1930s works on Mexican villages by Robert Redfield of the University of Chicago, who happened to be Park's son-in-law. *Suye Mura,* a study of a Japanese village by John Embree, a Chicago student of Radcliffe-Brown, appeared in the same year as *Peasant Life*. Malinowski may have been indulging in a bit of prefatory hyperbole, but nonetheless his judgment was not entirely groundless that *Peasant Life in China,* which was "not [about] a small, insignificant tribe, but [about] the greatest nation in the world . . . not written by an outsider looking . . . for exotic impressions . . . [but] by a native among natives," was "a landmark in the development of anthropological field-work and theory."

Fei's predilection against library research may have weakened his larger generalizations, but that is as nothing weighed against the contributions to be made by his sort of field work. He was surely right in arguing that not much can be learned about Chinese peasants from traditional literature, and probably right in thinking that the kinds of survey and statistical information that were beginning to accumulate in China in the 1930s were often erroneous and misleading. Though his field work was brief, he worked with remarkable speed and energy, and he had certain advantages: he knew the language, was familiar with customs, and came with good local contacts. In spite of the questions that can be raised about his numbers, the observations he made and the data he collected on the spot are undoubtedly much more accurate and more richly informative than other kinds of information we have about Chinese peasants. Fei and a few others, including a number of students he trained in Yunnan, were embarked on a study of Chinese society that was much more sound than what had gone before. Referring to this work of Fei's and others', Maurice Freedman has spoken of "a Chinese phase in social anthropology": "It could be argued that before the Second World War, outside North American and Western Europe, China was the seat of the most flourishing sociology in the world, at least in respect of its intellectual quality."[31]

As to the charge of class bias, this has surely been vastly exaggerated. Fei thought it more important to try to understand the interrelationships within the social system than to rail against social injustice, but it is nonetheless true that his sympathies were with the poor and oppressed. In Guangxi, it was for the Yaos against the Han Chinese, and for the landless Yao groups against the "long-haired" Yaos. In *Peasant Life,* he was against absentee landowners, corrupt rent and tax collectors, usurers, and the industrial expansion of the West, and on the side of the ordinary peasant, about whose economic plight he was deeply aggrieved: "It is the hunger of the people that is the real issue in China." Particularly in Lu-cun, he used terms like "shocking" and "criminal" to describe differences in standard of living and the exploitation of privilege.

Fei's functionalism with its conservative tendency to justify the status quo did not completely determine his view. His method had the great merit of bringing him into direct contact with social reality. Here is his account of his introduction to the village of Lu-cun:

> We first arrived . . . during the period of winter inactivity. Walking from the district town, we were impressed by the absence of workers in the fields of luxuriant broad-bean plants. As we entered the village, we observed many men idling about, some talking in groups, others squatting at the door of their houses, puffing their pipes. Catching sight of strangers in city garb, they immediately gathered around to ask questions. They welcomed us cordially when it was learned we were from the university, and the master of the primary school immediately invited us to lunch. Their hospitality and the warm, leisurely atmosphere of the village brought to my mind the old Chinese poem:
>
>> The harvest's wealth this plenteous year
>> Has gladdened us, for we may share
>> With welcome guests who travel from afar.
>
> But this mood was quickly dispelled when we saw, stumbling along the roughly paved paths of the village, lines of heavily laden coolies with lean, hungry faces and in worn, ragged clothing. On their backs they carried huge blocks of salt, burdens beneath which their bodies were bent almost double. Inquiries directed to our new friends elicited the information that these people were salt-carriers, whose job it was to transport salt on their backs from the well to the district town—more than a full day's walk. For this they paid a wage of twenty cents a day. So, almost at the moment of entering the village, we were

introduced to the startling contrast between the two classes who inhabit it: those who do not need to work during the slack agricultural period and those who must work continuously. (*Earthbound:*40–41; LCNT:38–39)

Much of the 1957 criticism of Fei's village studies, in fact, relied on three sentences from *Peasant Life,* taken out of context. One was on how "it is incorrect to condemn landowners and even usurers as wicked persons." Actually, Fei's point here was that it was the whole credit system that needed to be changed to relieve "a vicious circle which saps the life of the peasants." Another was on how land reform was not the "final solution" of agrarian problems in China; but he went on to say that it was "necessary and urgent" and "an indispensable step in relieving the peasants." Finally, much was made of Fei's 1938 remark that the Communist movement was a product of peasant hunger, when his point seems to have been to criticize the Nationalist Government for spending its revenues on fighting the Communists instead of carrying out land reform (*Peasant Life:*284–285).

As for the charge that Fei's work was irrelevant to the needs of peasants, right from the beginning he said that his goal was "to understand China in order to remake China" (1936F12; *HLY:*50). Because his ultimate purpose was "to improve the people's livelihood" (*Earthbound:*311), he concentrated on economic matters rather than topics like magic, myth, religion, and kinship, which had been the traditional concerns of anthropology—or the book on Chinese ancestor worship Malinowski urged him to do. It was just this practical orientation towards building a foundation of knowledge on which social change could be based that most impressed Malinowski and made him feel "genuine admiration, at times not untinged with envy" for *Peasant Life.* If some of Fei's work was hasty, it was precisely because of the urgency he felt about contributing to social reform at a time of national crisis.

Fei was doubtless over-sanguine about the possibilities of social engineering once a little research had been done, but he was surely right in arguing that the Nationalist Government had made wasteful mistakes in its attempted reforms and promulgated inappropriate policies because of ignorance about rural conditions, and it does not seem unreasonable for him to have thought that the kind of research he was pioneering might prove beneficial to China's peasants. To object that this work never really was, as he hoped, used in "directing cultural change" (*Peasant Life:*4) blames him for what was not his fault. As he wrote in the 1930s, there had to be a division of labor between knowing and doing, between scientifically trained researchers, who forget practical problems to concentrate on analyzing reality, and government administrators, who lack the time to study anything in depth. The researchers could not help it, however, if their research was not used. "If there is reliable research, but feasible policies for relieving the world and saving the people are not instituted, and an enemy seizes the advantages, then that is the fault of the administrators" (1936Jl22).

FEI AS A TEACHER:
THE YUNNAN RESEARCH STATION, 1939–1946

Fei spent most of the war years living a few miles outside of Kunming, the capital of Yunnan province, where he was a professor in the Sociology Department of Yunnan University and field director of the Yanjing-Yunnan Station for Sociological Research. Yunnan is the most southwestern province in China and Kunming, on a plateau six thousand feet in altitude, and has a pleasant climate, warm and sunny year-round, with flowers in bloom in all seasons. Fei said it was almost a paradise, and he was very sorry to leave (*MZ, XF, RQ:*11, 78).

But it was also one of the most economically underdeveloped parts of China, into which in the late 1930s streamed a flood of refugees from the Japanese-occupied coastal regions. The result was a life of hardship and poverty, at least for those unable to profit from activities like black-marketeering. Robert Payne, who taught English at the other university in Kunming, Southwest Associated University (Lianda), has written vividly of the dreadful living conditions of the professors (and also the students), the hardship and hunger, undernourishment, inflation, poverty, bombed buildings, crowded rooms, rats, disease, lack of drugs, the terrible shortage of books and journals, of information from outside, even of paper—students used the blank side of allied government propanganda bulletins for their notes. He spoke of "the heartache of seeing my professors worrying their heads off for the sake of their children . . . What is so disconcerting in Kunming is the beauty of the place and the terrible poverty of my friends."[32]

Fei remarried in about 1939, and his only child was born in late 1940, a daughter named Zhonghui and usually called "Little Hui," after Wang Tonghui. His second wife, Meng Yin, was not an intellectual as Wang Tonghui had been, but less well educated and of rural background:

> My wife is from country. Her father is a villager, if not actual farmer. I like her because she retains something I am lacking, simplicity and "near-to-the-soil." She does not like the cinema but working in the house and on the land. She is hospitable, a character of country-breeding. (5/17/44 to MPR)

To her he dedicated a book published in 1946 (*NDNC*), "in memory of seven difficult years in the interior." They lived in Kunming briefly until the Japanese air raids became so frequent they had to be evacuated. In October 1940, after scurrying out of the city on footpaths into the surrounding hills during an air raid (Meng Yin was pregnant), they returned to find that their house had been hit, and a gaping hole in the roof made it uninhabitable. They then moved to a village near the town of Chenggong, fifteen miles southeast of Kunming (thirty to forty-five minutes by train), where they took some rooms in a peasant's house.

Caring for a family was not easy under wartime refugee conditions. The baby was due to be born soon after their move to the village and, as it was too expensive to go to a hospital, Fei made arrangements for a midwife to come. But their old rustic landlord would not allow a baby of another family to be born in his house because of a local belief that this would cause the termination of his family line. So they found a Cantonese lady in the town who rented them a dark room in which the child was delivered (*NDNC:* 55-58). Medicine was unobtainable or frightfully expensive, as was powdered milk, which the baby needed. One time when his daughter was sick, Fei had to borrow money to pay for medical care (*CFYL:*70).

In the sociological articles about the family that Fei wrote at that time, we find a striking emphasis on how burdensome parenthood is, what sacrifices are necessary to raise children. He wondered if religious celibacy did not originate in a selfish desire to avoid such sacrifices, and maintained that artificial cultural mechanisms were needed to induce people to have children (1941Ag30). A series of articles describing a trip to western Yunnan (*JZS*), he later said, expressed his desire to run away to a mountain monastery to escape from the burdens of life during the war: living in the country, cooking, carrying water, being a father, a meager salary, a child crying from hunger, and a wife worn out from work (*CFMG:*7-8).

Not only were they refugees (nostalgia for his native place is the theme of one article, [1943Ap10]), not only did they suffer shortages and dislocations; inflation had made them poor. In the 1930s, university professors had been well paid, but, in the 1940s, their salaries, like those of other government employees, did not keep up with inflation. The result was a redistribution of wealth, and Fei now found himself poorer than many members of lower social classes. For "a college professor . . . to share a house in common with a peasant," was in itself, he thought, "unprecedented in Chinese history" ("Harris Lecture":54). He regretted that his wife had to learn to get along without servants and do her own cooking (*NDNC:*49). He complained about rich villagers storing up money or gambling for extravagant sums (*NDNC:*81, 86). He found, during the harvest of 1942, that male field workers in the village where he was living earned more than he did ("Harris Lecture":54), and he was shocked at how much the peasant in whose house he lived was said to have made the year before

(*NDNC*:81). It was a serious social problem for China, he suggested, that "uneducated minds" should suddenly become rich ("Harris Lecture":61–62).

Fei had become assistant professor in the sociology department of Yunnan University in 1939, and in 1941 was quickly promoted to full professor and chairman. Apart from his classroom duties,[33] most of his time was spent at the Yanjing-Yunnan Station for Sociological Research which Wu Wenzao, representing Yanjing, had set up in cooperation with Yunnan University. Fei became field director of the Station in 1940 when Wu went to Chongqing.

The Research Station had been evacuated from Kunming in October 1940 to half a mile or so west of Chenggong town where, inside "Old Walls Village," the former site of the town, it took over a three-story tower, built in 1818 to a star-god believed to bring success in the imperial examinations.[34] The name of the tower, shortened to Kuige ("Queike" in *Earthbound*), became the informal name for the Research Station (*XTZG*:98). Wilma Fairbank, as cultural relations officer of the American Embassy, visited Kuige in 1945, and in her report described

> . . . the crenellated wall of the village; inside, the narrow cobblestoned lanes lined with small dark shops and squatting vegetable vendors are barely wide enough for the . . . jeep to pass. Here the peasant women wear silver earrings, caps decorated with turquoise chips, and cross-stitched shoes. . . .
>
> The Yenching-Yunnan Station for Social Research is housed in a romantic Spirit Tower which stands foursquare with curving glazed-tiled roofs in the midst of a cypress grove. Each of its three storeys is a single room with windows framing enchanting views on each of the four sides. The top storey houses a furious wooden god and a brilliant young research assistant. There are no gods on the second storey; it holds three desks, a square center table with tea cups, and two or three shelves of books and manuscripts. This is the workroom for the research men and the center for meetings and discussions with the Director regarding the research in progress. The first storey is a kitchen and entrance-way . . .
>
> The material plant of this institution is practically nil but the spirit, hard work, and purposefulness of the bright young men who constitute it is impressive.[35]

The Yunnan Research Station, 1939–1946   101

Wartime conditions made research difficult. The researchers had very few books. After the Rockefeller funds ran out, they got grants from the Farmers' Bank, the Ministry of Education, and other government agencies. By 1943, they were supported mostly by the Yunnan Provincial Economic Council under the Yunnan industrialist Miao Yuntai, whereupon the "Yanjing" was dropped from the Research Station's name. But they did not have money for large-scale research projects, for assistants, for secretaries, or even for such simple equipment as a camera and film. Publication mostly meant mimeographing, and Fei himself spent hours writing out stencils and operating the machine. In this penury, however, there may have been some hidden advantages; without books or assistants, forced to live in the countryside, they developed "guerilla tactics" based on firsthand observations, attacking this problem and then that in small-scale studies which built on each other. They had a sense of unity and purpose, feeling that their social research would provide the basis for postwar reconstruction. Morale was high.

There is no question Fei excelled as a teacher. He and his research fellows, perhaps half a dozen at a time, lived and worked very closely together. At one time

> we had six research fellows living together in the same place with my family. This gave us a wonderful opportunity for intimate discussions. We gathered together after we had scattered for a few months in the field and held regular discussions in group which we called a seminar, following the Malinowski tradition. It always lasted for a whole morning or whole afternoon in a most stimulating and enjoyable atmosphere. ("Chicago Talk":12–13)

Fei's enthusiasm attracted and inspired students, one of whom has since written of the extraordinary atmosphere at Kuige: the climate of free inquiry, the respect for individual expression, the open debate, and the spirit of camaraderie. The older type of Chinese teacher seemed by comparison haughty, dogmatic, intolerant of criticism, possessive about his theories and materials. Fei let his students study what interested them, stood at their sides training them and aiding them at all stages of research, urged them to put forward their own ideas in sometimes heated seminar discussions, and helped them publish their own work.³⁶ Wilma Fairbank, in the report quoted above, wrote:

> The Director and moving spirit of the Station is Fei Hsiao-t'ung, who . . . seems to have a gift for gathering around him bright young men . . . His creative mind, enthusiasm, and warm impulsive nature encourage and develop them it is plain to see. In turn, the general spirit of camaraderie and their lively uninhibited participation in discussions on all topics attest their faith in and affection for him.

The bright young men Fei gathered around him and instructed in social research numbered more than ten over the course of his several years at Kunming, although there were probably usually fewer than half a dozen there at any one time. Some dozen monographs were produced, but only a couple of these were printed in book form; the others were circulated in mimeograph, and are unfortunately not available now.³⁷

Fei's students made a brilliant and promising group of scholars in the 1940s. Zhang Ziyi, a 1939 Qinghua (Kunming) sociology graduate, helped with Fei's study of Lu-cun. Then, under Fei's direction, he carried out similar studies of two Yunnan villages in which, unlike Lu-cun, rural industry was important; one won an Academia Sinica prize as the best sociological work of 1942,³⁸ and the two were translated by Fei as Parts II and III of *Earthbound.* Zhang then did a study of the petty farming economy of another village.³⁹ Shi Guoheng, another 1939 Qinghua graduate in sociology,⁴⁰ was guided by Fei in a study of labor problems in a Kunming factory, which Fei translated into English as *China Enters the Machine Age* (1944). Shi later wrote on Yunnan tin-mining, and after the war Fei got him to Harvard for a year.⁴¹ Tian Rukang studied female workers in a Kunming cotton mill. He next did research on non-Chinese people on the Yunnan-Burma border, and then went to England and took a PhD in anthropology at the London School of Economics.⁴² Li Youyi, Yanjing BA (1935) and MA in sociology, wrote on Chinese-Lolo relations in a mixed community in Yunnan, which was summarized by Fei in *3 Types.*⁴³

The Yunnan Research Station, 1939–1946

Gu Bao did a study of the power structure in a Yunnan town. Hu Qingjun, a 1942 sociology graduate of Qinghua, made an investigation of the basic power structure in Chenggong.[44] Yuan Fang was also a 1942 Qinghua sociology graduate, with a thesis on urbanization in Kunming.[45] Francis L. K. Hsu (Xu Langguang), who had taken a PhD with Malinowski at L.S.E. in 1940, was not a student of Fei's but was associated with the Station. He did field work in western Yunnan in the early 1940s, published as *Magic and Science in Western Yunnan* (New York, mimeo., 1943) and *Under the Ancestor's Shadow* (New York, 1948), and served as acting director of the Station when Fei was in the United States in 1943–1944.[46]

Apart from Hsu, all of these men stayed in China after 1949 and have more or less dropped out of sight. Occasional articles, mostly non-scholarly, appeared under most of the above names in China in the 1950s. Yuan Fang was in 1957 an assistant professor at a Labor Cadres' School[47], and in 1972 American visitors found Shi Guoheng working as Qinghua's librarian; but, otherwise, it is not known what they have done in the last quarter of a century.

FOUR

A Chinese Anthropologist Looks at the United States

> Only abroad did I discover I was truly Chinese.
> —*CFMG:*97

Fei had once written that people with educations like his were middlemen between Eastern and Western cultures who were in a position to make great contributions to China's modernization (*JCTX* #4). It was a role that he was good at and devoted considerable energy to: traveling to the West, making American and British contacts, serving as a go-between for institutions on both sides, writing about China in English and about England and America for Chinese readers, and making translations both ways. He was abroad three times in all (before the late 1970s, when he began traveling again): for two years in London in 1936–1938, a year in the United States in 1943–1944, and three months in England again in 1946–1947. But it was on his American visit that Fei's activities as a cultural mediator were especially apparent. Out of this trip would come several English publications about China, no fewer than three books and countless articles in Chinese about the United States, and several close and enduring friendships with Americans.

VISIT TO THE UNITED STATES, 1943-1944

In 1942, the State Department's Division of Cultural Relations invited six Chinese universities to choose one professor each to be sent to the United States for a year, to study, make institutional contacts, and talk about China. Their passage was to be handled by the State Department, which would pay them $10 a day while they were in the United States and in transit and a lump sum of $500 to buy equipment in the United States; presumably part of this would be remitted to China for the support of their families. It was no doubt a munificent opportunity for someone struggling to live in the deprived conditions of 1940s China, and it must have been an honor to be selected to go; in the four years that the program continued, a number of famous scholars and writers were included, such as Tao Menghe, Lao She, and Cao Yu.[1] Of the first group of five professors, the youngest, at 32, was Fei Xiaotong, chosen by the President of Yunnan University, apparently with the understanding that he would translate into English some of his Station's studies, of which mimeographed abstracts in English had already attracted some foreign attention.[2]

Fei was in the United States from June 1943 to July 1944. I have been fortunate in being able to see letters Fei wrote during this period to Margaret Park Redfield, the daughter of Robert Park, with whom Fei had studied at Yanjing, and the wife of the Chicago anthropologist Robert Redfield; to Wilma Fairbank of the State Department's Division of Cultural Relations, who was in charge of his trip; and some to the Institute of Pacific Relations (IPR).[3] From this correspondence emerges a richer picture of Fei's week-to-week activities than is available to me for any other period of his life. It is a picture of an energetic and resourceful international scholarly entrepreneur, working closely with Americans to establish what he hoped would be the basis for long-term academic cooperation in the social sciences between Americans and Chinese.

Most of his time was spent preparing English versions of his and his students' works. During July, August, September, and October he was in New York at the offices of the Institute of Pacific Relations, translating his own *Lucun nongtian* into what was to become Part I of *Earthbound China*, with the aid of Paul Cooper, a graduate student of the Columbia anthropologist Ralph Linton. The IPR paid Cooper and provided Fei office space, secretarial help, and eventually a subsidy for the book. Parts II and III, Yunnan village studies by Zhang Ziyi, he translated in November, December, and January at the University of Chicago with the help of Margaret Redfield. February and March he spent at the Harvard Business School, translating (with the aid of Dorothea Mayo, wife of Business School professor Elton Mayo) a book by Shi Guoheng into *China Enters the Machine Age*. In April and May he was back in Chicago revising *Earthbound China* and writing an introduction and conclusion for it.

He also found time to travel within the United States, making a number of trips to various places on the east coast and upper midwest,[4] and to establish and cultivate contacts with American social scientists. He spent time with Linton, Robert Redfield, William Ogburn of Chicago, whose *Social Change* he had translated into Chinese a decade before, and George Taylor of the University of Washington, then working for the Office of War Information (OWI). On trips to Cornell, Michigan, and Minnesota, he gave talks and made contacts. At the University of Wisconsin, he was stimulated by conversations with a rural economist named Leonard A. Salter, Jr. At Harvard, he found the sociologists a little standoffish, except for Talcott Parsons, with whom he got along; he never even met Pitirim Sorokin. As for the Harvard Sinologists, Fei complained that they were dull and lost in the past (10/21/43 to WCF), but at the Business School he found that Elton Mayo and T. North Whitehead were greatly interested in discussing his work and concerned that China avoid making the West's mistake of neglecting the "human factor" in industrializing.

Much effort was devoted to trying to arrange for a prominent American social scientist to spend a year in China. Fei's hope was to enlist such a key person's sponsorship of cooperative research, which would involve considerable student exchange financed largely from the American side. After a couple of months in Chicago, he got no less a scholar than Robert Redfield, then Dean of the Division of Social Science at Chicago and Chairman of the Social Science Research Council, to agree to come to China for a year to survey the various institutions carrying on social research and the possibilities for American help. The State Department promised to provide wartime transportation. Several trips to New York finally secured financial support for Redfield's trip from the Rockefeller Foundation. There followed a long period of discouragement when it looked as though the project would be undone by the Chinese government's refusal to issue Redfield an official invitation, until at last in June an elated Fei could declare that this was straightened out and he had achieved success after all. Redfield set out on a sea voyage to China in the fall of 1944, but then, alas, all Fei's efforts were undermined by a dental problem which forced Redfield to disembark at another port and cancel the trip. When he and his wife finally came to China four years later, the Civil War was too far advanced for him to do field work with Fei or to stay very long.

Considerable time and travel went also to getting his students and colleagues in Yunnan fellowships or appointments to come to the United States. The Harvard Business School was happy to have Shi Guoheng, but unable to give financial support, which Fei solicited from several sources before finally succeeding with the Harvard-Yenching Institute; Shi came the next year. Several trips to Madison (and elsewhere) resulted in an assistantship in rural economics for the other of Fei's "two sons," Zhang Ziyi (3/8/44 to WCF); but, in the end, Zhang was unable to come. Fei also arranged with Linton and Karl Wittfogel for Francis L.K. Hsu and Qu Tongzu to come to Columbia the following year.

Fei's other big undertaking was to raise money for his Research Station. On this he did rather well. He asked the IPR for $10,000, a big sum in those days, and got part of it; the Harvard-Yenching Institute provided $4,000 for the coming year, and several talks with Yunnan industrialist Miao Yuntai in New York resulted in a grant from the Economic Council of Yunnan Province. He also got the University of Chicago sociology department to send to his Station and other Chinese institutions books solicited through an appeal in the *American Journal of Sociology* (5/16/44 & 4/29/44 to WCF).

Other projects included getting the China Institute to give a grant to the University of Chicago for a Chinatown study and finding someone to do it; and talking with Chinese students in the United States, whom he found generally unhappy. Fei was also writing articles about America for his Kunming weekly newspaper, *Shenghuo dao-bao;* for this he had an arrangement with George Taylor of the Office of War Information whereby OWI supplied him with materials about the United States (his article in praise of the American rationing system, for example, was based on such materials) and transmitted his articles to Kunming. In return, Fei promised to give them a list of topics on which they might publish pamphlets in Chinese and the names of Chinese in both China and the United States who might write them (10/11/43 from WCF). Fei was also instrumental in getting his friend C. K. Yang, with whom he stayed in New York, a six-month State Department appointment to write a Chinese guidebook to America, which was apparently a big success.[5]

In all this, Fei was aware of his own energy and resourcefulness. His natural exuberance—Jin Yuelin (one of the other professors on the United States trip, a philosopher and symbolic logician with whom Fei became close) said affectionately that he was only half civilized—was stimulated by the desire to make the best of his stay in the United States and to establish contacts here that would give him the edge over rival social researchers, such as Lin Yaohua and Chen Da. He referred to himself as a "promoter," and spoke of the importance of "able and efficient executives" who could run things single-handedly, as he had run his Station in Yunnan. Busy, energetic, productive, he felt himself the embodiment of the American spirit of enterprise, hard work, self-reliance, and creative energy. He wrote in a letter, "I am in fact more American than Chinese. In China such [a] personality ... is too disturbing" (11/11?/43 to WCF).

Indeed he seems to have fit in well in the United States and to have flourished. Wearing Western clothes, speaking fluent bubbling English, discussing social theory at universities with fellow professors and social scientists, he was more or less right at home. He felt difficulty in learning to address Americans senior in age and status by their first names; he worried that he had offended Mayo by alluding to his age; he couldn't handle cocktails very well. But these were minor problems, and he formed warm friendships with several Americans. In particular he accomplished much by enlisting the support of intelligent and able women: Wilma Fairbank, Margaret Redfield, Dorothea Mayo. Fei tended to speak of enjoying the "mothering" or being in the "motherly care" of these women (11/8/43 and 1/20/44 to WCF; 2/9/44 to MPR), and wondered if he didn't have "a psychological complex": "I do not know why I usually get encouragement from that end [women] . . . It can not be only chance. There must be something wrong with me" (2/19/44 to WCF). To Margaret Redfield he wrote: "I must confess that I feel really at home when I come to your family. I cannot find any essential difference from China and America when I am staying with you" (6/16/44 to MPR).

Fei was to pay a price for his close and successful foreign ties, for they were later sharply criticized in China by nationalists on both the right and left. In 1947, he complained that "conservative elements" were attacking him for cooperating with foreigners and publishing about China in English (5/12/49 [i.e. 47] to WCF). In the Communist press of the 1950s, Malinowski's admiration for his "absence of national prejudice and national hatred" (*Peasant Life*:xxv) would be quoted against him, and it would be said that his activities had amounted to selling intelligence about China to imperialists.

It is true, of course, that his career was advanced by foreign support. Indeed, a far longer and more detailed list could be made than was ever published in the 1950s of close contacts with Americans and Britons and of ways in which he benefited from these ties. He had studied at American-financed and controlled schools, and then gone abroad on a Qinghua scholarship from British Boxer

Indemnity Funds (money which, though coming from the Chinese government, was owed to and partially controlled by foreigners). In Yunnan, he held a British Boxer Indemnity Fellowship directly from the British Council, and his Research Station was founded and supported by Rockefeller Foundation money as well as Chinese funds. After Fei returned from his trip to the United States, paid for by the State Department, the American Consul General in Kunming was pleased to report to Washington that he had "contributed to Kunming newspapers and magazines several articles indicative of strong pro-American feeling."[6] His book on the United States, *Chu fang Meiguo,* was published by the Office of War Information, the propaganda agency of the American government. He invited GIs into his home (1/29/45 to WCF). He seems to have been friendly with some Consulate and OWI people in Kunming, and in the summer of 1946 he and a dozen others, fearful of assassination, took refuge in the Consulate for several days. His American friends, many of them government employees, performed countless favors, from sending back his articles through government channels while he was in the United States, to sending him asthma medicine, books, and articles after his return to China, and helping get his protégés to the United States. He obtained a grant from the State Department for a symposium, and a personal research grant from the Institute of Pacific Relations. The royalties from his books published in England and America, paid in foreign currencies, were an important source of income in these years when his salary was eaten away by inflation.

Yet in all these activities—most of which, it should be remembered, were carried on in the wartime atmosphere (so different from that of the decades that followed) of China and America fighting together against their common Japanese enemy—Fei's goal was the betterment of Chinese society, for which he felt great concern and attachment. Although he more than once had the opportunity to advance his career through a job in the West, Fei— unlike so many Western-educated Chinese—rejected the idea of becoming an expatriate. He was a patriot, though not in a narrowly nationalistic sense. He had been educated in Yanjing's spirit of internationalism and the anthropological tradition of tolerance and respect for other cultures. He believed that the airplane was making the globe smaller, walls were being torn down, and the need for global understanding was greater than ever (*CFMG:*175–177). Most people think of their own culture as the standard, he said; this attitude strengthens them in time of war but, now that "a world society is coming into being," such blind faith had become a source of international friction (*MGRXG:*73–74, 87–88). Fei's efforts as a cultural mediator were intended to help relieve these dangerous tensions.

CHANGING PERCEPTIONS OF AMERICAN CULTURE

Interestingly, the time when Fei sounded most like a Westernizer was probably before his trip to the United States. Articles from early 1943, a few months before leaving China, expressed impatience at the conservatism of Chinese culture. He urged China to learn from the West more dynamic, progressive, Faustian values, and criticized the Chinese attitude of passively enduring time and life. Chinese saw themselves as passengers on a ferry, he said, accepting what comes, hoping for good fortune instead of actively seeking it, whiling time away instead of using it industriously as capital. They were like plants; even in war, they passively waited for victory as frozen trees await spring, rather than making sacrifices, running risks, or taking the initiative. "We are old monks in an ancient monastery ringing the evening bell in the dusk, unable to imagine that there are girls at dawn wildly singing at the top of their voices." Life was short and should be lived to the full; and when it couldn't be lived happily one should not be unwilling to die (1943Ja1).

In order to insure material support for their old age, he said, Chinese maintained control over their children even when they were grown. The result was that their society was perpetually in the shadow of the old and decrepit. For a society to change, reform, be progressive, it had to be child-centered and future-oriented. To free China of the domination of the aged, he said, the state should assume responsibility for providing for old people (1943 Ja30). In another article Fei maintained that Chinese society was stagnant because it lacked wild dreams, utopian visions, and ideals. Such natural yearnings and dissatisfaction with the present were what spurred people to creation and progress, but Chinese culture had rejected them in favor of an accommodation with the status quo. Chinese values were those of acceptance, not creation; "in politics, returning to the past; in art, classicism; in ethics, staying within bounds." "A people so poisoned are as paralyzed—not dead, yet not alive." "Traditional Chinese culture has shown it cannot preserve the existence of our race; we must create a new culture" (1943Mr20).

Fei's first impressions of the United States he described in a series of articles for a Kunming weekly, articles that were subsequently collected and reprinted under the title *Renqing yu bangjiao* (Human feelings and international relations; *RQ&BJ*). The earlier ones are full of praise for the fairness of American wartime measures and the unstinting public support for the war effort; praise, and surprise too, for it was very different from what he had just come from in Nationalist China. Stopping at U.S. airbases on his way to the United States, he was impressed with the good treatment given American soldiers: good food, freezers full of meat (indeed civilians faced shortages because so much had been sent to the military), decent pay, medical care, housing with two or three in a room, movies, playing fields, reading rooms, chapels, and cemeteries. It was not just that America was rich, Fei wrote; the average citizen was paying a 35 percent income tax to support this. And then he went on to speak of civilian hoarding and profiteering in wartime China (*RQ&BJ*:1–4).

He described the American rationing system in detail, saying it had succeeded in preventing the inflation that was plaguing China, and had also eliminated hoarding. A black market existed, he acknowledged, but most people observed the law. Most remarkable, the system extended even to the White House, where it was said the head cook dreaded the arrival of important guests like Churchill, for how could he provide enough meat and butter (pp. 19-24)? Fei was impressed with the extent of popular support for the war effort, the willingness of Americans to make sacrifices, to fight, and to die. He was amazed to meet a company president serving in the army, and chafing at being far from the action at that. In China, by contrast, people thought only of avoiding the draft and of profiting from the war. It showed, he said, that the best way to concentrate people's strength and build a powerful nation was through democracy and not fascism—not coercion but popular participation (Chapters 2 and 9).

He praised American women. They were not the frivolous creatures Chinese saw in American movies, interested only in dancing, love affairs, marriage and divorce. ("I think our Shanghai women and a portion in present-day Kunming are perhaps closer to the movie pattern than the average American woman.") American women were busy with social responsibilities—in addition to housework, for few had servants. While their husbands manned the front lines, millions had taken jobs in factories, making a great contribution to the war effort. Others were in the military, and in Washington more and more women were performing important jobs. This, he wrote after a talk with Congresswoman Clare Booth Luce, would undoubtedly make American government more humane, compassionate, and peaceful (pp. 29-33).

Crossing the Hudson by ferry on his first trip to New York, he was awed by the sight of the Manhattan skyline. The skyscrapers and smokestacks, and the power and wealth they represented, stood out in overwhelming contrast to China. He visited the home of a cabdriver in Miami, a little, carefully furnished house with a small garden full of flowers, and when the man's tanned, well-fed wife apologized that they were just poor people, Fei could only exclaim, "Even we professors don't enjoy such happiness." Staying overnight at a farm in Minnesota, he reflected that the average American farm of five hundred *mu* was as big as a whole village in Yunnan, where the average farm was but five *mu*. One family on that much land could have security, a radio and an automobile, plenty of food, a college education for the children; but how could a hundred families hope for this? He quoted that bitter line from Du Fu: "Inside the red gate wine and meat spoil, while on the road corpses freeze." But the Americans had worked hard for what they had. They had not always been rich; indeed the memory of poverty was painfully close, as the Broadway success of *Tobacco Road* showed. Coming out of this play, which he said showed poverty as brutal as anything he had seen even in the Yao mountains, into Times Square, he was overcome with the magnitude of the progress that had been made—made as a result of hard work and self-reliance (*CFMG*:13–22).

Such were the articles expressing his initial enthusiasm for America. It is clear that, to a considerable extent, he was looking on the United States as a model for China in the future. In a letter, he stated explicitly his expectation that "the China [that] will come" would be "an industrial China which cannot be too different from the America of to-day" (10/21/43 to WCF), and it distressed him to think how far China had to go to catch up. But, as the months went by and his enthusiasm and energy wore off, he began to think more fondly of his homeland. "I am getting more conservative," he wrote in a letter (4/21/44 to WCF), and in another spoke of "struggling between two cultures"; "I am not trained in a classical way, but I love the [Chinese] tradition and hope it should not die away in a sheer compact [conflict-impact?] with the West (2/23/44 to MPR). In an article about Chinese students studying in the United States—he was harsh with those who came just to avoid the draft and to further their careers—he wrote of the need to be a member of a group with which one shares sympathy, a sense of mutual responsibility, and standards of conduct. In a strange society, one feels airless and uneasy. Ice cream and bread and butter cannot relieve the sense of listlessness and emptiness (*RQ&BJ*:67–71).

The tone of his articles began to change. Writing from Harvard in the spring, he complained about the fickle weather, overheated houses, the ugly smokestacks and smoke "which could make only a Wu Jingchao [famous as an advocate of industrialization for China] appreciate industrialization"; Western food which "except for breakfast I more and more dislike"; Harvard's aristocratic atmosphere (which he said he resented "because I come from a poor background"); the Harvard Faculty Club's exclusion of women from the premises; and finally the fate of an old retired professor he met, discarded after so many years of teaching and left to live there alone. Fei began to feel that "there are some things in Western culture which we need not bring to China" (*RQ&BJ*:45–52).

Whereas earlier Fei had criticized the Chinese veneration for age, he now felt repelled by the way Americans treated their old. On Thanksgiving Day, he had a turkey dinner at the home of an American friend, who took out his father's old diary and read the entry for Thanksgiving 1901; the passage spoke of the children growing up, and of the sad fact that they would soon be leaving home. Fei reacted strongly:

> I know well all the tragedies of the [Chinese] big family, but at that moment I became a reactionary and felt that to make sacrifices to bring up children and then watch them fly away like swallows, leaving one able only to sit on a cold park bench and feed sparrows, is just too cruel ... I am glad I was not born in America. (*RQ&BJ*:53–59)

He wrote movingly of how terrible it must be to live in a culture where age is not respected, where "old" is a term of abuse meaning useless, broken, about to die—where old women wear make-up and even men dye their hair, and the young dread approaching age. By contrast, he remembered how his father's friends had felt proud to be nearing fifty. The difference seemed to be between a society in which knowledge based on tradition and experience, which the old have, is valuable and valued, and a new culture in which experience is less useful. Science compresses experience into quickly learned formulas—the discoveries that took Newton a lifetime can be mastered by a schoolboy in a week—and Fei wondered sadly whether science, which China needed for economic development, would destroy its traditional respect for old people (*RQ&BJ*:53–59).

He pitied Americans for living in a world without ghosts. Ghosts represented tradition, a sense of history and continuity with the past. Fei told of how comforting it was, as a body, to seem to see his grandmother, who had recently died, walk through the room in her accustomed way, and of the beautiful feeling that separation in time could be overcome. American children, however, did not listen to ghost stories, but instead read Superman comic books. It seemed to Fei that an approach to reality that ignored the past was shallow, empty, and false, for the present was built upon and contained all that had gone before. Traditionalism, he admitted, had its bad aspects, specifically privilege and resistance to change; but still, "I feel Chinese culture at its base is beautiful—to live in a world with ghosts" (*CFMG:*106–16).

In another article, he was astonished to see hanging on Wilma Fairbank's living room wall a Chinese ancestor portrait, for she had no Chinese ancestors. And he related in bemused detail his experience in a Chinese restaurant in Washington, where those cultural bastards, chop suey and chow mein (which he had to write in English letters and describe for his Chinese audience), served by Chinese waiters in Western dress (Cantonese who answered his Mandarin in English), were eaten with knife and fork and (*horribile dictu,* for it makes the oil congeal in one's stomach) washed down with ice water; all to the accompaniment of girls doing Spanish dances to American jazz ("I don't understand how it can be called music") and a Cuban singer introduced by an announcer with a southern European accent. In the original version of the article on these episodes, he spoke not disparagingly of the American melting pot in which different cultures fused; and he said such gaucheries showed the boldness and lack of inhibitions of a young culture. The American spirit was like that of a sixteen-year-old boy, boldly setting out to tame the wilderness; and it was this spirit that, in little over a century, had turned a wild frontier into "a utopia where doors are not locked at night nor lost items picked up from the road" (a classical Chinese description of the ideal state). In contrast, China's long history and traditions "restrict us and make it hard to modernize quickly" (*RQ&BJ:*24–28). But in the revision of this article, done after his return to China, the tone of admiration is gone. Fei now felt this spirit of daring, experimentation, and recklessness could come only if there was opportunity, which the American frontier had provided. But, he wondered, now that the frontier was gone, would American culture grow up, take fixed form, and settle down? China had had a youthful atmosphere in the Spring and Autumn Period in the first millenium B.C., but then matured. In the last century, Western industrial culture had been young and growing, but perhaps maturity was near—the English already were said to crave quiet and contentment (*CFMG:*33-44). Thus, Fei no longer spoke only of China's learning from the West; there might also be ways in which the West would become more like China.

Fei seems to have thought of the basic difference between Western and Chinese culture as the contrast between ceaseless productive energy and leisurely contentment with poverty. The attitude of villagers he had seen in Lu-cun, content to sit in the sun and smoke a pipe and enjoy the prestige of wearing a long gown even though they were very poor, was strikingly different from the Protestant ethic of endless work for the sake of ever-deferred future pleasure and the "acquisitiveness" that Tawney said moved the modern economy. (Later, using concepts from Spengler, Fei would speak of China's as an Apollonian type of culture, classical, trying to preserve an already established order, and the West as Faustian, finding the meaning of life in ceaseless struggle, creation, and change; *XTZG:*46).

Fei's own emotions about work and leisure seem to have become connected with his feelings about the West and China, and also city and countryside. When he was feeling energetic and productive, he thought of himself as American, and was positive about American culture. But, after finishing a project, he would become depressed and often physically ill until he became caught up in new work. At such times he would yearn to be away from "the whip of work and its scanty rewards" (*CFMG:*7-8), talk of retiring somewhere to write a novel, complain about the pace of life in American cities, dream of a lonely mountain monastery in western Yunnan to which he had gone for escape in early

1943, and wonder if he was not mostly Chinese and never really to feel at home in America after all.

He would dream of the countryside, in spite of the fact that "not only am I unable to recognize a rose; I don't know the names of even a dozen flowers" (*RQ&BJ:*12). "You have seen that I am not a real gardener, but . . . like to live in the country, perhaps in the way of a Chinese gentleman-leisure-class," he wrote to an American friend, adding that he thought happiness was to "have a garden but . . . not need to work on it" (5/17/44 to MPR). This peaceful, Chinese countryside he sometimes thought of so broadly as even to include his childhood Suzhou, a city by any measure.[7] In the following passage, Fei linked together ideas of leisure, rural life, Suzhou, and Chinese traditional culture:

> I am still turned to the countryside; my character and prejudices are still traditional. I cannot feel at ease in the tumult of Shanghai or the night life of Hong Kong. I seem unable to get rid of the ideal of life of one raised in Suzhou: a silk gown, satin shoes, and leisure in a teahouse. (*CFMG:*7)

Thus, in American cities, did Fei become nostalgic for what he thought of as a more rural China.

On his return to China, Fei found himself regarded as an American expert, with a considerable audience for talks and articles about China's wartime ally and the model of a modernized society which China had set out to become. In order to supplement his visitor's impressions (for he had, in fact, spent much of his year in America in offices making translations), he began to read books and articles about the United States, and out of this came a more systematic analysis and critique, found in his second book about the United States, *Chu fang Meiguo* (First visit to America; *CFMG*), published in 1945. Although this book does contain some anecdotal material from articles written during his visit, it is less a travelogue than the title implies, but rather an attempt to explain American culture in terms of its history and environment.

The American spirit, its values and traditions, Fei said, were shaped by European immigrants opening up a vast new land, a frontier full of opportunity. If he had previously spoken of American culture as urban, he now asserted that the American spirit was really essentially pre-industrial and formed by rural life. Most middle-aged and older Americans even in the 1940s, he said, had been brought up on farms; this was the basis of the American spirit of hard work, self-reliance, equality, and love of freedom (*CFMG:*14–16). America was originally a poor country, a wasteland opened up by poor people fleeing poverty and oppression in Europe. Rebellious types to begin with, on isolated, dispersed, one-family farms, without the protection of a feudal lord, they had to rely on themselves for defense against the Indians. Without traditions, in a "cultural vacuum" (p. 36), for they were fleeing from the old culture, they relied on their own experience and judgment. They disliked interference and distrusted government (pp. 24–32). With uncultivated land waiting to be opened up, there was opportunity; all it took was strength and work. The American frontier fostered an "acquisitive" spirit, daring and heedless of consequences (pp. 37–39).

This analysis in terms of environment could still lead to some comparisons very unflattering to China. In a society where another's success opens doors for everyone, people feel happy at the happiness of others, he said; but in China, with its scarce resources, another's gain is often one's own loss. That is why Americans freely displayed happy emotions in public—husband and wife kissed and hugged at a train station in a way that seemed quite undignified and improper to Chinese, but hid their tears at a funeral. With the Chinese, however, it was just the opposite; grief is displayed and gladness hidden so as not to arouse spiteful envy:

> When westerners see another's happiness they feel happy, but with us another's happiness makes us unhappy . . . Jealousy is our basic spirit. Joy at disaster and unwillingness to help others out is our tradition. We can pity another's hardship, but this is not sympathy but a kind of feeling of comfort at our own security. (pp. 118–119)

His view of America was now much more political than it had been before, and it contained shadows, in part the result of his reading of such radical American social critics as Charles Beard and of what he termed "progressive" journals like *The Nation* and *The New Republic* (p. 154). The "two wheels of the cart to happiness," science (the basis of industrialization) and democracy, he said, had developed at different speeds. Bourgeois financial and industrial interests were able, in the Constitution, to block the passion for equality expressed in the Declaration of Independence. The development of large-scale industry meant the economy was increasingly dominated by great concentrations of industry and commerce, trusts, and millionaire robber barons, with whom the common people could not hope to compete and so no longer had real liberty and equality (pp. 45–55).

Fei did not show much interest in the Jeffersonian idea that cities were inimical to democracy, which was based in rural life. Jefferson's ideal small farmer no longer had a place, he said, and it was the big-city factories that absorbed the immigrants, giving them jobs and freedom from hunger (pp. 56–58). The trouble was that American democracy was merely negative, stressing freedom from government interference, in the mistaken faith that Adam Smith's invisible hand would ensure that individuals pursuing individual interests would result in the greatest happiness of the majority. Only slowly, after many periodic depressions and one Great Depression with twelve million out of work, did social legislation and laws opening the way for labor unions begin to emerge. This Fei welcomed, of course, though he had some critical words for American labor unions for perpetuating the gulf between management and labor, and failing to concern themselves with people's need for a feeling that their actions had social significance and that they were working toward a common goal (pp. 69–78).

America had its problems, but Fei was sanguine that they would be solved, because Americans had ideals. These were in part grounded in Christianity, which Fei called "an important pillar of Western culture," even if Americans did not go to church very much any more (p. 129). The Christian spirit was the opposite of Chinese selfish disregard for others. Because of their belief in an omniscient God, Americans did not try to cover up their sins, but had the courage to admit the shortcomings in their society, such as the race question. The rich felt solicitude for others and uneasy about their wealth, and were much more apt than Chinese to contribute liberally to colleges, hospitals, social work, and research institutes. In short, Christianity had given Western culture "an ideal of perfection, spread deep in each man's heart." Thus Fei returned to the importance of ideals, utopian visions of the future, as the psychological impetus behind social progress. And what about China? China had no religion in the sense of selfless devotion to something outside; Chinese feared, tricked, bribed, and begged from their gods, who represented power and wealth, not ideals and principles. Fei seemed unsure whether China could acquire the idealistic spirit:

> I am not a Christian . . . I don't believe one must be a Christian to have love, selflessness, ideals . . . But . . . I feel what we have lacked is this [guide], and it is most difficult to obtain . . . What is worthy of our admiration is not everything they have but their process of creation and the spirit which moves them to create. And, what is worth our studying from them I think is nothing other than the ideal they have of a world of love and sympathy which Christ symbolizes. (pp. 137–38)

An article on the Chinese in the United States told of the various abuses and inequities they had suffered, but also defended the Americans. He maintained that their anti-Chinese prejudice was understandable, given the Chinese immigrants' strange customs, lack of education, and the real economic threat they presented because of the low wages they were willing to accept (How would we treat such people in our midst? he asked, and gave examples of Chinese intolerance of outsiders). He added that new opportunities for advancement were now opening up for Chinese-Americans (pp. 79–86).

He concluded the book with three optimistic articles about how the excessive power of big business was being curbed and American political democracy was leading to economic democracy.

First, the working classes were becoming educated to their true interests—the CIO's Political Action Committee had made a great contribution towards this in 1944—electing more progressive leaders and combating the ability of big business to buy the friendship of politicians with campaign contributions. Second, he was encouraged by the New Deal policies of controlling big business for the sake of public welfare. Finally, he felt "overwhelmed" reading David Lilienthal's book on the TVA (6/19/45 to MPR). The success of the TVA (which he greatly regretted not having visited), proved, he said, that society's interests need not be incompatible with individual interests and that society's prosperity was good for private enterprise, and it had given people a sense of participation in a common social goal (pp. 137–173).

CRITIC OF AMERICAN POLICIES, 1947–1948

By 1947, Fei had come to consider that the hope he had felt for America two years before was mistaken. The New Deal promise of economic democracy was being undone, since the end of the war, by the anti-labor and anti-New Deal legislation of the Republican-controlled Congress, and by Truman's foreign policy, which seemed to seek American paramountcy in the world. He no longer felt hopeful about the possibility of political and economic democracy going together (CFYL:77–80). The main cause of his increasing bitterness towards the United States was unquestionably the American aid and support for the Nationalist Government in China, from which, as we shall see, he had become strongly disaffected—support which, he no doubt felt, strengthened rightist elements within the Guomindang and blocked the formation of a coalition government with the Communists. "I have no doubt your government has done something very bad to us," he wrote to Margaret Redfield (11/27/46 to MPR).

This new attitude can be glimpsed only obliquely in the third book Fei wrote about the United States, *Meiguouren de xingge* (The American character; *MGRXG*), which appeared in 1947, for it had started out as a translation, which he then decided needed to be rewritten for a Chinese audience and, "once writing, my pen strayed far from the original" (*MGRXG:*72–75). The original was Margaret Mead's *And Keep Your Powder Dry: An Anthropologist Looks at America* (1942), an attempt by this famous social scientist to describe the national personality—the book was published in England under the title *The American Character*. Up to a point, Fei followed Mead's book faithfully enough. There are chapters in both versions on how Americans frequently moved from place to place, rejecting their past (*MGRXG,* Chapter 1), and moving up the social ladder (Chapter 2); how parental love was conditional on success (Chapter 3); the importance attached to school grades (Chapter 4); how success was associated with divine favor in the Puritan tradition (Chapter 5); how Americans valued fair play and did not like to start a fight (Chapter 6); and their ambivalent attitude to Europe (Chapter 8).

In some ways, however, Fei's book painted a less hopeful picture of America than did his rather up-beat source, which had been written in part to bolster American morale during the war. Where Margaret Mead described American cultural ideals, Fei added here and there statements to the effect that these ideals were not yet fully realized, that the American reality was less rosy. He added a section explaining the concept of national character as socially shaped common personality, in which he criticized Mead for describing as "the American character" cultural patterns which in fact were not shared by blacks, Chinese-Americans, and other minority culture groups (pp. 76–86). He added a whole chapter on racial prejudice in America, describing how blacks were denied equal opportunity in contradiction to American ideals, and hinting that this was an upsetting question for him, as though he had had some unpleasant experience; but, if so, he nowhere related it. (He had written elsewhere, "Americans are very conscious of race and skin color, but, since the outbreak of the war, we yellow-skinned Chinese do not run into public prejudice, at least not very often" [*RQ&BJ:*69].) Finally, Mead had asked whether the current generation had lost its sense of moral purpose as a result of, among other things, the New Deal (Fei toned down her criticism of the New Deal; he was very pro-Roosevelt), and she answered no, because child-rearing patterns were too deeply ingrained (Mead, Chapter 8). Fei said he was not convinced, however; he thought Americans had indeed lost their self-confidence, that World War II was fought without clear goals, and that the post-war anti-Soviet hysteria was due to these self-doubts—in a word, that Americans had been sick with fear for twenty years (*MPRXG,* Chapter 5).

Fei's disillusionment with the United States, and particularly its post-war domestic and foreign policies, is clearer in his writings on international affairs from the late 1940s. During the latter half of 1947 and all of 1948, several dozen articles flowed from his pen, some in a series called "Lu bian tianxia" (The world from firesides; *LBTX*), on the internal and foreign affairs of the United States, Great Britain, France, Italy, Greece, Japan, and on American policy towards China. The material for these detailed and well-informed pieces seems to have come from leftist British and American political magazines. At his request, friends in England and America regularly sent him clippings from journals of current opinion (6/20/47 to WCF; 1948My15), and his articles frequently refer to such journals as *The New Statesman, The Economist, The Spectator,* and *The Nation.*

These numerous and varied articles are marked by a recurring critique of America's actions in the world. Both American political parties were controlled by capitalist bosses, he argued, and American foreign policy represented the business interests' response to the threat of a post-war depression. Productive capacity had expanded during World War II to beyond what peacetime demand could consume; but, instead of seeking a solution in some kind of New Deal or socialist national economic planning, the United States was trying to avoid depression by securing markets abroad for its excess production, and it was this need for foreign markets that underlay both America's hostility to the Soviet Union and the Marshall Plan of loans to Europe (1945N10; 1947Ag1).

The Cold War Fei seems to have blamed largely on the United States. He wrote very little about the Soviet Union in these articles, but a passage here and there suggests that he saw it as weaker, preoccupied with domestic economic reconstruction, and responding to American provocation. The Russians were no real threat to the Americans, and American fear of the Soviet Union was irrational. In his earlier articles, Fei hinted that this anti-Russian feeling in the United States was being stirred up by Truman to serve other goals—to incite workers to make economic sacrifices, or to win public support for foreign aid, or to stimulate the arms industry, which helped to avoid depression. In the later articles, he pointed to a real conflict of interest with the Soviet Union: Russian-supported socialist governments refused to be "free" markets for American goods. The Cold War and American belligerence toward the Soviet Union, Fei felt, created a serious danger of a hot war, indeed an atomic war of unprecedented destructiveness. The American people did not want war—they were more interested in baseball than foreign affairs (*LBTX* 3.16:18)—but the fear of economic depression was also a factor, and propaganda in the business-controlled press had made Americans afraid of socialism and the Soviet Union. At times, Fei suggested that compromise between the United States and the U.S.S.R. was possible (1947Jl1; 1947N16), but often he feared that world peace was in serious danger (1948Ja1b). Cold War tensions were also damaging to those nations in between the two powers (1947Je15).

Fei had at first welcomed the Marshall Plan as a reversal of the Truman Doctrine, which had led to conflict with the U.S.S.R., and he denied that the Marshall Plan was necessarily anti-Soviet (1947 Jl2; 1947O1). But he subsequently began to see ways in which it was not to the benefit of Europe. Its purpose was really veiled self-interest: to create in Europe an economically healthy market for American goods, and thus avoid another depression at home. Aid was used to get political concessions out of the recipients, to try to reestablish the old order in Europe, and to prevent the rise of socialist governments. Fei also noted the Marshall Plan had the effect of cutting off western European countries from east Europe, which would be their natural source of agricultural products, and obliging them to buy these instead from the United States (1948Ja17a; 1948Mr1a).

The deleterious effects on other nations of free trade with the United States and its huge "international monopolies" Fei described in an article on the movie industry in England, which he found was being stifled by Hollywood imports. American movie companies controlled most of the movie theatres in England and bought away good English actors, with the result that the English movie industry could not really get going, and considerable foreign exchange was wasted on importing American movies. Such "free enterprise" really amounted to control by foreign capitalists, but it was difficult for nations accepting American aid to avoid this (*LBTX* 4.2:17-18). In countries other than England, too, U.S. policy had unfortunate effects. In France, Fei thought American loans had caused the government to move to the right and had put it in a position where it could ignore the demands of the workers, thus weakening the Communist Party there (*LBTX* 3.18:18-19). In Italy, the American insistence that aid would be terminated if the Communists came to power had caused a polarization between the popular leftists and the American-supported Christian Democrats, who were too close to the Fascists to be popular (*LBTX*, 3.22:17, 19). American efforts to strengthen Japan alarmed Fei, because Japan had not been really democratized, and might well become expansionist and threaten China again (1945S16; 1947Ag10; 1948F28). In Greece, the Truman Doctrine amounted to aid to an unpopular government which just made it more corrupt and unpopular (1948Jl20).

It all had implications for China, of course, implications which hardly needed spelling out. An article and part of an editorial on Greece which he translated from *The Nation* (166:3-5 [January 3, 1948]) told how the corrupt and oppressive fascist Greek dictatorship was using the existence of the guerrillas as a justification for terror and for getting more millions in U.S. aid dollars. Fei dryly explained that he had made a translation because he was afraid that, if he had written an article of his own on this subject, "people might suspect . . . I was using 'Greece' to talk about a certain oriental country" (*LBTX* 4.3:18).

What he did spell out, repeatedly, were reasons why the Nationalists should not take continued American support for granted—warnings no doubt made in the hope that the government would be more responsive to domestic pressures for reform if it were less sure of foreign backing. U.S. policy was fickle and apt to change, he warned. The American hostility to the U.S.S.R. was not an end in itself, but a means to economic goals that would be threatened by war. War between the United States and the Soviet Union, a war which some Chinese were counting on to bring all-out American support to the Nationalists, was not likely (1947Jl1; 1948My29; 1948Jl20; 1948Ag5b; 1948O20). American security did not require an anti-Communist China; the United States was looking more to Japan (1947Je1; 1947Jl19). China was not as important to the United States as was Europe, and did not warrant a Truman Doctrine or a Marshall Plan; the United States would not make a big loan to China, as this might provoke the Russians to enter the conflict there, Fei predicted in January 1948—incorrectly as it turned out (*LBTX*,3.20:18–19). During the presidential election campaign, Fei insisted that foreign policy was based on real interests and that, campaign promises notwithstanding, when it came to real interests there was not any basic difference between the two parties. Dewey's election probably would not bring increased aid to China, for the United States was aware it could not change the outcome of the Civil War (1948Jl3; 1948Jl20). Finally, in November 1948, Fei thought that, in view of Nationalist losses, the United States would probably cut off aid, step aside, and hope instead for markets in a Communist China not too closely tied to the U.S.S.R. (*LBTX,* 5.10:14–15).

Yet, though less than wished for and in spite of ups and downs, American support for the Nationalists continued to the end, and in the end Fei was disillusioned and bitter about the United States. He had followed the presidential election with great interest (1948Ja17a; 1948Ap24; 1948Jl3; 1948Jl31), for it involved policies towards China. His sympathies were with Henry

Wallace, who he thought alone represented the people's interests in peace rather than business's interests in belligerent anti-communism around the globe. Wallace's failure made Fei question the fairness of the election (there were some dishonest practices against Wallace, black suffrage was restricted in the South, and so on, he said). He doubted whether all the candidates could make their views known in news organs owned by businessmen, whether either party really represented the interests of the people, and whether those elected kept their campaign promises and were responsive to the people. "Democracy, democracy," he concluded. "When all these subtractions have been made, is there anything left but the name?" (1948N20).

In October 1948, when Communist troops were near Peking and few doubted their victory was at hand, Fei wrote that the Iron Curtain was really between the rich and the poor, between the United States and the rest of the world. Caring only for their own security and kept ignorant by a capitalist-controlled press, the Americans were unable to see that the Cold War policies that aided their own economy were causing untold suffering in Europe and China (*LBTX*, 5.10:14–15). He remained firm in his friendship for individual Americans (many of whom surely shared his views about American support for the Nationalists), such as the Redfields who stayed with him in Peking in October 1948. But the United States, because of its policies in China, had lost an influential friend and admirer.

URBAN INDUSTRY

Out of Fei's American experience, in large part, came his feeling that there was something wrong with "modern industrial civilization" as it had developed in the West, an idea that came to be interwoven with his argument for rural industry in China.

Prior to his visit to the United States, in 1940, before Japanese bombing forced the Research Station to move out of Kunming, Fei and his colleagues had begun to get interested in urban industry in southwest China, largely out of a desire to know what was happening to villagers who were leaving their farms and going to work in modern factories. Two researchers from the station, Shi Guoheng and Tian Rukang, made studies of labor in Kunming factories, interviewing and living with workers in 1940 and 1941. They found, in brief, a very unsatisfactory situation. Efficiency was low; both workers and management agreed that the workers were producing much less than they could. Morale was poor; there were frequent fights, disputes, and ill-feelings, and workers tended to leave their jobs after a few months. Fei was somewhat involved in this research, helping to plan it and visiting the factories several times, and in the United States translated the results into English (*Machine Age*).

In articles written at this time on labor problems in Chinese industry, he tended to take the view that the problems were caused by rural attitudes carried over into city factories where they were no longer appropriate. The economic calculus of enduring the present pain of work in order to enjoy the future pleasure of consumption was the foundation of modern capitalism, first in the form of the Protestant work ethic described by Sombart, Weber, and Tawney, whereby consumption was put off to the next world (this Fei called irrational and non-humanistic asceticism); and then, "as the religious tide receded," in the form of pell-mell production for the sake of consumption in this world, a drive that underlay socialist economics too. In rural China, by contrast, as he had found at Lu-cun, the basic calculus was simply avoiding pain, restricting consumption to avoid work. Such an attitude, rational enough when it came to the "sweat and blood" labor of Chinese agriculture, was inappropriate in urban workers, whose work was not so onerous. It had the unfortunate effect of making them work less as wartime wages rose (1940Ag5).

Similarly, an agricultural society's contempt for manual labor, he argued, was inappropriate in a modern factory, where the worker was no longer like an animal, but was a supervisor, a master over his machinery (precisely the opposite of what he would say later). The persistence of this attitude impaired the ability of new industries to attract workers—Shi and Tian found that most workers from villages were in Kunming just temporarily to avoid the draft or creditors—and created a gulf between blue-collar and white-collar workers in factories, which made cooperation impossible (1941Ja12; 1946a:220-24).

In another early article, Fei suggested that the inefficiency of factory workers was due to their not resting properly in their off hours. Agricultural work, though onerous, was carried on at a leisurely pace, so there was no need for rest afterwards. But, when people worked fixed hours and then spent their nights at mahjong or in boisterous activities in theatres, coffeehouses, and parks, they would doze off on the job the next day. "If we want to enter industrial civilization," he said, Chinese must learn to spend their leisure time in recreation that refreshes: music and literature and strolling outside the city and enjoying the scenery (1942D11). Thus, before going to the United States, Fei had seen the problems of factory workers in terms of the cultural lag between a changing economy and persistent rural habits and attitudes, and seems to have felt that those rural patterns should and would change.

In the United States, he began to take a different view. There is no indication that he ever visited an American factory but, while at the Harvard Business School translating Shi's book into English, he spent some time talking about the problems of industry with the industrial sociologists Elton Mayo and T. North Whitehead. The conclusion to Fei's translation of Shi's book was, in fact, largely written by Fei (an "editorial note" by Mayo and his wife hints at this [p. viii]); it maintains that the unhappiness of peasants in urban factories would not be resolved when, with the passage of time, they had changed their country habits. Perhaps the peasants were not to blame; they might be right in their dislike of Western-style factory life, for modern industrial organization had a "serious weakness," its lack of "social integrity" (*Machine Age:*160-164).

Fei's ideas about this serious weakness are spelled out most clearly in the long afterword, dated December 1944, which he contributed, this time explicitly over his own name, to the Chinese edition of Shi's book (1946a), as well as in a chapter in his book about the U.S. visit (*CFMG,* Chapter 6), and a 1946 pamphlet on machines and human nature (*RX&JQ*).

It is easy to see the sources for Fei's ideas. He discussed in some detail the famous series of experiments that had been carried out in the 1920s and 1930s at the Western Electric Company's Hawthorne plant in Chicago by Mayo and his colleagues at Harvard. In an attempt to test the relationship of working conditions to productivity, carefully recorded variations in lighting, temperature, rest periods, and so on, were made over a period of several years among workers assembling telephone equipment, but no constant relationship was found to productivity, which rose and fell independently. Eventually it was discovered that social factors were more important than the physical environment. Workers tended to form small informal groups, each with its own customs, routines, and norms, and these provided their members with a sense of belonging and with approval or disapproval that was more important than that of management's or than their wages (1946a:217–20).

Fei may have read about the Hawthorne studies (which have been described in several other places as well) in T. North Whitehead's *Leadership in a Free Society* (1936); at any rate, he knew the book, for he quoted from it in another context (*SYZD:*127–28). Whitehead, intending to help industrial managers raise the productivity of their workers, ended up with a serious indictment of large urban enterprises: "It is my central thesis that modern industrial society suffers from a dangerous lack of social integration" (p. 231). Human beings, he said, needed social living, the satisfaction of doing things together. But modern society made too watertight a separation between work and non-work, business and social life, with the result that people were unable to form satisfying social ties in either. Fei probably also knew Elton Mayo's *Human Problems of an Industrial Civilization* (1933); and later he spoke of rereading Mayo's *Social Problems of an Industrial Civilization* (1945) very carefully (1948O5). The Hawthorne studies and the "seamy side" of modern industry are the subjects of both these works.

Fei cited the views of the nineteenth-century French sociologists Le Play and Durkheim, who are also discussed in Mayo's books. Frédéric Le Play was a conservative Catholic mining engineer who made a pioneering series of empirical studies of workers' families all over Europe from 1829 to 1855. Fei noted his finding that, as industry and cities developed, the level of cooperation in work declined. In farming and fishing villages, there had been mutual trust, help, peace, and stability. But, in more industrialized parts of Europe, community life, social norms, family ties, and social coordination were weakened; people were discontented, and police were needed to maintain order. Durkheim, Fei said, showed that people's zest for life came from belonging to a group and identifying with it. When people were no longer part of a group, in industrial cities, they became beguiled by material pleasures but lost their sense of the significance of life. Under such circumstances, many committed suicide: the incidence of suicide was a result (and an index) of social disintegration (1946a:225–27; 1945Mr27). In a letter, Fei spoke of himself becoming "very much Durkheimian," feeling that "the joy of life must be derived from group life, not through symbiosis, but consensus" (2/5/47 to MPR).[8]

The problem with urban industry, in Fei's view, lay here. Machines, and the division of labor and large-scale organization which went with mechanization, had freed people from hunger and poverty; but they also made people unhappy. The modern industrial worker hated his work; this could be seen in his decreasing efficiency, feelings of fatigue, frequent illness, and restlessness. The reason was that he did not control the machine, but rather had to adapt himself to it and its needs. It was too big for him to understand. Production was broken up into small parts, and work became mechanical; the worker had no sense of creating. He was treated by the bosses as just a means of production, like a machine. But under capitalism, even the owner did not enjoy the fruits of production, for he had to reinvest them. Production was for its own sake; worker and owner alike were slaves to the machine. The real conflict was not between classes, but between man and the machine.[9]

Furthermore, machine production had destroyed community life, and the worker had no sense of belonging to a group. When the process of production was divided into tiny jobs done by many, the worker could not see the connection between his work and that of others. City factories gathered together men who had no bonds, who lived in isolation from each other, and had no shared goals. Capitalism encouraged competitiveness; people were concerned with their individual economic interests. They had no spirit of cooperation, and the result was social disorder. Rules had to be imposed and compliance coerced, for people lacked the group spirit that would make them voluntarily follow social norms. The worker's job seemed purposeless and burdensome and cut off from the rest of life (*RX&JQ*:15-25; *CFMG*:61-66; 1946a:228-34; 1945Mr27; 1947N8a).

The logic of Fei's analysis would seem to point to a critique not just of factory work but of urban life in general. He did not really develop this idea, nor did he make a connection between the social disintegration caused by urban industry and the disintegration of the American family which had so shocked him. But here and there he did speak of how, in a city, individuals floated rootlessly, meeting and parting without ties or feelings (*CFMG*:7), and of how city dwellers lived in isolation, lonely, without shared goals, lacking the completeness of community life (*RX&JQ*: 19-20).

Fei's visit to America and his reading of certain Western sociologists thus led him to the conclusion that the West was not a good model for China to follow. Whereas once he had thought China would become an industrial society not unlike the United States, now he began to write that "methods that have proved successful within a certain tradition and environment may not be transferable to another tradition and environment" (*CFMG*:166-67). He took issue with the common assumption that the choice for China's economic development was between the Anglo-American model and the Soviet model. China had its own deeply-rooted traditions, he said; the idea of "wholesale Westernization" was a delusion (*RX&JQ*).

In a speech at the London School of Economics in January 1947, Fei was ready to speak quite unequivocally of the failure of Western civilization to achieve social integration. It had achieved great abundance but failed to provide "a social order which will make these advances of benefit to mankind." Le Play and Durkheim had demonstrated this defect of modern industrial society, but it was perhaps less apparent to most Westerners, who had grown accustomed to it, than it was to a Chinese factory worker with "a recent memory of another way of life in which, in spite of poverty, he was able to enjoy a personal intimacy with others and share the common purpose of a group." China should adopt Western material technology, but, in the realm of human relations, he suggested the West might learn from China's Confucian tradition:

> . . . the one sided emphasis on material achievement without due consideration of a corresponding development in social relations is . . . dangerous. It is therefore clear that the process of social change in China should not be a mere transplantation of western culture, but should [be] in conformity with the inherited spirit of harmony and integration. . . . Unless China is to perish we have to find our own solution from our inheritance of experience over thousands of years. ("L.S.E. Speech": 9 ; cf. *Gentry*:142, and *XTCJ*:14–15)

FIVE

Plaintiff for the Chinese Peasants

We must use the scientific method to explain the Chinese way of life and the concepts it has engendered, one by one from the point of view of our history and environment. Only after such a crystal-clear reckoning will our next steps not be as stupid and wasteful as present ones.
—*MGRXG:*90

A systematic presentation of the actual conditions of the people will convince the nation of the urgent policies necessary for rehabilitating the lives of the masses.
—*Peasant Life:*6

. . . we are the plaintiff for the Chinese peasants . . . we shall . . . appeal for certain actions, to improve their way of life.
—*Earthbound:*297

Fei returned from the United States, convinced that China's modernization ought not follow the pattern of the United States (or of the Soviet Union), but rather "seek for our own society a way which will be suited to our own tradition and environment" (*CFMG:*167). To find such a way required understanding that tradition and environment: "An analysis of culture is the basis of planned reform" (*XTCJ:*152). That had been the stated purpose of his study of sociology and his field research in China, and now he went on to the next steps. Based on his research and on his sociological understanding, he developed a general analysis of Chinese society and culture, and concrete proposals for reform. And, to promote these ideas, he publicized them not in scholarly works but in dozens of popular articles and books written to appeal to a broad urban public and influence their attitudes toward the rural masses.

FEI AS A POPULAR WRITER

On his return to China in late 1944, Fei became more and more caught up in teaching and writing. He was not again to have the opportunity, the time, and the funds to do field work himself; nor does he seem to have spent as much time supervising, editing, and translating the research of his young colleagues at the Research Station. By early 1945, he and his wife and daughter had moved out of the Station in the Kuige temple to a house which had once been a watch house for the graves of a rich family, on a hill inside the Chenggong town wall where, for the first time, he did some gardening and raised chickens (2/19/45 and 9/3/45 to MPR). Then, later in the year, after the war and the bombs were over, he moved into Kunming to the Yunnan University campus to be closer to his teaching responsibilities. He had been, since the early 1940s, not only Director of the Yunnan Station for Sociological Research, but a full professor of social anthropology and acting head of the tiny sociology department at National Yunnan University. He gave courses on rural sociology and on the family, courses that led to books to be discussed below.

Although still a young man, he was coming to have something of an international scholarly reputation and his star was rising in Chinese academic circles. He thought of himself as part of "the coming generation of Chinese intellectuals" and in opposition to the older generation which had monopolized power and position without using it to advance "the academic movement in China as a whole." In letters to American friends, he spoke of the "conflict between older and newer generations in university circles," and declared, "I have no trust in the old Victorian scholars in

China" (10/21/44 and 11/13/44 to WCF).¹ He was ambitious and competitive; as he confided to a friend while in the United States:

> I like competition. As a youngest son, I know what is meant by competition. To play a game there must be someone to combat with. I have beaten Ta Chen, the old man [Chen Da was a well-known sociologist and demographer]. He is a good competitor because he is really serious in his work. I seize his weakness and develop my line ... This is perhaps also my unconscious reason of not seeing Buck and Yu-tan Lin [John L. Buck and Lin Yutang]. One day I will come up and challenge them. (4/29/44 to WCF)

In early 1945, he was offered a job with the United Nations Rural Rehabilitation Administration doing practical rather than academic work. But, just as ten years before he had gone to graduate school instead of working on rural reconstruction with Liang Shuming, he declined this chance too to leave the university, saying that, although he felt a duty to serve the war effort, he did not know how the Yunnan sociology department could get along in his absence (1/28/45 to MPR, 1/29/45 to WCF). Then, in the summer of 1945, only thirty-four years old but with several significant books to his credit, he was offered a position at Qinghua University, one of the two best universities in China. During the war (and continuing in 1945–1946), Qinghua was merged with Peking University and Nankai University into Southwestern Associated University (Xinan Lianhe Daxue, or Lianda for short) in Kunming. It was the top of the academic world, and Fei accepted without delay. He continued, however, to run the Yunnan department without pay, in effect doing two jobs and lecturing twelve hours a week in 1945–1946. By early 1946, he was famous enough to warrant a biography in the "Who's Who in China" series of the Shanghai *China Weekly Review* (101:85 [March 23]).

Not only for his scholarship was he becoming well known, but increasingly in the mid-1940s for his newspaper and magazine articles directed to a general educated public. The articles he had sent back from the United States had been well received and, after returning to China, he found himself becoming more and more a popular writer:

I have become a journalist since I came back. I write four editorials every week for various papers in Kunming. *Ta Kung Pao* [*Dagong bao*] has published two of my articles (first appeared in my weekly "Liberty Forum") and asked me to contribute more frequently. (1/29/45 to WCF)

His "Letters from America" were published in the Kunming newspaper *Shenghuo dao-bao,* a four-page weekly "mosquito paper" (a class of publication so called, it is said, because "they could bite at anyone and anything,"[2] particularly the authorities). Fei had become involved with it shortly before going to the United States, contributing articles almost every week. The editor had been a student of his, and Fei advised him about the paper and attributed its success partly to this advice; he spoke of it as "our" paper. He brought a file with him to the United States, which he gave to Harvard (the only copies anywhere outside of China, I believe), and in letters described the paper, its policies, and contributors in great detail. He was proud of its growth in circulation to 15,000 or 20,000, the biggest in Kunming, with editions in Guiyang and Guilin in neighboring southwestern provinces. The readers, he said, included high-school and college students, factory workers, shopkeepers, soldiers, lower and middle civil servants, and even an occasional peasant. He had hopes that "our paper" might one day overtake in circulation even the *Dagong bao,* the leading independent daily in China, but in late 1944 it was closed down by the local government, apparently for personal and not political reasons (1/23/44 and 10/21/44 to WCF).

He immediately joined with some others to found a successor journal, called *Ziyou luntan* (Liberty forum). Fei pledged full support and sold his fountain pen to raise money for newsprint, which wartime shortages had made very expensive. He was responsible for contributing one-quarter of every issue, but I have not been able to locate any copies of this weekly outside of China.[3] For several months in late 1945 and early 1946, he put out a weekly he edited himself, called *Shidai pinglun* (Time review). The political authorities apparently found it too independent and, after several issues, government agents "advised" the printer to stop (the same thing happened to several other liberal publications); Fei continued to bring it out in mimeograph.[4] This too is not available outside China to my knowledge, but many of Fei's articles from it were reprinted in book form.

His writing was also appearing with increasing regularity in a number of other periodicals of national circulation and importance. By 1947 and 1948, after the war was over and he was back in Peking, his pieces were a regular feature in Shanghai (such as *Shiji pinglun, Guancha, Zhong jian*), as well as in the newspaper *Dagong bao*. He wrote no less than five to eight articles a month during most of this period, and in 1947–1948 was the most frequently published author in *Guancha,* perhaps the most highly regarded journal in China. The *Dagong bao* included him as one of sixteen famous writers in a feature on "Writers and their Works," indeed featuring him in the headline along with illustrious Hu Shi and Ba Jin. (In the United States, *The New York Times* referred to him as an "eminent Chinese political analyst," and *Time* magazine, quoting him, called him a "sociology professor and one of China's sharpest political commentators."[5])

His books too were popular. His *Xiangtu Zhongguo,* for example, consisting of articles on general features of rural society in China, was published in an edition of 3,000 in April 1948, sold out in less than a month, and went through successive printings of 2,000 each in June, July, August, and November of that year and January 1949 (it has since been reprinted in Taiwan and in Hong Kong). Many who were high school or college students in the late 1940s have told me of their excitement in reading his articles; he received letters (which he answered) from "common readers . . . from high school students to managers of factories" (12/4/47 to MPR).

The reason for his popularity is not difficult to fathom. He wrote in an informed way about matters people were concerned with: Chinese society, politics, the world abroad. His point of view was independent, critical, not tied to dogma of right or left. And he developed an admirable prose style, clear and full of vivid and apposite anecdotal detail. He knew he had writing ability; he even thought of writing a novel about his life in Kunming and the "variety of psychological reactions to the war" (6/16/44 to MPR). Here is how he himself described his style and its impact:

> I have become a popular writer in China. I do think the readers like my writings because I write in a very simple language, different from most. . . In addition to that, I usually draw concrete evidence to illustrate my point. This catches the imagination of common readers . . . For the civil servants, household wives, students, they begin to learn sociology from me. (6/30/47 to MPR)

He devoted much of his energy to this kind of popular writing partly because, in the ever-worsening inflation, he needed the money. By early 1945, Fei was making more from writing than from his regular salary (3/4/45 to WCF). Of his numerous articles on international affairs in 1947 and 1948, he wrote, "If I could now enjoy the living standard of a pre-war teacher in China, I wouldn't be writing essays like this" (*LBTX* 3.16:18). "When there is no rice in the pot and no coal in the stove," he said to the editor of *Guancha*, "don't worry; even without your urging, my essays will inflate too" (*LBTX* 5:10:14). But he was also aware of a powerful civic duty in a time of crisis:

> Formerly, I wrote for myself, for my own enjoyment or perhaps for different reasons essential for my own. But now, I feel I must constantly write to convey my idea to the public who I feel are in great need of such readings. . . I simply do not feel good to enclose myself in the university circle and be a nice boy. (12/4/47 to MPR)

RURAL CHINA'S CULTURAL PATTERNS

One of the most popular of Fei's books was *Xiangtu Zhongguo* (Rural China; *XTZG*), based on the course he taught on rural sociology and originally serialized in the Shanghai magazine *Shiji pinglun* from June 1947 to March 1948. These essays, written for a broad non-specialist audience, discuss peasant life on a more general level than had his village studies. Once he had argued that each village was a community with its own way of life which should be studied the way ethnologists study individual tribes (1933N15), but now he was willing to generalize about "rural China." This was the second stage of his sociological work, he said; he had passed from investigating and describing specific communities to synthesis: comparing, finding patterns, and analyzing social structure (*XTZG:*97-98, 103-104).

His discussion now encompassed much from the high culture of China's past as well. Whereas he used to insist that the literate tradition in China was irrelevant to peasant life, he was now reading in the Classics, and this book on "rural China" is, unlike any of his others, sprinkled with quotations from the *Analects* of Confucius. In a letter, he explained that he had previously been opposed to the study of traditional Chinese culture because he thought it consisted only of ideals which were not put into practice and thus did not represent reality. But now he had changed his mind. "These ideals . . . are [a] real force, a social force in shaping individual life. To understand a culture, the ideal pattern is as real as the actual practice" (6/16/44 to MPR).

It is clear that, following his visit to the United States, Fei was thinking about Chinese society and culture more and more as a whole. He was not, however, inclined to see Chinese culture as unique so much as just one example—though he discussed no others—of a social type, "rural society." He was, he said, "using Chinese facts to explain the characteristics of rural society, just as Miss Mead used American facts to explain the characteristics of a society of immigrants" (*XTZG:*106).

Much of Fei's book is concerned with contrasting rural or Chinese society with modern or Western society and, in making these sweeping social contrasts, he applied to China several of the grand conceptual dualisms which had been so prominent in the Western sociological tradition. There are explicit references to Tönnies's contrast between *Gemeinschaft* (close community which comes from living together) and *Gesellschaft* (relationships individuals enter into for specific purposes); to Durkheim's distinction between "mechanical solidarity" based on shared attitudes and "organic solidarity" based on the division of labor; and to

Spengler's dichotomy (which Ruth Benedict had used in *Patterns of Culture*, 1934) of the stable classical Apollonian personality and the modern Faustian type striving ceaselessly for the infinite. There are also reflections of Maine's contrast between society based on kinship and status and society based on territory, contract, and formal political controls; of Cooley's distinction between primary, face-to-face relations and secondary, indirect relations, which Park had said predominate in rural and urban life respectively; and of various anthropological ideas about the differences between primitive and civilized cultures.

Some of these contrasts had originally been meant to describe the difference between feudal and capitalist societies; others pre-modern and modern, agricultural and industrial, rural and urban, primitive and civilized, or simple and complex societies, but they were often, in the West, too, lumped together into a single great dichotomy. Robert Redfield, for example, had brought many of these ideas together in trying to construct a bi-polar continuum between village and city on which various communities could be located, in his *Folk Culture of Yucatan* (1941) and in his January 1947 article on "The Folk Society." Redfield is not mentioned by name in *Xiangtu Zhongguo,* but most of his characterizations of folk society can be found there.[6] Fei touched on and explained a host of other Western social concepts as well—Gresham's law, Adam Smith's invisible hand, Malinowski's kulu ring, Spengler's life-cycle of societies, Durkheim's God as a symbol of the social group, to say nothing of more fundamental notions, such as "culture" and "function." Fei's popular writings are surely significant for, among other things, introducing to a wide Chinese public the basic categories and ideas of Western social science.

The basic theme of this book is how various Chinese cultural patterns have grown out of the realities of Chinese agriculture and village life. Just as the American spirit had been shaped by the frontier, he thought, Chinese culture was based on its rural foundations. China's was "A Culture that has Grown out of the Ground," as he had vividly put it in the title of a 1946 article describing Chinese culture as a response to the environment of scarcity in an agrarian economy using primitive technology (1946Jl1). When goods are strictly limited there is likely to be social conflict, he explained elsewhere; the Confucian ideology of contentment, which taught that each person had his role in society and should be content with his lot, contributed to stability and happiness (*XTCJ:*1–9).

In *Xiangtu Zhongguo,* Fei emphasized the intimacy of village life. Unlike nomads or factory workers, he said, farmers were tied to the land and, except in times of crisis, lived and died in the same place. In China their society was the village, a world without strangers where one seldom encountered anyone other than those one had been brought up with, because villages were more or less isolated and had little contact with each other (it seems odd to find this claim, which he had not made in his village studies, here, where he is concerned with the unities of Chinese culture). From this long contact came understanding, closeness, and trust. Villagers were intimates, almost like family members (indeed Chinese villages were often really kinship groups, closed to outsiders; pp. 76–83). They habitually acted considerately to one another, out of familiarity, without need of law or contracts—that was stuff for a society of strangers. As Confucius said of himself at the highest stage of moral perfection, villagers "can do what their hearts desire without transgressing what is proper" (pp. 1–7, 59–60).

Rural society was marked, too, by the importance of custom and tradition. When a person lived in the same place and did the same things as his parents and grandparents before him—acting out the same play on the same stage—he could rely on the experience of his ancestors. In dealing with an unchanging environment, traditional ways were effective; they really worked or they would not have been handed down (pp. 19–20, 54, 93–94). These customary ways of behavior (*li*) were internalized in childhood and made habitual. One reason people could safely follow their own desires is that, though they were often unaware of their true social functions, these desires had been shaped by handed-down culture (pp. 51–57, 96).

Out of the importance of learning the traditional customs—life was a journey, Fei said, filled with more and stricter rules than are posted at any inn, rules the traveler does not know at the outset—arose the importance of elders. In modern society, where culture is not stable, people must depend on abstract principles rather than experience, habit is an obstacle, and intelligence and specialized knowledge are respected instead of age. But in a stable society one learned from one's seniors how to deal with problems, for they had coped with the same difficulties (pp. 70-75). In a society dominated by elders, however, open disagreement or opposition to authority was not tolerated; the "face" of those with authority demanded at least nominal compliance. Slow change—for no culture is absolutely static—resulted in a tendency for name and reality to diverge, a kind of hypocrisy seen, for example, in the scholarly tradition of accepting the authority of a classical text while changing its meaning through annotations (pp. 84-89).

Rural society was controlled, then, by a paternalistic rule by elders. It was lightly governed for, although there was no choice about mastering the *li* and in that sense people were coerced, once internalized, *li* maintained the social order without being enforced by the power of the state or threat of punishment. Disputes were mediated by elders, an educational process usually involving moral lectures for both sides. Going to court was considered shameful, and there were no lawyers, for everyone knew the customs (pp. 59-63). There was little exploitative control by one class or group over another—rural society was too poor for exploitation to be very important. But neither was it democratic; democratic consensus, the social contract, was based on cooperation and the division of labor in society, for which Chinese peasants, basically self-sufficient in everything except salt and iron, had little need (pp. 64-69).

In an interesting reversal of the common view of Western individualism and Chinese collectivism, Fei argued that in Western society, but not in Chinese, social relations were shaped by the idea of a group with clearly defined boundaries and no ambiguity about who was a member. Members of such a group were usually thought of as equals with certain rights and duties vis-à-vis the group, whose interests were represented by the idea of God. This corporate consciousness, which perhaps originated among nomads, for whom the tribal group was important, was lacking among the Chinese, whose agriculture demanded little cooperation. When a Westerner spoke of his family he meant his wife and children, but among the Chinese the concept was unclear and could be expanded depending on circumstances to a large lineage or clan. With the Chinese, a web of social relations radiated from each person like ripples in a pond. How far this network extended depended on the influence of the individual at the center. A powerful man's "neighbors," those who are included in his family's weddings, births, funerals, could include a whole village, while a poor man's were just the two or three families next door.

Chinese social relations were not thought of as between equal members of a group, nor were they governed by a universal ethic thought to derive from God, but were individual-centered and particularistic; how one acted to another depended on the strength and nature of one's particular relationship with that person. This is why, Fei said, Chinese were willing to sacrifice family for self, clique for family, nation for clique, and the world for the nation (later, in 1957, this was called a libel on the Chinese people). A pattern of individual-centered, particularistic social relations, then, was the explanation for the "selfishness" (*si*) and lack of public-spiritedness rural reformers complained of, exemplified by the dumping of garbage in Suzhou's canals, which everyone used for washing and by the proverb "Everybody sweeps the snow from in front of his own door, but no one concerns himself with the frost on his neighbor's roof" (pp. 22–27).

Fei also took issue with the conventional view that Chinese value family more than Westerners do, or that the Chinese social structure should be characterized as "familism."[7] He had long been struck by the emotional shallowness between husband and wife in rural society. In Lu-cun, having rented a room that was separated by only a thin wall from his landlord's bedroom, he discovered that the wife came into the room only to sweep; they did not sleep together. Similarly, in another peasant house, he found that not only did husband and wife not share a bed, they worked together without talking and parted when there was no work. "There was never any laughter or happiness between husband and wife." Of course, Chinese were not entirely without romantic feelings—he cited examples from traditional novels—but these were not the norm. Two images—Western couples who kiss in public, and Yunnan husband and wife who don't even speak to each other in private—presented a stark contrast (1941O30; *SYZD*:55-57). The Chinese, constantly stressing respect for parents rather than love between the sexes, he said, were incapable of experiencing or understanding romantic love and were reserved about their emotions ("except for tears . . . which we never lack") to the point of being "emotionally numb" (*CFMG*:119; cf. *SYZD*:61).

After he had been to the United States, Fei wrote that the Western "madness" of romantic love, of forgetting self and the world to think only of one another (a madness that he said he had never experienced himself; *SYZD*:65), was a luxury that American women could indulge in because (paradoxically) marriage was not so important to them, for modern conveniences and city jobs had given them independence. In China, in spite of legal equality, women were still very much tied to their housework and dependent on their husbands. Since "marriage determines our women's whole lives, how can they let emotions run loose and give over their whole lives, and those of their children, to luck and chance?" (*CFMG*:125).

Elsewhere Fei put forward the striking idea that the Chinese peasant family was not a locus of shared feelings, attitudes, and values, and perhaps not really a transmitter of culture. Its economic activities required little social communication, just as there was no need to converse with one's rickshaw puller. In America, where people were constantly on the move and did not live and die in their native place, home was a castle, a refuge in a world of competition with strangers. Sunday in the United States, which everyone spent with his own family, had seemed strangely quiet to a Chinese, for whom Sunday was a day of social visits and hubbub outside the home (*MGRXG*:18-19). In rural China, people did not find companionship, "relationships of laughing and talking," within the family, but with age- or sex-mates: men with other men on the street or in teahouses, wives with neighboring wives, and children with each other away from adults (1947S6). "In Chinese villages, [it] is not the family but the neighborhood ... that really generates the community feeling, the feeling of enjoying life together" (2/5/47 to MPR).

The key difference, Fei suggested in *Xiangtu Zhongguo*, was that, while the Western family had little business outside of child-rearing, the Chinese family had political, economic, and religious functions as well. For this a different structure was appropriate; the "small lineage" (*xiao jiazu*) centering on vertical relationships, particularly that between father and son, rather than on the husband-wife tie, was not necessarily more numerous than the Western nuclear family but was more permanent and extendable in size according to need. As a practical, task-oriented organization, the Chinese family required discipline, with which personal emotions, which are exciting, upsetting, destabilizing, are apt to interfere. There was no impulse to overcome the gap between men and women with romantic love in rural society, which did not find life's significance in a Faustian struggle to overcome obstacles, in the process of creation, in novelty, ceaseless change, and adventure with the unknown (*XTZG*:38-50).

At times, Fei seemed concerned to defend peasant ways against the contempt of urban intellectuals, just as Malinowski had sought to show Europeans that the antics of savages had their practical utility. Trying to puncture the sense of superiority of city dwellers who ridiculed peasants for not knowing enough to get out of the way of cars,[8] he told of his city students in the fields mistaking wheat for corn, and of how peasant kids were better at catching grasshoppers than professors' children. Rural reformers, concerned with peasant "ignorance," overstressed literacy education; in fact, Fei said, peasants were not ignorant, they just had a different kind of knowledge. Theirs was a practical knowledge based on accumulated experience, and it worked; Fei's Yunnan landlady knew how to cure his baby's gum problem without understanding a thing about germs (pp. 7-9. 54-55). Peasants might be illiterate, but in a face-to-face society they did not need to communicate at a distance, nor did they need to record things in writing when one generation's experience was the same as the last's and the whole culture could be transmitted orally from parent to child (pp. 10-20).

There is little disharmony in Fei's picture of rural life. We do not see class conflict, oppressive landlords, bandits, peasant rebellions, famine, or disease. Yet this functional view of culture involved no sentimental romanticizing about peasant goodness or the idylls of rural life. Though Fei occasionally spoke in a letter of a desire to get away from urban hubbub, he also felt no sympathy for "the romantic escape of the retired city dwellers [in England] . . . [who] keep themselves outside of the community and praise rural life in abstraction" (2/5/47 to MPR). He was no Daoist advocating a return to a rustic simplicity and naturalness—indeed, in his view, rural ways of life, like all culture, were neither particularly simple (Malinowski had needed volume after thick volume to describe the culture of one primitive society) nor natural at all. Nor did he believe, as did those Chinese, including many Communists, inspired by the Russian populist tradition, that peasants had a special goodness or virtue, that they would be the creative force shaping the future, or that intellectuals would be improved by going to villages.

Some of Fei's generalizations about Chinese society, as a critic would note in 1957,[9] were similar to the ideas of the Confucian rural reformer Liang Shuming, who had also emphasized custom, ethics, ritual, and contentment in his contrasts of Chinese civilization with that of the West.[10] Liang had been the leading theorist of the rural reconstruction movement in the 1930s and, though Fei did not acknowledge any debt to him (probably considering him a hopeless old reactionary), it seems not unlikely that Fei's understanding of Chinese culture should have been influenced by this noted philosopher. But their attitudes towards this culture, the value they placed on it, were very different. Liang, steeped in traditional Confucian (and Buddhist) learning, was trying to preserve in village life what he thought was the essence of Chinese culture. Fei, the social scientist, never claimed the patterns he described were uniquely Chinese or of ultimate worth. Culture for him was merely a means for sustaining life; life must not be sacrificed for culture, he said (*XTCJ*:149-150). "Values and norms are tools for people to use to satisfy their life's needs; they are not absolute commands, but practical rules established according to the time and place" (*MGRXG*:78).

Fei thought Chinese cultural patterns should be understood in the context of the rural society that produced them, and that traditional ways had worked in a stable society, but—the familiar refrain comes at the end of several of these essays—when the environment changes, old ways are no longer effective. "In the process of going from rural to modern society, many of the patterns of life cultivated in rural society produce defects" (*XTZG*:7). "To want to keep the spirit nurtured in rural society at this time is dangerous" (p. 95). Only as rural society's tradition is destroyed can China be put on the road to modernization (p. 62). The pattern of interpersonal relations based on familiarity won't work between strangers, and law and force become necessary to get group cooperation (p. 56). Kinship and similar close interpersonal ties inhibit commerce (pp. 81-83). Illiteracy must disappear in modernizing (p. 14).

Trial and error were all right for adapting to slow change, but unequal to a rapidly changing situation. In a changing society, internalized tradition and individual desires are no longer safe guides for action—social planning, based on conscious knowledge of needs and the conditions for survival, is needed (pp. 90-96). When old ways are no longer effective and new ways have not yet been found, there is a time of confusion, psychological tension, doubts, and uneasiness. In such a situation, instead of light government, there is a need for a great leader with the power to create new ways and to suppress dissent, that is to say, the sort of political power found in a rapidly industrializing nation such as the USSR (pp. 85-88). As he had put it in another place:

> ... China's traditional values were suited to the traditional society and interacted with it ... [But], for better or worse, ... the situation has changed. By the side of a West which had industrialized, there is no possibility of preserving in the East an economy of scarcity. The way of life suited to an economy of scarcity and the value system supporting this way of life can no longer help us live in this new situation. (*XTCJ*:9-10)

Yet he did think the face-to-face intimacy of village life was the source of social harmony, a sense of community, a feeling of closeness between the individual and his society, and a happy willingness to work together which China should strive to preserve.

THE GENTRY AND SOCIAL EROSION

In addition to his essays on Chinese cultural patterns, another aspect of Fei's move away from village studies toward synthesis, at a time when Civil War and inflation made field work extremely difficult, was his work on a major book about China's social structure—its social classes, the relationship between countryside and cities, and how these were changing. The book was never completed, but his ideas on the subject were published in a number of articles in the late 1940s, particularly "Peasantry and Gentry: An Interpretation of Chinese Social Structure and its Changes," which appeared in English in the *American Journal of Sociology* ("Peasantry"); his three articles in the book he edited with the Qinghua historian Wu Han called *Huang-quan yu shen-quan* (Imperial power and gentry power; *HQ&SQ*); and several of the newspaper articles on reviving the countryside reprinted in his *Xiangtu chongjian*. English versions of seven pieces from these two books, versions that he dictated to Mrs. Redfield when she and her husband finally got to Peking in late 1948, were subsequently published as *China's Gentry*.[11]

This work on China's social structure involved more thought and research about China's past than had his work on peasants. As we know, Fei was not by inclination much of a historian; on the one occasion since college when he did some real digging in historical documents, collecting data on social mobility with Pan Guangdan, we find him complaining, "It is a dull job" (11/7/47 to WCF). But these sociologist's speculative essays on the traditional social structure are among the earliest scholarly work on the gentry as a social class, social mobility, and the differences between market towns and walled cities, and they have stimulated and influenced subsequent historical scholarship on these subjects. In their own time and place—China in the midst of social revolution—they must have helped to convince many gentry sons and daughters that, though the gentry had not been oppressive in the past, change was urgently needed now to make them useful to society.

Fei maintained that in China, where commerce and industry were little developed, there were only two important social classes, peasantry and gentry (though he did come to show some interest in doing research on the emerging Chinese "business class"). Interested in continuities with the peasant, after the end of the old civil service examination system, he tended to think of the Chinese "gentry" less as officials and those eligible for office by virtue of examination degrees (he once even suggested they were not necessarily all literate; "Gentry Draft":6), as a local elite essentially dependent not on the political power of the central government but on the economic power of landowning. Above all they were those with leisure, "those who in an agricultural economy enjoy the fruits without physically laboring" (*HQ&SQ*:9), for leisure was a source of great status in a technologically underdeveloped economy where manual work, with primitive tools, was indeed most onerous and unpleasant. Further prestige accrued from the moral authority which the gentry's control of ethical knowledge, of the traditional codes of conduct and old rituals, gave them. This knowledge—essential in a civilization at once traditional and complex—was based on literacy and familiarity with ancient texts, which the gentry could monopolize.

The gentry had their own culture or way of life, based on leisure, and so different from that of the peasantry, Fei thought, as to warrant use of Disraeli's phrase "two nations" ("Peasantry": 1). Needing larger social organizations to protect their property, the gentry tended to have—in contrast to the peasant family averaging four to six persons—"big families" of sometimes dozens and dozens of people under one roof, plus servants, living together under the rule of a single patriarch—"an empire by itself," Fei called it ("Peasantry":5). The "clan" (or lineage), an organization of separate families with a common ancestor, he also thought primarily a gentry organization based on ownership of property; unless the clan corporately owned land it would tend to fragment and wither away. The gentry were distinguished in addition by long gowns, distinctive shoes, hats, hair style, way of sitting and walking, refined speech, and elegant houses, located often in towns rather than villages. The town teahouse was the center of gentry culture: "From morning until nightfall, the leisured gentlemen gather in the teahouses to amuse themselves sipping tea, in listening to the storytellers, in talking nonsense, in gambling, and in smoking opium" ("Peasantry":7).

Fei felt ambivalent towards these people. He thought of himself as of gentry background, and illustrated gentry characteristics with pleasant anecdotes from his own family and happy childhood; he would speak warmly of the "charm" of gentry towns and the "cultured eloquence with which the average customer [at a Suzhou teahouse] talks and the mellowed and humorous outlook on life he has achieved" ("Peasantry":7). But he also was repelled by the lack of productivity, energy, agressiveness, and creative power of these gentlemen. He called them "parasites" who lived through exploitation and privilege. The gentry child was

> . . .detached from the life of the people. He lives in a big house devoid of sunshine; he grows up in the reverence of the past, in the shadow of his ancestors, from whom his privileges are inherited. From the petty court politics among the family members he learns to put on a feigned obedience, is imbued with a sense of futility of all efforts, and is trivial, resigned, conservative, and cowardly. Physically he is weak, slender, and sometimes sterile. ("Peasantry":12)

Fei had once written that the existence of a leisure class was a goal stimulating farmers to work hard, because there was a real possibility of social mobility in traditional China. "A lower-class person if willing to work could in a moderate amount of time raise either himself or his sons or grandsons into the upper class" 1946a:224). Now, together with his friend and colleague in the Quinghua sociology department, Pan Guangdan (to whom we shall return in the next chapter), he made a careful and path-breaking study of the extent of social mobility through the civil service examinations. He and Pan gathered and quantified information from published examination essays on the family background of almost a thousand successful candidates, most from the nineteenth century. They found that 67 percent had had fathers who were also degree-holders, and 87 percent had had degree-holders somewhere in the last five generations on the male line. Inequality of opportunity was also indicated by the finding that somewhat fewer successful degree candidates, even among the newly risen 13 percent, came from rural areas, where most of the population lived, than from towns and cities, where the gentry were more concentrated. It seemed that few peasants were moving into the gentry; even those without official forebears were likely to be from landlord families, rural or urban, or to have an economic base outside agriculture.

Pan and Fei's conclusion was ambivalent—the glass was both half full and half empty. Their research showed that "the opportunity for upward social mobility provided by the examination system was not too great," and common sense confirmed that, except for the occasional poor boy educated with scholarship funds from friends, community, or local government, families had to reach a certain economic level before they could provide the leisure for their sons' education. Yet 13 percent from families without degree-holders for five generations indicated significant social mobility through the examination system, comparable to the proportion of people rising from farming backgrounds to high-status professions in the United States, and much greater than mobility out of the peasantry in pre-revolutionary Russia (1947Oa; "Social Mobility").

Not only were the gentry not a closed caste, but as local leaders first and government officials only second, in Fei's view, they performed a positive function as protectors of local interests and the common people against the central government (*XTCJ*:160-161). It was his opinion that official position was not generally lucrative, that the gentry took office not to gain power or riches but to try through personal connections to protect their family property against the administration, and that even in office they did not really share power. Political power was monopolized by the throne; the Emperor was all-powerful, and officials just took orders (*Gentry*, Chapter 1). Fei described imperial power in decidedly hostile terms, perhaps not uninfluenced by his feelings about the Nationalists. It was tyrannical, despotic, oppressive, fierce as a tiger; it was based on violence and military force—dynastic founders were nothing more than successful bandits. He seemed disappointed that the gentry had not been more vigorous in resisting such power, that they had not banded together to force the monarch to accept a Magna Charta like the European aristocracy, but had been politically passive, limiting themselves to moralistic talk about how power should be wielded, content to be merely ethical arbiters instead of political actors (*Gentry*, Chapter 2).

But, although gentry power was negative and their motives quite selfish—it was in their interest that the social order not be upset by excessive government exactions on the people—they were nonetheless effective in protecting themselves and their communities against government tyranny. They relied on their moral authority to promulgate a philosophy of passive and limited government (*wuwei*) and on their ability to resist government orders at the local level. The central administration extended down only to the county level; below that orders were transmitted by low-status *yamen* runners to figurehead village headmen. When these orders were unacceptable to the people, the gentry, who were the real local leaders but not bound to obey because not part of the track transmitting orders down, could informally approach the county magistrate as social equals and get the orders modified. The gentry thus provided a separate, informal track of upward influence from the people to the administration—Fei called this "two-track government"—and the result was much de facto local self-rule (*Gentry,* Chapter 4; *XTCJ*:42-64).

The gentry also provided local leadership for community affairs—irrigation, self-defense, the mediation of disputes, and other matters not handled by the government. He cited his own father's efforts in running a school, organizing a county assembly, and putting forward schemes for local development (1948Ja1a). Under pressure from critics who charged him with being too kind to the gentry,[12] Fei admitted that they sometimes became local tyrants (1948Mr20), but continued to maintain that they were of benefit to the community because "serving the locality was protecting their own interests as landlords, it was raising chickens to get the eggs" (*XTCJ*:71). The traditional values of contentment and restricting desires, furthermore, had caused landlords to live frugally and not accumulate enormous holdings, and Confucian morality had inspired them to charitable work and the like, with the result that landlord-tenant relations were not tense (*XTCJ*: 92-93).

But, if the gentry had once been not very oppressive and often useful to local society, Fei was adamant that in modern times they had become pernicious economic parasites. For one thing, they were no longer restrained by the ethic of frugality; Western influence had brought a desire for higher living standards (1946 Jl1). Then, because of the collapse of rural handicrafts, the rural economy could no longer support land rent, which had once been more readily borne.[13] Further, with the demise of the philosophy of passive government, no longer appropriate for the modern age, and with the extension of government administration to below the county level (the *baojia* system), it was no longer possible for the gentry to resist harmful government orders on the local level.

The principal reason why the gentry could no longer be useful as local leaders, however, was simply that more and more of them had deserted the countryside and gone to live in large cities. Fei's father, for example, had served his community, but Fei himself and his brothers had all left for the city, leaving only their sister. This pattern, Fei thought, was general and deleterious. The fact that in the past a considerable proportion of the gentry lived in the countryside was indicated by his and Pan's study of degree-holders which found that a sizeable proportion had come from rural areas (even though a minority—41 percent of those with degree-holding forebears and 47 percent of those without). Now gentry sons were going to modern schools and colleges in cities and were becoming urbanized and Westernized. College graduates were not willing to return to the village, where they felt there was no one they could talk to and where there were no suitable jobs. Fei knew of seven people from the primary school in his county who had gone abroad to study on public scholarships before the war; not one had returned to the county.

The urbanization of the gentry meant that the villages were losing men of talent and influence who could lead and protect them, in a process Fei called "social erosion," comparing it to the leaching of the soil in the Tennessee Valley before TVA. On top of this, feelings of local solidarity, emotional ties to the community, were disintegrating, and selfishness and corruption were spreading throughout society. Fei looked back with yearning to the old gentry habits, strengthened by Confucian morality, of local service and informal leadership. He also spoke admiringly of the public-spiritedness of the English gentry, which he had observed in an English village in 1947: doctors, public servants, scholars, retired from the cities, serving the rural community in myriad capacities, apparently without pay (*Gentry*, Chapter 7; 1948Ja1a; *XTCJ*:59–61).

The urbanization of the gentry was harmful to the countryside partly because Chinese cities had always had a one-sided parasitic relationship with the countryside. Theoretically, Fei said, cities should provide manufactured products to villages and markets for their agricultural goods. But the Chinese situation was abnormal because so much handicraft manufacturing was down in the countryside, which received little from cities. Rural-urban relations were basically not commercial but financial; the countryside supported cities with its payments of rents, interest, and taxes. In some pioneering articles on types of settlement in China, Fei argued that they should be distinguished not by size or population density—for some cities were smaller than villages—but by function. Villages were clusters of largely self-sufficient family units, with little division of labor. What little trade was required by the rural economy was carried on in temporary periodic markets (*shi*) or permanent market towns (*zhen*). The walled city (*cheng*) was a government seat, situated for defense rather than communications, which attracted landlords who wanted protection and government ties, some of whom also engaged in moneylending or dealing in rice. Urban craftsmen produced goods for these government and landlord classes, not for the countryside—peasants did not shop in the city, Fei said (though the walled city and market towns were sometimes combined, the market towns also attracted landlords and artisans). The modern treaty port was also not a productive industrial city but a consumption area, draining off money from the countryside which was spent on foreign imports. The Japanese War, which cut off the countryside from the cities, had been a relief to the rural areas (*XTCJ:* 16-32, 153-155; *Gentry,* Chapter 5; 1948Mr20).

The solution Fei urged, though only in general terms, was for the gentry and the cities to become productive and useful. They would have to give up their privileges, that is to say, their dependence on land rents which they did not earn and which the peasants could no longer afford. For their own good, he urged, landlords should do this voluntarily and peacefully; otherwise economic hardship would drive the peasants to violence. Of course, other sources of support for the gentry would have to be found; his hope was that they would become productive by taking part in modern industry. But for this their old habits and attitudes were a formidable obstacle.

Gentry culture—normative, literary, and conservative, concerned with values, human relations, and the manipulation of symbols—Fei said, was ill-suited for modern industry. The gentry had been taught to feel contempt for manual skills and technical knowledge, avoiding contact with things and nature, going around with their hands in their sleeves, and relying on servants to fetch things for them. They were concerned with social roles, status, and "face," insisted on wearing clothes that marked them off from the working class, and found happiness in ordering subordinates around. Among Fei's own generation, even those who studied science and technology abroad tended, after returning, not to use them but to live the exalted life of the ruling class (*Gentry*, Chapter 3; *XTCJ*:89–98; *HQ&SQ*:20). If the gentry was to become productive and if Chinese industry was to develop, the psychological gap between the educated and the productive would have to be overcome. Towards this end, he praised a friend who had invented a construction toy for teaching Chinese children to use their hands (1948Ap10).

China's modern urban intellectuals, successors of the old gentry, must learn a new kind of practical, productive, technical knowledge and, like missionaries, take it to the countryside (*RX&JQ*: 28):[14]

> What I hope is that the sons of the landlord class, who have enjoyed traditional privileges as well as the opportunity for modern education, will in various ways serve the rural villages . . . How otherwise, I ask, are villagers going to get a chance to have modern technology? (1948Mr1a)

REFORM PROPOSALS: RURAL INDUSTRIALIZATION

Perhaps the principal message of Fei's 1940s popular articles was the worsening crisis of the rural economy. Peasants were becoming unable even to sustain life by farming. China's agrarian economy was different from an industrial economy of interdependent parts, which, like a complex machine, breaks down easily when one tiny part goes wrong, but is also easily fixed. In China, he wrote in mid-1947, the economy was gradually becoming paralyzed in each of its countless independent cells as peasant families were being forced to leave the land. Though the crisis was less visible than an industrial depression or a natural disaster, the prospects for recovery were much worse (*XTCJ*:33-41).

From the beginning Fei had said that the purpose of his social research was to provide the basis for planned social reform. As early as 1940 and 1941, just after he had finished the Lu-cun study, he had started writing articles for Kunming journals, many of them later collected in a volume called *Neidi nongcun* (Villages of the interior; *NDNC*), putting forward proposals for rural economic policies in the "hope that this field research of ours can one day change the currently fashionable atmosphere of empty talk and bureaucratic making up of numbers behind closed doors" (*NDNC*:i). Later, back in Peking, he wrote the pieces for the *Dagong bao* which were collected in *Xiangtu chongjian* (Rural recovery; *XTCJ*), published in 1948, a long and probing series of articles on what should be done to solve this rural crisis.

The causes of peasant distress, he thought, were several. There was the fighting, first against the Japanese and then the Civil War between Nationalists and Communists, which ravaged many areas, taking only a few days to destroy a whole season's crops. Press-gang conscription removed millions of men from their farms and caused others to flee. The burden of excessive taxes, supplemental levies, and labor service was crushing. We have seen how he thought the gentry's desertion to the cities was leaching the countryside of its human talent and draining its wealth, in the form of land rents and interest payments. In Kaixiangong, he had found that some 70 percent of the peasants were tenants who had to pay about 40 percent of their rice crop as rent to absentee landlords. He estimated that about half China's farmland was owned by non-farming landlords or by rich peasants who hired laborers, and so at least a quarter of the total agricultural production was being taken from the producers, going to a landlord class which constituted 10 percent of the population. He assumed that most of this wealth was leaving the countryside (*XTCJ*:79-88, 129-33; *Gentry*:110-126).

Fei called, of course, for an end to land rents, as well as for reducing the burden of taxes and conscription. Land reform was a "necessary and urgent . . . step in relieving the peasants," he had written in *Peasant Life* (p. 285). During the war, he said that policies such as peasant loans, rent reduction, and "using 'land to the tillers' to stem the flow of land into the hands of the long-gowned class"—such policies, "if sincerely carried out," would reduce hardship and enable the traditional agricultural system to continue functioning (*NDNC:*41). Later on, he would call tenancy "exploitation" and landlords "parasites," as we have seen, and warn the landlords that rent was becoming insupportable and they would have to give up their unreasonable privileges or face violent revolution. But, at the same time, he thought that land reform measures would only ease somewhat, and not fundamentally solve, the rural crisis. Even without having to pay rent, the average Kaixiangong family, he said his figures showed, would be unable to live from agriculture alone. High tenancy he thought was not the cause but the result of rural economic decline.

Writing from wartime Yunnan, he was markedly unenthusiastic about land reform measures. The Nationalists' policy of "land to the tillers" had been worked out in response to tenancy problems in villages of the coastal provinces, he said, and was not suited to the interior (*NDNC:*26). In the interior, at least in a village like Lu-cun, there were very few tenants, and they rented mostly on favorable terms from temples or clans, and were not in need of relief. Most landowners hired labor and managed their own lands. The life of the laborers had been bitter in the past, but the wartime demands for soldiers and for workers in new industries had created a labor shortage in the villages of the interior, driving wages up to where now "a bearer smokes cigarettes a professor can't afford" (*NDNC:*101). And the labor shortage was finally forcing the landowners to work in the fields themselves; thus, perhaps even without land reform, they would gradually turn into petty owner-cultivators. A government proposal for loans to enable tenants to buy land elicited from Fei a very negative response, based on some questionable arguments. He calculated that interest and loan repayments for new peasant-owners might come to more than the rate of return from land he had found in Lu-cun. (But was it reasonable to assume, as he did, that there would be an interest rate as high as 12 percent?) He argued that land rent is customarily reduced in years of bad harvest, and that interest on government loans would be less readily reduced. A laborer might not be better off tilling his own land if it was poor, infertile land. (But would he not still be better off than as a tenant on that land?) Such a program might make land prices rise and, if the current inflation was reversed, borrowers would be paying more in real terms. If everyone had land, each would have very little. (But would not most still be better off?) Indeed, his remarks were so negative he felt it necessary to add, "I hope the reader will not misunderstand me as defending landlords" (*NDNC:*97–104).[15] In later articles (for example *XTCJ:*79–88), he was more outspoken about the urgency of relieving the peasants' burden of rent, and castigated the rural reformer James Yen for neglecting land reform in his program (1948Ag28). But still he maintained that it would not solve the basic problem.

The basic problem was too many people on too little land. In Lu-cun, Fei had found that people remembered being much better off a generation earlier when the population had been smaller and farms considerably larger, but the habit of the wealthy of having many sons had resulted in the division of estates. In fact, Fei argued his studies proved, China's rural population was too large in proportion to the arable land to be supported by agriculture. Calculations based on figures collected in Kaixiangong, Lu-cun, and Zhang Ziyi's two villages—figures about average farm size, fields, family size, food requirements, and other expenses (see the chart in *Earthbound:*298–299)—showed that most peasants, particularly the majority who paid rent on some or all of the land they tilled (a majority, at least, in these four villages), had to have some outside source of income.

Given this problem of overpopulation, Fei was sharply critical of the Nationalist Government's policies of encouraging births in order to "strengthen the nation"; indeed an article of his on this subject apparently prompted the authorities to close down the magazine that carried it (*NDNC:*47–55, vi–vii). (The same party founder whose word had made land reform orthodoxy had, ironically, caused population limitation to be heresy for the Nationalists for decades: Sun Yat-sen had written that China's large population was one of her great assets.) But birth control was too slow a solution to offer much hope for China's crisis, in Fei's view.[16]

Another strategy for relieving rural population pressure would be to develop urban industry and so provide city jobs for peasants. In his early articles (and in spite of the fact that he had argued in the case of Kaixiangong that proximity to cities had caused the high tenancy), Fei took the view that peasants would benefit from the development of urban industry and commerce—to cite one curious argument, he thought urban investment opportunities would draw city capital away from farmland and so decrease rural tenancy (*NDNC:* 8–11, 80). But he later argued that urbanization was not the solution to China's rural problems. Merely to halve the number of people pressing on China's tiny farms would require cities of unprecedented size and number and, if possible at all, would take many decades at least. It had required sixty years for the agricultural portion of the American population to decline from 80 percent to 40 percent, he noted. Even if 200 million Chinese moved to cities—making China the most urbanized nation in the whole world—it would only double the size of China's tiny average farm, leaving it nowhere near the 100-acre farms common in the United States (*RX&JQ:* 11). In the meantime, the development of urban industry would bring further decline to rural handicrafts and peasant welfare. Moreover, urban industry would require rural markets for its products but, without higher income, China's villages could not become markets for anything.

There was another problem about reducing the rural population: in his village investigations, Fei had discovered that Chinese agriculture needed this large population. In Lu-cun, he had gathered information about the agricultural calendar: the various farming activities performed at different times of the year, how much labor each required per unit of land, and how much leeway there was as to when each task had to be carried out. He found that the busiest time, in the case of double-cropped land (and perhaps

70 percent of the land in Lu-cun was double-cropped) was in the spring, in April and May, when the winter crop of broad beans had to be harvested and threshed, and the land hoed and otherwise prepared for the transplanting of rice. All this had to be done within about sixty days, and required for each *gong* of land (about one-seventeenth of an acre) some six days of male labor and three and a half of female. Thus, one couple working alone could not cultivate more than about ten *gong,* or three-fifths of an acre (*Earthbound:* 22–23, 34ff). This maximum could be increased if labor were exchanged with a neighbor who staggered the dates of his planting; and these figures should not be taken as precisely accurate. But it is clear that—with the technology then in use—the average Lu-cun family of 5.7 persons was not capable of tilling much more land than the average Lu-cun farm of 1.33 acres. From this resulted the ironic but tragic fact of Chinese agriculture: it required a larger labor population than it could support.

The problem was compounded by primitive technology. China's huge population, unemployed for much of the year, had made labor cheap, and this, Fei thought, meant there was no incentive for developing more efficient techniques. In the early 1940s, he seemed to be looking towards the transformation of the agricultural economy into something more like the American pattern, stressing advanced technology, chemical fertilizer, and mechanization (*NDNC:* 24, 29, 45–46), though he never showed much interest in the details of agricultural tools or techniques. To prepare for the use of machinery, government policies should be directed towards increasing the size of farms rather than further fragmenting them with land reform. It is not clear exactly what Fei was proposing—it sounds like primogeniture—in the following passage, with its blunt implication that production mattered more than social justice:

> If we are to think of ways of avoiding the fragmentation of fields due to population pressure, it would seem that we must adopt the principle of unequal inheritance and give the right to inherit land to a special minority. Such talk seems very unfashionable, because these days the power of abstract words like freedom and equality is too great, and

everyone seems to be willing to sacrifice economic interests for them. (*NDNC:* 23)

In another essay, he softened this line of thought by noting that what was needed was large-scale farm management and not necessarily concentrated ownership. The idea of small, equal ownership combined with large management led him to consider the possibility of mutual-aid teams or collective ownership (with large fields being prepared for tractors), but he made no specific proposals. He suggested only that something might be developed out of the extensive collectively owned temple and clan lands, and he noted the advantages of exchanging labor in busy seasons and of cooperation in the use of irrigation water (*NDNC:* 31–32).

But, in later writings, Fei changed his view about the hope of a technical transformation of agriculture. Improved technology, he was told by agricultural experts, could only bring increases in yields of 20 percent to 100 percent at the most, which would not raise peasant income enough (*XTCJ:* 100–102).

Rent and taxes, overpopulation, and technical stagnation all contributed to rural poverty, but the real cause of the current crisis, Fei argued, was something else—the collapse of handicraft industries in the face of competition from cheap machine-made goods—"the invasion of Western industry" (*XTCJ:* 164). In the past, Chinese peasants, though poor, had enjoyed, as the title of one article put it, "The Moderate Standard of Living of Freedom from Cold and Hunger," and this had been due to rural industry, mostly handicrafts, which Fei claimed had always been widespread and indeed an essential part of the peasant economy. It was because they had supplemental income from rural industry that Chinese farmers had been able to bear the burden of land rent in the past (*XTCJ:* 79–88). He liked to say that China did not lack industry; it was just widely dispersed in rural areas, so that "most of the farmers of China are, at the same time, craftsmen" (*Earthbound:* 300). Kaixiangong's silk industry or Yi-cun's basketry and paper manufacturing were examples of myriad industries in villages all over China. Even in a primarily agricultural village like Lu-cun, most people made their own clothing, cushions, and baskets.

Rural industry provided supplementary income for the large farming population Chinese agriculture required but could not by itself support, and off-season employment for the many hands needed in agriculture only during certain busy periods. Fei claimed that for many there was no work for two-thirds of the year; even for those who grew winter crops, he had found in Lu-cun, there was very little farming to be done during the long winter months. In other words, Fei was arguing not only that rural industry *was* widespread in China's villages (which he really did not have the data to prove) but also that an analysis of the rural economy (and here a sampling of a few villages was more persuasive) showed that it could not depend wholly on agriculture but *had* to have rural industry to complete the system. China's large population, agricultural technology, and rural industry were all in "organic adjustment" (*Gentry*:116), a harmonious integration that was being destroyed by the influx of machine-made goods and the decline in handicrafts.

The solution, and Fei's answer for China's peasant poverty, which he put forward in writing many times from a long 1941 preface to Zhang Ziyi's book *Yi-cun shougongye* to the 1948 newspaper articles in *Xiangtu chongjian*,[17] was to revive and develop rural industry. In urging this, Fei wanted to restore the old equilibrium of the peasant economy, but he was not arguing for the restoration of old-fashioned handicrafts. Gandhi's promotion of home cotton-spinning, for example, Fei thought quite impractical, for the importation of modern goods could not be cut off (*XTCJ*:10-11). What was needed were machines and modern technology to make rural industry competitive with them. Nor was he arguing that all industries should be located in the countryside; heavy industries such as steel mills would always have to be in cities. But, he maintained, a much more rural industrialization was possible than the West had known.

This was now possible because electricity and modern transportation had ended the necessity for the big factories of the nineteenth-century West, which had had to be built around a central source of power, the steam engine. With electricity, men and machines could be dispersed in rural homes or small workshops. Indeed, Fei claimed that 71 percent of the factories in Shanghai employed fewer than 90 persons, and enterprises of this size could easily operate in villages (*XTCJ:*110). Similarly, the earlier necessity of locating factories in cities, close to supplies and markets, was lessened by the development of better transportation. Fei noted, in fact, that there was at present a tendency in the West for industry to disperse to rural areas.

Small-scale rural industry lacked the economies of scale of big urban factories, but had the advantage of cheaper land and labor costs; it was fair for rural labor to be paid less because it cost less to live in the country. There would also be savings in transportation costs for agricultural processing industries. On the whole, Fei seems to have thought rural industry, if technologically modernized, could compete effectively with larger urban manufacturers, although at one point he suggested there might be some economic cost to the nation as a whole in encouraging rural industry, a cost quite small in comparison with the gain in peasant welfare (*XTCJ:* 102–103).

Fei proposed both reforming old handicraft industries and setting up new village industries (1947N8a). Both of these would be mostly agricultural processing industries, making use of locally available raw materials to produce finished or semi-finished manufactures, although he also mentioned the possibility of turning semi-finished factory products into consumers' goods. Some possible products were: sugar, paper, porcelain, alcohol, paint, ink, candles, varnish, lubricating oils, soap, various kinds of cloth and cloth products, leather and metal objects (*NDNC:*128–130; mostly quoting from an article by Han Dezhang). Modern technology meant, of course, machines—small, relatively inexpensive machines, run by electricity, including some very simple ones in farmers' homes as well as larger machines in small village factories. Fei thought many manufacturing processes could be broken down into stages, some of which could be done at home by hand, and some by machine in local factories; and that the parts for many industrial products could be separately made in rural areas and then assembled in central plants. The household labor would be seasonal, in the idle months of the farming year; it is not clear to what extent he imagined the factory labor to be seasonal.

One of the appeals of rural industry for Fei seems to have been the prospect of local control and funding. Where, he asked, is the capital for industrializing China to come from? Foreign aid and foreign investment were usually made, especially to a country which is going through a period of instability, for political and not purely economic reasons, and were apt to entail some loss of sovereignty. It would be preferable for China's capital to come mostly from domestic savings, Fei felt. For the government to raise capital for industry through taxation was a possibility—in England the Labour Government was doing just that. But for China, which had not yet developed democratic institutions, this would involve a dangerous concentration of power in the government and the risk of dictatorial abuses. Far better would be voluntary investment by peasant families in tools and machines for household or local collective industries. The savings for such investments, Fei thought, would be possible after land reform had lifted the burden of rent payments, for China's peasants were by tradition thrifty (*XTCJ*:125-143).

By modern technology Fei meant not just machines but new forms of organization as well—in particular, the cooperative. For some industries, home production was appropriate, but if they were to avoid exploitation families would have to band together and cooperate in buying and selling and in introducing new technology. In other cases, small factories would be required in order to make efficient use of modern techniques. The experience of the paper mills at Yi-cun had shown that rural industries using expensive machinery were apt to be controlled by a few capitalists; to avoid this, cooperative ownership was needed. In the case of larger enterprises, public-service factories like the silk factory at Kaixiangong, capitalized by loans from government banks, should be instituted.

Rural industry was not only, in Fei's view, the fastest way of getting the benefits of industrialization to peasants (far from being conservative), but it also would be a form of modernization which would avoid the loss of social integration which, as we have seen, he thought plagued the West, a way of making industrial activity complement and not harm community life. If machines were set up in villages rather than cities wherever possible, the community life of the village could be maintained. If the worker felt himself part of a community, and production was carried on on a relatively small scale in homes or small workshops, then the psychologically healthy handicraft traditions of love of tools and pride in work would not be lost.

If all this were to happen, however, dedicated, public-spirited educated people would have to go to the countryside to spread new techniques of production and organization. The model for Fei's plan and the source of his enthusiasm for rural industry was, of course, his sister, Fei Dasheng, whose work improving sericulture in Kaixiangong and the Suzhou region has already been described. As he wrote in 1946:

> My proposal is not without factual basis. In fact it is the plan my sister tried successfully twenty-odd years ago in a Jiangsu village. There are many aspects of it which need improvement, but in its principles it is suited to the needs of China's peasants. (*NDNC*:vi)

Fei was not the first person to advocate developing China's rural industry[18]; in fact, there had been a few real programs to stimulate rural industries in some of the rural reconstruction efforts of the 1930s and later to compensate for the loss of industrial cities to the Japanese in the war.[19] Nonetheless, rural industry was not a common idea at the time; it was quite contrary to the widespread assumption that the route to industrialization in China as elsewhere was through city factories. Critics accused Fei of a sentimental attachment to inefficient handicraft industries doomed to extinction, of an impractical nostalgia for the past, and an irrational hatred of machines.[20] If there is merit to the notion of rural industrialization, it was not obvious to most.

To be sure, it is possible to raise a number of questions about Fei's analysis of the situation, such as how widespread was peasant dependence on rural industries to maintain a subsistence income, or whether Chinese peasants were not busier than he supposed during the winter months in agricultural tasks, such as repairing tools and water works (one of his own examples of rural industry, the Yi-cun paper mills, did not rely on seasonal labor). He tended to blur the distinction between peasants making things like clothing or baskets for their own household consumption and manufacturing goods for sale. The former was no doubt widespread, and was what Fei meant when he called most farmers craftsmen, but only the latter, which he had found absent in Lu-cun, would provide the supplemental income he was talking about. And it was only the latter which Fei seems to have thought had been hurt by imports of industrial goods; he did not think modern goods had entered the village so much as displaced rural manufactures in city or town markets.[21]

Fei did not foresee the vastly increased yields that can now be produced by improved techniques in agriculture. He probably also underestimated the difficulties of rural industrialization. He did not pay much attention to the costs of rural electrification or transportation in a big mountainous country like China, or the great economies of scale sacrificed in small village industries. He may well have been overly sanguine about the possibility of building village factories with voluntary investment from peasants' savings. He did not deal with the contradiction between using seasonal labor and getting full use out of capital plant; expensive factories would go idle part of the year if their employees were also farmers. He never thought of the enormous problem of maintenance and repairs for machines in out-of-the-way places. Finally, he doubtless underestimated the difficulty of getting technical knowledge into the village; educated people all over the world seem to prefer to live in cities.

Yet, when all is said and done, Fei was probably basically right in his perceptions that the development of urban industry would not bring immediate or substantial benefits to the rural population; that China's rural population was its main concern and problem; and that, to some degree, another kind of industrialization, directly beneficial to the rural population, was possible and preferable. There is no question that there are grave disadvantages, especially to the rural poor, in the situation found in much of the world, where rural migrants live in the slums or shantytowns of industrial cities.

China's experience in the last two decades with promoting small-scale rural industry and limiting urban growth shows that the kind of alternative Fei was thinking about was not impractical. After several years of following the Soviet pattern of giving priority to the development of urban heavy industry, the Communist Chinese government began in the late 1950s and early 1960s to encourage dispersed rural industries, such as chemical fertilizer, cement, electricity, iron and steel, tools and machines, repair services, and diverse manufactures, depending on local conditions and needs. Some are owned by local collectives, using local savings as capital, and some apparently depend on loans from the state. Today, we are told, there are over one million rural commune and brigade industries in China, employing 17 million workers, and providing 23 percent of the total output value of communes, brigades, and teams. "Many commune workers operate machines at township workshops a few kilometers or less from their houses. They work in small factories most of the year and go to the fields in the busy farming season."[22]

In the late 1960s and early 1970s, also, tens of millions of educated young people were sent to the countryside (*xia xiang*) to serve the people and break down the gap between city and village and between mental and manual labor. (To be sure, the language used, in contrast to Fei's, stressed that intellectuals were to learn from the peasants and from manual labor as much as they were to teach.) In addition to limiting urban growth, this migration of educated youths has doubtless contributed to improving village education, agricultural techniques, public health, and economic accounting.[23] It is not certain that these policies have been altogether successful; in particular the rustication of educated youths, which was motivated perhaps as much by the problem of urban unemployment as by the goal of rural development, has involved, among other problems, too high a degree of coercion to be continued indefinitely, and since Mao's death it is being de-emphasized. Rural industry, however, though it has doubtless involved inefficiencies in the use of resources, seems on the whole a successful strategy which may make China's modernization significantly different from that elsewhere.

Fei was talking in a practical kind of way about real needs of Chinese society, and the kinds of sociological analysis which led to his conclusions were potentially useful for arriving at a prescription for China's ills. In the end, of course, China's problem was less a matter of sociological knowledge than of politics. What was essential was getting the government concerned with rural needs and getting intellectuals to become more useful to society. These are the ends Fei was trying to promote with his popular writing of the late 1940s, and the significance of these articles is political rather than scholarly. His writings were avidly read by many, and surely not a few urban readers of the time must have been affected by his sympathetic analysis of peasant life and the rural economic crisis, by his concern for preserving China's village social integration through new methods of development, and by his call to intellectuals to make themselves of service to Chinese society and its peasant millions.

SIX

Politics, 1945–1948

For a force which the people do not control to serve the people would be a miracle.
—*XTCJ:*140

No matter which party the government is formed by in the future, it will have to do much more than did government in the past; the traditional idea of passive government is no longer meaningful, and the institutions which limited abuse of power in our cultural heritage have altogether atrophied . . . Are we to sit and watch centralized power expand without limit and local self-government wither? If we are unable to learn the representative institutions of England and America, what alternative have we?
—*STCJ:*63–64

In the course of the 1940s, Fei and many others became increasingly repelled by the Nationalists—by their pursuit of civil war instead of a negotiated settlement and economic reconstruction; by their corruption, brutality, and suppression of dissent; and by their seeming unconcern for the suffering of the masses. His revulsion was made sufficiently explicit in articles and speeches for Fei to feel himself in danger, and even to fear for his life. His disgust with the Guomindang and his desire for a government that would be effective and dedicated to progressive social change and peasant welfare drew him leftwards and, by 1948 and 1949, he could welcome the Communists with apparent enthusiasm.

But to say he was an implacable foe of the Nationalists is not to say he was really close to the Communists in his political views. As late as 1947, he was still writing longingly about Anglo-American democracy and constitutionalism, freedom of the press and rule by law, and the peaceful democratic socialist revolution of postwar England. These political values kept him somewhat aloof from the Communists in the 1940s and were to cause friction between him and them in the 1950s. Yet, if Fei himself felt reservations about Mao's movement, they were not stressed in his writings. A few people who were students at the time have told me of being radicalized by Fei's articles in the late 1940s, and it seems not unlikely that many young readers must have been encouraged to join cause with the Communist revolution by the persuasive and popular writings of this calm and reasonable scholar about rural distress, Guomindang oppression, American international capitalist exploitation, and *minzhu* (democracy), which, meaning "rule by the people," seemed close to the goals of the Communist movement. The disaffection of intellectuals from the Nationalist Government was a significant factor in the eventual success of the Chinese revolution, and it is worth a close look to see the process by which one so little inclined to radicalism as Fei Xiaotong came to support the Communists.

KUNMING, 1945-1946

Kunming had been a sleepy, backward little provincial capital upon which the cream of China's intellectual elite descended in the early years of the war with Japan. The best of her scientists, scholars, professors, and writers, many with American or European doctorates, were concentrated here in greater density than they ever had been in the large coastal cities of the east. Conditions were appalling—poverty, illness, lack of equipment and books—but morale was kept up by the feeling that a new China would be built in the post-war world and that these men and their students, their ideas and knowledge, would be of crucial importance in building it.[1]

At the same time, the political situation in Yunnan was peculiar. The province, far from the seat of the national government in Chongqing, was controlled by Long Yun, an old warlord general who had been governor for almost two decades. Nominally subservient to the national government, his power was in fact quite independent of the Guomindang, and he had every wish to maintain his independence. Although this rough, part-aborigine warlord had little in common with the intellectuals from the eastern cities, it served his interests to allow them a measure of freedom to criticize the Guomindang. To be sure, he occasionally closed their journals; they were also sometimes harassed by the Guomindang secret police; but, compared to Chongqing, criticism in Kunming was outspoken and the universities there, particularly Lianda (Southwest United University), formed a "fortress of democracy."[2]

Few of the professors and students in Kunming were truly radical; those whose sympathies lay with the Chinese Communists had already gone to join them in Shaanxi in the northwest in the late 1930s. There was surely considerable diversity in political outlook, but the predominant orientation was perhaps towards the United States, where many of the professors had been educated, and which stood in their minds for democracy and political liberties. Americans were also visible and well-liked allies against Japan, particularly in Kunming, which was an important air base for supplies coming "over the hump" from India and had a large number of GIs passing through.

Things were quiet for most of the war, but by 1944 dissatisfaction was growing among students and teachers. In January 1944, Zhang Xiruo, an American- and British-educated professor of political science, is reported to have given a speech in which he said that the present regime was the most tyrannical in Chinese history, that the Nationalist Party and Government regarded criticism as a crime and a sin, and that their only saving grace was their inefficiency—harsh words from a non-Communist scholar. In July and August 1944, American diplomats reported bitter criticism of Chiang Kai-shek and the Guomindang by Kunming liberals, and said student dissatisfaction had begun to grow about six months before and was stronger than in Peking in the 1930s.[3] In October 1944, a mass meeting calling for coalition government and basic freedoms for the people, sponsored by the Democratic League and, it is said, attended by over 10,000, was disrupted by Guomindang secret agents until local security forces restored order.[4]

An atmosphere of opposition began to grow between the central government and the universities, students, and professors, an opposition intensified by the measures taken by heavy-handed government agents. Robert Payne wrote in his diary on February 18, 1945:

> We live, in this age of nightmare, with the secret police around us. A student has disappeared. No one knows where he has gone, or whether he will ever return; no one doubts that he has been spirited away by the secret police . . .
>
> You see them sometimes hovering round the University gates, men with lawless and broken faces, the excreta of prisons, the refuse of this civilization which is in danger of making us all refuse, men with American guns in their pockets and a price on their heads. It is easy enough to understand why they are there. Of all places in China this University is the most glorious, because it is dedicated to democratic government, and believes in democracy, not knowing what democracy will bring China, because it has never been practiced . . . Universities, democracy— the two words most disliked by the soldiers who are in power.[5]

Tension in Kunming between the intellectuals and the Nationalist Government came to a head in the year following the end of the war against Japan, when the central government finally took control of Yunnan by force. In October 1945, after Long Yun's army had been sent to Indochina to receive the Japanese surrender, Central Government forces marched into Kunming; during the ensuing shooting between central and local troops, Fei hid his wife and daughter under the bed and lived off a neighbor's garden for three days (10/17/45 to SCF). Long was taken to Chongqing where he was given a lofty official title and put under house arrest. New provincial officials were installed by the Nationalists, who proceeded to enrage the intellectuals by taking away that measure of freedom of expression they had enjoyed under warlord Long.

The Chinese Democratic League was the chief agent for the expression of this political dissatisfaction.[6] The League claimed to be a third force, representing those educated Chinese who found themselves in agreement with neither the Nationalists nor the Communists. It called for constitutional democracy and civil liberties, and later, after the Civil War had started, for an end to the fighting and the establishment of a coalition government which would include the Communists.

Just what the Chinese Democratic League stood for politically is hard to state with precision for two reasons. First, it was both a political party and an umbrella organization for other parties. It had been formed in stages during the war, from 1939 to 1944, out of six or so small independent political parties or groups, some quite old but none with a very large following or organizational strength. These parties, while joining the League, continued their independent existence, and in addition the League had a number of individual members unconnected with any of the constituent groups. League membership was never very large, a few thousand probably, but nonetheless quite heterogeneous. The leadership, made up largely of prominent intellectuals, was itself sometimes seriously divided, and to what degree it spoke for the membership is another question.

Second, the League changed over time, moving closer to the Communists. This was due, no doubt, in large part to the clumsy treatment it received at the hands of the government, which tended to see the League as an agent of the Communists and finally outlawed it in October 1947. The League seems to have tried at first to steer a middle course between the Nationalists and the Communists; then, in October 1945, a shift in leadership brought it closer to the latter with the result that some of the original constituent groups pulled out. Nationalist sources claim that, in November 1945, a secret agreement was made between certain League leaders and the Communists, providing for cooperation, exchange of information, and a financial subsidy for the League, and that, from this time on, it was completely a Communist tool. Even if this is true, however, it proves nothing about the views of most League members.

Fei probably only became really interested in politics during the war, in 1943 or so. As a boy and in college, he had been unconcerned with such things. He later mentioned a "radical atmosphere" at the London School of Economics (*RQ&BJ*:49), but there is no indication he was caught up in it. In *Peasant Life*, written in 1938, he fleetingly criticized the government for its inability to carry out practical rural reforms because of spending so much money on anti-Communist campaigns (pp. 283-285), but he also suggested that political issues were unimportant, the result of mere factual misunderstandings which would be dispelled by books such as his about "actual conditions" (p. 5). Similarly, in his articles on rural policy written during the early war years (*NDNC*), he offered suggestions to the government, but his criticisms were mild and the tone calm.

A little later, just before and during his trip to the United States, Fei seems to have become more concerned over the Nationalist Government's behavior. In April 1942, he signed with eight others a long statement protesting the harmful effects of inflation, and proposing government controls and heavy taxes on the rich.[7] While inflation was something that touched him personally, for the salaries of government workers, including teachers, always lagged behind rising prices (he complained that he had seen his former maid in the theatre with a fur coat; "Harris Lecture":54, 61-63), he was also developing a more disinterested political consciousness. Shortly before he left for the United States in 1943, he published under a pseudonym a short story about a power-mad dictator who rules the world by virtue of a monopoly of atomic power (a startling idea two years before Hiroshima). He kills all intellectuals in order to secure his monopoly of this secret, but then when he becomes ill there are no doctors to cure him and, crazed with anger, he blows up the world (1943Ap3). In a letter, Fei described the number of the weekly in which this story appeared as a special issue "attacking dictatorship" (1/23/44 to WCF & JKF), and we may well see in this story a lampoon of Chiang Kai-shek's authoritarianism.

Before the Nationalist Government would give Fei and the

other professors passports to go to the United States in 1943, it required that they undergo several days of political training in Chongqing, which no doubt irked them considerably.[8] In letters written while he was in the United States, we find vague hints that Fei felt himself working with his American friends for liberalism and democracy in China. One letter spoke approvingly of an "offense against C. C.," by which he meant an "offensive" against the more conservative and authoritarian faction in the Nationalist Government, called the "CC clique" after the brothers Chen Lifu and Chen Guofu. The offensive doubtless had to do with protesting the Chinese government's restrictions on Chinese students in the United States; Fei had expressed fear it would provoke "more reactionary action" on the part of the Chinese government (4/29/44 to WCF). He spoke of trying to influence political opinion in China through the Kunming weekly newspaper *Shenghuo dao-bao,* which he called "one of the most outspoken papers of the liberal China" (10/21/44 to WCF), and whose policies he described as: "(1) arouse enthusiasm about social problems; (2) maintaining a liberal standing; (3) attacking profiteers and dictatorship; (4) fighting negative spirit of 'waiting for victory'." He discussed the possibility of buying the paper to make it an organ of "our group" (not identified), and sending one or two of the present staff, who had no definite political ideas, to the United States to "convert them into good fighters" (1/23/44 to WCF and JKF). He thought the paper could grow to become a major influence if only "we can enjoy less restriction on public opinion . . . perhaps it will be only after a revolution" (12/12/43 to WCF; such free talk about revolution is not characteristic).

Finally, his articles from the United States praising the American war effort implicitly threw Chinese wartime policies into a bad light. In the preface to the first collection of these, dated October 1944, Fei's disgust with the Nationalists' corruption and demoralization was explicit and bitter:

> One thing is the same in each article, and that is that I was taking the United States as a mirror to ourselves. I hope what I saw and wrote was

my prejudice and mistaken . . . [But] facts are facts and not to be denied. Their inflation is less than onefold, ours is a thousandfold. In their society the distance between rich and poor is decreasing because of the war, with us it is increasing daily. In order to win the war they have devoted half their citizens' total income to military expenses, with us it is probably less than one tenth and most of the nation's wealth is locked in foreign banks. Their sons all do military service without regard to rich or poor, high or low; we have a special class which enjoys honor without the responsibility of protecting the country. They go without coffee and meat at home so that the front lines won't lack these; with us the rear consumes ceaselessly and frontline soldiers die on the road. The sons of their leaders are first in the line of fire; the relatives of our important people use foreign exchange to travel abroad. I need not give further examples of the differences between the two. I just want to ask, how can we be this way—are we richer, stronger, less afraid of national extinction, more shameless? What can I say? Happy he who has not seen the world, for he can close his eyes and await the blessings of victory. (*RQ&BJ*:ii–iii)

Fei's association with the Democratic League may have been through the Democratic Socialist Party, which was a constituent group within the League and of which Fei was identified as a member by an apparently well-informed writer in 1946.[9] The Democratic Socialist Party, earlier called the National Socialist Party, had been formed in the early 1930s by Zhang Junmai (Carsun Chang) when he was teaching at Yanjing, and consisted of a few hundred students and professors. It was Zhang Junmai who got Fei his research appointment to Guangxi in 1935, but there is no reason to think that Fei was connected with Zhang's party at that time. His brother Fei Qing, however, may well have been, for he contributed frequently to the party journal *Zaisheng* in the 1930s. Fei Qing came to Kunming in about 1943 or 1944 from Japanese-occupied Shanghai, where he had been Dean of the Suzhou University Law School (12/18/43 to WCF), and perhaps he drew Fei Xiaotang to Zhang Junmai's party. At any rate, Zhang is one of the few older Chinese intellectuals Fei spoke of favorably in his letters, calling himself an "admirer" and "intellectual follower" of Zhang (1/28/45 to MPR), and in 1946 a number of his articles appeared in Zhang's *Zaisheng*.

Fei's relationship with the Democratic League was ambiguous. The League had a branch in Kunming, founded in December 1944, and said a year later to have some 200 members, mostly academics (it also sponsored a Chinese Democratic Youth League with several hundred students from the two universities).[10] "I have refused to join their League," Fei wrote in January 1945; he disliked the leader of the Kunming branch, Luo Longji, an American-educated political scientist and journalist, whom he called "a second-rate politician," aloof from the common people (1/29/45 to WCF:3). Robert Payne, not always correct on such matters, thought Fei an independent.[11] He was not one of the several Kunming professors on the League's Central Executive Committee.[12] Yet Fei did write for League journals and did work for the democratic movement; and by mid-1946 at least he was being referred to as a League member.[13]

Fei's ties with the Democratic Socialist Party and the Democratic League and his increasing concern with politics were strengthened by his growing friendship with Pan Guangdan (Quentin Pan), with whom he later did the study of social mobility via the examination system. Pan was twelve years older than Fei, of a scholar-merchant family in Paoshan county right next to Shanghai and not far from Fei's native district. He had gone to the United States as an undergraduate and was graduated from Dartmouth College, Phi Beta Kappa in zoology, in 1922. He then took an MA from Columbia in 1924, and had become famous in China in the 1920s for books and articles advocating eugenics. In 1930, he became professor of sociology at Qinghua University, where Fei apparently studied with him, for he acknowledged his help in the published version of his BA thesis (1934Je). Pan was a member of the Democratic Socialist Party, and also active in the Democratic League, serving in October 1945 as a member of the League's Central Executive Committee and as a leader, with Luo Longji, of the League's Kunming branch.[14] Fei had gone on a trip with Pan to western Yunnan in early 1943 (*JZS*) and two years later we find him writing, "the one-legged Pan [he had lost his leg long before] . . . has become a most active fighter for the liberal movement. He is wonderful. We meet every week . . . He encourages me to write and talk. I do" (1/29/45 to WCF:3).

When he returned to China from the United States in 1944, Fei found that his articles from America had made him a popular writer and much in demand as a speaker. "During the last three weeks," he wrote in October 1944, "I have at least given a dozen speeches in closed meetings, in governmental meetings, in factories . . . So far I still maintain my principle: never refuse any opportunity to express my ideas to the public" (10/21/44 to WCF). In the next two years, his articles appeared regularly in what he called "liberal" journals such as *Ziyou luntan* (Liberty forum, which Fei termed "very progressive" [1/29/45 to WCF:1]) and the Kunming *Minzhu zhoukan,* organ of the Democratic League.[15] He continued to give speeches on current topics,[16] and it was in this role that he experienced the incident in November 1945 that would greatly harden his opposition to the Guomindang.

The end of the war with Japan had found Fei not exultant, but profoundly worried about the likelihood of civil war in China. A few days after V-J Day he confessed to being "depressed . . . Things look dark and discouraging" (9/3/45 to WCF). By November, he was writing articles warning against an even greater danger: that the fighting between Nationalists and Communists in China, by then a reality, could set off a third world war between the United States and the U.S.S.R. in which mankind would be destroyed by atomic weapons (1945N?; 1945N26).

On the evening of November 25, 1945, Fei was one of the four speakers at a large outdoor rally to protest and discuss ways of settling the daily widening Civil War.[17] The night before, the Nationalist Party, Government, and military authorities in Kunming had issued an order prohibiting all mass meetings; but the sponsors of the rally, student organizations of Lianda, Yunnan University, and two smaller Kunming colleges, decided to go ahead anyway. School authorities, under Guomindang pressure, refused them the Yunnan University auditorium they had planned to use, so they moved to an outdoor site on the Lianda campus. Several thousand people came (six thousand according to one eye-witness), mostly college and high school students. The first speaker was Qian Duansheng, an American-educated political scientist who called for a coalition government as the only way to end the Civil War. Next, the economist Wu Qiyuan spoke of the financial disaster civil war would bring. Both, though critical of the government, were known to be members of the Guomindang and hardly radical. While they spoke, shooting could be heard outside the campus walls.

Then Fei Xiaotong mounted the platform to speak on how American foreign policy increased the likelihood of civil war in China. This policy expressed, he said, the wishes of American financial and military barons, not of the American people as a whole, who should unite with the Chinese people to oppose the war and U.S. militarism. While he spoke, the shooting got louder and closer. Rifle and machine-gun fire and grenade explosions could be heard; the lights went out, and bullets could be seen whizzing right overhead:

> I stood on a platform high above the ground. It was in the dark evening with the twilight of the dim stars. About five thousand students sat on the ground making a very impressive scene. We were surrounded by soldiers who were sent to threaten the meeting. Machine guns and mortars were firing over our heads. The light was gone; only a gas lamp besides the speaker. Death was so near to us. Bullets flew only few feet over me. I had to calm myself and continue my speech (in fact I did not know what I was saying) in order to keep the audience attentive. Any disturbance in the meeting might cause massacre on the spot. (12/12/45 to MPR)

He finished speaking to much applause. A fourth speaker, Pan Dakui, called for coalition government and the withdrawal of American and Russian troops; then a resolution was passed to send a protest to the government condemning the Civil War, and to the United States a demand for the withdrawal of American troops. After the meeting, soldiers harassed students trying to return home. The next day, the newspapers carried a story from the official Central News Agency that troops had fired at armed bandits trying to rob some houses in the vicinity of the university.

Most of the students from the colleges and high schools in Kunming went on strike in protest over the incident. In the following days, they continued to disobey orders to return to classes and, instead, took to the streets, passing out handbills, writing slogans such as "Chinese should not fight with Chinese" on the walls, and talking to townspeople. They were harassed by soldiers and secret police, and the atmosphere became more and more tense. Then, on December 1, the climax came. Large groups of soldiers and rowdies in plain clothes broke into Lianda and several other schools, where they destroyed property and beat up students and teachers. When the day was finally over, ten students had been injured, and four people—three students, one a girl, and a young high school teacher—lay dead, killed by hand grenades.

The December First Incident, as it immediately became known, aroused public opinion both in Kunming and in other cities in China. The four bodies were carried into the Lianda library, where they lay for weeks, symbols of martyrdom in the battle for democracy and against fascism. Much of the press, including most daily newspapers, gave the story scant or no coverage, but a few magazines such as those associated with the Democratic League, in Kunming, Shanghai, and elsewhere, gave it wide publicity, and the Kunming students started their own weekly. Many of these anti-Guomindang periodicals were forced to stop printing, but a few, including the *Shidai pinglun,* which Fei edited, were able to continue in mimeograph. A wide spectrum of the public was apparently shocked by the incident. "The entire public is bitterly against the criminals" responsible for the killings, wrote Fei (12/12/45 to MPR), and tangible evidence of public support was seen in donations to the student cause. In several cities, one in Shanghai in January 1946, for instance, was attended by several thousand people and addressed by prominent intellectuals.[18]

The students were finally talked into going back to classes in January after being assured by their teachers that the government would investigate and punish those responsible for the incident; indeed, Chiang Kai-shek himself had spoken out to this effect. The two top officials in the province, acting governor and party head Li Zonghuang and garrison commander Guan Linzheng, who the students thought were ultimately responsible for the killings, were transferred out of the province, but they were never punished. This left a smoldering feeling of dissatisfaction in the early months of 1946, and the sense of a movement, the "democratic movement" it was sometimes called, continued long after the strike was over. The concerns of this movement went beyond the December First Incident. Demands and slogans typically called for an end to the fighting between the Nationalists and Communists, withdrawal of foreign (that is, American) troops, and the establishment of a coalition government; democracy instead of one-party dictatorship; personal liberties, including freedom of speech, press, assembly; and an end to secret police abuses. In the government-oriented press, this movement, when it was mentioned at all, was depicted as stirred up by Communist agents, but in fact it was not openly pro-Communist and did not call for the overthrow of the government or the Nationalists or Chiang Kai-shek.[19]

Fei was very active in this democratic movement. He had been badly shaken by the episode of November 25—what he called his "battle with fascists" (12/12[/45] to WCF)—but nonetheless affirmed the next month that "we are doing everything possible even at the risk of our lives to turn the tide in China... Democracy must be born to us" (1/8/45 [i.e. 46] to MPR). After the December First Incident, he signed with 70 other Yunnan University faculty and staff members a statement of sympathy and support for the Kunming student "anti-civil war and pro-democracy movement," and calling that day's slaughter "unprecedented in the history of the republic."[20] The next month, he was one of 194 Kunming educators to sign an open letter to the Political Consultative Conference, then meeting in Chongqing with representatives from the Nationalist, Communist, and third parties, demanding a cease-fire, coalition government, democracy, and civil liberties.[21]

Then came a long open letter welcoming General Marshall, who had recently arrived in China on his lengthy mission to try to stop the Civil War, signed by Fei, Pan Guangdan, Wen Yiduo, and Wu Han, but apparently written largely by Fei ("I have just completed a draft of a memorandum to your general which will be sent in the names of many professors in Kunming," he wrote an American friend at the time. "I belief it is one of my best articles. I wrote from my heart" [1/8/45 (i.e. 46) to WCF]). It called for civil liberties and the opportunity for expression of dissent, disbandment of secret police organs, rapid demobilization of swollen armies, new elections to a national assembly, and the elimination of a number of economic abuses. Three words glow on the page: "democracy" is spoken of thirty-seven times, "freedom" twenty-five times, and "peace" fifteen. Government oppression, corruption, and dictatorship are execrated unequivocally. The Communists are referred to only once; their resort to armed resistance is explained as caused by the government's intolerance of peaceful dissent, but it is not justified: "We are opposed to any party having its own army" (1946Ja12).

In May, we find Fei's signature on another open letter to General Marshall, this one from twenty Kunming professors, calling on the Nationalists to purge themselves of the "reactionary elements" who have broken the cease-fire, are trying to establish a fascist dictatorship, and have sent secret police everywhere to suppress the people; and asking the United States to stop arming and transporting Nationalist troops and to make no further loans to the government, as this just made it possible for the Nationalists to slaughter more Chinese and delay democratic government.[22] He wrote a series of articles on democracy and civil liberties, to which we shall return. No doubt he was active as a speaker too. We know that, on February 18, he spoke at a big student meeting sponsored by the Kunming Student Federation, several magazines including the Democratic League's *Minzhu zhoukan* and Fei's *Shidai pinglun,* and the Sino-Soviet Cultural Association; the chairman was Wen Yiduo, and the other speakers were Fei Qing, Pan Guangdan, and Wu Han.[23]

Fei was keenly aware of the danger of being a leader in the democratic movement. His letters spoke of a "state of terror in Kunming, of rumors that he was to be arrested, of being watched constantly, and of a sense of risking his life (12/12/45 to MPR; 12/12[/45] to WCF; 1/8/45 [i.e. 46] to MPR). Then, in May and June of 1946, as the cease-fire broke down and fighting between the Nationalists and Communists in Manchuria intensified, the atmosphere in Kunming became even more frightening. Posters accused local Democratic League leaders such as Wen Yiduo, Li Gongpu and others of being Communists, and there were rumors the Democratic League was plotting violence, rumors which it was feared would be used to justify violence against the League. At three receptions given by the League to try to scotch these rumors, Fei, Pan Guangdan, Wen Yiduo, Li Gongpu and others, stated the League's positions and history; the meeting was harassed by the secret police and subsequently all were kept under surveillance.[24] There was talk of the secret police being given a free hand to "take care of" the situation. There were also rumors of a blacklist of names active in the democratic movement who were slated to be arrested or assassinated, and Fei's name was said to be on it.[25]

Then Li Gongpu was assassinated. Li was an American-educated professor, a Christian, and onetime Y.M.C.A. worker, who had become involved right before the war in political protest against the government's policy of not resisting Japan and had been arrested (as one of the "seven gentlemen") in 1936. In Kunming he was active in the Democratic League, and was an editor, with Wen Yiduo, of its weekly *Minzhu zhoukan*. In the late evening of July 11, after getting off a bus on his way home from the movies with his wife, he was shot in the street by three men with American-made pistols with silencers. He died in the hospital early the next morning.[26]

In the following days, various journals printed many pages of sad and bitter statements by non-Communist intellectuals. Fei Xiaotong's which was carried by a Communist magazine, read:

> This is the beginning of the end. Li Gongpu's blood marks a new

turning point in the history of the Chinese people's struggle for democracy; a turning point which is without doubt already nearing the light. I grieve that Gongpu will not be able to see the coming of the light, but his blood itself has made it possible. "Shameless," was his final accusation against the powers of darkness which assassinated him. But let me comfort the dead; when shamelessness reaches this extent it will soon be past. Have faith in the people, they will carry on the fight. (1946Jl21)

Next, an apparently crazy woman appeared at the house of Wen Yiduo to shout that Li Gongpu was dead, and that Wen and Pan Guangdan would be next. Wen had also studied in the United States for a few years, and had then become a poet and classical scholar of considerable reputation, and during the war a professor at Lianda. His interest in politics came rather late, in 1944 apparently, but he then became a very active leader in the Democratic League. "He believed the present government of China to be corrupt, and said so openly, with no shadow of fear on the fine high-boned face," wrote his friend Robert Payne.[27] In spite of warnings of danger, on July 15, Wen went to a memorial meeting for Li Gongpu and stood up to speak before a crowd of a thousand; returning home a few hours later, he too was shot and killed, and his son wounded, by four or five men with pistols outside the Lianda faculty dormitory.

The cold-blooded murders of two Democratic League professors on the streets of Kunming just four days apart, plus various rumors of blacklists, warnings, and other ominous signs—Fei, for example, found a hole in his back wall with Garrison Command troops stationed nearby who would not permit Yunnan University workmen to stop it up[28]—were a clear indication that there was an organized effort of violence against leaders in the democratic movement and that the lives of others were in danger. That night Fei Xiaotong, Pan Guangdan, Zhang Xiruo, and eight others, mostly professors and Democratic League members, took sanctuary in the U.S. Consulate General. One account of the incident indicates that the Americans took the initiative, sending a vehicle to bring them to the Consulate, and Harold C. Roser, Jr., Vice-

Consul at Kunming, told me that he and Fei rode around in a jeep picking up all the people on an alleged assassination blacklist the Americans had come into possession of. On July 19, after Kunming had seemed quiet for a few days and the Garrison Command had guaranteed to the Consulate that the group would be protected, the eleven went home. Then, two days later, threats, various ominous incidents, and a general atmosphere of terror brought them back again, and they stayed on in the Consulate, guarded day and night by a small group of armed American soldiers, until about the 28th, when arrangements were complete for some of them to leave the city.

Fei and the others thus spent some eleven days under American protection. He never mentioned it in anything he later wrote and perhaps was a bit ashamed of the incident. That a group of almost a dozen prominent intellectuals should have to seek refuge in the American Consulate was of course an extraordinary event and indicative of the lawlessness of China at that time. The Consulate officials were reprimanded by the Embassy in Nanking for creating an embarrassing situation, but it seems clear that the lives of some or all of these men were in fact in danger. The incident also indicated the still friendly feeling between anti-Nationalist liberals and American government officials, in spite of American support for the Nationalists.[29]

The assassinations brought forth considerable press comment both in China and abroad. The Democratic League conducted its own investigation, which found ample evidence to blame the Yunnan Garrison Command, and more generally the Guomindang and its secret police.[30] In late August, two junior officers in the Yunnan Garrison Command's secret police branch (*tewu*, literally "special affairs") were tried, convicted, and executed for Wen's murder; but the official explanation that they had acted on their own initiative seemed to most people not credible.[31] In retrospect, it is clear that these assassinations by government agents were responsible for a considerable erosion of public faith in the legitimacy of Guomindang rule.

The Central Government and the Americans sent officials down to Kunming to arrange for safe conduct to the north for the refugees.³² On July 31, two days after leaving the Consulate, Fei and Pan, together with Fei's wife and daughter, flew out of Kunming to Nanjing accompanied by an official from the Ministry of Education. They refused to talk to the press on the way, and after a week in Nanjing disappeared from public view.³³ The Feis and Pan remained in hiding for the next three months, staying with Fei's sister Fei Dasheng and with his father in Suzhou (8/11/46, 9/3/46, 10/10/36 [i.e. 46], 10/14/46 to WCF).

During these "several months of rest in my native town," Fei felt depressed. A "certain feeling of futility possessed me . . . a vast and roaring tide of adversity attacking a small vessel in the midst of a big ocean." He felt "bewildered by the cruelty of human history" (12/4/46 to MPR). He had reunions with his relatives, who had been under Japanese occupation during the war. He met with old schoolmates from Zhenhua Girls' School. He went over old family genealogical records. He was badly in need of money, and Wilma Fairbank gave him $150. But mostly he spent the time trying to arrange to leave the country. A few months before, he had been invited to attend the Princeton bicentennial, but felt he couldn't get away from his Qinghua duties (5/19/46 to Holland, 5/19/46 to Rowe, in IPR 98). He had planned to move back to Peking in September (5/19/46 to Holland, in IPR 98), but now felt it too dangerous to stay in China, in spite of Wilma Fairbank's advice that "some of your Tsing Hua [Qinghua] colleagues have spoken of your exaggerated fears," and that it would cause whispering for him to leave now (10/16/46 from WCF). He got an invitation to go to England for three months (an invitation James Yen had previously turned down), but his wife was not included. John Fairbank tried to bring him and his family to Harvard, to teach regional studies and social relations for a year. He thought of applying for a job with the United Nations in the United States. Finally, he decided to leave his wife and daughter (who was just starting school) with his father in Suzhou and go to England alone. He got a leave of absence from Qinghua and, after some delay, the government finally issued him a passport (8/11/46, 9/7/46, 10/14/46, 11/11/46 to WCF).

SECOND VISIT TO ENGLAND, 1946-1947

Fei was in England for about three months from November 1946 to February 1947, as the guest of the British Council. He stayed in London with Tian Rukang, who had been his student at the Research Station in Yunnan and was now studying anthropology at Fei's old alma mater, the London School of Economics. He gave a public lecture to "a big audience" at L.S.E. (2/5/47 to MPR) on "Social Change in Modern China," sat in on seminars, and spent some time with Malinowski's successor, Raymond Firth, but he seems to have missed his old master sadly:

> Malinowski died and has left no shadow or inspiration in his old seminar room. I sit in the same chair I used to sit ten years ago, but I feel quite sad in it. I miss something, the thing I have in Queike [his Research Station]. (12/28/46 to WCF)

He visited Parliament and was introduced by an English friend to some young Labour backbenchers with whom he had several talks. He spent three days in a village near Oxford interviewing local leaders. He wrote weekly articles about England for the *Dagong bao* and worked on a manuscript on Chinese social structure in English for IPR. He instituted a personal foreign aid program to England, asking Margaret Redfield to use his royalties from *Earthbound China* to send American books on China to England where they were hard to get (2/5/47 to MPR). And, at a cocktail party the British Council gave for him when he first arrived, Fei met Arthur Waley, the great English translator of Chinese and Japanese literature, of whom he had apparently never heard: "I met a translator, named 'Willy' I think, who asked questions about Po Chü-yi's relations with his wife" (11/26[/46] to WCF; Waley's *Life and Times of Po Chü-i* was published in 1949). Fei left London on February 18, passed through Singapore, and stopped for four days in Hong Kong and then a week in Shanghai, where he picked up his family. On March 3, 1947, he arrived in Peking, which he had not seen since 1936.

After he returned, the *Dagong bao* articles about England were collected into a slim volume called *Chong fang Ying-lun* (Second visit to England; *CFYL*). It is personal and anecdotal, full of charming conversations with a woman on the plane, his landlady in London, a school teacher, an innkeeper; stories about Lord Nelson and Lady Hamilton, and Laski's libel suit, and inspirational biographies of the Labour leaders Aneurin Bevan and Ellen Wilkinson. But these easygoing narratives are never without a point. Fei had hailed the Labour victory in the July 1945 election at the time as the coming of the century of the common man (1945Ag6). Now he continued and developed this theme. The book is pervaded with excitement, admiration, and hope for the new government's socialist policies. It is a warm and happy book; "I love England," he declared unabashedly on the first page.

England filled him with hope that bloodless revolution was possible, that freedom and equality, political and economic democracy could be conjoined. He had felt similar hopes about the United States a few years before when Roosevelt was President; but now it seemed to him that the United States had failed to solve the problems of monopolies, depression, and unemployment, or to achieve real social and economic equality. Conversely, the U.S.S.R. had economic equality but at the cost of political liberty. It was England that promised both. The Labour Government was on the way to redistributing wealth and economic power, raising living standards, recognizing the right of every person to a job, health care, and education, and giving each the opportunity to serve society to the best of his ability, free of want or threat. In just two years in power—and in most difficult circumstances, with empire crumbling and industry declining—the new government had alleviated an unbearable housing shortage, weathered a severe coal shortage, and solved England's basic economic problems. And all this had been done democratically, without violence, in a revolution by consent (pp. 77-88).

His glowing discussions of Labour's socialist policies emphasized the welfare state aspects, direct government services to the public, rather than state ownership of the means of production. One chapter described admiringly the National Health Insurance Bill, which was then in Parliament (pp. 69–76). Two chapters on education noted a trend away from aristocratic schools to a system offering opportunities to all children, rich or poor (pp. 44–60). Here and there he praised the construction of public housing, government aid to people buying and restoring war-damaged buildings, and a policy of rationing milk for adults in order to supply it free with lunch to all school children "for the sake of the next generation." He hardly mentioned the nationalization of basic industries or state economic planning (in a chapter on the coal industry, his point was not the benefits nationalization had brought to the workers or its economic rationalizing effects, but that the current coal shortage was caused by factors beyond the government's control and was thus not to be taken as a failure of socialism pp. 36–43). He saw socialism as a spirit, a spirit of working together for the sake of the future common welfare.

Above all, socialism meant to Fei the abolition of special privileges. Fei listened to the Parliamentary debate about abolishing the pension for Nelson's heirs, and he approvingly concluded that the English had come to feel that special privilege, in this case rewarding a man's descendants and making a hero of the admiral while forgetting the common sailors, was unreasonable (pp. 27–35). The old educational system which had provided elite education for a privileged few was being changed. Fei described the debate on health insurance as between those interested in the welfare of all the people and a few private doctors afraid of not being able to sell their practices when they retire. Post-war rationing, he said, indicated public acceptance of the idea that those with money should not be specially privileged to purchase scarce commodities. And a chapter on how Harold J. Laski, Labour Party theoretician and professor of political science at L.S.E., lost his libel suit blames the verdict on the system of "special juries," upper middle class by virtue of high property and educational qualifications, another instance of special privilege which he predicted would be reformed (pp. 17–26).

In view of his advocacy of rural development in China, an article criticizing the English government for promoting rural development is worthy of notice. In England, he argued, urban industrialization was already an accomplished fact, and 80 percent of the population lived in cities, which were the centers of culture and opportunity. Rural life could attract only retired or weekending city people who wanted a garden to putter in; the rural areas were no more than backyard gardens to the cities (pp. 61–68).

His only serious complaint about the Labour Government was in the realm of foreign policy. England was wrong, he wrote, in attempting to maintain the Empire. The naval and industrial technological hegemony on which the Empire was built could not be continued, and attempting to keep it now would lead only to economic drain and conflict. Empire amounted to special privilege —monopolies of markets and raw materials—and England should learn to live without privilege (pp. 1–9). Fei thought that, because of England's dependence on American loans to pay for imports for post-war reconstruction, the Labour Government had been forced to capitulate to the United States in foreign policy, adopting an anti-Soviet line, maintaining troops abroad, and buying food from America instead of Eastern Europe. So far they had managed to avoid compromising their domestic socialism, but soon another big loan would be needed and what conditions would be exacted could not be foreseen. Fei saw the United States, hostile to socialism, as Britain's major problem, the only dark cloud on its horizon (pp. 88–91; 1947Ag29; 1947N1).

Fei's mood of wistful, almost dreamy idealism when he was in England is clearest in an article about his hopes for future international relations. The piece is constructed around his conversation with a fellow passenger on the plane to England, an English businesswoman from Hong Kong. She complained to him about the constant nuisance of customs and visas, and that her business was greatly affected by the outcome of American elections in which she had no vote. This provoked in Fei the thought that the old Chinese ideal of one world (*tianxia yi jia*) had now been made necessary by modern developments. National boundaries made no sense in an age of rapid air travel. National sovereignty was unreasonable when nations were economically interdependent. The only reasonable way was a united world without separate nations (pp. 10–16).

On returning from England, Fei set out to translate (with the help of one Shi Jing, who did the last few chapters) a book about *Labour's First Year* (London, 1947) by J.E.D. Hall, a British journalist. Hall's book was a non-partisan summary of the debates in Parliament on both the new socialist domestic measures and also foreign policy questions during the first session the Labour Party was in power, from the summer of 1945 to the summer of 1946. Fei's Chinese translation was published under the title *Gong dang yi nian* (*GDYN*) in September 1947. For his Chinese audience he thought it necessary to provide a long introduction explaining the British political system and the Labour Party's brand of socialism. British socialism was milder and gentler than that of the U.S.S.R.; it involved buying big and basic industries, not confiscating all means of production; supervising private enterprises but not comprehensive economic planning; slow rather than radical change; and no violence (*GDYN*:xx–xxv). British politics, he said, though retaining old forms such as the King, the House of Lords, and various quaint customs from a truly autocratic age, was nonetheless pervaded with a thoroughly democratic spirit (pp. v–xx). Old forms with new contents was just the opposite of China, he said, where no real democracy, but only empty slogans and democratic forms without substance, were all that had been accomplished in the almost half century since the Republican Revolution of 1911:

> In China, we tend to change names. If a child is seriously ill, we pretend to give him to another, changing his name in order to fool the evil spirits. In politics it is the same; the revolution for democracy succeeded only in changing names [as though] if the name were changed then the content would change with it. Still today, democracy is thus uncertain. (p. ix; cf. 1947Jel4)

POLITICAL IDEALS: DEMOCRACY AND SOCIALISM

The closest thing to a political credo Fei ever wrote was a series of articles he had done in the spring of 1946 at the height of the "democratic movement" in Kunming. They were first published in the journal he edited in Kunming, *Shidai pinglun,* quickly reprinted in a couple of Shanghai magazines, and then again, with a preface by Pan Guangdan, in a short book called *Minzhu, xianfa, renquan* (Democracy, constitutions, and human rights; *MZ,XF, RQ*) published in Shanghai in August 1946. It is written in the simplest style, dialogue and anecdote, the point always clear, and was obviously intended for a very broad audience; Pan's preface calls it "an uncensored citizenship textbook."

In this book, Fei referred with feeling to the December First killings (and the mendacious reporting of the student movement by the Central News Agency), inequities in conscription, arbitrary arrest for purposes of extortion, secret police activities, and new regulations permitting the police to enter homes at will (not permitted, he asserted, even in Germany under Bismarck or the Nazis). These excesses Fei thought very stupid, for "government power cannot be maintained against the opposition of the people" (p. 83), and he suggested that the Nationalists were in effect committing suicide.

The alternative, and the main theme of the book, was Anglo-American constitutional democracy. Fei praised American political parties, which exact no oath of discipline, but express popular opinion and put forward men of talent (Chapter 1). He described Hyde Park and freedom of speech: in spite of the variety of opinions expressed, England was an orderly country, he said, for free expression leads to mutual understanding, compromise and consensus, and in a free country people do not try to trick others for fear of losing their credibility (Chapter 2). He lauded constitutions, contracts between the government and the people which restrict government and prevent abuse of power, and recounted at length the "admirable story" of the formation of the American Constitution (at times his admiration went too far; forgetting the

American Civil War, he said the American Constitution laid the foundation for 160 years of stability; Chapter 3). He praised British success in getting power away from the King in a series of relatively bloodless steps from Magna Charta to 1688 (Chapter 4), and cited Beard to the effect that the right of *habeas corpus* is the greatest contribution of the Anglo-Saxons (Chapter 6). Above all, he admired the tradition that rulers are subject to law. "What we must do now is take the Anglo-Saxon spirit of constitutional government and transplant it to China" (p. 35). Fei did not, however, suggest just how such a transplant was to be made.

The theme of restraining government power came up again in *Xiangtu chongjian,* which described how the old Chinese checks were no longer effective. The philosophy of passivity (*wuwei*), which taught a ruler not to try to do too much, was no longer feasible in modern times. The *baojia* system had extended government administration down to the local level, and the desertion of the rural gentry to the cities had left unchecked a corrupt and ineffective local administration unresponsive to local interests (*Gentry:*75–90). In answer to critics, Fei said that he was not opposed to strong centralized government, indeed that it was necessary for modernization (although, as we shall see, he thought that in the early stages of democracy it would be better if government were not too big), but wanted to make it responsible by means of a constitution defined as "a contract limiting governmental power, established between the people and the government," and democracy in the sense of "ways of expressing the people's opinions and structures for representing the popular will" (*XTCJ:*56).

Since positive checks on government were not well developed in China, "we must learn from the West, especially England and America" (p. 57); "in my opinion the only way probably is to study the Anglo-American representative system" (p. 63). To this, two well-known scholars, Liang Shuming and Zhang Dongsun, objected that Western-style institutions had not worked very well in China and were not suited to Chinese culture,[34] but Fei replied that there was no real alternative: "Traditional *wuwei* has lost its meaning, and the institutions in our cultural inheritance for preventing abuse of power are totally feeble . . . Are we to sit quietly and watch centralized power expand without limit? . . . Is our past failure to learn the Anglo-American system due really to inability or rather to unwillingness?" (pp. 62–63). He admitted, however, that full democracy could not be instituted all at once, that Chinese peasants, who had been oppressed for thousands of years and consequently had a low level of political consciousness, needed political leadership—"I'm not one of those with a superstitious faith in 'the people'" (p. 61).

Fei tended to think of politics, I believe, less as a struggle between irreconcilable conflicting interests than as a means of finding solutions to social problems through analysis and discussion. "The major problem of collective life is how to get out of people's differing opinions a consensus which all can accept" (*MZ,XF, RQ:*15). Each person's experience and hence his understanding is only partial; through free expression and exchange of views there is compromise and mutual understanding, and in this way it is possible to reach a common view and sense of common interest on the basis of which behavior can be harmonized (*XTCJ:*43, 147–148). Thus the importance of a free press and accurate news reporting (1942Ag10; 1946Je6a; 1948S5).

Although Fei wanted constitutional safeguards against misgovernment and for freedom of speech and press, he was not a champion of individual liberty. Since individuals are dependent on society for their survival, he tended to think of society as the source of ultimate value and that people should devote themselves to social goals. He did not seem interested in encouraging the development of individual selves, nor was he concerned with protecting a realm of individual autonomy against the demands of society. Unlike "democracy," the word "liberty" appears seldom in his writing, and how far Fei was from thinking it always desirable may be seen from the answer he gave to a critic of his views on urban life. Wu Jingchao had written, taking issue with Fei, that cities were centers of freedom against the restrictions of custom; that they offered more choices and amenities of life, and were preferred by most people who had lived in them, including Fei himself.³⁵ To this Fei replied:

> I think "freedom" and "restrictions" are meaningless terms. Culture itself can be called "restricting"; language restricts one's manner of expression, but we don't therefore seek freedom from language—on the contrary it is only through the restriction of language that we attain the freedom to express ourselves. Freedom is only meaningful if it contributes to the goals of our life. The urban freedom Wu admires has elements sociologists like Le Play and Durkheim called social disorganization, because this freedom is the cause of divorce, crime, poverty, unemployment, and suicide. (1947N8a)

In his book on England he sometimes seemed to suggest that the purpose of liberating individuals was so that they could serve society. Equal educational opportunities, he said, were valuable because, if educated, persons of ability from among the common people could make great contributions to society (*CFYL*:56). He admired the attempts and hopes of Labour to free all from the threat of want or unemployment, and thereby "allow each person to develop fully the opportunity to serve society" (*CFYL*:80). Elsewhere, he said that life was meaningful only when lived in society: "Once a man leaves the group and no longer identifies his interest with the group's interests, he no longer feels any value in existence or interest in his work" (*RQ&BJ*:68).

Capitalism seemed to him to be inherently exploitative—competition demanded this—and was unfair because the economically weak could not protect themselves against those with accumulated wealth. He was concerned lest the fruits of the coming industrialization of China go to a handful of privileged capitalists to the detriment of the majority; for this reason he advocated cooperatives, and, for those industries that required large-scale urban production, such as steel, state ownership.

But there was a problem with state socialism. It was fine in a country like England, Fei thought, but it put too much power in the hands of the government in the case of a nation in the early stages of democracy (he was speaking not of China's present but of some future government):

I do not want to underestimate the political level of our people, but after several thousand years of authoritarian government it seems unrealistic to hope that they can all at once assume the responsibilities of modern citizens and oversee the actions of the government. At a time when the people are not yet able to control the government, to enlarge government powers will necessarily tempt those with power to abuse it. So I think that, if one day China truly takes the road of democracy, in order to make the government responsible to the people and controlled by the people, in the early stages government duties should be light and government power weak . . . That is to say many duties and powers should be given to various non-governmental groups directly managed by local people. This broadly based democracy is the only guarantee that democratic government will not change its character. (*XTCJ*:139; "Financing":111)

This, of course, is another argument for preferring small-scale rural industry, owned cooperatively by local peasants who have voluntarily invested in it and who profit from it, to large-scale urban industry built by the government with funds raised through compulsory taxes. To force people to pay taxes for heavy industry they did not directly benefit from would require considerable coercion, and "under these conditions the sprouts of democracy are easily crushed . . . For the sake of preventing the emergence of bureaucratic capitalism and dictatorial government, I cannot [but[36]] feel frightened of having the government coerce savings out of the people and itself manage industry" (*XTCJ*:140; "Financing":112).

The theme of land reform runs through *Xiangtu chongjian*. Landlords consume but do not produce, Fei said; they are "parasites"—he used the word countless times, and urged them to give up their privileges voluntarily. But he seems to have envisaged some form of compensation, presumably by government loans to peasants who would buy the land, and, as we have seen, he hoped the former landlords would invest in and actively manage industry, as well as provide rural leadership. For such views, he was accused by leftists of being soft on landlords, of wanting to protect landlord interests and even turn them into capitalists.[37] His response was that they had to be provided some alternative livelihood or they would fight for their land. He wanted to make them producers; to eliminate landlordism, not the landlords (*XTCJ*:89-98, 163-165):

> I admit that, although I am from the "fallen landlords" who have lost landlord status, I still feel a responsibility to think about the future of this stratum caught in a dilemma with nowhere to go . . . I am not calculating how to maintain the privileges of the landlord stratum, but how these people can seek a reasonable solution: how to make them relinquish the privileges they in fact cannot easily retain and do not deserve to. (*XTCJ*:97-98)

China needed radical political and social reform in Fei's analysis, but he wanted it to come without violence. How often he wrote of his desire for peaceful political change! That was what was so attractive about England to him; there the privileged had given up their privileges without a drop of blood being shed. He hoped it could be done in China too (though by 1947 he admitted to being less optimistic than previously), and he ended his book on England with a quotation from Laski: "Violent revolution is a possibility, but for the sake of culture we must always progress in the direction of avoiding violence" (*CFYL*:91-92). Peaceful change was the theme of his obituary of Sidney Webb, who had been one of the founders of the Fabian Society (1947N8b), and indeed Fei held much in common with the Fabian ideals of democracy, socialism, and peaceful change—as well as with the Fabian tradition of intellectuals writing about social reform. Fei's article on Gandhi's death, too, was a panegyric on peace and non-violence. Some think that peace is a religious illusion, he wrote, that the realities of politics are violence and conflict, and that Gandhi was a dreamer, but his success proved that he was in fact a practical realist (1948Ja31).

It is natural that, in time of war, a person should yearn for peace; it is understandable that, living under the Guomindang, one should yearn for democracy. In 1947 and 1948, in the midst of one of the greatest armed revolutions in all history, however, there is something a bit odd, indeed pathetic, about Fei's hopes for non-violent change, for landlords voluntarily relinquishing their land rights, for studying Anglo-American representative institutions. Yet he was certainly not alone in wanting these things; the powerful appeal of the ideals of Western-style democracy and human rights was felt by many Chinese intellectuals in those years.

FEI AND THE COMMUNISTS BEFORE 1949

How far was Fei radicalized by the events of the late 1940s? There can be no question of his profound hatred of the Nationalists following the events of 1945 and 1946, but that does not tell us much about his feelings toward the Chinese Communists. The answer is elusive, for before 1949 Fei wrote little, practically nothing in fact, about the Communists. It was simply too dangerous to write on such topics; he confided in a letter that he was "very much on guard of what I can put on paper without once more to invite unnecessary danger" (12/4/47 to MPR). In addition, he was not very well informed. He knew little of Marxism; he had read a bit, but not much, about the Soviet Union; and of the Chinese Communists, with whom he had no direct contact and about whom little published information was available in China, he was most ignorant of all.

Earlier, during the war, he seems to have thought of himself as a moderate and a liberal. While critical of the government, he wrote in praise of "the coming generation of Chinese intellectuals (not too radical, much less actionalist [that is, activist])" of which he doubtless felt himself a part (10/21/44 to WCF). In this he was no different from many around him in Kunming, where, as Robert Payne put it, the general attitude of Democratic League intellectuals was "a plague on both your houses," and "we heard little of Yenan."[38] Persecution by the Nationalists subsequently drove many such intellectuals left toward the Communists, who were very friendly to them. In 1946, a scholar and League leader could write:

> Communism . . . is at least very much better than fascism . . . Without the cooperation of the Chinese Communist party, it would be impossible to emancipate the Chinese people from the yokes of the Gestapo

service and to give them the minimum amount of freedom so essential for the establishment of a democratic state.[39]

(What seemed to make the Communists palatable to this writer was his conviction that they "have no intention of introducing communism—nay, not even the Russian type of socialism—into China at the present stage, nor for a generation to come.") By the time the League was dissolved by the government in October 1947, its leaders were working very closely with the Communists. But not all who had been associated with the "democratic movement" went so far toward the left. A recent study of the magazine *Guancha* —the leading non-party journal of opinion, highly critical of the Nationalists, and a magazine in which Fei published regularly— from 1946 to 1948, has found that independent intellectuals admired much of what the Chinese Communists had done but felt that communism as a form of government was basically undemocratic and undesirable.[40]

Fei wrote often about the foreign policy of the Soviet Union in his articles on international politics, but there are only fragmentary references to its domestic conditions, which he felt he knew little about ("We have no way of knowing how people live in what is reported to be a forbidden land locked behind an iron curtain" [*LBTX*, 3.16:18]). It is clear that he admired the "economic democracy" of the Soviet Union, apparently meaning more equal distribution of wealth and income, and economic decisions made for national rather than private goals, as compared to the capitalist United States. But, as a handful of fragmentary remarks indicate, he had little esteem for the Soviet political system. Political democracy, he thought, had been sacrificed to economic democracy and it might not be worth the price (*RX&JQ*:3; *CFYL*:75). Strong leadership and suppression of dissent were perhaps necessary if a backward nation was to modernize rapidly, he wrote elsewhere. This was not tyranny, as English and American scholars charged, for it was not exploitative; but it was not democracy based on popular consensus either (*XTZG*:85–88). The Soviet Union had inherited from its feudal past a tradition of despotism, and it was hardly to be expected that democracy, "the highest stage of politics," could be carried out there. Harsh secret police methods would probably continue to be necessary to control internal opposition (1947N16:5).

The few references to the Chinese Communists in Fei's pre-1949 writings indicate his general ignorance about them and his distaste for their violent methods, but also a measure of admiration for what he understood to be a peasant movement representing peasant interests. A solitary remark in *Peasant Life* described the movement as motivated by peasant "hunger and . . hatred of landowners and tax collectors," called the Long March "heroic," and revealed he was familiar with Edgar Snow's glowing account in *Red Star Over China* (p. 284). A few years later, he seemed to approve of what he "had heard," that the Communists had moderated their radical land reform policy of many years "for which they had not hesitated to spill blood fighting" (*NDNC:*28). A letter hinted: "The real people's movement is yet to come . . . Perhaps far in the north" (1/29/45 to WCF), and another said that a social revolution was in progress in which the traditional leadership by scholars, who had proved inadequate in a changing world, was being replaced by peasant leadership, adding, "I do not think ideology plays any important part in the struggle, much less the interference of the Red Empire" (12/4/47 to MPR).

That Fei approved of the Chinese Communists precisely to the extent that he felt they were moderate agrarian reformers and not "Communistic," radical, or connected with the Soviet Union, is apparent in the only extended piece we have from his hand about them. In May 1945, he reviewed for an American magazine a Chinese report of a one-month visit to Yan'an. Formerly, Fei wrote, the Chinese Communists had been radical, and, although he had "always been sympathetic" with their "ideals," their practice had led to "disorder." But they had learned from painful experience and were now striving for only gradual reform, carrying out policies that were not at all "Communistic," but quite similar to those of 1930s rural reformers in Ding county and Zouping, and worthy of study and imitation by non-Communists. "This is a great improvement." He was still somewhat apprehensive, however, that they would try to extend to all of China the simple life without division of labor or modern industry found in the economically backward Yan'an area. "We think that the world cannot be made into one uniform mass... As the different classes of Chinese people have many common interests, there is no reason why they cannot exist together" ("Review of Zhao").

As late as November 1948, when the Communist victory in north China was almost complete, Fei could still write, "Subjected to a news blackout and propaganda tricks, we really don't know what conditions are under the Communists, and what we don't know we can't criticize" (1948N5). There was something stand-offish and hesitant in his relationship with the Communists; one senses he did not want to get involved with them. If he had really felt attracted to them, late 1946, when he was a fugitive from Nationalist terrorism, would have been the time to go to Yan'an, but instead he hid out in Suzhou and then went abroad. Or he might have followed a course similar to that of his Qinghua colleague Wu Han, with whom he collaborated on a seminar and a book of essays (HQ&SQ). Wu had been a middle-of-the-roader in Kunming, criticizing the government and calling for Western-style democracy, but, by the end of 1947, he was secretly reading Mao's works, carrying messages, protecting underground Communists, and in August 1948 he went to Communist territory.[41]

Fei does not seem to have been very active politically in 1947 and 1948. There was a widespread anti-government student movement with frequent demonstrations and strikes in Peking during these years, but, apart from one article expressing sympathy with the students (1947My3), there is no indication that he was involved. His signature was one of 90 on an open letter from Peking professors protesting a speech by the local Guomindang boss;[42] he spoke out at forums on the role of intellectuals to say that they should become more practical (1948My16 and 1948Ag5a); and he wrote in praise of an old scholar's controversial anti-government speech (1948N5). But he had a feeling of general helplessness about the current situation; he withdrew and played mahjong for most of one spring vacation in an attempt to put it out of his mind.⁴³ And, in a letter, he admitted that "I remain silent on the major political issue on which I am not in the position to say anything," and that not a few students were dissatisfied with "my inactivity" (3/3/48 to WCF).

His remarks that intellectuals should learn to work with their hands were quoted with approval in a Communist magazine, and his books were published by a leftist publisher,⁴⁴ but for the most part his work, and especially the *Dagong bao* articles which were to become *Xiangtu chongjian*, was "criticized by left-wing writers as 'too conservative,' though 'not yet reactionary' " (3/3/48 to WCF). His proposals for restoring rural industry were seen as an anti-progressive nostalgia for pre-machine-age handicrafts. His theory of "two-track politics," according to which the gentry had served a useful purpose in the past in restricting government power and protecting local interests, was taken as advocating a restoration of gentry power. His idea that intellectuals could play a useful role in taking modern knowledge to the countryside, and his fond words for the English gentry were said to betray a desire to protect the privileges of the landlord class. And his caution that more than land reform was required to raise significantly the rural standard of living was understood by some as opposition to land reform. These charges were widespread and apparently plausible enough for Fei to feel that he had to respond to them at length (1948Mr1a; 1948Mr20; *XTCJ*:144–69).

If some of these leftist criticisms of Fei's articles were unjust, there were, nonetheless, some very real and basic differences between him and the Communists. His strictures about the need for constitutional democracy to prevent abuse of power were not meant just for the Guomindang:

> In order to maintain the health of the political structure in the face of gradual centralization and strengthening of government power we must . . . study the representative institutions of England and America . . . This question is not directed against any particular man or party; from now on, no matter what party constitutes the government, it must do more than government did in the past. (*XTCJ*:63)

He had reservations about state socialism, as we have seen; he was not attracted to the idea of class struggle, and hoped for peaceful reform. He blamed the Nationalists most for the Civil War, but one comment suggests he was not convinced the Communists should be held blameless. The continued destruction and suffering caused by the war, he said, "forces me to suspect that at least one and perhaps both sides are not concerned with the betterment of the nation and the welfare of the people" (1948N5).

Finally, his scholarly ideals and intellectual style had been influenced by the critical spirit and opposition to dogma which have characterized modern science as it developed in the West in the centuries since the Renaissance. The main reason Fei was not attracted to Marxism was that he found it doctrinaire and unempirical, and thus at odds with his most basic attitudes about knowledge. This view is clear in his criticism of the 1930s Chinese social history controversy ("Unfortunately the 'iron law' they upheld has no basis in fact. Social change is not so simple as they imagined" [*LCNT:*190])[45], in his rejection of any unilinear historical determinism (*SYZD:*75), and in statements like "I . . . cannot feel satisfied with the deterministic view that our future is decided solely by the logic of history" (1947N8a:10).

Yet for all his distance and differences from them, when the Communists entered the Qinghua campus outside of Peking on December 16, 1948 (six weeks before they took Peking itself), Fei was still there. Nationalist troops had left two days before, there had been no fighting, and Fei could easily have left.[46] The government provided an airplane to fly intellectual leaders out of Peking, including, for example, Mei Yiqi, the President of Qinghua. Fei had no love for the Nationalists (nor they for him), of course, and would not have wanted to go with them to Taiwan. He might, however, have gone to England or the United States as he had considered doing in 1946; he knew English, had a Western PhD, a reputation among Anglo-American anthropologists, and enough academic friends in those countries so that he would have had no trouble finding a suitable position, most likely in an American university, as did so many Chinese at that time. To be sure, the great majority of Chinese professors and scholars stayed, and Fei's decision should not be considered something extraordinary. But still, we may speculate on his reasons.

There was a feeling of patriotism. This (together with the fact that it was difficult to study Chinese society away from China) was what had made him decide to return to China before, in early 1947. At that time he had written, "I feel much better that I am going through the dark period with my people" (6/30/47 to WLH, in IPR 330), and "I think I shall have much more work to do in China, training students to study China" (7/28/47 to WCF). He also wrote: "I am glad that I decide to return home instead of run away to foreign countries. The sense of belonging and rooting which grows responsibility is essential to human life. It makes one's life rich" (12/4/47 to MPR). Then there were his positive feelings about the Communists as an honest and constructive people's movement.

Finally, it seems clear that he hoped he would be able to continue his work, to contribute to the building of a new China by doing sociological research and training students. To be sure, he was not free of doubt on this point. He was perhaps thinking of the Nationalists, who had been arresting intellectuals and students, when in July 1947 he wondered "if in the future we still have the opportunity of free thought . . ." (*MGRXG:*90). But that was probably not the case in March 1948, by which time a Communist victory seemed likely. At that time, he followed a statement about how he had been criticized by leftists with the ominous declaration, "I shall continue to voice until I am forced to silence" (3/3/48 to WCF). And, in late 1948, the focus of his anxieties was clearly the Communists—but he was optimistic: "I hope I will not be lost to social science, instead I do think the future is rather bright; on this point, I need whole night to explain to you" (10/28/48 to RR). He told the Redfields, who were with him at Qinghua in November 1948, that he thought he would be able to continue his work with the Communists and even to criticize as part of a "loyal opposition." He also told them he thought his brother (Fei Qing?), who was closer to the Communists, would afford him some protection.[47]

Fei hoped and believed that as a social scientist he would be able to be of use to his country under its new government. Socialism needs social planning, he wrote, and "I definitely believe sociology is helpful in social planning" (1947O15; also 1947Ob, 1948O5). His hopes were clearly expressed in the concluding remarks, written in June 1948, to *Xiangtu chongjian,* his last important work before Liberation:

> A prerequisite for rebuilding the countryside is a government that serves the people. If this prerequisite doesn't exist, all my discussion has no immediate significance... But I can't believe China can go on like this forever. One day the prerequisite for rural rebuilding will exist, and then the questions I have raised here will need to have been carefully examined. So I feel my views are of some use... Furthermore, what else can a bookworm like me do to serve the nation? (*XTCJ*:169)

SEVEN

The Bourgeois Intellectual in the People's Republic

The relationship has not been an easy or untroubled one between intellectuals like Fei Xiaotong and the new authorities in China since 1949. The millions of non-Communist intellectuals (in the broad Chinese sense of those with college or even high school education) had valuable skills that could not be dispensed with. As teachers, scientists, technicians, economic managers, government bureaucrats, writers, and so on, they were vitally necessary for the all-important tasks of national construction. Yet, to the Communists, many of peasant background, who had spent hard decades in rural organizing and guerrilla war, these urban intellectuals often seemed arrogant, impractical, selfishly individualistic, and slavish to foreign ways. The Communists took ideas seriously; their success had been due in no small part to the power of their ideology to inspire and motivate people, and they naturally wanted to keep a close watch on non-Communists' expression of thought. They controlled the press and education much more tightly than the Nationalists ever had, and expended great efforts on the "thought reform" of intellectuals, in the hope that the study of political texts, small group discussion, and criticism and self-criticism, such as the Communists themselves had long practiced, would in time succeed in changing their attitudes and habits.
   It is hard to know how most intellectuals felt about this greatest

of revolutions, in what ways it changed their lives, or how much they really accepted the new ideas of thought reform. Fei Xiaotong, however—unlike most—continued to publish a good bit in the 1950s. There are, to be sure, special difficulties in interpreting his post-1949 writings. He was surely much more anxious than he had been under the Nationalists not to write articles that would displease the authorities. It was natural that he should tend to accentuate the positive, to write about those changes and policies he could agree with and keep silent about the others. Yet, with careful reading, particularly because we have his writings from before to compare them with, his post-1949 articles can be revealing about his response to the revolution and, by extension, about the countless other intellectuals like him.

EARLY ENTHUSIASM, 1949–1950

Between mid-December 1948, when the Communists arrived at the Qinghua campus, and the end of January 1949, when Peking itself was liberated, Fei journeyed to the Communist capital at Shijiazhuang, Hebei (*WZYN*:6). It was later said, and it is not impossible, that he was introduced (by Zhang Dongsun, the Yanjing professor, who was negotiating the surrender of the city) to Mao himself, and that as a result of this interview Fei was treated particularly favorably.[1] In the early years, just after the Communists had marched into the cities with their peasant armies, they doubtless found the public support of a prominent scholar and writer like Fei Xiaotong useful in bridging the gap between rural revolutionaries and urban intellectuals, and winning needed support for the Communists from educated city-dwellers. Widely known and respected, his name in the organs of the new government could help legitimize and gain acceptance for it. His articles, persuasive as always, could explain new policies to a wide audience of literate Chinese. To the Communists, Fei was a bourgeois intellectual, but he was a progressive one by virtue of his record of opposition to the Nationalists and he was enthusiastic and eager to participate.

In 1949 and 1950, he was appointed to a number of relatively prominent positions. These must not be thought to indicate real power—important decisions were made ultimately by the Party (that is, the Communist Party), of which he was not a member—but they doubtless conferred prestige and perhaps some measure of influence with the new leaders. He was a member of the University Affairs Committee which ran Qinghua. He was a member of the Congress of Representatives of Various Circles in Peking which established a new municipal government for the national capital. He was a delegate (from the Democratic League) to the Chinese People's Political Consultative Conference, which, meeting for ten days in Peking in September 1949, passed the Common Program and other organic laws which were the legal basis for the new national government. He was a member of the important Culture and Education Committee of the central government administration. He was also, in 1949, Vice-Chairman of the Democratic League's Culture and Education Committee; a director of the Sino-Soviet Friendship League; a Director of the Chinese People's Foreign Affairs Institute; and on the editorial board of the journal *Xin jianshe* (of which his brother Fei Qing was Editor).[2]

A sense of being treated well and a patriotic joy that China was now on the road to modernization are evident in a June 1949 letter to Margaret Redfield, delivered by hand and thus presumably not written for the eyes of the authorities:

> It will be a long story if I begin to retell the history of the last six months. I think my decision to stay at Peiping was correct. I have been learning many, and very fundamental too, precious experience from the process of liberation. It is altogether unusual and marvellous. It at least gives me an opportunity to reflect on many fundamental problems and criticize my own work that I had done before. I have again become a student and enjoyed deeply the "reintegration" process of my own thought reform. . . I am also convinced that if the Western world would let us alone to develop our country, China will catch up the modern world in my life time. The word liberation is not a slogan, it means business. I had visited the old liberated area and came back with full confidence of China's future. Trust me, I am not a light hearted person and I had my worry before I saw the reality with my

own eyes. . . Once the human resources are liberated, that is, everyone begins to see the hope in front, the creative force is enormous. . . I cannot see any deep anti-foreign sentiment in our new China. . . The new regime is most sincere in learning modern method of dealing with things. Even in most difficult time, our salary has been increased, it is taken as an indication of appreciation of science and knowledge. No one in our university has suffered any discrimination on political grounds. Classes go on as usual and students become disciplined in their class work. I was encouraged to develop my teaching method of putting my students in field observation as my lecture proceeds. I am again put on the committee on City Planning of Peiping in order to develop our city research. (6/24/49 to MPR)

Fei began to publish again in mid-1949, after half a year of silence and, from then until mid-1950, some two dozen articles of his appeared in new China's newspapers and magazines. He was impressed, above all, with the extent of popular support for the Communists, the degree to which the people were united, and the resulting spirit of democracy. On his trip to Shijiazhuang in early 1949, he saw long lines of peasant carts bringing provisions for the Communist troops. The sight of these seemingly endless uncoerced donations of the fruits of peasant sweat and blood was moving, he said, and made him realize that the power of the people united by a common purpose was greater than even English warships lined up in port or the Allied airfields in Africa which he had seen on his way to the United States (*WZYN:*6–7). He had had no contact with Communists before Liberation, but since then had come to admire them for their honesty, hard work, ability, and dedication (*WZYN:*2). They had unified all the people around a common program and given them a sense of being one family working together with neither haughtiness nor subservience, and Fei said he felt a new joy. For the first time he had learned to say *zanmen* (a north Chinese form of "we" which includes the person addressed; *WZYN:*13–18).

This unity and popular support for the government, he claimed, showed that new China was truly democratic. He had earlier become disillusioned with American democracy because of its capitalist contradictions, and with English democracy under

Labour for continuing its colonial policies and cooperating with America's evil foreign policies. Now, he wrote, after attending the Congress of Representatives of Various Circles in Peking in September 1949 and seeing the wide variety of people from all walks of life dressed in uniforms, work clothes, long gowns, minority nationalities' costumes, and so on, he realized that this was truer representation than England or America had[3]; real democracy did not depend on elections or opposition parties. The safe atmosphere for free discussion showed that Communist dictatorship, which suppressed the kind of reactionaries who had shot at him while making a speech in Kunming in 1945, was not incompatible with democracy but rather made it possible (*WZYN:*1-5).

As a member of the Congress of Representatives of Various Circles in Peking, Fei apparently participated in discussing and ratifying municipal policies. He wrote with satisfaction of what had been accomplished: law and order had been restored, mass organizations were being promoted, plans had been made for various municipal services, brothels had been closed, unemployment insurance had been instituted, and after-work schools established for workers previously unable to get an education (1949D6). He gave a long series of reasoned arguments justifying the Congress's decision to raise municipal taxes (1949D31).[4]

Other articles stressed that even the bourgeoisie, including intellectuals such as himself, were to be included in this democratic unity and had an important part to play in new China. According to Mao's doctrine of new democracy, China at its present stage was to be ruled by a coalition of four classes, including the petty bourgeoisie from which most intellectuals were held to come. The four classes, Fei explained, were all revolutionary by virtue of having been oppressed by feudalism, imperialism, and bureaucratic capitalism, and Mao himself had declared their united front essential to the success of the revolution. Fei predicted that the bourgeois classes would continue to play a vital role because capitalism in its early, competitive stage was progressive, promoted science and technology, and would be useful in developing the economy. Although socialism and communism were the ultimate goals, socialism required a modern industrial base and it was leftist infantilism to demand communism immediately. He quoted Zhou Enlai and Liu Shaoqi to the effect that socialism was a long way off and that it would come only when all the people wholeheartedly wanted it (1949O6). In fact, the transition to socialism came quite soon, in the mid-1950s; but Fei's expectation that the stage of new democracy would be lengthy was not just wishful thinking but the general expectation in those early years.

In most of these articles, Fei is of course explaining and justifying official policies, and a few follow the standard line so closely as to give little sense of his personal views. For example, some pieces on foreign policy seem hardly distinguished by an individual outlook. An article on the U.S. State Department's "White Paper" on American China policy in the 1940s maintained that these documents proved the real aim of the United States had been all along "to make China into an American colony" (1949S8). Another article, on the British recognition of China, called this a victory for the Chinese people, but also a new tactic of imperialism carried out in league with Washington as part of a plot to try to divide the socialist camp by diplomacy (1950Ja29). Finally, a piece on the Sino-Soviet Treaty said it guaranteed world peace by deterrring American imperialism, and that the U.S. charge that the U.S.S.R. had territorial designs on China was a poisonous lie (1950F26). Yet, such articles aside, for the most part, Fei's own voice, which we know from his earlier writings, can be heard in what he wrote at the time.

The majority of his 1949–1950 articles were on two topics—thought reform for intellectuals and the reform of the universities. Fei had, of course, written before 1949 of the need for scholarship to serve society, for foreign learning to be adapted to China, for intellectuals to be less contemptuous of peasants and of manual work, less parasitic and more practical and productive; and, in fact, in his articles on thought reform, most collected in a little volume called *Wo zhe-yi nian* (This year for me; *WZYN*), occur criticisms of the habits and character of Chinese intellectuals of a sort he had made earlier. When he was a boy, Fei said, he was told to study hard or he might end up having to work in the fields; it was considered shameful for boys of his class even to be seen outside carrying a burden. Fei's father had insisted on wearing a long gown, which signified the status of not having to labor, even in the heat of summer, right up to Liberation. Now, though, Fei had learned from working in his garden that nothing is produced without labor, and that to enjoy the fruits without working is exploitation (*WZYN*:51-59). The suggestion that he had been reformed by gardening seems a bit far-fetched, but the theme was an old one for Fei.

His criticism of the selfish individualism of Chinese intellectuals, too, developed themes that he had written before. Most intellectuals, he said, were from the petty bourgeoisie (a class which included urban poor, government servants, artisans, free professionals, and small tradesmen). Politically they tended to be weak and vacillating. In the past, this class had been exploited rather than exploiters, and did not share in political power. In imperial China, seduced by the examination system, coerced by the literary inquisition, and dependent on others for employment, the intellectuals tended to adopt the apolitical stance of serving any master and worrying only about their own livelihood. More recently, they had tended to be suspicious of all government power, thinking it always oppressive (1949O6; *WZYN*:19-25). The class personality of the petty bourgeois was one of individualistic self-reliance and hard work, spurred on by the fear of losing the little he had and by the hope of rising into the upper bourgeoisie. Although such a personality was more appropriate for America of three hundred years ago than for twentieth-century semi-feudal semi-colonial China where economic opportunity was severely limited, it nonetheless came to prevail among the intellectuals in China's universities. There it took the form of the good student who studied hard, lived frugally, did not waste time on girls or anything else, and strove to master a skill with which to make a living after graduating. Such a petty bourgeois student was certainly more progressive than the sons of landlords who wasted their time in school and then used connections to get ahead afterwards; but his individualism stood in the way of cooperation, and he was apt to feel competitive and jealous of others' success, sometimes even hoarding library books so that others could not use them (pp. 43–50, 60–67).

"After decades of Anglo-American education" virtually all intellectuals had "democratic individualistic ideas in their bones" (p. 71). It was vital that such individualism be changed through thought reform. After the coming of socialism, Fei warned, there would be no further role for the petty bourgeoisie. Nor would it do just to sit back and wait for one's ideas to change with social conditions; it was necessary to work on reforming one's thought in order to keep up with the changing social reality (pp. 34–42). Even "progressive" intellectuals who, oppressed by the reactionary government and threatened by the secret police, had worked for the revolution, were tainted by bourgeois ideas which needed to be changed; they should guard against self-satisfaction, which Fei admitted had been a problem for himself (pp. 68–76).

Thought reform, based on techniques developed in Yan'an in the early 1940s for rectifying the ideology and work habits of Communist cadres, was a lengthy process of study, lectures, small-group discussion, criticism and self-criticism, and writing of "thought summaries," by means of which one was supposed gradually to shed the burden of feudal, bureaucratic, and compradore (that is, foreign-serving) ideas and attitudes carried over from the old society.[5] Fei wrote partly from the point of view of a teacher explaining thought reform to students and other intellectuals, and in his articles can be glimpsed some of the reality as well as the theory of this process which was so important in the lives of China's millions of intellectuals. He recorded objections most often heard from students and offered answers, such as: "My thought doesn't need reforming" (Everyone's does, for we are all products of the old society); "If China is an alliance of four classes, why should proletarian ideas prevail?" (The proletariat must lead if we are to advance to socialism and then communism); and "I want to concentrate on practical courses" (You need also to cultivate an ardent desire to serve the people). He took some pains to explain why political study was not thought control, pointing out that the discussions were free, uncoerced, and carried on in a supportive and friendly spirit, because Marxism-Leninism would inevitably prevail in an open and extended debate. Perhaps he was hoping to influence group leaders to maintain this ideal.

He described the political study class in Marxism-Leninism which was required of all at the university—students, faculty, and staff. Since it was an internal process, thought reform required new educational methods, particularly self-study and small group discussion in which students and teachers helped each other, and only occasionally large lectures. Students inevitably went through a process of resistance to the assault on their old ideas; then, after the resistance crumbled, a period of feeling that they were worthless and life was meaningless. At this stage, it was helpful to have the support of others in the group, friendly criticism and self-criticism, and models to identify with and emulate. Finally, the feeling of emptiness would be replaced by a new outlook on life (*DXGZ*:93-100). Despite this positive and sympathetic description of the thought reform process, an uncomfortable strain and tension seem reflected in Fei's uncharacteristic use of military metaphors in an article about the fervid activities at Qinghua in late January 1950 when everybody wrote his "thought summary." It was, he said, an ideological battle, a war between old and new ideas, in which Marxism-Leninism and criticism and self-criticism were used as weapons; after careful planning for D-Day, a speech by Party ideologue Ai Siqi was a cannon barrage against the fortress of individualism; and so on. The atmosphere on campus was apparently very tense for several days. People stayed up all night trying to write their thought summaries; there were many tearful confessions of past errors. Afterwards, however, all had a joyous feeling of proletarian unity and of being one family (1950Mr16a).

But, while much of this criticism of Chinese intellectuals and of his own past attitudes was surely sincere, Fei also felt constrained to keep silent about things he did not agree with. His convictions about rural industry, for example, were contrary to Party policy of the early 1950s, which followed the Soviet Union's pattern of giving priority to urban heavy industry. Fei once or twice suggested that his old views were defective—that he had advocated a second-rate kind of development for the Chinese because he had failed to appreciate the power of the people, once united, to achieve real industrialization (*WZYN:*7; "Old Friends":16). Yet these occasional brief sentences seem scanty and unconvincing and, as we shall see, he was later to return to some of his old ideas about rural industry and peasant income—as well as about parliamentary democracy and the utility of bourgeois sociology.

As part of his own thought reform Fei would have had to criticize himself and his past ideas. We have only fragmentary indications of what he actually said:

> I should say that reformism was my basic ideology in the past . . . I was born of a landlord family, which declined in the hands of my grandfather. My father was educated in Japan, and had been a bureaucrat and teacher. I therefore have been imbued with the ideology of individualism . . . Prior to the liberation, I was dissatisfied with feudalism and captialist monopoly [but] did not trust the people's strength and the Soviet Union . . . I should say my reformist ideology of the past was basically reactionary and was based on the petty bourgeoisie. (1951D9)

The only article we have on Fei's own thought reform, "This Year for Me," first published in the official Party newspaper *Renmin ribao* on January 3, 1950, and widely reprinted subsequently, was about 1949. It had been a year of study for him, he said, beginning with the sight of long lines of peasant carts attesting to the strength of the people—a strength he had previously failed to appreciate. He had bowed his head, felt worthless and confused, and wished to be magically transformed into a new person. Such a wish, however, he now realized, was really just a dream of being prominent again; real reform was not sudden enlightenment but settling down to long, hard study. Then another problem arose: the intellectuals in his group developed a competitive attitude toward reform, instead of cooperating with each other. This made Fei want to find a purer environment, and he considered leaving to join a land reform group. In short, after half a year, he had hardly made a start in real reform. He only started to make progress, he said, when he began to take part in school affairs, deciding salaries, allocating housing, and so on. Busy with these objective matters, he stopped thinking about himself and feeling competitive, escapist, or depressed. Having to relate to others, he not only came to see the need for their thought reform, but also the inadequacy of his own theoretical understanding (*WZYN*:6-12). He was clearly eager to participate in responsible work, and we may detect here a certain impatience with the thought reform process.

Fei seems to have had responsibilities that first year connected with the reform of Qinghua University, where he was a member of the University Affairs Committee. He wrote a number of articles on this subject, and on university reform in general, which were collected into a volume called *Daxue de gaizao* (University reform; *DXGZ*), published in May 1950.[6] As with the individualism of intellectuals, Fei had long been dissatisfied with some aspects of the old educational system.

Under the Nationalists, he said, the universities had been concerned not with the needs of society but with individualistic scholarship for its own sake. Teachers were aloof and haughty towards students. Autonomous departments set their own curricula, passing on scholarly traditions rather than teaching practical skills. University courses were overspecialized, too theoretical, and blindly copied from abroad ("That China needs to accept Western culture is unquestionable; . . . [but] to combine Western science with Chinese native practice . . . requires creativity"; p. 47). Rather than training students for useful work, universities bestowed status with which graduates could get good jobs regardless of ability. Students were too concerned with examinations and credits, and trying to get ahead of other students. Middle schools were exclusively oriented to college, so that the majority who failed the traumatic college entrance examinations (Qinghua could take only 500 out of the 10,000 who applied every year) felt useless (pp. 13-34).

He applauded reforms that were making the universities more efficient in their mission of providing society with the cadres needed for national development ("cadres" are local leaders, particularly those on the state payroll). More students were being admitted, receiving more practical training, and a spirit of serving the people was being cultivated. He approved of reducing excess personnel (some universities had had as many as thirty teaching and seventy non-teaching employees per hundred students!), but warned that this should be done with care—it would be a mistake to judge teachers simply by how many students they taught (pp. 39-45). He described in considerable detail—which shows his enthusiasm—a cooperative hospitalization insurance program for faculty and their families (which he said could overcome the "iron curtain" which in an individualistic society separated the majority of individuals from the benefits of scientific knowledge; pp. 67-82), and a plan to generate investment funds for the government through a voluntary, group, payroll-deduction time savings account (pp. 83-92).

The universities were becoming more democratic, too, he said, describing a conference of 256 representatives of Qinghua faculty, students, staff, workers, and spouses, which gathered hundreds of suggestions on all aspects of university affairs from the whole university community and distilled them into 51 formal proposals (pp. 107-117). "Extreme democracy," however, was a danger to be guarded against; education required leadership—teachers must not be treated by students like a deposed ruling class, nor was it appropriate for university guards and laborers to have a say about academic policies or students about staff benefits (pp. 16, 49). (He said nothing about the real structure of power in the universities, however: of how hiring or budgetary decisions were made, of the composition of the University Affairs Committee, how it was chosen, its powers, or the process of assuming control over departments. There are but the vaguest references to guidelines from the Ministry of Education or the government and, most striking of all, not a single reference to the Communist Party.)

About some university reforms, however, he was much less

happy, particularly the plan, eventually adopted, to turn Qinghua into a purely technical school. Regular academic programs, he insisted, should not be cut back (pp. 23-30); theory as well as practical training was needed to produce creative and innovative cadres (pp. 9-10, 60); teachers should continue to be given the time and facilities for research, which was not a dispensable luxury but necessary for progress; research should not be segregated from teaching in research institutes (p. 20). In one of the last articles he wrote on the subject, this cautionary tone is quite clear. He went into some detail to point out the ways in which the old universities had been useful and should not be scrapped entirely: they had produced intellectuals who played a role in the revolution and in post-revolutionary construction; and even foreign-supported education in China had raised people's cultural levels, spread modern knowledge, and created a powerful weapon against imperialism. In particular, he repeated his warning against turning universities into vocational schools (1950My21).

Reading Fei's 1949-1950 articles on thought reform and the reform of the universities, one is struck by the theme of social unity that runs through them: the enormous power of nation and people united in common purpose; the importance of intellectuals overcoming individualism, factionalism, and divisiveness so that they could unite with the laboring masses; the benefits of cooperation and of pooling risks and resources; and so on. In those first two years, Fei must have thought the social cohesion he had looked for for so long was increasing, and he and the other intellectuals, instead of being cut off from most of society, were at last going to be able to contribute their skills to constructing a new China.

NATIONAL MINORITIES WORK, 1950-1956

Fei had surely hoped, at first, that in this unified society he would have a responsible role and be able to put to use his knowledge and abilities as a researcher, teacher, and writer. A Democratic League leader who defected in the 1950s says the Communists "misled the democratic parties and groups into believing that the Communists would let them participate in the administration of the affairs of the country and bring about a 'united democratic New China.'"[7] But it was not to be. In 1951 and 1952, in the tense atmosphere following China's entrance into the Korean War, the intellectuals found themselves much more stringently controlled and excluded from power than they had been in 1949 and 1950. The thought reform and university reform movements were radically intensified, and in the campaign to suppress counterrevolutionaries thousands of intellectuals were executed and the rest terrorized.

Fei's friend Jin Yuelin, who had gone to America with him in 1943-1944, declared himself "an instrument of American cultural aggression" who had fallen into the "bottomless pit of the degenerate philosophy of the capitalist class"; the eminent philosopher Feng Youlan said his past writings were "crimes against the people"; the archeologist Luo Changpei declared "I hate myself"; and Qian Duansheng, the American-trained political scientist who had shared the podium with Fei in Kunming when bullets flew overhead, gave "all thanks to Chairman Mao and the party for curing my disease and saving my soul."[8] Fei, perhaps specially treated, does not seem to have had to make the kind of humiliating public confession that many higher intellectuals did. He continued to hold various prominent posts (Democratic League Central Committee, Chinese People's Political Consultative Conference, Sino-Soviet Friendship Association, Chinese People's Institute of Foreign Affairs), and was even appointed to a few new ones: the Culture and Education Committee of the Peking Municipal Government (1953), Director of the Chinese Political Science and Law Association (1953), First National People's Congress (1954).[9] But he was not able to publish much any more, a heavy blow for one who had been such a publicist. From 1951 to 1955, there was little more than a few articles about national minorities, for the most part trivial and non-controversial, pale successors to his earlier work.

A second heavy blow was the elimination of sociology from the university curricula. Fei was later criticized for having opposed certain aspects of the radical reorganization of the universities,[10] probably mainly the abolition of sociology. An article written in March 1950 desperately proposed reasons to save the discipline. Recounting the history of the discipline, in the West and in China, he suggested at several points that sociology had certain redeeming characteristics not shared by other social sciences. In the West, sociology had exposed the social problems of capitalism and, as social work, it had palliated the contradictions of capitalism; thus it was neither as uncritical of capitalist society nor as centrally important to it as were the disciplines of law, politics, and economics. Then, both social investigation and social work were more empirical and less theoretical than the other social sciences, and so had been more easily Sinicized. Finally, a part of Chinese sociology had been politically progressive. It needed to be cleansed of bourgeois elements and become totally Marxist-Leninist, which would take time; but many sociology courses were still useful in New Democratic China, and sociology departments could train people for work in household registration, child welfare, factory inspection, and minorities work. A conference of Peking area sociology professors, in which Fei had participated, had recommended that sociology merge with other social sciences to form new university schools of social science, within which sociology would provide the theoretical base and the other social sciences more vocationally oriented areas of concentration. Fei went on to suggest for such schools a whole curriculum consisting of courses on Marxism-Leninism, Chinese, foreign languages (English and Russian), statistics, research methods, history, and professional courses including sociology courses on rural and urban society and national minorities (*DXGZ*:52-65).[11]

Fei's hopes that sociology could be useful to new China were dashed, however; the discipline was eliminated in the reforms of 1951–1952. I have not found any public discussion of this, but it is possible to speculate on the reasons. These were years of great Soviet influence in China. In the universities, Soviet textbooks, syllabi, and lecture notes were adopted and Russian language study stressed. Russian advisers urged reducing concentration on the humanities and social sciences in favor of technical specialties which would be of immediate use to industry. Sociology was not then permitted in the Soviet Union on the grounds that it was a bourgeois pseudo-science: the only true science of society was Marxism-Leninism. We have at least one report of a Russian adviser at an educational conference in China pointedly referring to the absence of sociology in the U.S.S.R.[12] The abolition of sociology in China was surely modeled on the Russian precedent.

When the sociology departments were eliminated, the "old sociologists," as they came to be known, were transferred to various other lines of work. Some taught or did research on labor or demographic problems; some went to miscellaneous unrelated jobs (Fei's one-time student Shi Guoheng was Qinghua librarian for many years); and not a few, including Fei, his friend Pan Guangdan, and his old college teacher Wu Wenzao, were transferred to national minorities work. Qinghua became an engineering school in October 1952, its science and liberal arts departments transferred to Peking University (which moved out of the city to the old Yanjing campus). Fei was still listed as a Qinghua professor of sociology in April 1951,[13] but in fact he seems to have been transferred to nationalities work well before, in July 1950, when he went off on a six-month visit to minorities peoples in Guizhou province. Fei had, of course, had some experience with minorities, long ago in Guangxi in 1936, but at that time he had evidently decided that the countless millions of Chinese peasants were much more important to study. It seems likely that he would have preferred to have been given responsibilities in the area of education, rural policy, or social research. But, naturally cheerful and ever curious, he may well have found his new work interesting, and China's minorities are certainly not unimportant.

China has scores of different minority nationalities (including ten with populations of over a million), varying widely in culture and economy. In the 1950s they accounted for some 35 million people, or about 6 percent of the nation's population, and for the most part occupied rugged and sparsely inhabited border areas comprising perhaps 60 percent of China's land area; the strategic importance of many of these border areas gave them a political significance even beyond their large numbers. From 1949 to 1955, the Party, generally weak in minorities areas, carried out a conciliatory policy. Refraining from the kind of forced assimilation that the Nationalists had attempted, they tried instead to win acceptance.[14] In June 1951, a college-level Central Institute of Nationalities (Zhongyang Minzu Xueyuan) was established in Peking to train both Han (ethnic Chinese) and minority cadres for service in minority areas, and also to do research on minority nationalities.

Fei was named one of three vice presidents of the Central Institute of Nationalities. It was a prestigious post, which got his name in the newspapers from time to time,[15] and brought a good salary and a pleasant house with a garden on the Institute's campus in Peking's northwest suburbs, not far from Qinghua and the former Yanjing campus (in the 1970s he was still living there). In August 1951, he also became a member of the important Nationalities Affairs Commission of the Central Government Administration. But it is not clear what his duties were. He did not teach at the Institute at all. In 1956, he said his time had been spent largely on "administrative work" ("Old Friends":15). He made a few trips to minority areas, and wrote occasional articles about them. He was connected with the Institute's research bureau, founded in 1952 to study minorities languages, history, culture, society, and economy, and to translate Russian materials on the nationalities question[16]; but it is hard to find signs of serious scholarship. His 1950s minorities articles are often thin—superficial and unsubstantiated allegations of how in the past these groups had been oppressed by Han Chinese and how today they are making great progress. Yet some of his accounts of the rich cultural and social diversity of these peoples are lively and interesting, and suggest that he may have enjoyed this work and especially the trips to minority areas.

In 1950, he spent six and a half months in Guizhou province as the head of a government goodwill delegation to explain the new government's nationalities policies to the minorities peoples there and gather basic information about them. This visit resulted in a series of articles then reprinted as a book, *Xiongdi minzu zai Guizhou* (Brother nationalities in Guizhou; *XDMZ*). It is a popularly written introduction to the complexities of that province's many nationalities, based mostly on information gathered by the team on its visit to various parts of the province.[17] Guizhou is, like its neighbor Yunnan, where Fei had spent the war years, a mountainous province of the southwest, difficult of access and incorporated into the Chinese empire only in recent centuries. Fei estimated its minority population at four million, or 30 percent to 40 percent of the province's total. There were at least twenty or thirty non-Han ethnic groups, varying in size from a few thousand in a handful of mountain villages to the Miao and Zhong peoples with over a million each. Some were assumed to be aborigines, while others were thought to have been pushed out of central China by the southward expansion of the Han Chinese over the centuries.

Fei found them poor and backward economically and in social organization. Most eked out a meager existence on mountain farms by dint of terribly hard labor. Some ate mostly potatoes (considered the poorest of food by the Chinese); many went barefoot; and he was shocked to see children without clothes playing outdoors in the December cold. Serf-like obligations from tillers to masters were not uncommon, and part of the Yi people (formerly called Lolos) just across the border in Sichuan actually still practiced slavery. Fei also found some bright spots; the Miaos' love of labor, lack of class distinctions, freedom of choice in marriage, expressive singing and dancing, and lovely embroidery are all described with pleasure and admiration.

He spoke repeatedly of the terrible suffering these peoples had endured at the hands of the Han Chinese. Centuries of armed conflict with Han troops had cost untold thousands of lives and reduced some groups almost to extinction. Some, to be sure, were exploited by ruling classes of their own nationality or oppressed by other minority nationalities (the Miaos dominated several smaller groups), but it was Han pressure that had pushed most into poverty and social stagnation in desolate mountain areas, and those who had come under Han political control were oppressed by a government that did nothing for them and were exploited by Han landlords. "You can't make a pillow of a stone or a friend of a Han," was a common saying in the southwest and, under the Nationalists, Miaos had been fearful of going into the towns, where Han troops might conscript their men and assault their skirt-wearing women (*XTMZ*).

All this, Fei said, was changing now. The oppressors of minority nationalities (according to Stalinist doctrine) were not the Han people in general but the ruling classes and, now that these were overthrown, exploitation was naturally replaced by friendship and cooperation. The life of minorities was getting better in other ways since Liberation. In an article intended for foreign consumption, Fei spoke of better trade terms and economic development, public health improvements, population increase, schools, and a measure of self-rule for China's minority nationalities. China had become a big family of free and equal brother nationalities ("Free").

In the fall of 1954, Fei made a visit to Mongolian nomads on the Hulumbuir Steppe and northern Inner Mongolia (in between Heilongjiang province and the Mongolian People's Republic) and, in writing about this, his emphasis was no longer on oppression and relations with Han people, but on how the minorities' way of life, formerly governed by the severe environment, was now changing. On this high flat grassland, unsuited for agriculture because winter snows came so early, people lived by raising sheep, cattle, and horses. They ate nothing but cows' milk, dried milk products, and enormous quantities of mutton—no vegetables, for they did not stay in one place long enough to grow them. They rode horses from childhood, lived in tents, and moved with their flocks from summer to winter pastures and back. This economically self-sufficient, nomadic style of life, with virtually no division of labor or trade, had probably gone on for centuries, but was now beginning to change—"The red sun of Chairman Mao has shone on the steppe." Fei applauded the progress that had been made: improved transportation had increased trade so they were able to vary their diet with imported flour, and experimental mutual-aid teams and cooperatives pointed the way to more efficient use of labor; machine harvesting of grass for livestock made it possible for some to give up their nomadic life and settle in permanent communities (*HHC*).

In spite of the gains for this and other nationalities, however, Fei felt they were still plagued by Han contempt for their cultures:

> Many Han people, not excluding some government workers, still suffer from vestiges of a "big-Han" chauvinist outlook in relation to the minorities. This has manifested itself in a lack of respect for their customs, habits, languages, and religious beliefs, and in reluctance to accord the minorities the right to administer their internal affairs. ("Free":20)

Despite the draft Constitution and before it the Common Program, which guaranteed minorities the freedom to develop their own written languages, many Hans, "due to the influence of remnants of past greater Han chauvinism," felt those who lacked writing systems should be obliged to learn Chinese, but Fei thought this would slow down their education (1954Ag21). We should help our brother nationalities rid themselves of backward customs, he said, but their right to reform themselves, in keeping with their national cultures and by means of their own local administration, must not be intruded upon by government fiat or outsiders' interference (1956My). Their own dance and other art forms, too, were not sufficiently respected. These were excellent media for propagating policies among them, especially among the illiterate minorities; but outside cultural workers should guard against a tendency simply to translate propaganda meant for Hans or to use Han art forms, as if the minorities' art were inferior. He pointed out that the Han people needed propaganda as well, to make them understand, respect, and sympathize with the non-Han peoples (1951Je1).

Fei was later to be accused of abusing Han workers and the Communist Party with his criticism of Han chauvinism, defense of the old culture of the minorities, and attempts to keep Han cadres out of minority administrative, social, and Party organizations,[18] in a word protecting minority interests against the Chinese government. But, in fact, policy at that time was very much to appease border nationalities by giving them some local autonomy and the freedom to preserve their customs, and injunctions against Han chauvinism were part of the official line then.[19] Such a line was surely congenial to Fei, tending like most anthropologists to want to protect his natives against the interference and the contempt of the more civilized.

These articles were all rather non-scholarly and do not indicate Fei was engaged in serious research. One exception was a 1952 detailed examination, without reference to Mao or Marx, of the murky problem of the historical origins of the six million Zhuang people of Guangxi. Quoting from historical sources from the first century B.C. *Shi-ji* onward, and drawing on complex linguistic arguments of others, he advanced the tentative hypothesis that the Zhuang might be descended from the Yue people of ancient times (part of whom perhaps became assimilated, leaving linguistic traces in southeast coastal dialects of Chinese, and part of whom, further west, continued to speak their own language; 1952Ja). It is possible, of course, that he did other scholarly work that is not available to us—scientific papers sometimes circulate only in mimeographed form—or that was part of a collaborative effort. I have seen references to a paper by Fei on the Kawa people of Yunnan (1955), and to an unpublished manuscript on the She people (of Zhejiang and Fujian), though both papers were later said by an unfriendly critic to have been largely based on the work of junior colleagues.[20]

Then in 1956, the Hundred Flowers policy offered scholars increased opportunities for research, and Fei's response seems to indicate he was eager for scholarly work. "Starting last year," he wrote in 1956, "I have partially resumed research. Last spring I spent four months in Guizhou to learn something of the history of nationalities there. Now we are drawing up a twelve-year plan of ethnological research . . . into the life and history of all the nationalities in China. . . ("Old Friends":15). His other activities during the Hundred Flowers period will be discussed later, but we should mention here articles he published in 1956 urging scholarly research on nationalities. He started with archaeology, which is politically comparatively safe. In a speech to an archaeologists' meeting in February 1956, he asked that they turn their attention away from Chinese cultural origins in the north to the minorities-rich southwest, and called for a multi-disciplinary study of national minorities in an area such as Guizhou or Yunnan (1956My10). Elsewhere he urged that the masses be educated to preserve and report artifacts they turn up, and he gave examples of objects found by peasants which throw light on minorities' history (1956Ap27).

Fei's desire for intellectually probing ethnological research is clear in another article setting forth an interesting series of justifications for such scholarly work. It was necessary to understand the characteristics of each nationality's society in order to know what reforms were appropriate in the transition to socialism. These societies were changing so fast that their original social features soon would be forgotten if they weren't studied now. Minorities peoples themselves, as they developed, were eager to find out about their own history and to have their place and contributions to national history made clear. Minorities research was also of general theoretical interest: Marxist understanding of social development, currently based largely on foreign materials such as the Greek and Roman examples of slave society and L.H. Morgan's writings about American Indians, would be deepened by information on Chinese minority nationalities, which include living examples of societies at all stages of development from primitive to feudal (in the Marxist progression from primitive communism to slavery to feudalism to capitalism—a unilinear scheme Fei had once, of course, contemptuously rejected). Finally, in what was no doubt a revelation of his personal feelings, Fei spoke of the desire of intellectuals to utilize their skills in active and creative service to the people, and to put to use the Marxist-Leninist theory they had learned from books, by combining theory and practice in the study of living human society (1956Jl27).

Then, together with his colleague at the Central Institute of Nationalities, the Harvard-trained anthropologist Lin Yaohua, he set out under the title "Tasks Which Current Nationalities Work Raises for Ethnology" an ambitious program of research topics they said needed study as a basis for government policy toward the national minorities. Four categories of questions were proposed. Just what should be the criteria for deciding if a group was an independent nationality was a basic question fraught with difficulties, and there were many unclear cases needing further investigation. The analysis of the social character of minority nationalities constituted another avenue of research. This was a complex topic which could not be dealt with in a doctrinaire fashion but required careful, patient collection of concrete data. For example, one society could have elements from different social stages; different groups within one nationality could be at different stages; even at the same stage each nationality had its own peculiarities; and some jumped over stages. The culture and way of life of each minority should also be studied, including material culture, social customs and habits, and art and literature. Finally, religion should not be neglected, for it played an important role in people's lives (1956Ag).

Most of this long and important justification of social research (except, interestingly enough, the section on religion) was reprinted in several installments in the authoritative *Renmin ribao,* in connection with a major research project then being planned under the sponsorship of the Nationalities Committee of the National People's Congress. This project, which Fei as an eminent scholar in the field and a member of the Nationalities Committee had surely helped shape, was intended to involve some two hundred scientific researchers from various disciplines and institutions over the course of four to seven years making systematic studies of the social history and socio-economic structures of minority nationalities, including productive forces, systems of ownership, class structure, historical development, and customs (1956Jl27). From August 1956 to February 1957, Fei himself spent six months in Yunnan as part of a team working on this social history project.

He never published a formal report of this work, which was cut short in 1958,[21] but a rather superficial newspaper piece he wrote told of many things they had found: neolithic implements, possible archaeological sites, inscribed stones, statues, and old documents, including two trunks of old Buddhist sutras, some as old as eight hundred years. He deplored the fact that such things were being lost or destroyed because people didn't realize their scholarly value (1957F8). Such were the hopeful beginnings of real social research on minorities in 1956.

A number of foreign visitors who had talks with Fei in the 1950s thought him contentedly busy with work he felt constructive and convinced that the new order in China was for the best. He had put on a good bit of weight in the early 1950s and looked well fed and jovial. The British economist Joan Robinson found him in the summer fo 1953 "in a very good state and happy in the work he was doing."[22] A year later, Cedric Dover, an Anglo-Indian biologist and writer on race, had dinner at his house and Fei told him that "he had at last become an 'anthropologist in action' in an exhilerating atmosphere where 'cooperative work with minorities' has already produced such outstanding results," and that, if Dover had had better sense, he would have arranged to have been born in China like Fei.[23] Kingsley Martin, the editor of *The New Statesman and Nation,* who was critical of the lack of intellectual freedom in China, had a long visit with Fei in the spring of 1955 and wrote (apparently about Fei):

> My friend was fatter and, I should say, happier than he used to be. He had . . . work that satisfied him; once he had proved his wholehearted acceptance of the New China and shaken off the dust of the West . . . he had been given more scope and recognition in China . . . than he could have had under the Kuomintang. . . I do not think my friend was pretending to be contented; if he had doubts, they were probably hidden even from himself.[24]

W.R. Geddes, an Australian anthropologist, had a long talk with him in the spring of 1956, finding him "the most impressive advocate of the Communist approach whom I met in China":

With the joyous excitement of complete conviction, Dr. Fei had argued powerfully for the rightness of the Communistic approach to the national problems of China and was enthusiastic in his praise of the virtues of the present regime.[25]

In 1955, a minor controversy about Fei in the British journal *Encounter* was ignited by Karl Wittfogel's allegation, in a review of *China's Gentry,* that Fei was no longer permitted to study the Chinese peasantry or discuss social questions freely, and that, given his earlier concern for peasant welfare, he must now be very unhappy about their tragic fate under communism. To objections from various people that this was malicious speculation, Wittfogel reiterated that Fei could be an "enthusiastic supporter of policies that were formerly alien to his way of thinking" only if his "moral fibre is weaker than I . . . believe."[26] Fei himself contributed a letter, charging that Wittfogel was concocting venomous rumors to slander new China (though he did not refute him point by point), and that had he been asked he would not have consented to the publication of *China's Gentry,* for his views had greatly changed since 1948 when the articles translated in it had been written (*"Encounter* Letter").

He pursued this discussion in a piece in an English language magazine published in China, in which he insisted that he had not been brainwashed—"It is ridiculous to imagine one can control another's thought"—but had simply decided some of his old ideas were wrong. For instance, his opposition to violent revolution and his proposal that landlords voluntarily give up their privileges was an unrealistic fantasy which just served to perpetuate landlord interests. His proposal for rural industry was partly mistaken because he had failed to realize, first, that the defects of Western industrial society were due to capitalism and would not occur in socialist China; and, second, that a China built on rural industry would be easy prey for imperialism. Life had become much better for him and hundreds of thousands of other intellectuals:

> We love China, we love our present-day life. We have realized what life can mean, realized that we, with our hands and brains, can create true

happiness. Facts give us confidence that as long as we serve the people our ideals will become reality . . .

Friends! Do I really seem the downtrodden worm of Mr. Wittfogel's imagination? If he believes that, he would believe anything. And I'm only one of thousands who constitute the Chinese intelligentsia. Wen-tsao Wu, Quentin Pan, Yao-hua Lin and others whom many sociologists and anthropologists abroad must know are now working with me: we are enthusiastically pooling our efforts for the sake of a great ideal.

We love our present-day work, we love New China. Is there anything incomprehensible about that? ("Old Friends")

It would be possible, but I think mistaken, to read a hidden message of dissent in the assertion that a person cannot be coerced to change his ideas, in his silence about Wittfogel's charges that the peasantry had suffered under communism, or in his vagueness about how his old ideas had changed. Fei was too prudent and cautious to risk public dissent, however veiled, and his tone seems too ebullient and self-confident to mask sullen resistance. Life seemed to be improving for most in China in the mid-1950s; there was in the air a spirit of construction, of building a better future, and Fei with his naturally sanguine temperament doubtless felt a good bit of elation at this. But we should not take a declaration of total happiness, intended for foreign consumption, at face value. We know enough of his feelings and situation to be sure that much of his early enthusiasm had been replaced by frustration. His patriotic desire to participate in the Communist-led effort of national reconstruction—and no doubt the same is true of many other intellectuals—must to a greater or lesser extent have been dampened by the mistrust and the restrictions placed on his participation. Fei was certainly unhappy at not being able to contribute as he thought he best could through research, teaching, and writing about the peasantry and other social problems the way he had before. His eagerness to return to such concerns and activities would become unmistakable during the Hundred Flowers period.

EIGHT

The Hundred Flowers and After

> Professors—we have been afraid of them ever since we came into the towns. We did not despise them, we were terrified of them. When confronted by people with piles of learning we felt we were good for nothing. . . . We must not tolerate it any longer. . . . They may have studied more natural science than we have, but they do not necessarily know more social science. . . We should not feel ashamed of ourselves.
> —Mao Zedong (March, 1958)[1]

Fei emerged briefly from the obscurity of minorities work in what is known as the Hundred Flowers period, a period of about a year and a half, from early 1956 to mid-1957, when a new policy of more favorable treatment and enhanced responsibilities for intellectuals was in effect. The new policy was based on the perception that there was a gulf of mistrust between Party members (the new elite), who felt intellectuals looked down on them because of their inferior education and humble social origins, and non-Party intellectuals (the old elite, now without power), who felt the Party would not allow them responsibilities or even keep them informed; and that this gulf inhibited cooperation and full use of the intellectual's talents which were needed for economic development.

In January 1956, in a long speech "On the Question of the Intellectuals," Zhou Enlai said that continued socialist construction would depend on the support of intellectuals and better use of their skills. "They must be given jobs and authority, their views must be respected, the results of professional research and work must be valued." The Prime Minister promised better working conditions, including a guarantee that no more than one sixth of their time would have to be spent on political study, meetings, administrative duties, and other non-professional activities. Finally, he said that, with continuing reeducation, it was planned to bring a third of the nation's higher intellectuals into the Party by 1962.[2] In the following months, intellectuals found their living and working situation improved, they were given new privileges, there was a substantial increase in funds allocated to scientific research, and in all fields far-reaching plans were formulated for vastly stepped-up research.[3] One such plan was the project on minority societies mentioned above.

Part of this new policy was the revival of the democratic parties, as they were called, of which the Democratic League was the most important. These small anti-Guomindang political parties had been allowed to continue after 1949, in keeping with the theory that China was governed by a united front, but they had gradually become inactive. Then, starting in late 1955, forums and meetings were held under their auspices to discuss the problems of intellectuals and the new policy toward them. In April 1956, Mao Zedong, in a major speech "On the Ten Major Relationships," said that the relationship between the Communist Party and the democratic parties should be one of "long-term co-existence and mutual supervision."[4] Membership in democratic parties is thought to have trebled in 1956 to some 100,000. The Democratic League grew to an estimated 30,000, drawn from "cultural and educational workers (faculty members in universities, middle schools, and primary schools), university students, technical personnel, professional people, government personnel, businessmen, and patriotic democrats among Overseas Chinese."[5]

In May 1956, under the exhilarating slogan "Let a hundred flowers bloom, let a hundred schools of thought contend" (*bai hua qi fang, bai jia zhengming*), Mao called for free discussion. His speech has never been published but, according to the Party's Director of Propaganda (Lu Dingyi), the slogan meant encouraging "freedom of individual thinking, of debate, of creative work; freedom to criticize and freedom to express, maintain and reserve one's opinions on questions of art, literature, or scientific research"; and Party members were told to unite with intellectuals and give up "sectarianism," holding aloof from people outside the Party.[6] Publishing and related activities increased, and for intellectuals there was a perceptible relaxation in the political climate.

There was also, however, opposition to the Hundred Flowers policy among many in the Party and reluctance to implement it, apparently, until Mao reaffirmed it in February 1957, in his widely publicized "On the Correct Handling of Contradictions Among the People."[7] Contradictions within "the people" (which includes even the bourgeoisie, excepting counter-revolutionaries), the Chairman pronounced, were for the most part non-antagonistic and should be dealt with gently with persuasion and education. If the government responded with coercion and terrorism to the grievances of people who basically supported socialism, they would become alienated. This had happened under Stalin and, more recently, was the cause of the uprisings in Poland and Hungary.[8] As Mao summed it up in April 1957:

> We must change the relationship between the Party and the intellectuals... Between Party and non-Party there is a ditch, which is very deep...
> Can we do without the democratic parties? No. The Soviet Union does not have them and does not hear contrary opinions... If we strike down the democratic personages, they will rise to oppose us. It is quite necessary to learn from them with an open mind...
> "Let a hundred flowers bloom, a hundred schools of thought contend" is a policy for winning over the intellectuals...
> It is the fault of the Communist Party that it has not been close to the intellectuals.[9]

Meanwhile Mao had become concerned about bureaucratic tendencies within the Party, which had grown rapidly in the 1950s, and in late 1956 the leadership had agreed that, sometime in the future, the Party would have a rectification movement to combat "subjectivism, sectarianism, and bureaucratism." Then, in the spring of 1957, Mao apparently decided to combine Party rectification with the Hundred Flowers and invite intellectuals to criticize Party members. Rather than conciliate the Party and the intellectuals, it has been argued convincingly, Mao wanted to set them against each other in a controlled conflict in order to correct rightist tendencies in both.[10] The result was five weeks of relatively unrestrained criticism, from about May 1 to June 7, with a growing torrent of strongly worded complaints about the Party's monopoly of power. This was too much for most of the leadership and the Hundred Flowers policy was abruptly ended.

INTELLECTUALS AND POLITICS

Fei's activities during this year-and-a-half may be divided into three categories. We have already seen his efforts for research on national minorities. Then there was his role as a leader of intellectuals: writing articles on matters concerning them, meeting with intellectuals in various parts of the country, listening to their grievances, encouraging them to speak out and perhaps to play a more active political role. Finally, there were tentative steps towards restoring sociology, culminating in a three-week re-study of Kaixiangong village.

In the new atmosphere, Fei was able to publish much more easily, on more than just national minorities, and thus we find articles quite unlike those of the preceding years. There was, for example, a little piece criticizing the aesthetic shortcomings of the monuments and tombs around famous West Lake, which set off a minor controversy in the press in nearby Hangzhou (1956Jl26; 1956O16). Much more striking, because such pointed remarks about the Chinese political system are most rare in the People's Republic, is an article about the National People's Congress. Fei had been named a delegate (from his native Jiangsu) in 1954, but at that time had written only an innocuous article saying that the Constitution the Congress had approved was different from the bourgeois constitutions he had once talked about in his 1946 book *Minzhu, xianfa, renquan*, which only protected the rights of the bourgeoisie (1954Jl16).

Now, following the third session of the Congress in June 1956, he wrote more openly about political matters. When he attended the Peking Congress right after Liberation he had thought that that was true freedom and democracy, he said; but later he recognized that what had impressed him was really just the feeling of personal security under the new government and the broad popular base present at the meeting; it was not living democracy. He had now come to feel that new China had democratic forms, but that in this country without a tradition of democracy the content did not always correspond to these forms. His little niece had raised a very serious question, he said, when she had asked, "How can Uncle be our representative when he doesn't even come to see us?" When he was in England he had loved to read or listen to Parliamentary debates, but in China the Congress meetings had not been very lively. This year, however, things seemed to be changing. He had made an inspection trip in part of Jiangsu, talked to many people, and gained a much better grasp of concrete conditions. And the most recent session of the Congress had had a remarkably fresh and open atmosphere in which criticisms of government officials had been frankly expressed. He thought now that when foreigners asked about democracy in China he could say he and the other representatives were members of both the party in power and the opposition, supporting socialism and opposing anything hindering it even within the government (1956Jl16).

In the light of such views, Fei's extensive travels and contacts with intellectuals take on political significance. As a famous and respected scholar, who had also been relatively progressive and activist, he was one of those selected (perhaps by Zhou Enlai?) to implement the government's new policy of winning over intellectuals by better treatment. In his January 1956 speech, Zhou had said the State Council, or cabinet, was preparing to set up an Experts Bureau to solve administrative questions concerning the treatment of intellectuals; on October 19, Fei was appointed Vice-Director of this Bureau. He was also named to a Scientific Planning Committee. As early as October 1955, he had been involved in Democratic-League-sponsored forums in which intellectuals were, apparently, invited to talk about their problems.[11] He organized such meetings with faculty members at Peking University, for instance, and also on his frequent trips around the country.

The amount of traveling he did during this period is remarkable. Towards the end of 1955, he made a tour of Nanjing, Suzhou, and Hangzhou to investigate questions concerning intellectuals, and while there he met with local Democratic League organizations and encouraged them to organize forums to discuss intellectuals' problems. From August 1956 to February 1957, on a six-month trip to the southwest for research on minorities' social history, he investigated the situation of intellectuals there for the Experts Bureau, and held forums with intellectuals under League auspices in Chengdu and Kunming.[12] In May and June 1957, he again made an inspection trip in southern Jiangsu. In Wuxi, on May 27–29, he met with educators, the Democratic League committee, and local cadres, and he urged intellectuals to write about their grievances and use newspapers to influence a wide audience.[13] Similarly, in Suzhou, he encouraged middle school teachers to speak out about their problems and write essays for *Guangming ribao*, *Wen hui bao*, and *Xin guancha*.[14]

In February 1957, he reported on the conditions of intellectuals around the country to the Democratic League Central Committee. Their problems, he said, had been caused by "two lids." One was restrictions on scientific research; this lid had now been lifted, at least partially, releasing their scholarly activism. The other suppressed their participation in political affairs; this had not been lifted and Fei thought it should be, to release their political activism (1957My31). These themes he expanded on in a long article called "The early spring weather of the intellectuals," carried in *Renmin ribao* in late March. It was his most widely read article of the period, encouraging intellectuals to speak out at a key moment in the Hundred Flowers period, and one for which he would later be denounced countless times.

The material conditions of the intellectuals, he said, had greatly improved since Zhou's January 1956 speech and were no longer a problem. Those who before could only afford food and clothing were now able to buy books, and in many places they were often given preferential treatment in barber shops, clinics, markets, and theatres. Before, many had felt lonely and excluded. Zhou's speech was like a second Liberation for them, assuring them there was a place for them in the new society. Some applied to join the Party; others started buying books and planning projects; old scholars who had not been heard from for years were engaging in research and publishing articles. Spring had come. Now what teachers in institutes of higher education wanted was, as one put it, "a room and two books"—the opportunity for study, research, scholarly conferences, and perhaps even study abroad. Finding enough free time and appropriate facilities was still a problem in some places, but the major need, Fei thought, was for leadership in research: concrete support and direction from superiors and those with experience in designing and carrying out research projects, organizing cooperative efforts, combining research with teaching, and arranging conferences.

It was also important, he went on, that intellectuals engage in freer discussion, even of ideology and politics. If their thought reform was to progress further, they had to learn to master ideas, to distinguish idealism from materialism. As it was, many tended to call theories from bourgeois countries idealism and those from socialist countries materialism, like a little boy at a play who understands only that the red faces are good and the white ones bad. Intellectuals were still cautious and reticent, unwilling to reveal their thoughts, as though afraid that it was early spring and the weather might turn cold again. A few feared a trap, that opinions would be collected and there would then be a rectification campaign. More were afraid of being labeled idealists or backward elements, something he said was not just a question of face but would affect the attitude of their students in class, salary and promotion, going abroad to study, even finding a spouse. Moreover, their superiors were sometimes unwilling to carry out the policy, or wanted to limit free discussion to scholarly questions only, and apt to cry out with alarm when an idealistic idea was expressed. Especially on political matters, Fei said, the intellectuals should speak out more. For instance, the incidents in Poland and Hungary had evoked little response. Of course the Party's leadership should be trusted, but intellectuals should not be passive or without opinions in national affairs (1957Mr24).

Mao later said that the blooming and contending were meant to apply only to literature and art and academic matters, and that it was rightists who wanted to extend it to politics.[15] The policy had indeed been originally so limited, but it seems clear that, by February and March 1957, Mao himself was calling for political debate. He invited non-Party people to participate in Party rectification, calling for "opening wide"—"let all people express their opinions freely, so that they dare to speak, dare to criticize and dare to debate"—and said that blooming and contending were good, not just for science and the arts, but "for all our work ... [for] truth develops through debate between different views."[16] I suspect Fei had approval, and perhaps even encouragement, from higher-ups before urging intellectuals to political discussion, and he later told how cautious he had been in putting this article forward. After reporting to the Democratic League on intellectuals in February, he said, he had been encouraged to write an essay, but did not dare send it out. He revised it repeatedly and showed it to friends. Then he heard that the climate was not right, and a magazine reporter told him orders had come down to be careful in what was printed; but others said things were relaxing and he should submit it. He completely rewrote it and finally sent it off on just the morning of Mao's February 17 speech on "Contradictions Among the People." After hearing about the speech from an excited Pan Guangdan (Fei could not attend because he had been receiving a foreign friend), he revised the second half yet again (1957My31)! It seems unlikely that the article would have been published in the Party's highest newspaper if it were not in accord with the views of at least some of the leadership, and indeed Fei is supposed to have claimed that it was praised and supported by certain leading cadres on the Party Central Committee.[17]

At any rate, only the less touchy of the two themes in "Early Spring," the advocacy of greater research opportunities, was continued in Fei's articles of April and May. There was no contradiction between teaching and research, he said in one, for good teaching requires the kind of active understanding that comes from trying to put theory into practice in research, even if the research does not contribute to human knowledge. For instance, his understanding of the theory of a nationality's four characteristics had been greatly increased by trying to apply this theory in research on Chinese minorities and, were he to go back to teaching now, he said (perhaps wistfully), he could teach the theory better (1957Ap). The desire for a room and two books did not mean intellectuals wanted to neglect political study; they hoped rather to improve their professional abilities to meet the increasing needs of socialist construction and thereby to serve the people; it was really a form of political activism (1957My31).

It is clear that Fei was in touch with a large number of intellectuals in various parts of the country, that he asked them about their needs and desires, and that he encouraged them to speak out. It would be absurd to think he did these things on his own initiative; they were in line with the Hundred Flowers policy and doubtless done on instructions from higher authority. Whether he went beyond these instructions cannot be known. It is to be expected that he would want to reduce Party influence in higher education, and this was also in accordance with the new policy of giving more authority to non-Party intellectuals; thus, it seems quite plausible that he suggested replacing Party committees in institutes of higher education with university affairs committees, as he was later charged with doing.[18] He was said to have complained that at the Nationalities Institute the Party secretary and fellow Vice President Su Kejin was a layman (*waihang*) and that the Institute was a "Party school."[19] It was also reported that he argued that political factors should not be considered in admitting and advancing university and graduate students—all should be treated equally.[20]

He seems to have tried to cultivate his influence over a segment of the press and to use it to air his views. It was later charged that he had great influence on the magazine *Xin guancha* (a biweekly of national circulation and descendant of the *Guancha* magazine in which Fei had published frequently in the late 1940s), in part through a member of the editorial board called Huang Sha who had been a sociology student of his at Qinghua before Liberation; and that, in the spring of 1957, he twice came to talk to the magazine's editorial board about the thaw.²¹ It was said that the Democratic League leader Luo Longji had used his influence with the Shanghai newspaper *Wen hui bao* to give Fei publicity,²² and that other League leaders had tried to form a new advisory board for the Peking newspaper *Guangming ribao*, on which Fei would have served.²³

It is possible that Fei was trying to organize the intellectuals into a political force with some real influence. He was a leader of the Democratic League, a growing party of intellectuals which, the doctrine of "long-term coexistence and mutual supervision" seemed to suggest, might come to play a more important political role and perhaps even become a kind of countervailing force to the Communist Party. He was later said to have complained that the Democratic League in the past had done nothing except on instructions from the Communist Party's united front department,²⁴ that the Soviet Union lacked democracy, that Stalin had been a dictator, and that how to create a socialist democracy in China was a problem still to be solved.²⁵ He was also said to have interceded with government officials in the interest of various people with grievances in the province he was supposed to represent in the National People's Congress.²⁶

Fei was out of Peking, safely in a village, during late April and all of May when others were becoming reckless in their criticism of the Party. He returned to Peking only on May 31,²⁷ but then, on June 6 at a small meeting with five other professors and Democratic League members, he is supposed to have made the following inflammatory statement on the subject of student unrest and outpouring of bitterness against the Party at Peking University. The words are quoted in a later denunciation and should probably not be regarded as a verbatim transcript of what he said:

> A new emotion arises in my heart today. I sympathize with the students

in these matters that are brought to light [there had been tearful accounts of students being wronged in the campaign against counter-revolutionaries in the early 1950s]. . . The students are looking for leaders everywhere. . . [He went on to say the trouble was the fault of a system in which non-Party people had no authority and Party members usurped power.] I think it is not a question of the style of work of individuals but a question of system. I have declared I will not join the Communist Party as an expression of my attitude. . . Some say without Party nomination I cannot be anything. I don't think so. Let us see whether the masses support me or not in an election campaign.[28]

RETURN TO SOCIOLOGY AND KAIXIANGONG

Fei had written clearly and repeatedly of the importance of national minorities research in 1956, but it was not until 1957 that he began to make tentative, hesitant suggestions that there might be a place in new China for sociological research and the "old" sociologists. This was radical stuff; ethnology of national minorities, which was studied in the Soviet Union too, had never been considered illegitimate, but sociology was a bourgeois ideology which had been abolished. Zhou Enlai, in January 1956, had said nothing to suggest it might be restored, only that the neglect of "social science" (a term often used very broadly in China, to encompass the study of Marxist theory, history, literature, and so on) in comparison with natural science should be corrected; and Lu Dingyi's speech on blooming and contending, too, spoke only of correcting the tendency of social sciences to be "monopolized" by Party members.[29] But in the Soviet Union, following Khrushchev's February 1956 anti-Stalin speech, there had been the beginnings of discussion about the attitude toward sociology, and in August, for the first time, the Soviet Union and several East European countries sent scholars, some of whom gave papers, to the (Third) World Congress of Sociology in Amsterdam. This significant development did not go unnoticed in China; indeed, *Renmin ribao* carried a translation of an article about the conference by one of the Russian participants.[30]

The opening shot in China did not come until January 1957 with a short article by Wu Jingchao, Fei's former colleague in the sociology department at Qinghua. Wu noted the Soviet participation at the meeting and suggested that there was a need in China for a critical acceptance of the rational parts of the old sociology, and for courses on subjects like "population theory and statistics, social investigation (including both urban sociology and rural sociology), problems of marriage, the family, women, and children, and the criminology part of social pathology."[31] In addition to Wu, other once-prominent sociologists surfaced during the Hundred Flowers period, talking about research on society. Chen Da, for many years professor of sociology at Qinghua and China's leading demographer before 1949, who had since been in such eclipse that he had not even participated in the 1953 census, came forward in early 1957 with a comprehensive plan for research on population problems; this was discussed in an important meeting at the Labor Cadres School, the first meeting since Liberation to consider research on population, according to Fei (1957Ap3). Li Jinghan, another well-known old sociologist and the principal author of the 1930s survey of Ding county, had after the reform of the universities prepared three separate new courses in three successive years and not been allowed to give any (1957Mr24). Then, in early February 1957, no less a newspaper than *Renmin ribao* carried a series of articles by him on a re-survey of current conditions in some villages in the suburbs of Peking which he had first investigated and written on in the 1920s.[32]

Fei followed Wu Jingchao with his own article agreeing that there was a place for sociology in new China. What is most striking about this article is its cautious tone—a caution that is in contrast to his writing and activities concerning intellectuals and that adds weight to the notion that the latter were not unauthorized. Fei started by saying that he had not thought about sociology for some time and was writing only in response to a request by the Shanghai newspaper *Wen hui bao* following Wu's article. His own relationship with sociology had been peripheral; he was trained in social anthropology, part of what is now called in China *minzuxue* (ethnology or nationalities studies) and had taught in sociology departments only because there were no anthropology departments. The abolition of sociology and sociology departments in China, he lamely protested, had been no hardship for him—he was happy using his old training to make field researches of minority nationalities, and had no wish to return to sociology.

Nonetheless, since he had been asked, he would set down a few thoughts. He did not want to discuss the question of whether abolishing sociology several years ago had been correct or not, but felt that, as society changed, new questions arose. Some, such as those concerning political relations or use of personnel, were studied by government and party organs, but others were not. There were, he said, questions of interpersonal relations, relations between the sexes, marriage, child-rearing, care of the old, population questions, and others that would arise. These would not go away by themselves and should be studied; and they are studied better, he asserted, by experts than by Party and government cadres. As systematic research leading to scientific generalizations, this study constituted a discipline; the name did not matter—if people objected to "sociology" how about "social investigation" (*shehui diaocha*)? As to who could do it, there were the old sociology teachers and students, who, once their viewpoint was rectified, had valuable skills and comparative knowledge of the old society. Some had never found suitable positions since sociology departments had been eliminated, and would be happy to return to work. As to organization, Fei suggested a sociological (or social) research institute in the Academy of Sciences (1957F20).

Then, on March 12, at a propaganda work conference called by the Communist Party Central Committee, Fei openly called for a change in the official attitude towards bourgeois sociology.[33] In April, he chaired a forum sponsored by the magazine *Xin jianshe* on problems connected with developing sociology, which was attended by twenty-odd people, including such old sociologists as Wu Jingchao, Wu Wenzao, Pan Guangdan, Chen Da, Li Jinghan, and three who had been students of Fei's at Kunming, Zhang Zhiyi, Yuan Fang, and Hu Qingjun; the magazine later published most of their statements.³⁴ Fei wrote some short pieces in April and May reiterating his arguments for the usefulness of sociology and the old sociologists. Socialist society had questions that needed to be studied, and bourgeois sociology, while it should still be criticized, had elements that could be used, particularly research techniques. A new sociology could be developed and, while it was "too early" to establish sociology departments in universities, there were concrete problems that should be studied scientifically right away (1957Ap10), for example, various demographic questions (1957Ap3). It would be faster to reform the large number of old social scientists than to train fresh people. After they had been reformed, the old social science workers would have a deeper understanding of society than those who had not been through this struggle; their potential was now being wasted (1957My).

The Democratic League Central Committee commissioned a special group in that spring of 1957 to study how China's scientific work could be improved. Fei was not a member of this group but apparently participated in some of its discussions and had a hand in revising the group's report which was published June 9. In particular, it was later charged, Fei had written parts of the section on social sciences, which argued that social science should not be totally neglected in favor of natural science; that, to develop social science, "we should change our attitude towards the old social sciences," remolding them and retaining what was useful instead of rejecting and ignoring them ("In the past many who studied sociology, political science, or law have changed fields, and many courses were eliminated because the U.S.S.R. didn't have them."); and that social scientists should be encouraged to put forward their views on government policies, and government organs should provide them with data and support.³⁵

Of course, Fei was not alone in hoping for the restoration of sociology. In April, in a forum in Tianjin, Wang Ganyu said that many had suffered when fields of study were abolished just because they did not exist in the U.S.S.R.; that it was wrong to reject everything in bourgeois social sciences; and that he hoped the study of sociology and politics would be restored.³⁶ In Shanghai in May, a meeting of old sociologists agreed that sociological research should be restored; they formed a sociology work group, and one of them published a long article saying flat out that the disbanding of sociology departments in 1952 had been a mistake.³⁷ Not all agreed; Sun Benwen, who had been another prominent sociologist in the 1930s and 1940s, wrote a scathing critique of "capitalist sociology," concluding that it was all anti-Marxist and could not be useful to socialist China.³⁸ But there was plenty of ammunition for those who later charged there had been a conspiracy to restore bourgeois sociology, and the names of once-prominent sociologists said to have been involved include, besides Fei, Wu Jingchao, Chen Da, Li Jinghan, Tao Menghe, Zhao Chengxin, Pan Guangdan, and Wu Wenzao.³⁹

The climax to this "conspiracy" came in June. The Academy of Sciences' Section on Philosophy and Social Science had on April 23 appointed an eight-man group, which included Fei, Wu Jingchao, and Li Jinghan, to make preparations for establishing at a later date a Social Problems Research Work Committee, circumstances which suggest a measure of official encouragement. This group then, it was later charged, privately met on June 9 at Chen Da's house, and on its own initiative changed its name to Sociology Work Committee with Chen as president, started getting in touch with other sociologists in order to form a Chinese Sociological Association, and made plans for getting sociology departments restored at the universities.⁴⁰ That they did in fact do these things seems independently verified by an interview Chen Da gave a visiting Japanese scholar in July. The goals of the Sociology Work Committee, Chen told him, were: (1) to reestablish contact among old sociologists in China (a hundred had already been reached) and with international professional organizations; (2) to organize a national sociological association which would meet annually and publish research reports; (3) to work towards reestablishing sociology departments in universities to offer courses on population, labor, family, urban administration, the peasantry, nationalities, and crime; and (4) to promote research projects, such as a compilation on the peoples of the world, to be done mostly by Central Institute of Nationalities researchers under Fei Xiaotong; a study of various social changes in the Peking area under Li Jinghan; and a demographic study of one county in preparation for the 1960 census.[41]

The high point of Fei's efforts to restore sociology came during twenty days in late April and May 1957 he spent in Kaixiangong, the south Jiangsu village he had studied twenty-one years before and written about in *Peasant Life in China*. It was, interestingly enough, not the first time the village had been revisited by a social scientist making comparisons with Fei's 1936 findings. A year before, in May 1956, W. R. Geddes, an Australian anthropoligist on a visit to China, was able to spend four days in the village. It was not a very long time but, an experienced field worker who knew Fei's book well and had two people helping him, he was able to take a full census of the village and gather some economic data, sufficient to make an interesting short monograph published in 1963 under the title *Peasant Life in Communist China*.[42]

Presumably Fei knew what Geddes was doing, for he saw him when he was in Peking, and perhaps this is what gave him the idea of going back himself. His talk with Geddes would surely have indicated to Fei that there was still interest in *Peasant Life* and in Kaixiangong in the English-speaking world. He is supposed to have said before going that his investigation would have international significance (which prompted the magazine *Xin guancha* to send a reporter and photographer along)[43] and to have corresponded with Routledge and Kegan Paul in London, the publishers of *Peasant Life,* about the possibility of a book in English about changes in peasant life under the new government.[44] On this return visit, Fei was once again accompanied by his sister Fei Dasheng, now a delegate to the Provincial Congress, and also by some young assistants who helped collect data. His findings were published in two long installments in *Xin guancha* in June; a third part never appeared.

It was an extraordinary article. The village had undergone vast changes, he said, going from an exploitative to a non-exploitative society; socialism had improved the life of most peasants. At the high tide of the collectivization movement a year or two earlier, it had been appropriate to emphasize these improvements and thus increase enthusiasms, but now to go on making a lot of windy propaganda about what had improved did not do socialism any good. It was more important to take a hard-headed look at the obstacles that still lay ahead.

Getting enough food was still a problem for many families, and most children still could not go to school because they had to gather grass to feed the sheep, penned so that the dung could be collected for fertilizer. Rice production had increased greatly, from 350 catties per *mu* in 1936 to 559 in 1956 (unhusked; a catty, or *jin*, is 1.1 lb.),[45] due to more extensive double-cropping, improved irrigation, and increased fertilizer. But income from secondary industries, which had been an important part of peasant income in the past, had not increased, and Fei calculated that the average increase in income was very slight, a scant 30 catties per capita. It is true that 1936 had been a good year and, after the Japanese occupation, things became much worse; and it was also true that the poorer farmers were much better off now. But Fei said that a majority felt things had been better in the past (1957 Je1:3–4)!

As in the old days, he emphasized the importance of subsidiary industries. In 1936, he wrote, every family had raised silkworms, but now production was down to only 60 percent of that year because of a shortage of mulberry leaves. Formerly, the cocoons had been unraveled in the village, in homes, and then in the cooperative factory Fei's sister organized. But now the cocoons were sold, and that income was lost, as were the technical skills involved. In 1936, most of the boats in the village had been used for transporting and selling goods, but now this had been stopped as a capitalist activity. Before, the village had had about a thousand sheep, now there were only two hundred odd. Rabbits were being raised instead, which would have been fine except they too kept children out of school cutting grass. Many families were raising pigs now, but there was a problem supplying them with feed—land was too valuable to use to grow fodder. Fei admitted that his pre-Liberation writings on rural industry had underemphasized the importance of heavy industry, but he thought rural industry was still worth considering. Many light industries did not need to be in cities; small factories could produce high-quality goods. Rural industry could be a force for technical improvement, provide waste products for fertilizer, and avoid urban problems. But agricultural cooperatives were concerned only with agriculture, and processing industries, even milling grain, had been taken over by the cities. If the Kaixiangong silk factory were to be restored, Fei thought the villagers would welcome it (pp. 5-7).

Since income had risen considerably, at least to 1936 levels, and well above what it had fallen to after 1936, and this was furthermore a rich area with average income higher than the national average, how could it be that the villagers did not have enough to eat? Fei found that grain production came to about 380 catties (husked) per capita (presumably after deducting expenses, taxes, and sales to the state), which was about equal to what the villagers ate (as was true in 1936 once rent was deducted).[46] In 1956, however, after people had eaten more than usual in anticipation of a bumper harvest (because of increased fertilizer), a typhoon damaged the crops. Food could have been bought from other areas, but there was no money, largely because the old sources of outside income, such as reeling silk and using boats for buying and selling, were now not permitted (pp. 11-13).

Fei thought the peasants' standard of living was fairly high, though he didn't have comparative figures from 1936. They dressed rather well—some had sweaters and sneakers. They ate about 20 catties of pork a year each, and the previous year it had been more. They drank tea, smoked cigarettes, used toothbrushes and toothpaste. Some had flashlights. Indeed, he thought the living standard had increased faster than production, which had only just reached 1936 levels, and that explained why they had no savings with which to weather emergencies. Under capitalism, capital was accumulated by puritanical capitalists. In China it had to depend on the peasants, and could not be accumulated if, as in this village, they spent all they earned. The problem was that they had lost their old habits of frugality, in part because of one-sided propaganda which emphasized only the benefits that socialism had brought and not the difficulties still ahead, and had come to depend on the cooperative's cadres to solve their problems (pp. 13–14).

The third part of Fei's article on his revisit to Kaixiangong never appeared, so we cannot know what conclusions he was working towards. (It was later charged that he had meant it to concentrate on "backward phenomena" in the village's family, marriage, cultural and educational patterns.[47]) It does not seem impossible, however, that he was going to advocate his old solution of cooperative rural industry to encourage voluntary peasant investment and raise supplementary income. It should be said that he was not alone in thinking that it had been a mistake for the rural cooperatives to concentrate so much on agriculture; the commune movement of the next year would cause rural industry and sideline occupations to mushroom. Nor was he alone in raising questions about the benefits of collectivization. Mao said in early 1957 that, in view of the fact that some cooperatives had brought a decrease in peasant income, "certain Party cadres" were asking whether the agricultural cooperatives were worth preserving at all.[48] I do not think Fei's article was going to go this far, but it does seem possible that he had been encouraged to do this sort of investigation and write this sort of article by certain factions high in the Party who thought more attention should be given to village sideline production.

It is clear, at any rate, that many of Fei's ideas had not changed much since 1949. His interest was as before in peasant welfare, thought of in terms of average income for a village, and with increasing it through sources of income outside basic agriculture. He still felt that sociological community studies by expert scholars were useful in formulating policies that would benefit the people. He was still drawn to representative government, open discussion of social and political issues, and greater freedom for scholarly research. It must have seemed for a while in 1956 and 1957 that these things were coming nearer, and those months of the Hundred Flowers period were surely a happy and hopeful time for Fei.

THE ANTI-RIGHTIST MOVEMENT, 1957–1958

The Chinese leadership was apparently surprised and alarmed by the bitter criticisms released against the Party in May 1957 (where open dissent is not allowed, it is probably natural to underestimate discontent), and when, in early June, university students were aroused by revelations of Party wrongdoing to the point of rioting, the opponents of the Hundred Flowers liberalization won out and the policy was reversed. It was evident that many intellectuals greatly resented the Party's monopoly of power (what Chu Anping stingingly called "the Party's empire," *dang tianxia*), and this indicated to the Party that they had not been transformed by thought reform but were still rightists at heart. For the latter half of 1957 and most of 1958, much of the nation's energies were devoted to an Anti-Rightist Movement to criticize, discredit, and remove from responsible position tens of thousands of "rightist" intellectuals. The two most prominent targets were both cabinet ministers and Democratic League leaders, Luo Longji and Zhang Bojun, who were accused of an anti-Party conspiracy. Among the next half-dozen most important and most loudly abused rightists was Fei Xiaotong.

It started gradually, but the movement was in full force in a few weeks. On June 8, the *Renmin ribao* asked editorially, "What Is Going On Here?" and in succeeding days talked more and more about the need to counterattack criticisms which had gone too far. On June 10, the Democratic League's Central Committee had a small group meeting to "criticize anti-socialist opinions," at which Fei tried to soften the growing counterattacks. Discussion should be based on common acceptance of socialism and Party leadership, he said, and with this understanding, freedom of speech should be protected. People should continue to speak out, trusting the Party's guarantee that those who do so may meet with opposition but not with punishment. He suggested that the atmosphere be made less tense by having smaller meetings of four or five persons without reporters present, and giving people a chance to emend their remarks overnight.⁴⁹ But, instead, the atmosphere got tenser, and meetings to criticize rightists more frequent and harsher. A few days later, at a forum of non-Party people convened by the State Council, Fei was fully on the defensive. He said that he had been mistaken in thinking (as he had stated in "Early Spring") that thought reform had basically converted the intellectuals to genuine supporters of socialism. He had been too warm-hearted, had not criticized dangerous rightist ideas, and his comments a few days ago about guarantees against punishment just served to protect the rightists. But now, he said, he was determined to cut himself off from them.⁵⁰

It was not so easy, however. His name kept coming up—newspapers, for instance, were criticized for printing his articles and interviews with him.⁵¹ On June 19, he admitted to a reporter that he had been wrong to stress professionalism in "Early Spring."⁵² He was required to speak out at meetings.⁵³ To judge from fragmentary news reports, at first this was mostly a matter of making accusations and revelations against others. On June 25, at a Democratic League Central Committee small group meeting, he accused Luo Longji of praising ideologically backward intellectuals and of calling progressives doctrinaire and opportunist.⁵⁴ He revealed what Qinghua President Qian Weichang (who would deny it) had said at the meeting of six professors on June 6, that with teacher leadership the students were ready to revolt. A few days later Qian, under fire from students and teachers at Qinghua, said Fei had drawn him into the Zhang-Luo conspiracy and introduced him to Chu Anping ("rightist" editor of *Guangming ribao* and a friend of Fei's from the time he had edited *Guancha* in the late 1940s).⁵⁵ By early July, Fei was regularly being named as one of Luo Longji's anti-Party anti-socialist clique,⁵⁶ and the inflammatory remarks he allegedly made about student riots at the June 6 meeting were revealed in the newspapers.⁵⁷ He admitted at a Democratic League anti-Luo forum that he had been used by Luo for years, saying that Luo had tried to befriend him in order to use him as a contact with intellectuals. "Fei claimed that he was pulled down into the rightist pit and he wanted to be a witness in exposing the conspiracy," a news account reported.[58]

At the National People's Congress meetings, too, Fei was denounced. Li Da said the two "Early Spring" articles were propaganda for the Zhang-Luo alliance, opposing the leadership of the party in intellectual matters and calling for a Hungarian incident in China.[59] Xia Kangnong, like Fei a Vice President of the Central Nationalities Institute, called him a strategist of the Zhang-Luo alliance, and gave what he called evidence of Fei's sustained anti-Party, anti-socialist activities: his article on the National People's Congress of a year before had expressed joy at hearing the government criticized; his "Early Spring" article, alleging that the government's policy toward intellectuals had failed, was applauded in Taiwan; and so on.[60] Others also pointed to the "Early Spring" article, saying it had expressed feelings of bourgeois melancholy intended to move dissatisfied intellectuals to political activism.[61] And even Bing Xin, Wu Wenzao's wife, who had helped with "Early Spring," said the article reflected the feelings of just a few intellectuals who were alienated from the people, were bourgeois in their hearts, and never saw the sunshine of big change.[62]

Then, on July 13, Fei himself rose in the National People's Congress, to "Admit my Guilt to the People," in a fourteen-point 4,000-word list of wrongdoing. The tone was abjectly confessional:

> . . . I have committed the most heinous crimes, treasonous crimes. . . Directed and influenced by the Zhang-Luo alliance, using the Democratic League's organization, standing on the side of the bourgeoisie, I embarked on an anti-Party anti-socialist political course and committed a series of crimes injuring the Party and injuring the people. How could I commit such crimes? I am still examining myself, but the main reason is that I failed to relinquish the reactionary stand of the bourgeoisie, resisted party education, and did not reform myself as I should have. . . .
>
> I hate my past; I must change my stand . . . I am grateful to the Party for keeping the door of reform open to us who have committed mistakes and fallen into the rightist's quagmire, and for doing its best to educate us. Let me bravely enter this door, embark on the road to life, thoroughly reform myself, and find an opportunity to atone for

my crimes to the people. I have only recently awakened and my understanding is not profound; I still need to explain in detail and examine in depth my crimes and my thoughts . . . I resolve to accept Party education and under the Party's leadership to follow the socialist road (1957Jl13).

In the next months, the meetings continued. Fei was criticized further at the National People's Congress.[63] In late July, the Academy of Science held five days of meetings, with over a hundred scientists present, to criticize the Democratic League's proposals for scientific work, and Fei was held responsible for the passage advocating a change in attitude towards the old social sciences.[64] The magazine *Xin guancha,* in which Fei had published such articles as the ones on revisiting Kaixiangong, held meetings all through July; it was said the magazine had been infiltrated by Fei in conspiracy with his former student, the reporter Huang Sha, and its policies corrupted by Fei's rightist influence.[65] The State Council Experts Bureau, of which Fei was a Vice Director, held meetings to criticize him.[66] The Democratic League continued to have meetings in August, at one of which Fei spoke again (as presumably he did at many of the others) confessing that he had been conspiring for a long time to incite intellectuals against the Party.[67] The Central Institute of Nationalities held a number of meetings to criticize Fei's minorities work, and he was denounced by wall posters there (and elsewhere no doubt) as well as in articles in its house publication.[68] Outside of Peking, too, there were meetings; for instance, the Democratic League organizations in Wuxi held a series to expose the poison Fei had been spreading there.[69]

Beginning in late August, the Academy of Sciences' Department of Philosophy and Social Science held a high-powered and well-publicized series of meetings to denounce what was called the plot to restore bourgeois sociology and economics, in which Fei was held to have played a major role. With more than a hundred members present, a large number of prominent intellectuals made speeches against Fei and Wu Jingchao, Li Jinghan, and the economist Chen Zhenhan. Then, in late September, the Academy as a whole sponsored an even higher-powered series of five days of meetings with over two hundred people present from the Academy, Peking's universities, the Central Government, and also some scientists from Shanghai and Tianjin. Fei himself made a confession on September 18, and, many a speech later, the meetings finally wound up with a pronouncement from Guo Moruo, President of the Academy.[70] The speeches and statements made at these Academy of Science meetings were later published in a volume of 700-odd pages, of which a sizeable proportion concerns Fei.[71] In late September, the Nationalities Committee of the National People's Congress held a four-day meeting to expose Fei and Pan Guangdan's conspiracy in nationalities work.[72] And so on and on.

It is frightening to imagine what these meetings must have been like for Fei. One co-worker at the Nationalities Institute who subsequently left China (and wishes to remain anonymous) told me that, in the harrowing experience of being publicly denounced and excoriated for weeks on end, Fei lost a great deal of weight. A foreign eyewitness to similar meetings at Peking University, where the long meetings and conferences, which went on for months, drove many students and teachers to suicide, has described them this way:

> The so-called rightists had to stand, facing hundreds of their onetime friends and colleagues, and hear that they were treacherous enemies of the people and reactionary agents of Chiang Kai-shek or imperialist America. Sometimes emotions ran so high that the frenzied crowds became mobs howling for blood... These maniacal meetings, the shrieking voices of condemnation and the accusing fingers, the abuse, the venom—I find them hard to forget.[73]

Another description of struggle meetings, based on interviews with refugee cadres in Hong Kong, gives an idea of the inner dynamics:

> In major political campaigns there had to be specific human targets to "struggle" against; errors and evils, as well as virtues, had to be personified.
>
> These "struggle meetings," as described by ex-cadres from central ministries who have participated in them, are psychologically unnerving, even terrifying, experiences... They are carefully planned and

directed by Party personnel, and the hapless victims are pilloried with torrents of abuse in a succession of public meetings that may last several days. The victims must stand with bowed heads while accusations are shouted at them; and . . . they cannot speak in self-defense except when specifically instructed to do so by the Party leaders directing the meetings. The charges made in these accusation meetings generally include ones to which large numbers of cadres in the audience may feel vulnerable . . . Those who do so often feel under the greatest compulsion to join publicly in the denunciations, fearing that failure to do so might suggest that they secretly sympathize with the persons under attack.[74]

Apart from the meetings, there was an enormous campaign against Fei in the press. Newspapers and magazines were full of denunciations of Fei and other rightists for many months, continuing well into 1958. I have seen perhaps a hundred articles criticizing various aspects of Fei's life, works, and deeds.[75] There were even a few books published about him.[76]

Most of this great campaign concerned Fei's activities in 1956 and 1957 regarding intellectuals and the Democratic League, and his moves towards reviving sociology in China, with special emphasis on the visit to Kaixiangong. There were, to be sure, many other charges thrown in. There was a small amount of shrill name-calling, of which the following is an example:

> Fei Xiaotong was a hard-core leader in the Zhang-Luo alliance. He is a bourgeois, individualistic, political opportunist, posing as a "scholar," and an obsequious loyal stooge of imperialism. In addition, he has all along been a schemer and strategist for the feudal landlord class, and his views on rural questions, whether political or economic, have been consistently reactionary, plainly revealing his feudal landlord standpoint.[77]

There were other charges of unscrupulous opportunism. It was said that he had not worked very hard at his scholarship but relied on his foreign connections to get ahead. A colleague at the Nationalities Institute claimed that most of his 1950s articles on minorities had been stolen from the work of others, usually drafts of younger, less-prominent colleagues,[78] a charge which is surely overstated, though it is possible that, to get them published, Fei's name was put to articles that were collaborative efforts (on a few he did acknowledge the help of others).

Lin Yaohua, who had been a friend in college and co-worker at the Nationalities Institute, in a vicious and quite untypical article entitled "The Ugly and Treacherous Fei Xiaotong," described him as a man who would sacrifice others for personal advantage and fame. Lin said that, in 1935, Fei had fallen in love with another woman one week after his wife Wang Tonghui died; that, in 1941–1942, he had conspired to expel Tao Yunkui from the chairmanship of the Yunnan University sociology department, with the result that Tao fell ill and died and his wife attempted suicide; and that, in 1957, he had boasted falsely that *Peasant Life in China* had been translated into eleven languages.[79] (The first accusation seems absurd; about the second, I know only that Fei wrote a rather affectionate obituary for Tao [1944My7]; as to the third, it is true that eleven translations were mentioned in the newspapers,[80] but it seems inconceivable that Fei himself could have been the source of such an obviously false claim.) In *Xiangtu chongjian,* Fei had warned that landlords would violently oppose land redistribution unless they were offered another economic foundation; by this, it was said, he was "openly calling on landlords to resist land reform with armed force."[81] But most of what was said about him was much less far-fetched.

Fei's pre-1949 books, particularly *Peasant Life in China* and *Xiangtu chongjian,* were cited to show his fundamentally rightist stance. In his field investigations, he had relied for information on landlords and local government officials; in Kaixiangong he had lived with the village head, a landlord bully named Zhou Baoshan, whom he praised but who had been sentenced to death by a people's court in 1951 for killing and robbing the people.[82] He had ignored class analysis in his studies, and various passages were cited to show his sympathy with the landlord class: in *Peasant Life,* he had said (p. 284—the passage was often quoted in 1957) that landowners and usurers were not evil but provided credit for peasants, and that land reform and rent reduction would not solve the rural problem. In *Xiangtu chongjian,* he had expressed sympathy for the plight of the landowners, had depicted them as frugal and not much better off than the peasants, had had good words for the gentry as local leaders, and had argued against violent revolution.

Fei's urging landlords to become productive industrial managers was called advising them to become capitalist exploiters as land-based exploitation became untenable. Blaming the rural problem on overpopulation and external economic pressure, it was said, was a cover-up of the real evil, private ownership and landlord exploitation. His proposals for rural industry were for the purpose of preserving the feudal land system by enabling peasants to pay rent, interest, and taxes. Rural cooperatives, which had also been promoted by the Guomindang, would inevitably be dominated by landlord types, as had happened (it was claimed) with the Kaixiangong silk cooperative.

He was also accused of having been a slave to the imperialists. One critic called him a "cultural compradore" who lacked a national sense and was willing to betray his country for money and academic advancement: Fei's career had consisted of selling intelligence about China's economic and political conditions to the imperialists, and selling bourgeois theories in China in order to anesthetize the Chinese in preparation for an imperialist cultural invasion.[83] He had curried favor with and followed Malinowski. He had praised Anglo-American political democracy and urged China to imitate it. He had maintained close relations with people like the Fairbanks, who were U.S. government agents (true), and he had taken refuge in the American consulate after the Li-Wen assassinations.

Of his activities and writings from the early 1950s there was surprisingly little criticism. It was said he had conspired with Qinghua President Qian Weichang and others to oppose the reorganization of universities which resulted in the elimination of sociology departments. Lin Yaohua, off the mark again, made a half-hearted argument that *China's Gentry* could not have been published in the United States in 1953 without Fei's consent, which showed he must have kept up his connections with imperialists.

There were vague charges that he had neglected political study and had not even read newspapers and that, in spite of being well treated with over twenty important positions, he had still grumbled and been dissatisfied.

Practically nothing was said about his work on nationalities affairs. Apart from the statement that his articles had been stolen from others, one can find only a few vague and brief comments accusing him of resisting the Party's direction in nationalities work; maintaining that socialism was incompatible with the preservation of national forms; overemphasizing the superstructure of minorities societies and neglecting the determinative role of the economic base; and stirring up friction between Han and minority nationalities with his complaints about greater Han chauvinism.[84] But these were just a few passing remarks, not sustained argument.

Most of the scores of articles against Fei in 1957–1958 attacked his activities during the Hundred Flowers period, both on behalf of intellectuals and also with respect to the restoration of "bourgeois sociology." It was, perhaps significantly, charges regarding the first, his Democratic League work with intellectuals, that came earliest in the course of the Anti-Rightist Movement.

His confession before the National People's Congress on July 13, for example, mentioned only briefly his efforts for bourgeois social science and the old social scientists, and only briefly his articles on Kaixiangong (he said they had stressed the negative, sowing discord between the peasants and the Party). The emphasis, rather, was all on having urged the organization of forums for intellectuals to discuss, off the record, their concerns. He had, he confessed, both in Peking and in his travels around the country, encouraged backward intellectuals to express their grievances. His article on "Early Spring" had publicized their dissatisfactions and had been a signal releasing anti-Communist and anti-socialist attacks from them. His recommendation to intellectuals to concentrate on their professional work and on raising their professional level amounted to saying that ideological reform should be secondary. He had cooperated with League leaders Luo and Zhang, providing unfavorable information about intellectuals' conditions for their speeches. He had wanted the Democratic League to speak for intellectuals, to support their demands in the People's Congress and the Political Consultative Conference in order to influence public opinion and Party policy. This, he now realized, would have had the effect of driving a wedge between the intellectuals and the Party, and (since it was backward intellectuals he had been encouraging to speak out) would have made the League into a political party of the bourgeoisie. He had said he wanted all to share in the work of the state advancing to socialism; this was equivalent to advocating seizing power from the Communist Party (1957Jl13).

Others developed these themes, particularly the idea that, in his Democratic League work with intellectuals, Fei had tried to stir up discontent by encouraging them to express their grievances. He had collected grievances in Yunnan, one writer there wrote, as though he were an imperial commissioner sent to uncover wrongdoing.[85] Many condemned his "Early Spring" article. It was said to have played on the mentality of those intellectuals who wanted more professional research and less teaching, politics, and Marxist leadership. He had meant to turn intellectuals against the Party by suggesting that it had shut them out, that it could not lead scientific research, and that Marxist education was simplistic.[86] Lack of faith in the Party had been expressed in the statements about fearing the return of cold weather (when in fact the sun was so warm) and about intellectuals greeting Zhou's 1956 speech as a second Liberation (which implied they had not been liberated in 1949). Fei's admonition to intellectuals to take an interest in events such as the uprisings in Poland and Hungary were called an inflammatory incitement to similar anti-socialist, anti-Party politics in China.[87] His talk of lifting the two lids suppressing scientific research and intellectuals' political expression was said to have amounted to opposing Marxism-Leninism and Party leadership.[88]

Fei's opposition to Party leadership in institutes of higher education and his desire to increase the influence of the Democratic League proved, to his accusers, that he wanted to change the relationship of leaders and led, to equalize power and then, with the other rightists, to seize it in order to restore capitalism.[89] In the early stages of the Anti-Rightist Movement, there was much attention paid to contacts and ties between Luo Longji, Zhang Bojun, Fei, and other arch rightists, contacts which allegedly proved there was a real political conspiracy. Intellectual contending and even criticism of Party leadership and socialist construction were permissible, it was said, but not political conspiracy. Fei and the others had been attempting to use the freedom of the Hundred Flowers policy deliberately to set fire to and burn down the whole house of the nation.[90]

Fei's suggestions for a limited revival of social science were depicted as part of a plot to replace Marxism. After the first couple of months of the Anti-Rightist Movement, most of the writing on Fei shifted to documenting this attempt to restore bourgeois sociology and to analyzing why it was pernicious. We have already seen Fei's published remarks about the need for sociological study of the new society and his actions which contributed to the formation of the Sociology Work Committee. There is no question that Fei was indeed attempting to get old sociologists back to research, sociology back to the universities, and sociological writings back in print. The problem was to demonstrate to the reading public why this was a crime.

In late 1957 and 1958, a number of long and serious theoretical articles were published attempting to prove the reactionary nature of "bourgeois sociology."[91] This critique, which had its Soviet predecessors,[92] involved long excursions into the history of sociology and extended discussions of Comte, Spencer, and later schools of sociology. We need not follow this argument into its details; it is enough to note the general burden. It was said that bourgeois sociology had been progressive at first, when subverting feudalism, but had lost its revolutionary nature when the bourgeoisie became the ruling class. It had consistently supported the bourgeois capitalist order by justifying its social divisions, extolling social harmony, and generally depicting capitalist society as just and the highest stage of social development. The social reformism which had often been associated with sociology merely shored up the status quo without changing its economic exploitation and political oppression. European and American sociologists, fearful of the legacy of the French Revolution and of mass movements, had denied the irreconcilability of class conflict, and had opposed violent revolution and Marxism. Their theories were idealistic, depicting society as determined by factors other than the relations of production, as historical materialism held. Bourgeois sociology, finally, was not scientific, for it merely described facts and drew random conclusions; science should discover objective laws—the only true science of society is Marxism-Leninism.

As for anthropology, it had served imperialism by providing information on primitive colonial peoples that was used in controlling them. Firth's *Human Types,* which Fei had translated (*RWLX*), was quoted to show that anthropologists provided this service knowingly: "Modern anthropology is practical. . . . Colonial governments have known it is important to use anthropology in dealing with aborigines."[93] Functionalism, it was said, had not been concerned with explaining origins or the history of systems but with pointing out functions, in order that colonial administrators could handle peoples more effectively. It had stressed the unity of society, denied class war, and did not recognize that the cultural superstructure is determined by the economic base.[94]

Chinese sociology, it was pointed out, had been imported from England and America. The earliest sociology departments had been in missionary colleges, the first social research was largely carried out by Americans, and later Chinese investigations had been supported by foreign foundation and government monies, obviously for the purpose of colllecting intelligence about various parts of China. Subsequently, Chinese sociology was given limited support by the Guomindang Government, which found it useful in gathering information for police control, training cadres, preventing strikes, and directing attention to social "problems" and away from the basic cause of these problems which was feudal exploitation. Chinese sociology, in short, had been anti-Marxist and reformist, serving imperialists and the Guomindang.[95]

Fei and others had argued in early 1957 that, although the old sociology had not been Marxist, there were portions, particularly research methods, which could be useful in building a new socialist sociology. The answer to this argument was that Chinese Communists had developed excellent techniques of social investigation (*shehui diaocha*), going back to the Chairman's own investigations of the peasant movement in Hunan and of rural counties in Jiangxi in the late 1920s and early 1930s. Communists already had absorbed what was useful of sociological methods, and had the advantage of being trusted by the people who would give them information; hundreds of cadres, with the same language and habits as the peasants and taking a proletarian point of view, could conduct investigations that would represent the true interests of the peasantry. Moreover, they used Marxist objective laws and class analysis. The result was studies that were truly helpful in socialist construction. For instance, one author claimed, all 176 articles in the 1956 book *The Socialist Upsurge in China's Countryside* were better than the rightists' investigations, though the authors were not PhDs.[96]

It was in this context that the criticisms of Fei's pre-1949 work were made. His reliance on landlord informants, the desire to avoid violent revolution, and so on were held to invalidate the whole sociological research tradition. The point was not simply to criticize Fei for comments made long ago but to discredit completely the methods and practitioners of the old sociology.

That, too, was the reason so much attention was paid to pointing out flaws in his articles about the revisit to Kaixiangong. In September 1957, the Central Institute of Nationalities sent a team of eight scholars to the village to collect data to disprove Fei's assertions, particularly that the rise in per capita income had been at best very modest. They found that Fei's figures were wrong, and that, if corrections were made (such as deducting rent and interest from 1936 income, and excluding two other poorer villages from the 1956 average), there was indeed a substantial increase in per capita net income for the village. Just how much this increase was varies from article to article,[97] and in no case is it explained how the figures were obtained. I find most of these statistics—and Fei's as well—impossible to reconcile with each other and basically not very confidence-inspiring; I suspect that desire to refute Fei's findings may have led to some distortions. To be sure, some of the criticisms of his article are well taken. One was that, by giving average figures for the whole village instead of class by class, he failed to recognize the fact that life had improved enormously for the majority and that the gap between rich and poor had narrowed considerably; and class-by-class income figures for various years were given to show this. Fei might have replied that he had indeed mentioned that socialism had improved the life of the majority and that he did not have class-by-class figures for 1936 (where did his critics get theirs?), but there is probably merit to the point that, by neglecting class analysis, his articles missed one of the big changes.

As to Fei's major point, the decline in income from subsidiary enterprises, it was argued, on the one hand, that this had been overstated and, on the other, that it was due to reasons that could not be helped. Kaixiangong's sericulture had declined because the factory and the mulberry trees had been destroyed by the Japanese and the Nationalists, and also because sericulture was now being promoted in areas that used to export mulberry leaves to Kaixiangong. Furthermore, compared to 1948, income from sericulture had actually risen. As to the decline of boat commerce, this had been capitalist exploitation which increased the gap between rich and poor and diverted energies from cooperative agriculture. Fei overstated the 1936 income from sheep-raising, saying there had been a thousand in the village when, in fact, the villagers said there had never been more than four hundred and *Peasant Life* itself only claimed five hundred (p. 237). Moreover, other sideline industries, such as pisceculture, had developed. Fei's suggestion that the silk factory be reestablished was to be rejected on several economic grounds, mainly that it was not needed and would conflict with the interests of other silk-producing villages and urban silk workers, and that both villagers' and governmental investment funds would be better spent on other projects.

The argument was also made that it would have been fairer for judging the achievements of socialism to compare 1956 with 1948 rather than 1936. Since 1936 had been an unusually good year followed by considerable war damage, taking 1948 data as a base showed considerable greater improvement in villagers' income. The figures are given, all with great precision, though again it is not clear where they came from or whether Fei had access to them. Other points too seem plausible, if not all of great importance. It was argued that it was unfair to compare 1936 net income (after rent, taxes, and interest) with 1956 net income, some of the deductions from which went into the public accumulation fund and public welfare fund which benefited all. If there was some tightness in the food supply, it was said, this was because there had been a famine in other parts of the province that year, and therefore more than the usual amount of grain had been purchased by the state (with the result that nine million refugees were aided); and what was left (a later supplement brought it to the equivalent of 572 catties of unhusked rice per person) was plenty for all—with the exception of a few families with lots of adults, and for them the problem was really caused by the system of equal allocation regardless of age or sex. It was said that improvements in standard of living could be seen in new water wheels, boats, thermoses, sneakers, pens, suits, and houses—which Fei had in fact remarked on. Furthermore, schooling was greatly increased and illiteracy had dropped since 1948 from 66 percent to 11 percent for males and from 97 percent to 56 percent for females. Villagers could now see a movie about every month.[98]

In sum, it was said, Fei's study had understated the great achievements and improvements in the standard of living made since Liberation and concentrated on negative details. It was thus an attack on collectivization. Since sociology was anti-socialist and anti-Marxist, its revival was not an academic question, concerning which free discussion was theoretically guaranteed under the Hundred Flowers principle, but a political one. It involved ideology and an attempt to restore capitalism and bourgeois control. Fei's efforts for sociology were thus connected with the opposition of the rightists in the democratic parties to Communist leadership.

That, then, was the case against Fei Xiaotong. The facts were generally true, but the interpretations put on them were another matter. The sociological tradition in which he had been trained was indeed anti-revolutionary; Fei had certainly not been a Marxist in the 1940s and his pre-1949 works contain views which are by that standard heretical, such as his opposition to violent revolution. His functionalist outlook no doubt led him to understate the degree of class conflict and exploitation in rural China. But many more anti-landlord than pro-landlord sentences could be plucked from his works, and a fair-minded reading will find his chief sympathy was with the peasants. It was this sympathy with the plight of China's peasants and his consequent disgust with the inadequacies of the Nationalist Government that seem to have most impressed his readers in the 1940s. He certainly had close relations with foreigners and was influenced by foreign ideas but, far from being an agent of imperialism, he had been most critical of American support for the Nationalists.

His Kaixiangong article may have underplayed the accomplishments of collectivization but, all the same, the fact is the peasants were still terribly poor, and he was trying to make constructive suggestions in their interests. He believed it would be helpful to point out, for example, shortcomings in the management of cooperatives, such as the neglect of subsidiary industries. Criticisms of this sort were made by Party cadres without incurring charges of opposing socialism. The case against Fei really rested on the assumption that he was trying to damage the cooperative movement, an assumption that probably stemmed as much from that fact that his remarks were published and came from a non-Party, old intellectual as from what he actually said.

The real reason for silencing the likes of Fei Xiaotong, no doubt, had less to do with the bourgeois nature of sociology than with the charges against him that came up first in the Anti-Rightist Movement, about organizing the intellectuals and publicizing their views. Chairman Mao himself suggested as much in October 1957, in a passage now preserved in his *Selected Works:*

> Fei Xiaotong, for one, has over two hundred friends among the

higher intellectuals in places like Peking, Shanghai, Chengdu, Wuhan and Wuxi. He simply cannot break away from the group and, what is more, *he has made a conscious effort to organize these people and has aired views on their behalf.* That's the source of his trouble. I would ask, can't you change a little? Chuck your group of two hundred and seek another two hundred among workers and peasants.[99]

Mao had called for criticism of Party and government cadres to keep them from becoming aloof and arrogant bureaucrats, but he had wanted a "mass" democracy of the peasants and common people, not the "bourgeois" democracy of "the professors" and democratic parties.[100] To many Communists, no doubt, the activities of old intellectuals like Fei during the Hundred Flowers period seemed a direct political challenge.

The intellectuals' public criticism of Party leadership, their demands for a more democratic sharing of power, and the possibility they might even organize to exercise a modicum of political influence—these were alarming to revolutionaries whose experience had taught them that politics was a deadly struggle for power. Above all, what made intellectuals like Fei dangerous was their prestige and their ability to exercise influence by means of the press, which the Chinese Communists have seen as nothing more or less than a political weapon. Because Fei's views were published, it was feared they would dampen the popular enthusiasm needed for the great tasks facing China. Mao has spoken of the need to "preserve enthusiasm, encourage hard work and the spirit of surging ahead," and seems to have felt that the rightists' criticisms were intended to undermine this.[101] The agricultural cooperatives, for example, had not been a universal success, and there appears to have been some public sentiment against them; in this context, Fei's talk of problems with cooperative management must have seemed highly subversive.

Under the circumstances, the Communists inevitably saw much to fear in the tendency of intellectuals like Fei to be skeptical and critical, a tendency associated with the modern scientific tradition. Those trained as scientists, including social scientists, have believed it important not to accept ideas on authority, but to subject as much as possible to rigorous empirical testing. This attitude has, to be sure, often made them blind to their own biases or reduced them to collecting meaningless facts, but it has also made them skeptical about received doctrine and the declarations of authorities. It was this critical spirit, the threat that independent social investigation might not only cool off popular enthusiasm about current improvements but even call into question official social theory, which we may suspect made sociology unpalatable to the Chinese leadership. In that sense, then, the problem with the intellectual tradition of which Fei was a part was not that it was inherently conservative, but that it was radical.

Epilogue: Return of the Hundred Flowers

One part of the message of Fei Xiaotong's 1940s writings had been that the peasant economy was collapsing, and that it was the responsibility of intellectuals to do something about this. It was the Communists and not the intellectuals, however, who had the capability of bettering the life of the peasants and, sensing this, Fei and other intellectuals supported them. He must be pleased with much that has happened since. Many of the things he wanted for Chinese society seem to be coming closer. Peasant welfare is increasing materially, culturally, and in terms of social status and self-respect. Small-scale rural industry is helping develop the countryside. Vast numbers of young intellectuals have gone to villages both to be useful and also to overcome their contempt for manual labor and to bridge the gap between city and country. The social cohesion of the village community Fei wanted to retain has been strengthened by the production team, that collective unit of twenty to forty families who together own the land, till it, and share its produce. China is finding her own path, not blindly following either tradition or foreign ways, but developing new social forms built on the old and appropriate for modernization. These were all developments he had hoped for.

But the three things Fei stood for most of all—independent and critical study of society, pluralistic discussion of public issues in the press, and cosmopolitan openness to the outside world—have all been sharply curtailed in new China, particularly in the twenty years following the Hundred Flowers. Even the word for "sociology" is missing from a recent dictionary from China.[102] To be sure, it is possible to argue that there is a kind of sociology in China, though not that of the "old sociologists."[103] Social theory is regarded as important—so important that it is considered the exclusive province of the Party—and, because this theory has been widely propagated, there is among the masses an impressive awareness of social categories and forces.[104] There is also a Chinese Communist tradition of "social investigation," carried out by government cadres for specific purposes.[105] Indeed, Mao keenly felt the need for administrators to be well informed about social conditions and urged his Party cadres to undertake a kind of village study.[106] But Communist social theorizing and investigation are done by Party and government non-professionals; the results of investigations are not published; and they are surely colored by political preconceptions and political needs. This is quite different from the kind of sociology Fei stood for—scholarly research and writing by independent specialized professionals who think of themselves as scientists impartially seeking truth.

In the decades following the Hundred Flowers, Fei himself disappeared from view, disgraced, half-forgotten. He was not able to do research on Chinese society, to teach, to publish his views, to maintain his foreign contacts, or to contribute his skills to building a new China. Yet, compared to many others, he was treated most leniently. No fewer than 110,000 people, according to unofficial reports, arrested in the Anti-Rightist Movement were held in jail for twenty-one years until 1978.[107] Fei, protected perhaps by his national and international reputation, fared much better. The wordy campaign against him was intended to discredit him as an intellectual leader, destroy his influence and that of others like him, and educate all intellectuals who held similar views; apart from the pain of public vilification, he was not much punished. He was not legally classed a counter-revolutionary or enemy of the people (as were some rightists); he was not arrested, sent to labor reform, or in any way treated as a criminal.

He was relieved of his most important posts, particularly those of National People's Congress Deputy and Central Institute of Nationalities Vice President. But (according to my Nationalities Institute informant) he was kept on in the research department of the Institute, being dropped only one rank in the professorial scale and thus suffering only a slight reduction in salary, and keeping his comfortable house on the Institute campus. As early as late 1958 and 1959, he was reelected to the Democratic League Central Committee and named to the Chinese People's Political Consultative Conference's Third National Committee (impotent remnants of past united-front policies, to be sure, but nonetheless a sign of forgiveness). On December 4, 1959, it was announced that, as he had truly reformed, his "rightist" label would be removed.[108]

In the 1960s, little was heard of him. He was, I was told, part of an Academy of Sciences national minorities research team, working with Pan Guangdan and Wu Wenzao; but nothing with their names on it was published as far as I know. In 1962, an article by him appeared in the Hong Kong Communist newspaper *Wen hui bao*, telling about a visit to his father, then eighty-four years old, in Suzhou. It compared his father's happy, well-treated old age to the neglect of old people he had seen in America in 1943–1949, and went on to describe how enthusiastic everyone was under socialism where "everyone is master" and under the leadership of the Communist Party (1962Mr9). No doubt he hoped this might begin his return as a writer, but it was not to be. As far as I know, nothing by Fei Xiaotong was published in China in the long years from 1957 to 1979. In 1963, he wrote Routledge and Kegan Paul, his London publishers, asking that *Peasant Life in China* never again be reprinted, to which they agreed. In a way, there was symbolic truth in the published catalogue of the University of Michigan's Asia Library, which says he died in 1975.

During the Cultural Revolution, his name did not come up in the press, but it was doubtless a difficult time for him; his friend Pan Guangdan is said to have been driven to suicide. From

November 1969 to February 1972, he spent over two years in the countryside at physical labor and political study at what is called a May Seventh Cadre School. He came back proud of his biceps from growing cotton and building brick houses, and it may well have been a not unpleasant relief after the tensions of the Cultural Revolution.

Returning to Peking in early 1972, just after Nixon's visit so dramatically signaled the resumption of ties with the United States, Fei suddenly surfaced as a greeter of foreign visitors to the Central Institute of Nationalities. His reputation abroad and his fluency in English as well as his sociable temperament made him a fine spokesman, and in the next few years he was seen by dozens of foreigners; I have spoken or corresponded with many of them.[109] The majority, who were inclined to view the People's Republic favorably, found him cheerful, ebullient, enthusiastic about life in new China, and sincere in criticizing his old work as paternalistic and condescending to the peasantry. Others, predisposed to be skeptical, thought Fei acted as though he were playing a charade which everyone knew to be false. (One concludes that, in these brief and unnatural contacts between Chinese and foreigners, much depends on the eye of the beholder.)

His conversation tended to be more about the Institute than his own activities. Right after returning from his two years in the countryside, he spoke of how the experience of manual labor had finally enabled him to share the outlook of the peasants, something his old studies had fatally lacked, and the implication seemed to be that now he could engage in a new kind of anthropology, free of the defects of the old. Later that year, however, when the political atmosphere grew chillier, he stated flatly that there could be no more anthropology in China ("Interview"), and for several years we heard no more about research. There were some indications he was spending his time making translations from English.

Then everything changed. Following Mao's death and the arrest of the Gang of Four in 1976, China's new leaders, apparently alarmed at the economic stagnation and social disorder of the Cultural Revolution and following years, decided that "modernization" was more important than anything else. Anti-elitist and egalitarian policies have been de-emphasized. Academic education is being strengthened, cultural controls relaxed, and scholarly work depoliticized. The Hundred Flowers slogan has been revived, and indeed included in the 1978 Constitution. It is now admitted that, in 1957, although a few rightists took advantage of the policy, attacked the Party and socialism, and had to be opposed, most were branded rightists erroneously, and this had an unfortunate inhibiting effect on blooming and contending for twenty years. Intellectuals are now considered workers and not bourgeois, and mental work is said to be just as important as manual. Socialist democracy and intellectual liberation from dogma are regarded as necessary for modernizing. That China should learn from abroad has changed from heresy to the official line.

A strong effort to strengthen research and teaching in the natural sciences and technical subjects has brought in its wake new life for the "social sciences." A Chinese Academy of Social Sciences was established in 1977, parallel with the prestigious Academy of Sciences and headed by the old Communist writer Hu Qiaomu, who is said to have close ties with Deng Xiaoping. In addition to institutes for research and graduate education in various fields of economics, law, history, archaeology, linguistics, literature, journalism, philosophy, and even religion, there is also an Institute of Nationalities Studies (or ethnic studies, or ethnology), of which Fei is a Deputy Director. Research on national minorities is once again being encouraged. As early as late 1976, Fei was talking to foreign visitors about plans for social research concerning minorities on questions of practical use to the government, and in the spring of 1978 he addressed a meeting of two hundred people convened by the Academy of Social Sciences to plan research on minorities.[110] Periodicals concerned with national minorities are appearing again, and the publication has been announced of a series of histories of all of China's fifty-odd nationalities, apparently based on the work done by Fei and others from 1956 to 1964.[111] In the spring of 1979, a big national planning conference in Kunming mapped out a long series of nationalities research topics for the next five years, and established a Nationalities Research Society with Fei as one of the vice presidents.[112]

For awhile, it seemed that sociology and social research on Han Chinese were not to be included in this revival. Then, in early 1979 came the startling announcement that a Chinese Society of Sociology was being founded, with Fei Xiaotong as President. At the founding meeting, Hu Qiaomu spoke of the importance of sociological research, which had been suspended since 1957. Sociology is a branch of science and it is wrong to forbid its existence, he said, urging "sociologists" to study "current social problems, facts and phenomena inside China and try to furnish some answers."[113] The Academy of Social Sciences is setting up a sociological research institute, and there is even talk of reestablishing university sociology departments.

In this new atmosphere, Fei has returned to national prominence, just as in the 1950s. His name is in the papers again, and even occasionally a picture. He is a member of the standing committee of the Chinese People's Political Consultative Conference, newly important as an organization for democratic consultation and discussion of political affairs among people of various walks of life. He is associated with the Democratic League again, which had not been heard of in years.[114] He is on a committee appointed by the standing committee of the National People's Congress for strenthening the legal system (its chairman, Peng Zhen, once Mayor of Peking, fresh from ten years in jail).[115] As in the Hundred Flowers period, he is traveling, going in 1978 on trips to Sichuan, Ningxia, Guangxi, and even abroad—for the first time since the 1940s—to Japan. Then, in the spring of 1979, he came to the United States for a few weeks as part of a delegation of the Chinese Academy of Social Sciences looking at American social science and considering sending students to study here.[116]

The final element in the resurrection of Fei was publication. This came in the early months of 1979 when the foreign-language magazine *China Reconstructs* carried two articles by him on his recent trips to Sichuan and Guangxi ("Szechuan" and "Yao Revisit").

These articles are less significant for what they say than for being the first pieces from Fei's hand (as far as I know) to be published in China in the twenty-two years since 1957. That this reemergence into print should be in a magazine for foreign consumption is an indication of his importance once more in his old role of cultural mediator (in the mid-1950s, too, Fei's Hundred Flowers flurry of articles were preceded by some rather bland pieces in English— "Names" for example), but we shall probably soon be seeing more substantial works in Chinese from this notable writer.

Fei is finally moving back towards the kinds of work he had done before: social research, international communication, and writing. He is seventy years old now, however, and those long lost decades cannot be recovered. In the years that are left, what he himself can accomplish at these tasks is less significant than training younger successors to carry on this work. This, I suspect, is his urgent concern at the moment.

At this point, Fei seems vindicated. China has come again to value at least a good part of what he represented. Yet his experiences suggest that these trends may be vulnerable. He and his kind were products of a peculiar historical situation, of foreign influence over important sectors of Chinese economy and society, which no longer exists. Without any loci of power outside the Party and government, and without an institutionalized liberal tradition, the activities of intellectuals are apt to be subject to the whim of the authorities. Whatever kind of sociology develops in China, it surely will not be independent of government control.[117] A requirement that social research be on problems of concern to the government would not on the surface be distasteful for someone like Fei, for whom the goal of sociology had always been improving social policies. Yet it is all too easy to imagine how just this reformist impulse, calling for a focus on what needs correcting in society, can get sociology into trouble with leaders unwilling to have the defects of current social conditions exposed, and by implication their policies questioned, by muckrakers. This radical potential of sociology will surely result in much greater restrictions on it than on the natural sciences. Even more vulnerable is the publication of a wide variety of views such as we saw in the Republican period, now that the press is firmly controlled by a government and Party which strongly believe in the importance of propaganda and ideology. But perhaps, as the world grows smaller, as the problems and possibilities of social engineering grow, and as the empirical and anti-dogmatic values associated with modern science become more widely accepted, the long-term trend is toward international communication, social science, and public discussion of current issues. If so, Fei Xiaotong may one day be seen as swimming with the tide of history rather than against it.

POSTSCRIPT, MARCH 1981

Fei is now more and more in evidence as a public figure. He serves on various government bodies, such as a committee to oversee the granting of academic degrees throughout the nation.[118] He was one of the judges at the trial of the Gang of Four, and has written a preface for a book about it, expressing satisfaction at the progress towards rule of law.[119] In August 1980, his 1957 designation as a "rightist" was finally declared to have been in error.[120] He is mentioned in the press more often, occasionally at length, as in a recent full profile with photograph in a national newspaper.[121] His receipt of an international anthropology award in the United States made the front page of *Renmin ribao*.[122] He travels with astonishing frequency: in 1978 to Japan; in the spring of 1979 to the United States; in the fall to Canada, where he lectured at eleven universities; in 1980 briefly to the United States again; in late 1980 and early 1981 back to Canada and the United States—and a trip to Britain is planned for 1981.

Yet, in his sociological activities, Fei maintains a lower profile. Compared with the pace of changes in other areas of Chinese society and in Sino-American relations, the restoration of sociology is proceeding slowly, and Fei appears deliberately cautious. He is still as likely to be identified as Vice-Director of the Academy of Social Sciences' Institute of Ethnology as by one of his titles involving sociology.[123] The 1980 meeting of the Chinese Society of Sociology, addressed by Fei as President, was covered in the press, but little more was reported than that Fei stressed the importance of sociological investigation for China's modernization, and that the meeting resolved that Chinese sociologists should concentrate on finding solutions to social problems like population, marriage, and juvenile delinquency.[124] There seems to be little public discussion of plans for sociological research, and no signs that any is under way. In early 1980, a delegation of American social scientists found sociology yet to be taught in a single Chinese university, and sociological journals still only in planning stages. The Chinese Academy of Social Sciences' Institute of Sociology, of which Fei is Director, is taking shape slowly, with Fei and a staff of ten working out of an apartment in Peking. (Fei is still living in his same house at the Central Institute of Nationalities.)

A major difficulty in reviving sociology, not surprisingly, is the paucity of trained sociologists. Many of the names now being mentioned were Fei's colleagues or students in the 1940s. Zhang Ziyi, Yuan Fang, Li Youyi, who had been at the Yunnan Research Station, and Zhang Luoqun, a co-author of *Renxing he jiqi,* were seen in Peking in 1980 by visiting American sociologists. Gu Bao is said to be at a Nationalities Research Institute in Urumqi, and Hu Qingjun at the Institute for Nationalities Studies of the Academy of Social Sciences.[125] Among the vice-presidents of the Chinese Society of Sociology are Lin Yaohua and Tian Rukang, the latter recently at Cambridge University on leave from Fudan University, Shanghai. The Society's advisers include aged professors Wu Wenzao (Fei's old college teacher), Li Jinghan, Chen Hansheng, Li Anzhe, and Yan Xinzhe.[126]

Fei seems cautious in what he writes. He is publishing more, but compared to other things appearing these days—exposé literature, criticisms of cadres, doctrinal reexaminations—or even to his own writings of the Hundred Flowers period, his articles have a tone as though on guard against providing ammunition to the enemies of sociology. His tame 1979 English article, noted before, about a trip to the Yao mountains and the improvements there since 1935

(1979Jl15), has appeared in Chinese magazines. His contribution to the inaugural issues of the Academy of Social Sciences' Chinese- and English-language journals was about how to tell which groups constitute true "nationalities" (1980Ja10a; "Ethnic Identification")—an old question, of practical concern to the government, on which Fei had written similarly decades ago (1956Ag). An afterword to his Chinese translation of C.G. Seligman's *Races of Africa* told how his finished manuscript, on the verge of publication in 1966, was destroyed in the Cultural Revolution, so that he had to translate the work again in 1978–1979 (1980Ja10b). It is no small thing that works of Western social science can again be published in China, but this book seems an unexciting choice. Seligman, a British anthropological pioneer born in 1873, was a *predecessor* of Malinowski, and his book is now half a century old. Fei says he also made translations of H.G. Wells's *Outline of History,* which goes back to 1920, and of a 1932 *World History* by C.J.H. Hayes, P.T. Moon, and J.W. Wayland.[127]

Following his visit to the United States in April and May 1979, Fei wrote at length about how American society had changed since 1943–1944, when he had last seen it. "Fang-Mei lüe ying" ("Glimpses of America"; *FMLY*) was printed in 27 installments in the Shanghai paper *Wen hui bao,* and is also appearing as a booklet. With his prior experience, contacts with American social scientists, lively mind, and fluent pen, Fei is well placed to interpret the United States to Chinese, even after a visit of only a month. He wrote of air travel, the interstate highway network, the proliferation of automobiles, and the speed of American life. He was impressed with the long-distance telephone, which he said permitted a new kind of social community not limited to spatial propinquity, and by computers and electronic control devices. He described the affluence of middle-class American life, suburban houses, home appliances which make housework a pleasure, supermarkets and shopping centers, and a professor's family budget.

Yet all his positive comments were balanced with reminders about American social problems. Though poverty had been virtually eliminated, crime and drug addiction were increasing, and the growth of suburbs had left inner cities to decay. The race problem had been solved for blacks only of the upper stratum. Even for Chinese-Americans, who could now become professors in the universities because of government-imposed quotas, it was doubtful whether true equality had been achieved. Middle-class life made people prisoners of huge debts, while inflation and the energy crisis enriched big business. Yet, instead of asking the big questions of why so many people become criminals and addicts, Americans just put locks on their doors and discussed the legalization of marijuana. American social science had turned away from social theory to practical research; scholars, now in the service of government, political campaigns, and advertisers, worked mostly on solving problems and staving off crises for the ruling class. In the end Fei was somber, relieved to see less long hair than on American visitors to China in recent years, but appalled at the 50 percent divorce rate. He dared not visit Times Square, was made uneasy by a female professor discussing the erotic novel *Jin ping mei,* and wondered if the decline and fall of the Roman Empire was being repeated. The problem was, he said, that the social system was the same old capitalism and, while individuals were more and more dependent on others, they felt society was less and less dependable. Americans had lost faith in the political system and in traditional values; instead they were attracted to unconventional religions such as that which ended in Jonestown (*FMLY*).

The Society for Applied Anthropology gave Fei its annual award in 1980 in Denver. The award is named for Malinowski, and Fei's address, "Toward a People's Anthropology," was full of warm sentiment about his mentor and about being reunited after so many decades with "you who are my old friends." He then went on, skirting the difficulties of Chinese social science in the past years, to argue that much could be learned from the achievements of anthropology in the People's Republic. Malinowski, Fei said, had contributed greatly towards a more human relationship between the anthropologist and the people he studied, but he must have been frustrated by the distrust natives felt for him. Fei's own early work, though among his own people, had been hampered by class barriers. After 1949, things were different. "Compared to my former experience, I found myself warmly received when I carried out my field work among minority people. . . . It was simply because the people I studied knew and believed that I meant to help," for this research was "in the service of the state's political work," and in China "our politics is politics in service of the masses."

The only article specifically about sociology I have read (though I have heard the titles of others, perhaps in internal publications) is a recent newspaper piece, addressed to young people, on how he took up sociology. Among other things, Fei mentioned taking on the mission of reestablishing Chinese sociology two years ago, and of the trepidation he felt. But he offered no specifics about what kind of social research was contemplated, other than to suggest that, unlike natural science, social science cannot be imported from abroad (this, like his insistence that American social science is practical and untheoretical, suggests that Fei is heading off the charge that he is importing bourgeois social theory), and that it would be useful to society. "Many of my teachers and friends from the world of sociology did not survive the ten calamitous years. That I have some life left is unexpected, and I feel I should use it well to prove concretely that sociology is a discipline which can serve the people" (1980N1).

Fei (and many others like him) suffered much from 1957 to 1976. For most of those years he was unable to do scholarly work; when not actually being attacked as a rightist he was apt to be shunned by his colleagues;[128] survey data on minorities he and others had collected in the 1950s was destroyed in the Cultural Revolution;[129] and the strain has taken a heavy toll on his wife. That these years are over, and that Fei Xiaotong is once again able to travel, write, and work to rebuild Chinese sociology, is a joy not only to him but to all who share his ideals.

Notes

Bibliography

Glossary

Index

Notes

PREFACE

1. Fei's works are still cited today. The *Social Sciences Citation Index* (Philadelphia, annual), lists, for example, four citations of Fei's works in articles published in 1970, eight for 1973, and seven for 1976.
2. *Shen bao nianjian* (Taibei, 1966; reprint of 1935 edition), pp. S30–31 (994–995 in the reprint edition). In 1932, the United States had 73 students in schools of higher education per 10,000 population; China had 1 (*ibid.*, p. S47 [1011]).
3. *Quanguo Zhongwen jikan lianhe mulu* (National union list of serials; Peking, 1961).
4. R.E. Park, *Race and Culture* (Glencoe, 1950), pp. 356, 376, quoted in Lewis A. Coser, *Masters of Sociological Thought* (New York, 1971), pp. 365–366.
5. Y.C. Wang, *Chinese Intellectuals and the West, 1872–1949* (Chapel Hill, 1966), pp. 377, 374, 500.

1. FAMILY BACKGROUND AND EARLY SCHOOLING

1. Most of this information, unless otherwise indicated, comes from an uncle, an aunt, and several first cousins of Fei's, on both sides of his family, with whom I talked in 1969 in Taiwan, Hong Kong, and England.
2. I have concluded that Fei Xiaotong was not related to the powerful and wealthy Fei family of Wujiang which has been studied in some detail by the great Japanese scholar Muramatsu Yūji in *Kindai Chūgoku kenkyū* 5:1–184 (1964). This long article on the Wujiang Fei family bursary is summarized in English in Muramatsu's "Chinese Landlordism in Late Ch'ing and Early Republican Kiangnan," *Bulletin of the School of Oriental and African Studies* 29:566–599 (1966), and both articles are reprinted in his *Kindai Kōnan no so-san* (Tokyo, 1970). Muramatsu wrote that he

didn't know if Fei Xiaotong was related to this family (p. 181, n. 26), though he later told me in person that he believed he wasn't. The relatives I talked to (who were mostly on his mother's side, to be sure) also generally thought he was not. The strongest evidence, I think, is in Fei's statement that his family had come from Hubei twenty-odd generations before and were still known as the Fei's of Jiangxia (*XTZG*: 78–79); there is no mention of a Hubei background in the histories of the family Muramatsu studied.

3. In another place, he referred to several families of "relatives" who owned two or three hundred *mu* of land (*XTCJ*:93).
4. His other name was Cuiqing, changed after 1911 to Sumin.
5. *Xu Dantu xianzhi* (1930), 10:7b. This says Yang was a native of Zhenze county, which was next to Wujiang, shared the county seat with it, and was reincorporated into it in 1911, but was not where Tongli-zhen is located. Various issues of *Da-Qing jinshen quanshu* from 1890 to 1895 give Suzhou as Yang's native place. According to what his son Yang Xiren told me, both are wrong and he was a native of Wujiang.
6. *Hanzi muyin shi* (2 ce, Zhenjiang, preface 1904); *Zhuidao za yong* (written 1927 and privately printed; Yang Xiren kindly gave me a copy); and *Man-yi hua Xia shimo ji* (2 vols., photo reprint, Taiwan: Huawen shuju, n.d. [probably 1960s]). This last book was important enough to warrant a brief article in a Japanese historical encyclopedia: *Ajia rekishi jiten*, VIII, 381.
7. He is listed in such biographical dictionaries as *Zuijin guan shen lüli huilu* (Peking, 1920), p. 196, and *Dangdai Zhongguo mingren lu* (Shanghai, 1935), p. 339. Perhaps he was the "ex-magistrate" cited by Fei as an informant in *Peasant Life,* pp. 169, 192.
8. The Yangs believe themselves to have non-Chinese blood, and Yang Xiren, telling how Fei had always been interested in things anthropological, showed me something unheard of among Chinese, a thickly hairy chest.
9. This is from Fei Pu'an's own account given to interviewers for a 1961 collection of reminiscences: *Xinhai geming Jiangsu diqu shiliao,* ed. Yangzhou Teachers College History Department (Nanjing, 1961), p. 149. On page 124, it is stated that Fei Pu'an contributed a thousand Chinese dollars to the Red Cross society they organized, but this (which he does not mention himself) may be wrong; all the relatives I have talked to remember him as being not at all rich.
10. The date of her death is from *Zhuidao za yong,* last page. Fei Pu'an subsequently remarried and had several more children.
11. Fei Zhendong studied railway management in Shanghai at the Nanyang Academy (which later became Jiaotong University), and while in school joined the Guomindang. After Chiang Kai-shek purged the Guomindang of

Communists in 1927, he went to Indonesia, where he engaged in newspaper and educational work among the Chinese community for the next decade, and was editor of the Medan, Sumatra, *Min bao* and Secretary to the Medan Chinese Chamber of Commerce. In 1939, he published a translation of Amry Vanderboshch, *The Dutch East Indies* (*Ho-shu Dong-Indu gaikuang,* Changsha, 1939). After the war, which he spent in hiding, back in Medan and a member of the Democratic League, he actively opposed the Guomindang, and on the instigation of the Chinese Consul was expelled to Hong Kong in 1948. In China in the 1950s, apart from posts dealing with Overseas Chinese, he was on the Central Committee of the Democratic League and was a delegate (from Guangxi of all places) to the first National People's Congress. He was (like Xiaotong) criticized as a rightist in 1957, but in 1959 was still a member of the Committee on Overseas Chinese Affairs of the State Council. Most of this information is from *Xin Zhongguo renwu zhi* (Hong Kong, 1950), *xia ji* pp. 54–55; and *Gendai Chūgoku jimmei jiten* (Tokyo, 1966), p. 878.

My estimate of the years of birth of the Fei children starts by accepting as most reliable Yang Dunyi's remark, written in 1927, that, when his wife had died twenty-three years before, her eldest grandson (Fei Zhendong) had been 6 days old (*Zhuidao za yong,* last page). This would make Fei Zhendong a year or two younger than the 48 in 1950 indicated in *Xin Zhongguo renwu zhi.* Fei Dasheng must have been born soon after him, and Fei Qing soon after her, in order for Fei Qing to have been 52 at his death in 1957, August 8, 1957, as stated in *Renmin ribao,* which ought to be reliable, but perhaps was counting Chinese style, and conceivably was following the old practice of adding three years to a person's age in a funeral announcement.

12. Fei Qing was graduated from Suzhou University Law School, and later, in the mid-1930s, studied law in Germany on a national scholarship. He was Dean of the Suzhou University Law School in Shanghai before escaping from Japanese-occupied territory in 1943. He became a professor of law in Kunming during the rest of the war, and at Peking University afterward (he was chairman of the department in 1951). Articles on politics by him, critical of the Nationalists, were published in various journals in the late 1940s. He seems to have been close to Xiaotong in these years, and is mentioned in his writings. After 1949, Fei Qing was the Editor of the biweekly journal *Xin jianshe,* of which Fei Zhendong was a director and Xiaotong a member of the editorial board. He was also a member of the Supreme People's Court and Assistant Dean of the Peking Political Institute, among other posts. He died on July 24, 1957 at 52. See *Renmin ribao,* August 8, 1957; other scraps of information are from the *Qinghua tongxue lu, 1937,* p. 398; *Gendai Chūgoku jimmei jiten* (Tokyo,

1966), p. 878; and the Hong Kong *Dagong bao,* July 23, 1951. Fei Qing's articles can be found in *Zaisheng* in 1932-1933, and in *Zhishi yu shenghuo* and half a dozen other journals in 1947-1948. Fei Xiaotong talks about him in 12/18/43 to WCF, and *MZ, XF, RQ* Chapters 5 and 7.

13. Information on Fei Dasheng is mostly from Zou Jingheng and will be discussed further below in Chapter 3; an article on her and her husband in *Xin guancha* 1957, 13:8-9 has a photograph.
14. Li Changfu, *Fen-sheng dizhi—Jiangsu* (Shanghai, 1936), pp. 299-300; Fan Yanqiao, *Wujiang-xian xiangtu zhi* (1917), passim.
15. Most of this information is from Fei Chengwu, a maternal cousin who lives in London. See also *CFMG:* 109-110.
16. Shen Peixian, "Wujiang linian gaoxiao biyesheng diaocha baogao," *Xin jiaoyu* 7.1:95-116 (September 1923). Of these 113 graduates of the 14 upper primary schools in the district, 69% went on to middle school.
17. Chen Qitian, *Zuijin sa-nian Zhongguo jiaoyu shi* (Taibei, 1962; originally published in 1928 under the pen name Chen Yilin), pp. 225-229.
18. The course was called *xiangtu zhi,* and presumably they read the little book by Fan Yanqiao cited in note 14 above.
19. Japanese Government Railways, *Guide to China* (Tokyo, 1924), pp. 255-264; *Fen-sheng dizhi Jiangsu,* pp. 111-13, 293-295.
20. *Qinghua tongxue lu, 1937,* supplement, p. 7.
21. In 9/7/46 to WCF, Fei told of a reunion with old schoolmates from Zhenhua, including some men.
22. Jessie G. Lutz, *China and the Christian Colleges 1850-1950* (Ithaca, 1971), Chapters 4 and 6.
23. W. B. Nance, *Soochow University* (New York, 1956) has photographs.
24. *The Soochow Annual 1930,* pp. 83-86.
25. Nance, pp. 99-103; Lutz, chapter 7; Kiang Wen-han, *The Chinese Student Movement* (New York, 1948), Chapters 2 and 3; *Chinese Recorder* 58.7:456 (July 1927).
26. E. B. Cressey, *Christian Higher Education in China* (Shanghai, 1928), pp. 7, 67, 99, 105, 113, 168, 186, 191. These figures presumably include the law school in Shanghai.
27. To judge from photographs in *The Soochow Annual 1930.*
28. Pan Guangdan's introduction to Fei's *SYZD,* p. iv.
29. *The Soochow Annual 1930* (Chinese title: *Dongwu niankan*) pp. 43, 228; the photograph is on p. 326, and, unless I am mistaken, Fei is third from the left in the next to last row.
30. Unless otherwise indicated, information about Yanjing is from Dwight W. Edwards, *Yenching University* (New York, 1969), or an early draft of what was to become Philip West, *Yenching University and Sino-Western Relations, 1916-1952* (Cambridge, Mass., 1976).

31. Jesse Lutz, p. 201; *Shen bao nianjian* (1935), pp. S 32–33.
32. West; budget information from *Sili Yanjing daxue yilan* (Beiping, 1930), pp. 332–335.
33. *Guidebook for Students*, 1932.
34. *Faculty Bulletin*, February 13, 1932 (in archives of United Board for Christian Higher Education in Asia, New York).
35. Mrs. Maxwell Stewart, "Self-help for Students" (typescript, in United Board archives).
36. *Sili Yanjing daxue yilan*, pp. 320–331; percentages have been recalculated to exclude those not answering or whose fathers' occupations were not given because retired or dead.
37. Jessie H. Lutz, "December 9, 1935: Student Nationalism and the China Christian Colleges," *Journal of Asian Studies* 26.4:627–648 (1967); John Israel, *Student Nationalism in China, 1927–1937* (Stanford, 1966).

2. EDUCATION IN SOCIOLOGY AND ANTHROPOLOGY

1. Long Guanhai, *Shehuixue yu shehui wenti lun cong* (Taibei, 1964), pp. 79–80. Long appears to have relied heavily on Sun Benwen, *Dangdai Zhongguo shehuixue* (Shanghai, 1948), which I was not able to see while writing this.
2. E. H. Cressey, *Christian Higher Education in China*, pp. 40–44, 58–59; Leonard Shih-lien Hsu, "The Sociological Movement in China," *Pacific Affairs* 4.4: 283–307 (1931); Long Guanhai, *Shehuixue . . .* , pp. 88–89.
3. Chow Tse-tsung, *The May Fourth Movement* (Cambridge, Mass., 1960), p. 208m; Leonard Hsu, *Pacific Affairs* 4.4:289 (1931).
4. He Ganzhi, *Zhongguo qimeng yundong shi* (Shanghai, 1947), pp. 151–189.
5. Long Guanhai, *Shehuixue . . .* , pp. 79–80. The Shenghuo bookstore catalogue for 1935 lists 740 books on sociology, of which 322 are translations, but many of these are really works of Marxist theory.
6. Francis L. K. Hsu, "Sociological Research in China," *Quarterly Bulletin of Chinese Bibliography* n.s. 4.1/4:14 (March–December 1944).
7. Franklin L. Ho (He Lian) discusses this in his "Reminiscences" (1967) in the Columbia University Chinese Oral History Project, pp. 72–78.
8. Shirley S. Garrett, *Social Reformers in Urban China* (Cambridge, Mass., 1970), pp. 98, 111, 117, 133–135.
9. Useful bibliographies may be found in Li Jinghan, "Zhongguo shehui diaocha yundong," *Shehuixue jie* 1:79–100; Francis L. K. Hsu, "Sociological Research in China"; Long Guanhai, *Shehui diaocha gai shu* (Taibei, 1963), pp. 69–90.
10. West, *Yenching University*.
11. *Sili Yanjing daxue yilan*, pp. 234–248; Gideon Chen, "The College

of Public Affairs" (Yanjing pamphlet, 1933, in United Board archives), pp. 22, 25.
12. The requirements changed somewhat while Fei was there, so it is not certain exactly what he took; compare *Yanjing yilan,* pp. 234-236, and *Yenching University Bulletin, College of Arts and Letters, 1932-33* (in United Board archives), pp. 125-141.
13. *Shehuixue jie* 5:191-194 (1931).
14. For example, his *Nongcun lingxiu* (Shanghai, 1930).
15. *Shehuixue kan* 4.1 (July, 1933).
16. Granet's book was published in English translation in 1930, and Chen and Shryock picked up the suggestion in a late 1932 article in *American Anthropologist,* but Fei nowhere indicated that he was aware of these. Marcel Granet, *La civilization chinoise* (Paris, 1929), p. 187; translated as *Chinese Civilization* (London, 1930); T. S. Chen and J. K. Shryock, "Chinese Relationship Terms," *American Anthropologist* 34.4:629-630 (October-December 1932).
17. For English versions, see John Steele, trans., *The I-li* (London, 1917; Taibei, 1966), I, 22-24, 39; and Sidney D. Gamble, *Ting Hsien* (New York, 1954), pp. 380-381.
18. See, for example, articles by Yan Jingyao and Mai Qianzeng in *Shehuixue jie,* Vols. 2, 3, 4, and 5 (1928-1931).
19. See also, among other articles on the subject, his one on the significance and usefulness of contemporary community field research in *Chen bao,* January 9, 1935 ("Shehui yanjiu" no. 66), which was based on Fei's notes of a speech of Wu's.
20. C. K. Yang, interview, 1969.
21. *Shen bao nianjian* (1935), pp. S23-26 (pp. 987-990 in the Taiwan reprint).
22. Most of this information is from the "Foreword" to his magnum opus, *Social Organization of the Northern Tungus* (Shanghai, 1929). Other books are *Social Organization of the Manchus* (Shanghai, 1924), and two works of anthropometrics, *Anthropology of Northern China* (Shanghai, 1923) and *Anthropology of Eastern China and Kwangtung Province* (Shanghai, 1925).
23. Li Ji, interview, 1969.
24. *Social Organization of the Northern Tungus,* pp. 6-12.
25. *Anthropology of Northern China,* pp. 1-4, 118, et passim; *Anthropology of Eastern China,* pp. 113-122, et passim.
26. Chen Da, *Lang ji shi-nian* (Chongquing, 1946), pp. 212-213. Fei later recalled, "I had to remember all the names of the Western scholars, the dates of their birth and death, their publications and the dates of publica-

tion in order to pass my examination and to get my master's degree" ("Chicago Talk": 2).
27. L. S. E. *Calendar* for 1939–1940, p. 479.
28. The course numbers, for which I am indebted to the Academic Secretary of L.S.E., are I, 2a&b, 3, 4, 5, 6, 8, 10a, 11a, 29s. Course titles and descriptions, as well as recommended readings, can be found in the *Calendar* for 1936–1937.
29. R. Firth, ed., *Man and Culture* (London, 1959), p. 8.
30. Marvin Harris, *The Rise of Anthropological Theory* (New York, 1968), p. 546.
31. "Culture," *Encyclopedia of the Social Sciences*, IV, 636. This provocative statement was removed in the revision; cf. *WHL:*41.
32. *Dynamics of Culture Change* (New Haven, 1945) is concerned with these questions in regard to Africa.
33. *Dynamics*, p. 14; *Argonauts of the Western Pacific* (London, 1922), p. 10.
34. *Argonauts*, p. 514.
35. *A Scientific Theory of Culture* (New York, 1960 [1944]), pp. 4–5.
36. *We the Tikopia* (1936), p. 418.
37. Wu Jingchao, review of *SYZD*, in *Xin lu* 1.1:21–23 (May 15, 1948).
38. For instance, in arguing that birth control, abortion, and infanticide are widespread, he cites examples from Malinowski's Trobriand Islanders, Firth's *Tikopia*, his own observations among the Guangxi Yaos and Chinese peasants of Kaixiangong and Yunnan, the demographer Chen Da's estimate of the Chinese death rate, and the story of a Ming dynasty scholar (Gui Youguang) whose mother was harmed by taking a folk abortifacent (*SYZD:*5–11).
39. *A Scientific Theory of Culture*, pp. 28–29.
40. *Dynamics of Culture Change* (New Haven, 1945), Chapter 1; *A Scientific Theory of Culture*, pp. 9–11. An earlier argument that anthropological research was useful to colonial administrators, in his "Ethnology and the Study of Society," *Economica* 2:208–219 (1922), seems to me very forced.

3. FIELD STUDIES: GUANGXI, KAIXIANGONG, YUNNAN, 1935–1939

1. Study by Liu Yuren, cited in Zhao Chengxin, "Shehui diaocha yu shequ yanjiu," *Shehuixue jie* 9:159 (1936).
2. Information on her father is from Gao Xianggao, Taibei, 1969, and unconfirmed. Gao says his name was Wang Deqian.
3. Information about Wang Tonghui is to be found in the memorial articles

by various friends and colleagues in *Chen bao,* February 12, 1936 ("Shehui yanjin" no. 123). Her translations of articles by Park's student R. D. McKenzie, who developed the concept of "human ecology," can be found in *Chen bao,* June 12, June 26, and July 3, 1935 ("Shehui yanjiu," nos. 89, 91, and 92).

4. This and the previous statement are from *Chen bao,* January 12, 1936. The following on Zhang is mostly from Howard Boorman, ed., *Biographical Dictionary of Republican China* (New York, 1967-1971).
5. See, for example, Ren Guorong, "Yaoshan liang yue guancha ji," *Zhongshan daxue, Yuyan lishi xue yanjiusuo zhoukan* 4.46/47:1617-1649 (September 19, 1928) in the reprint volume; Pang Xinmin, "Guangxi Yaoshan diaocha zaji," *Zhongyang yanjiuyuan, Lishi yuyan yanjiusuo jikan* 4.1:45-82 (October 1932); and others in the bibliography to Hans Wist, "Die Yao in Südchina, *Baessler-Archiv* 21:73-146 (1938).
6. W. H. Oldfield, letter to J. Leighton Stuart, January 6, 1936, in the archives of the United Board for Christian Higher Education in Asia, New York. Oldfield was a missionary in Wuzhou, Guangxi, where Fei was hospitalized following the accident. This letter was apparently the basis for Wu Wenzao's account of the accident in his preface to *HLY,* which was also published in *Yu gong* 5.10:69-74 (July 1936). Walter Herbert Oldfield was the author of *Pioneering in Kwangsi: the Story of Alliance Missions in South China* (Harrisburg, 1936).
7. The text is in *Chen bao,* February 12, 1936.
8. 1936F12; *HLY:*49, 52; Zheng Dekun and his wife, who visited him in the hospital in Canton, interview, 1969.
9. *Yu gong banyuekan* 7.1/3:4 (April 1, 1937).
10. Compare the photograph in *Peasant Life* opposite p. 44, with that in *HLY* opposite p. 37.
11. *Mencius* 1.1.7; 1.1.3; 7.1.22; William Milne, trans., *Sacred Edict* (Shanghai, 1870), pp. 37ff; *Huang-Qing jing-shi wen-bian* (Qing essays on statecraft) 37:3a-b; Evelyn S. Rawski, paper at the Association for Asian Studies meeting, April 1, 1973; Mary Wright, *The Last Stand of Chinese Conservatism* (Stanford, 1957), p. 161; and Arthur Hummel, ed., *Eminent Chinese of the Ch'ing Period* (Washington, D.C., 1943-1944), II, 764-65.
12. Zhang Zhidong, *Quan xue pian* (Exhortation to learning; Liang-Hu shuyuan, 1898), *wai* 9:29a-30a; *Nongxue bao* 11:3, 26:2, 29:2a-b, 40: 2a-b, 41:2a-b, 77:3b et passim, esp. in *ce* 18, 20, 30, 49; *Zhongguo jindai nongye shi ziliao* (Historical materials on modern Chinese agriculture, Peking, 1957), I, 858-883; Yin Liangying, *Zhongguo canye shi* (History of Chinese sericulture; Nanjing, 1931), pp. 13, 59-60; E-tu Zen Sun, "Sericulture and Silk Textile Production in Ch'ing China," in W. E.

Willmott, ed., *Economic Organization in Chinese Society* (Stanford, 1972), pp. 107–108.

13. Suzhou Cansang Zhuanmen Xuexiao; when it later became a public school the name was changed to Jiangsu Provincial Girls' Sericulture School (Jiangsu Shengli Nüzi Canye Xuexiao). It should not be confused with another girls' sericulture school, a short-course school located right in Suzhou, Suzhou Nüzi Canye Jiangxisuo. Yue Sibing, *Zhongguo cansi* (Chinese sericulture; Shanghai, 1935), p. 151.
14. Zou Jingheng, Taibei, 1969; Mr. Zou was a friend of Fei Dasheng and had graduated from the same school in Tokyo.
15. *Zhongguo jindai jingji-shi tongji ziliao xuanji* (Selected statistics for modern Chinese economic history; Shanghai, 1955), p. 82.
16. Articles by Fei Dasheng describing her efforts with the Kaixiangong silk cooperative can be found in *Su nong* 1.5:6–8 (May 31, 1930); *Guoji maoyi dao-bao* 4.6:85–89 (November 1932); *Duli pinglun* 73:11–16 (October 22, 1933); *Dagong bao,* May 10, 1934, and October 25, 1934 (both in the "Xiangcun jianshe" supplement). Information on the cooperative is also contained in the Jiangsu-sheng Nongmin Yinhang's various annual reports for 1929–1935. Unrelated articles of Fei Dasheng's are in *Funü zazhi* 12.11:46 (November 1926) and 12.11:81–82 (December 1926), the latter calling for people to be sent abroad to study technology of artificial-fiber production. She also, no doubt, has articles in the Hushuguan school's publication, *Nü can,* which is not available outside of China. Finally, Fei Xiaotong tells about his sister's silk cooperative in *Peasant Life,* pp. 197–233, and elsewhere.
17. *Dagong bao,* May 10, 1934.
18. *Duli pinglun* 73:11 (October 22, 1933).
19. Kulp had also noticed this preference in China, but viewed it as irrational because marrying a cousin is (biologically) incestuous. More recently, there has been an enormous literature on the function of cross-cousin marriage around the world; see C. Lévi-Strauss, *Elementary Structures of Kinship,* for example (which cites Fei's findings).
20. Fei used Malinowski's theory of the difference between science and magic in contrasting peasants' knowledge of agricultural techniques, accumulated from long experience, with magical practices carried out by the district magistrate to deal with the uncontrollable, such as rainfall or locusts (pp. 165–169).
21. Wu Jingchao, in *Xin jingji* 1.11:305–307 (April 1939).
22. Elman Service, *Profiles in Ethnology* (rev. ed., New York, 1971), pp. 438–439. Another scholar, building models of different kinds of communities based on case studies, has used Fei's Kaixiangong as one of ten examples of a "folk village"; George A. Hillery, Jr., *Communal*

Organizations: A Study of Local Societies (Chicago, 1968), pp. 26–40, 203–250.

23. S. M. Shirokogoroff, "Ethnographic Investigation of China," *Folklore Studies* 1:1–8 (1942). The critical remarks in this article are oddly at variance with the favorable review Shirokogoroff gave *Peasant Life* in *Monumenta Serica* 4:377–378 (1939–1940): "The book is especially valuable because it deals with a definite unit, and a limited subject, in a rather exhaustive manner."

24. It was perhaps the same voyage described by Han Suyin in *Birdless Summer* (New York, 1972), pp. 6–17.

25. Not only is Fei sometimes careless with numbers; he does not always make clear what measures he is using, which can sometimes be very confusing. Grain quantities he gives in *Peasant Life* in terms of "bushels," a measure sometimes of dry volume and sometimes of weight, which varies widely in England and America from place to place and from commodity to commodity—or perhaps Fei is using the word to translate a Chinese measure. A 1936 article from Kaixiangong gave figures in terms of *dan* of polished rice, figures which are generally a third as large as those in *Peasant Life*—for instance, per *mu* yields of 2 *dan* instead of 6 bushels (*JCTX* #5). A *dan* is usually from 100 to 150 lbs., but it is not clear whether, in multiplying these figures by three for *Peasant Life* bushels, Fei was converting to a measure a third as large, changing to unhusked quantities, or both. In an article written a few years later, the Kaixiangong "bushel" is clearly treated as a measure of weight of 67 lbs. of polished rice (*XTCJ*:80; trans. in *Gentry*:110). But in 1957 Fei wrote that the Kaixiangong per *mu* yield twenty-one years before had been 350 catties (*jin*), which, at 1.1 lbs. to the catty and 67 lbs. to a bushel, comes to just six bushels—of unhusked rice (1957Je1#2:12).

In *Earthbound,* grain quantities are given in "piculs," and a rather curious footnote (pp. 28–29, repeated on p. 50), doubtless not written by Fei, informs us that, according to the *China Handbook,* a picul is usually about 110 pounds, and that, in Louisiana, a bushel of unhusked rice is 45 pounds. Neither of these two very different figures, however, comes close to according with the euqivalence of 7 piculs with 470 pounds he gives on p. 51, which works out to about 67 pounds. Now "picul" (a China-coast word of Malay-Portuguese origin) is the usual English translation for the Chinese *dan,* which is usually 100 catties, a catty varying from place to place between 1 and 1.5 pounds. But the Chinese version reveals that Fei is using "picul" not for the standard *dan,* but for the local Lu-cun *dou,* which is one tenth of the Lu-cun *dan.* The Lu-cun *dan* he says is about 3.5 hectoliters (*gong dan*), a measure of volume; it is also apparent that the Lu-cun *dou* weighs not 10 but 50 catties, and that these catties

are about 0.6 kg. or 1.33 lb., which comes to around 67 pounds for the Lu-cun *dou* (*LCNT:*56). It would seem, thus, that Fei's bushel and his picul and the Lu-cun *dou* are all the same, and we note that the "piculs" in the table on *Earthbound,* p. 70, had been "bushels" in an earlier English version ("Agr. Labor":161). In another place he makes clear that a "bushel" is slightly different from the Lu-cun *dou,* the former coming to 36.36 liters and the latter to about 35 (*NDNC:*4), which agrees with the statement elsewhere that in Lu-cun "the local picul equals 1.04 bushel" (*3 Types:* 13, n. 6; but note, incidentally, that the equivalence there of 15.78 Lu-cun *gong* to an acre is at variance with the 17.13 in *NDNC:*4).
26. Marvin Harris, *Culture, Man and Nature* (New York, 1971), pp. 214–216.
27. Huang Wanlun, *Zhexue yanjiu,* August 1958; He Zhiping, *Rennin ribao,* October 16, 1957.
28. There is a large literature on this question, which I do not pretend to have done justice to. Nor have I felt this is the place for a full discussion of the issue of conceptual bias and "value-free" science.
29. *Yi-shi bao,* May 19, 1937 ("Shehui yanjiu" n.s. no. 54).
30. Jack Potter makes this argument. "Although I grant the brilliance of Fei and Chang's fieldwork . . . it seems to me that *Earthbound China* is more an illustration of a preconceived notion than a test"; *Capitalism and the Chinese Peasant* (Berkeley, 1968), p. 200. I agree that the theory that the rural economy was hurt by the growth of treaty port cities has not been proved by Fei or others, yet I think Potter is on similarly weak ground in claiming it is disproved by his own synchronic study of a single village (atypical in that it is very near a big city which buys village-produced food and provides villagers with jobs) with the scantiest historical data.
31. Maurice Freedman, "A Chinese Phase in Social Anthropology," *British Journal of Sociology* 14:1–19 (1963), and "Sociology in and of China," *British Journal of Sociology* 13:106–116 (1962). It must be added that Freedman is critical of the tradition of village studies, speaking of the irony of the fact that this preoccupation with small social areas comes from anthropology's tradition of dealing with totalities. Another useful article on the same subject is Morton H. Fried, "Community Studies in China," *Far Eastern Quarterly* 14:11–36 (1954), part of a symposium on community studies in China and Japan with an introduction by Robert Redfield.
32. Robert Payne, *Forever China* (New York, 1945; also published in London as *Chungking Diary*), pp. 470–568 passim; the quotation is from pp. 545. A richly illustrated description of Kunming can also be found in Joseph E. Passantino, "Kunming, Southwestern Gateway to China," *National Geographic* 90:137–68 (1946).
33. *XTZG:*98, suggests his classroom teaching didn't start until he returned

from the United States in 1944, but this is contradicted by "Chicago Talk":19; *LCNT*:iii; and *SYZD*:i.

34. The Kuixing Ge is briefly described in *Chenggong xianzhi* (Chenggong county gazetteer; revised 1885) 4:39.
35. This report is in the Institute of Pacific Relations archives at Columbia University, box 91.
36. Hu Qingjun, "Fei Xiaotong ji qi yanjiu gongzuo" (Fei Xiaotong and his research), *Guancha* 4.23/24:23–24 (August 7, 1948). More recently, another former student has written of Fei as a teacher at Lianda, of how he encouraged students to express their own ideas, and how he put forward his own ideas not as doctrine but as one person's experience and thought, not fearing criticism. He Da, "Wo-de laoshi Fei Xiaotong xiansheng" (My teacher Fei Xiaotong), *Bo wen zazhi* (Hong Kong) 1.1:16–17 (1974).
37. Lists of works by Fei's colleagues in the Research Station can be found in *XTZG*, 98; *Earthbound*, x–xi; *Quarterly Bulletin of Chinese Bibliography* n.s. 3.1/2:38–39 (March-June 1943) and 4.1/4:52–53 (March-December 1944). But most of these were only mimeographed and are unavailable; I give in the list of Research Station personnel only those titles that were more formally published and are to be found in American libraries.
38. *Yi-cun shougongye* (Handicrafts of Yi-cun; Chongqing, 1943) has a preface by Fei.
39. His name was sometimes written Zhang Zhiyi; it is Zhang Ziyi in a December 1945 open letter (*Zhou bao* 15:10 [December 15, 1945]), but Zhang Zhiyi in a similar letter the next month (*Minzhu zhoukan* [Beiping] 2:19 [January 30, 1946]); and Chih-i Chang on the title page of *Earthbound*, but Tse-yi Chang on p. 12. He is presumably the same as the Zhang Zhiyi who participated in Academia Sinica studies of food marketing in Zhejiang and Fujian in the late 1930s, and who wrote on Xinjiang and Mongolia in the 1940s, contributing (to cite an example in English) to Owen Lattimore's *Pivot of Asia* (Boston, 1950). (He is not the same as the Zhang Zhiyi, written with a different character, who has been prominent as a Communist Party spokesman on national minority affairs.)
40. *Qinghua xiaoyou tongxun* (Qinghua alumni bulletin), n.s. no. 8 (Taibei, 1969), p. 33.
41. The Kunming factory study, *Kun chang laogong* (Kunming factory labor; Shanghai, 1946), with a long afterword by Fei (1946a), appeared after the English translation. Marion Levy has a manuscript of the Yunnan tin-mining study in English. At Harvard, Shi worked with Levy on *The Rise of the Modern Chinese Business Class* (New York, 1949).
42. One of Tian's border studies was published as *Mangshi bianmin de bai*

(The "Bai" cult among the Mangshi border people: Chongqing, 1946). The Kunming female factory worker findings are summarized as an appendix to Fei's translation of Shi's book (*Machine Age*). His L.S.E. thesis was published as *Religious Cults and Social Structure of the Shan States of the Yunnan-Burma Frontier* (London, 1948). He subsequently published pamphlets on *The Chinese of Sarawak* (London, 1953) and on Chinese shipping in southeast Asia in the seventeenth to mid-nineteenth centuries (Shanghai, 1957).

43. Li Youyi published articles on Tibet in the early 1950s.
44. Hu Qingjun in the late 1940s contributed articles to a book edited by Fei and Wu Han (*HQ&SQ*), and in the mid-1950s wrote about the Lolos (now called Yi people) of Liangshan, Sichuan.
45. According to Chen Da, *Lang ji shi-nian* (Ten turbulent years; Chongqing, 1946), p. 202; these are memoirs by the head of Qinghua's sociology department. Yuan Fang also contributed to *HQ&SQ*.
46. Fei's comments in letters from the period indicate he didn't get along very well with Hsu. Hsu has been a professor at Northwestern University for many years now, and has written numerous books and articles in English.
47. *Guangming ribao,* August 31, 1957.

4. A CHINESE ANTHROPOLOGIST LOOKS AT THE UNITED STATES

1. Wilma Fairbank, *America's Cultural Experiment in China, 1942–1949* (Washington, 1976).
2. The IPR republished some of these in 1943: Yu-i Li, Hsiao-tung Fei, and Tse-i Chang, *Three Types of Rural Economy in Yunnan;* Kuo-heng Shih and Ju-k'ang T'ien, *Labor and Labor Relations in the New Industries of Southwest China;* and Francis L. K. Hsu, *Magic and Science in Western Yunnan.*
3. The IPR records are at Columbia, but I have been able to find correspondence with Fei for only some years in the 1940s.
4. In June 1943, he stopped briefly in Miami before coming to New York; in early August, he spent ten days in Chicago giving a paper at the Harris Foundation conference ("Harris Lecture"). In September, he took a week's tour of the Lake Superior region, and then stopped at Minneapolis, Chicago, Ann Arbor, and Ithaca, New York. In October, there were trips to Washington and to Cambridge, before he left New York for Chicago. In January 1944, he attended an IPR conference in Atlantic City, where he took notes for the International Secretariat, and then went to Washington and New York before returning to Chicago. In February, he visited

Michigan and Wisconsin, where he gave lectures. After leaving Harvard in early April, he stopped at New York, Washington, and Cornell on the way back to Chicago. In May, he spent a week in Madison. In June, he made trips to Harvard and Washington from New York while waiting for a boat home.

5. C. K. Yang, *Meet the U.S.A.: Handbook for Foreign Students in the U.S.* (New York, 1948).
6. American Consul General, Kunming, Despatch No. 110 (November 11, 1944), p. 3, in the National Archives. I am grateful to Lloyd Eastman for giving me a copy.
7. Fei's association of Suzhou with the "countryside" would seem to support F. W. Mote's contention that a separate, urban culture never developed in traditional China; see his "A Millennium of Chinese Urban History: Form, Time, and Space Concepts in Soochow," *Rice University Studies* 59.4: 35–65 (1973).
8. Fei mentioned Le Play and Durkheim together in several other places (*RX&JQ:*20; *XTCJ:*9, 14; 1947N8a:12). I doubt he had read any of Le Play's massive *Les ouvriers européens* (6 vols., 1855–1879), and may have known him principally from Mayo's *Social Problems of an Industrial Civilization,* pp. 5–6, which is where Le Play's recent biographer discovered him; Michael Z. Brooke, *Le Play: Engineer and Social Scientist* (London, 1970), p. xi. Durkheim, too, he probably knew chiefly from secondary sources. He uses Durkheim's idea that God symbolized society once (*XTZG:*32), but elsewhere makes a mistake in equating Durkheim's organic solidarity with Tönnies' *Gemeinschaft* and mechanical solidarity with *Gesellschaft*—it should be the other way around, although perhaps this was just a careless slip (*XTZG:*5). But directly or indirectly communicated, I think these ideas made an impression on him.
9. Later, however, Fei said he was criticizing just the disharmony caused by machines under capitalism, not the machine itself (1947N8a); and that the appearance of socialism in England was a movement in the right direction (*XTCJ:*4).

5. PLAINTIFF FOR THE CHINESE PEASANTS

1. For all his complaining about the older generation, however, Fei was not entirely free of old-fashioned vices. On a list of Research Station personnel in 1945 may be found the name of Tang Dingyu, who was Fei Xiaotang's first cousin, and trained in European history, not the "Chinese social history" he is listed as doing research in; Wilma Fairbank, "Memorandum for the Consul General (on her visit to the Yunnan-Yanjing Station and the Qinghua Census Research Institute, Chenggong)," July 2, 1945, p. 3;

in IPR Box 91, Columbia University. It looks suspiciously like a case of old-fashioned nepotism.
2. K. C. Wu, *Lane of Eternal Stability* (New York, 1962), p. 426.
3. The Library of Congress has five issues of a Kunming monthly of the same title. That this is a different periodical from the weekly is clear from *Quanguo Zhongwen jikan lianhe mulu* (National union list of serials; Peking, 1961), p. 547.
4. *China Weekly Review,* 100:215 (February 23, 1946). Fei's friction with the government is discussed in the next chapter.
5. *Dagong bao,* December 11, 1947, p. 9; *New York Times,* July 8, 1947, p. 8; *Time,* September 29, 1947, p. 38.
6. Redfield said he was describing an ideal type which no actual society perfectly matches. Peasant communities, for instance, are not isolated but have economic, political, and status relationships with city people, and constitute a special kind of folk society. Viewed as a type, the folk, or primitive, society is apt to be small ("no more people ... than can come to know each other well, and they remain in long association with each other"), isolated, illiterate, homogeneous in physical type, beliefs, and activities, little changing, and united by a strong sense of solidarity. Behavior is conventionalized, conforming to customary norms, and the conventional ways are interrelated to form a culture which is "a coherent and self-consistent system," an "integrated whole." These folkways grow up out of long association of people with each other and are tacitly accepted rather than being purposefully designed or agreed upon; there is little critical or abstract thinking. The family rather than the individual is the basic social unit, and kinship tends to be the model for all social relations; that is to say the behavior one expects from another depends on one's particular relationship with him. The "sacred" is prevalent: strong feelings of value are attached to customary beliefs and ways, there is ceremony and ritual, and certain objects are thought invested with supernatural power. Folk thinking is apt to be magical and animistic. Finally, economic activity is carried on not for material gain but for social recognition. Robert Redfield, "The Folk Society," *American Journal of Sociology* 52:293–308 (1947). Fei's omission of the last three characteristics—on the "sacred," magical thinking, and economic activity for social status—is perhaps suggestive of Chinese peculiarities.
7. Fei was referring to D. H. Kulp, *Country Life in South China* (New York, 1925), which is subtitled *The Sociology of Familism;* see 1947S6.
8. Fei was presumably referring to Hu Shi; see Jerome B. Grieder, *Hu Shih and the Chinese Renaissance* (Cambridge, Mass., 1970), p. 153.
9. Li Da, "A critique of Fei Xiaotong's compradore sociology," *Zhexue yanjiu,* October 15, 1957.

10. I am indebted to Guy Alitto for letting me see a manuscript copy of his brilliant *The Last Confucian: Liang Shu-ming and the Chinese Dilemma of Modernity* (Berkeley, 1979). One could list other similarities in the thought of these two so basically different men, such as their distaste for industrial cities, hopes for rural industry, and desire to get intellectuals to take modern knowledge to the countryside.
11. The long essay on "Peasantry and Gentry" in the *American Journal of Sociology* for 1946, really more about gentry than peasantry, had been written in 1945 for a "symposium" funded by the State Department, a collection of articles in English Fei gathered from various Kunming scholars which was never published because of the low quality of most of the essays. He then got a $1,000 research grant from the Institute of Pacific Relations, which he shared with Pan Guangdan, to work on Chinese social structure; in mid-1947, they sent IPR a preliminary chapter, which has never been published ("Gentry Draft"). They also published the results of their research on social mobility in a scholarly article later that year (1947Oa). Three articles on the gentry in traditional China published in late 1947 led to a seminar on the subject the following spring with the Qinghua historian Wu Han; *Huang-quan yu shen-quan,* which includes Fei's three essays, is the volume of papers from the seminar. Fei's *Xiangtu chongjian* articles originally appeared in the Shanghai newspaper *Dagong bao* in late 1947 and early 1948. English translations of more articles from *XTCJ* had been planned but could not be completed before the Redfields had to leave in the face of the approaching Communists. *China's Gentry,* which Mrs. Redfield edited and had published, together with some other material not by Fei, in the United States in 1953, is not the systematic book on Chinese social structure Fei had wanted to write, but a reasonable selection of his ideas on the subject. In addition, he clarified his position on some of these matters in 1948 articles responding to criticisms (1948Mr1a; 1948Mr20: *XTCJ*:144–169).
12. For instance, Huang Mingzheng, in an article in the *Dagong bao*, November 16, 1947, p. 3, said that the gentry had always been oppressive, and that Fei overemphasized their positive functions.
13. Several critics objected to the notion that handicrafts had made the land system acceptable, and said that peasants had always been oppressed and exploited. For example, Jiang Qingxiang, in *Zhongguo jianshe* 5.5:34–37 (February 1, 1948); and Wan Dianwu, in *Zhongguo jianshe* 6.1:32–35 (April 1, 1948).
14. Even in 1947, he was accused of being elitist in this respect—it was said that, though he talked of "serving the people," it was clear that the people were to be led by intellectuals. "This opinion of Mr. Fei's surely reflects the present distress of 'educated people'; but it also reflects the sense of

superiority of 'educated people'," and Fei's prescription for restoring the organic relationship between city and countryside amounts to "restoring the rural order to the benevolent control of intellectuals." Xu Jiming, in *Shi yu wen* 2.15:6-8 (December 1947).

15. He could be said to have sided with poorer peasants against the better off in an article criticizing the government's peasant loan program for being too much oriented towards raising production. As a consequence of this bias, regulations favored loans to people with land (people who were "very possibly" using them in turn to exploit landless peasants, as Chen Hansheng and others had charged). Since, due to wartime shortages, no fertilizer, animals, or tools were to be bought, productive loans were now useless anyway; and Fei suggested turning the policy to a welfare purpose instead, by replacing with low-interest government loans the appalling burden of debt, mostly at interest rates of over 30%, which pressed on some three-fifths of China's peasants (*NDNC:* 90-96). Elsewhere, however, he urged the government to make spring loans to landowners to help them hire labor (*NDNC:* 105-111).

16. In accordance with his belief that China's villages had too many people, Fei felt the wartime rural labor shortage, caused by conscription and by the movement of industry to the interior, was not serious. He pointed to great pools of unutilized labor available in the idle class of landowners and in the mahjong-playing town women. More efficient work habits, better technology, and an exchange of labor between regions with different agricultural seasons could offset many labor shortages (*NDNC:* 33-39, 54, et passim). Other articles were likewise specifically concerned with wartime conditions. The rise in food prices had brought excess wealth to the villages, which Fei proposed soaking up with lotteries and other means. He opposed shifting land out of cash crops to food-grains, doubting there was a real food shortage. He warned that a lowered standard of living would be acceptable only if fairly and equitably shared by all (pp. 59-66, 81-89, 67-73).

17. See also in particular *RX&JQ* and 1947N8a; English versions may be found in *Earthbound:* 297-313, and "Problems" and "Financing."

18. J. B. Taylor, an English economist who taught at Yanjing (there is no reason to think Fei studied with him there, but he is mentioned in one of Fei's sister's articles), had in the late 1920s suggested the suitability of small-scale diffused industry for China. Another economist, H. D. Fong (Fang Xianting) of Nankai University, studied rural industries in north China in the early 1930s and emphasized their importance in the economy and their recent rapid decline; he felt that, with improved techniques and cooperative organization, they could still play an important role in China's reconstruction. In 1932 the sociologist Wu Jingchao, later remembered as

an advocate of urban industrialization, wrote in favor of promoting subsidiary rural enterprises and small industries in order to increase peasant income and make use of excess labor. A book on Chinese handicrafts published during the war by one Gao Shukang argued that China should take a different route to industrialization from the West's; in China, agriculture needed strengthening before industrialization could take place. Rural handicrafts, which absorb excess agricultural labor, were a part of agriculture and should be improved and developed at least in the early stages of industrialization. And Chaing Kai-shek himself is reported to have wanted "the establishment of a great number of widely distributed small plants," in order "to retain the best of the old traditions and to avoid the social dislocation of large-scale Western industrial development" while industrializing China.

See J. B. Taylor, *Farm and Factory in China* (London, 1928), pp. 91–92, and his "A Policy for Small-scale Industry in China," *China Critic*, March 26, 1931, pp. 292–295; H. D. Fong, *Rural Industries in China* (Tientsin, 1933), most of which is reprinted in Institute of Pacific Relations, *Problems of the Pacific, 1933* (Chicago, 1934), pp. 299–351; James Yen, *Ting Hsien Experiment* (1934), pp. 21–22; Wu Jingchao, "Jiazeng Zhongguo nongmin shouru de tujing" (The way to increase the income of China's peasants), *Qinghua zhoukan* 38.7/8:743–752 (November 21, 1932); Gao Shukang, *Zhongguo shougongye gailun* (A discussion of Chinese handicrafts; Shanghai, 1946 [first published 1940]); and Wendell Willkie, *One World* (New York, 1943), pp. 130–131 (the quoted words are Willkie's summary of Chiang).

19. An organization called the Huabei Gongye Gaizao She (North China Industrial Improvement Society) had been devoted to the reform of rural handicrafts. The Chinese Communists, blockaded in rural areas, had tried to develop rural industries. Likewise a response to force of circumstance, in this case the Japanese occupation of the coastal industrial cities, was the Chinese Industrial Cooperative Movement (Indusco) which, during the war, with Chinese government support and American money, organized some 1,500 cooperatives with over 20,000 members, making blankets and uniforms for the army, textiles, paper, candles, soap, tung oil, and so on. It is not clear, however, whether its members were mostly farmers working in their idle months, or skilled workers from the occupied coastal industrial areas; if the latter, which would account for the collapse of the movement after the war, it was not at all the same as what Fei had in mind. Fei mentions Indusco rarely, and then only as a model of cooperative organization, not of rural industrialization (*NDNC*:131). Earlier, in Japan's successful economic development, small-scale industries such as silk filatures or village bicycle-making shops had had an important role.

Fei, however, seems to have been generally ignorant about Japan, which he never visited, and of this aspect of Japanese industrial development, which he mentions but once (*NDNC*:130). See, for example, James Yen, *Ting Hsien Experiment*, pp. 21-22; *Xiangcun jianshe shiyan* (Experiments in rural reconstruction; 3 vols.; Shanghai, 1934-1937), Vol. I, Chapter 9; Mark Selden, *The Yenan Way in Revolutionary China* (Cambridge, Mass., 1971), pp. 254-262; Douglas Reynolds, "The Industrial Cooperative Movement in Wartime China (MA Thesis, Columbia University, 1967).

20. For example, Tang Deming, "Xiao shangpin shengchan de mengyi" (The daydream of small-scale production), *Lilun yu xianshi* 3.3:62-65 (October 10, 1946); and Wu Jingchao, "Zhongguo shougongye de qiantu" (The future of Chinese handicrafts), *Jingji pinglun* 1.20:4-7 (August 16, 1947).

21. Both are mentioned in *NDNC*:113; but, in the later *XTCJ*:20 (*Gentry*: 123), he is explicit that "foreign goods have not reached rural areas in any large quantities," but rather are "consumed in the towns in place of local handicrafts."

22. Foreign Broadcast Information Service, *Daily Report—People's Republic of China*, January 6, 1978, pp. E17-18. There have been numerous articles in the Chinese press in recent years about small local industry, and there is a growing Western literature on the subject of which the most important works are: Jon Sigurdson, *Rural Industrialization in China* (Cambridge, Mass., 1977); *Rural Small-scale Industry in the People's Republic of China* (Berkeley, 1977), the report of a recent delegation of American economists; and Carl Riskin, "China's Rural Industries: Self-reliant Systems or Independent Kingdoms?" *China Quarterly* 73:77-98 (March 1978). It should be noted that the concept of "rural industry" in China today includes, in addition to the sort of things Fei was talking about, some fairly large enterprises in county capitals, owned by the government and employing regular year-round wage workers.

23. On the rustication of youth, see Thomas P. Bernstein, *Up to the Mountains and Down to the Villages: the Transfer of Youth from Urban to Rural China* (New Haven, 1977).

6. POLITICS, 1945-1949

1. This atmosphere is vividly conveyed by Robert Payne, who taught at Lianda from 1943 to 1946, in *Forever China* (New York, 1945). My understanding of wartime Kunming was increased by hearing a talk by John Israel at Harvard in the summer of 1974, which has now become "Southwest Associated University: Preservation as an Ultimate Value," in Paul K. T. Sih, ed., *Nationalist China During the Sino-Japanese War, 1937-1945* (Hicksville, N.Y., 1977), pp. 131-154. See also, in the same

volume, Lloyd E. Eastman, "Regional Politics and the Central Government: Yunnan and Chungking," pp. 329–362.
2. The phrase is from *China Weekly Review,* December 8, 1945, pp. 22–23; the situation is succinctly described in Liang Shuming and Zhou Xinmin, *Li Wen bei hai zhenxiang* (The true picture of the assassinations of Li and Wen, n.p., 1946), pp. 6ff.
3. *Foreign Relations of the United States: 1944,* Vol. 6, *China,* pp. 315–316, 470ff, 491, 493ff, 526–527.
4. Liang and Zhou, pp. 7–8.
5. *China Awake* (New York, 1947), pp. 54–55.
6. Information on the Chinese Democratic League may be found in numerous places. Those I have found most useful are: Melville T. Kennedy, Jr., "The Chinese Democratic League," *Papers on China* 7:136–175 (East Asian Research Center, Harvard University, 1953), which summarizes well the material available in English then; Lyman P. Van Slyke, *Enemies and Friends: The United Front in Chinese Communist History* (Stanford, 1967), Chapters 8 and 9, which examines the relationship of the League with the Communists; and *Zhongguo ge xiao dangpai xiankuang* (Current conditions of China's small parties; n.p., 1946), apparently a secret Nationalist intelligence report and the best-informed source on the League through early 1946 that I have seen.
7. "Women duiyu dangqian wujia wenti de yijian" (Our opinion on the current inflation), *Dangdai pinglun* 2.9:130–135 (August 15, 1942).
8. Jin Yuelin, *Guangming ribao,* April 17, 1952, reprinted in R. J. Lifton, *Thought Reform* (New York, 1961), p. 478; Wilma Fairbank, *America's Cultural Experiment in China* (Washington, 1976).
9. *Guancha* 1.6:17 (October 5, 1946).
10. *Zhongguo ge xiao dangpai xiankuang,* pp. 16ff.
11. *China Awake,* pp. 202–204.
12. *Zhongguo ge xiao dangpai xiankuang,* p. 11.
13. For example: *Qunzhong* 11.12:34 (July 1946); *Dagong bao,* August 19, 1946; Liang and Zhou, p. 11; *Guancha* 1.1:24 (September 1, 1946).
14. *Zhongguo ge xiao dangpai xiankuang,* pp. 11–12; there is much on the Chinese National Socialist Party, including the information that Pan was a leader of the Kunming branch, on pp. 65–76. A biography of Pan may be found in Howard Boorman, ed., *Biographical Dictionary of Republican China.*
15. There were other editions in other cities with the same title; issues of the Kunming *Minzhu zhoukan* for 1944 and 1945 may be found at Harvard and the Library of Congress.
16. The late Professor Yin Haiguang of Taibei spoke to me vividly of the excitement Fei created as a speaker in Kunming, where Yin was a student.

17. The following account is drawn from articles in the Shanghai *Zhou bao* 14:13–15 (December 8, 1945) and 15:5–7 (December 15, 1945); the Shanghai *Minzhu zhoukan* 10:221–223 (December 15, 1945) and 11:257–260 (December 22, 1945); Liang and Zhou, *Li Wen bei hai zhenxiang,* pp. 9–10; an "eyewitness account" by Charles J. Canning in the Shanghai *China Weekly Review* 100.3:38–39 (December 15, 1945); and Robert Payne's long but secondhand (he was sick in bed) description in *China Awake,* pp. 201ff. The December First Movement is also treated briefly in Suzanne Pepper, "The Student Movement and the Chinese Civil War, 1945–49," *China Quarterly* 48:698–735 (1971); her account is based in part on Hu Lin, *Yi-er-yi de huiyi* (Recollections of December First; Hong Kong, 1949), which I have not seen.
18. *China Weekly Review,* January 12, 1946, p. 115; January 19, 1946, pp. 136–137; February 23, 1946, p. 215.
19. *China Weekly Review,* February 23, 1946, p. 215; March 9, 1946; pp. 36–37.
20. *Zhou bao* 15:10 (December 15, 1945).
21. *Minzhu zhoukan* (Beiping) 2:19 (January 30, 1946).
22. *Wen cui* 29:2–3 (May 9, 1946).
23. *Dagong bao,* February 22, 1946; *Minzhu zhoukan* (Beiping) 4/5:20–21 (March 6, 1946).
24. Liang and Zhou, pp. 10–11.
25. Liang and Zhou, pp. 10–13, 20; *Guancha* 1.1:22 (September 1, 1946) speaks of a long list of people to be arrested which included Fei; it also seems likely from what followed that Fei's name appeared on alleged blacklists that the American government heard about.
26. Information on the Li-Wen assassination and the refuge in the U.S. Consulate comes principally from: Liang and Zhou, *Li Wen bei hai zhenxiang,* which is the report of the Democratic League's investigation; an excellent article in *Guancha* 1.1:22–24 (September 1, 1946); virtually daily articles in the *Dagong bao* from July 16, 1946 to August 27, 1946; *Foreign Relations of the United States, 1946,* IX, 1380–1383, 1399–1401, 1410–1412, 1417–1419, 1440–1442; and *China Weekly Review,* July 27, 1946, pp. 200–201, 204. There is, without question, good material now available in the State Department records in the National Archives, which I have not seen.
27. Payne, *China Awake,* p. 419; Payne has much about Wen, whom he called "the greatest Chinese I ever knew" (p. ix), in this book, which is dedicated to him. There is also a biography in Boorman, *Biographical Dictionary,* and Kai-yu Hsu, "The Life and Poetry of Wen I-to," *Harvard Journal of Asiatic Studies* 21:134–179 (1958). Professor Hsu, who did a PhD thesis on Wen, is said to have a book

about him forthcoming. Information on Li Gongpu is much more difficult to come by.
28. Liang and Zhou, p. 23.
29. *Qunzhong,* 11.12:36 (July 21, 1946).
30. Liang and Zhou, pp. 29-32.
31. A postscript: in 1957 a former Guomindang intelligence officer was sentenced to ten years in jail for having followed Li and Wen (*Selections from the China Mainland Press* 1580:20).
32. John F. Melby, *Mandate of Heaven* (Toronto, 1968), pp. 140-142.
33. *Dagong bao,* August 2, 3, 10, 1946; *Guancha* 1.1:24 (September 1, 1946).
34. *Guancha* 3.7:3-6 (October 11, 1947), and 3.14:9-11 (November 29, 1947).
35. Wu Jingchao, "Zhongguo shougongye de qiantu" (The future of China's handicrafts), *Jingji pinglun* 1.20:4-7 (August 16, 1947).
36. Supplying a negative after *bu neng.*
37. See, for example, Jiang Qingxiang in *Zhongguo jianshe* 5.5:34-37 (February 1, 1948), and Wan Dianwu in *Zhongguo jianshe* 6.1:32-35 (April 1, 1948).
38. *China Awake,* p. 297, and pp. 237-296 passim.
39. Tseng Chao-lun, "The Chinese Democratic League," *Current History,* July 1946, p. 35.
40. Suzanne Pepper, "Socialism, Democracy, and Chinese Communism: A Problem of Choice for the Intelligentsia, 1945-1949," in Chalmers Johnson, ed., *Ideology and Politics in Contemporary China* (Seattle, 1973), pp. 161-218. The material covered in this article, and in the one on the student movement cited in note 17 above, has now been included in her *Civil War in China: The Political Struggle 1945-1949* (Berkeley, 1978). On the League's relations with the Communists there is much in Lyman P. Van Slyke, *Enemies and Friends: The United Front in Chinese Communist History* (Stanford, 1967), Chapters 8 and 9. See also Carsun Chang, *Third Force in China* (New York, 1952).
41. *Wu Han wenji* (Hong Kong, 1967), I, 7-11.
42. *Guancha* 4.10:2, 12 (May 1, 1948).
43. Shi Guoheng letter to Wilma Fairbank, March 12, 1948.
44. Hu Sheng, in *Qunzhong* (Hong Kong) 2.28:14 (July 22, 1948), quoted the talk summarized in 1948My16. Shenghuo Shudian's advertisement in the *Dagong bao,* December 8, 1947, p. 1, for example, listed Fei's *MZ,XF,RQ, CFMG,* and *GDYN,* alongside translations of Marx, Engels, and Lenin, books about the Soviet Union, and works by such leftists as Hou Wailu, Jian Bozan, Li Da, Hu Sheng, and Deng Chumin.
45. The full passage is as follows:
    Those in this country who discuss social change are often overly

influenced by nineteenth-century Western evolutionists and consider change in social conditions to be a fixed and immutable process: to get from stage A to stage C it is necessary to pass through stage B. This process is considered universal for all places and all times. According to this "iron law," if we want to know the future of a community, we need only be able to find what stage of evolution in this immutable process it is at now, and then the past and future will be immediately apparent. For this reason the mid-1930s controversy over social history was so clamorous. Unfortunately the "iron law" they upheld has no basis in fact. Social change is not so simple as they imagined. Even Marx himself had doubts about whether the process of evolution he deeply believed in could be applied to Asia. How much less are those without a thorough understanding of the formula likely to come up with interesting results. And so the controversy came to no conclusion, only a truce. Although I can't agree with their methods, I admit at least one point is worth our attention, and that is that they did not regard social change as the product of chance events, but as following a course; their mistake was to see this historical course somewhat too simplistically. (*LCNT:*189–90)

46. A. Doak Barnett, *China on the Eve of Communist Takeover* (New York, 1963), p. 316.
47. Robert Redfield, "Introduction" to *China's Gentry,* pp. 2–3; interview with Margaret Redfield, 1971.

7. THE BOURGEOIS INTELLECTUAL IN THE PEOPLE'S REPUBLIC

1. Lin Yaohua, *Renmin ribao,* August 2, 1957; trans. in *Current Background* (U.S. Consulate General, Hong Kong) 475:8.
2. *1950 Renmin nianjian* (Hong Kong, Dagong bao, 1950); *1951 Renmin shouce* (Shanghai, Dagong bao, 1951); *Gendai Chūgoku jinmei jiten* (Tokyo, 1966).
3. The Nationalists' National Assembly of 1948 had given another observer very much the same impression of social diversity as evidenced by sartorial variety; see A. Doak Barnett, *China on the Eve of Communist Takeover* (New York, 1963), pp. 60–61.
4. Higher Peking taxes were a good thing, he said, because: it was essential that the current 50% subsidy of Peking's expenses with revenues from rural areas be gradually stopped and even reversed; the new taxes, unlike old ones, were progressive; extra levies and tax evasion by big firms had been ended so the burden on the people would not be greater; the new

tax revenues would be used for popular welfare and constructive purposes; and the new taxes had been designed to encourage certain desirable economic developments (1949D31).
5. Standard sources of information on thought reform include Chalmers A. Johnson, *Communist Policies Toward the Intellectual Class* (Hong Kong, 1959); Theodore H. H. Ch'en, *Thought Reform of the Chinese Intellectuals* (Hong Kong, 1960); Robert Jay Lifton, *Thought Reform and the Psychology of Totalism* (New York, 1961); and *Current Background,* Nos. 169, 182, and 213 (1952).
6. On early university reform there is Chung Shih, *Higher Education in Communist China* (Hong Kong, 1953); Maria Yen, *The Umbrella Garden* (New York, 1954), which is the memoir of a Peking University student who defected; and Immanuel C. Y. Hsu, "The Reorganization of Higher Education in Communist China, 1949-61," *China Quarterly* 19:128-160 (1964).
7. Ching-wen Chow, *Ten Years of Storm* (New York, 1960), p. 39.
8. Johnson, *Communist Policies,* pp. 62-64.
9. U.S. Consulate General, Hong Kong, biographical files.
10. *Renmin ribao,* August 28, 1957, in *Xinhua banyuekan* 1957, 18:148-149; New China News Agency, Peking, July 16, 1957, in *Survey of the China Mainland Press* (U.S. Consulate General, Hong Kong) 1581:9; *Renmin ribao,* August 30, 1957, trans. in *Survey of the China Mainland Press* 1613:23.
11. Fei's article and similar materials are discussed in G. William Skinner, "The New Sociology in China," *Far Eastern Quarterly* 10:365-371 (1951), written at a time when it seemed sociology would be reformed and not eliminated.
12. Skinner, "The New Sociology," p. 368.
13. When he was appointed Vice President of the Central Nationalities Institute; New China News Agency, Peking, April 9, 1951, in *Survey of the China Mainland Press* 92:24.
14. June T. Dreyer, *China's Forty Millions: Minority Nationalities and National Integration in the People's Republic of China* (Cambridge, Mass., 1976).
15. For example: *Guangming ribao,* May 21, 1952; December 22, 1953; June 12, 1964; October 8, 1954.
16. *Renmin ribao,* August 25, 1956. In 1956, a history department was established at the Institute; *Minzu tuanjie* 1957, 3:18.
17. The German ethnologist Inez de Beauclair was still in Guizhou at the time and shared with him some of her extensive knowledge of the Miaos, she told me in Taiwan in 1969.
18. Such a charge is mentioned, for example, in Guo Shaotang, "Criticism of

some of the philosophical and sociological views of the bourgeois right-wing elements and revisionists in China (1957-1958)," translated from *Problemy Vostokovedeniva* (Moscow) 5:83-92 (1959), in Joint Publications Research Service no. 3091 (March 21, 1960), p. 10.

19. Dorothy J. Solinger, *Regional Government and Political Integration in Southwest China, 1949-1954* (Berkeley, 1977), pp. 180-192. In 1952, a review of nationalities policies found Han cadres had been guilty of serious mistakes of Han chauvinism, mechanical application of Han patterns, insufficient respect for minorities customs and traditions, and forcing adoption of the Chinese language, all of which were condemned. The 1954 Constitution granted minorities the right to take their time, think over reforms, and make their own decisions. See Dreyer, *China's Forty Millions,* pp. 120-127. Mao himself in 1955 wrote: "We must relentlessly fight Han chauvinism ... At present there is still a good deal of Han chauvinism, for example, monopolizing the affairs of the minority nationalities, showing no respect for their customs and folk-ways, being self-righteous, looking down on them and saying how backward they are"; *Selected Works of Mao Tsetung,* Vol. V (Peking, 1977), pp. 229-230.

20. Yu Shengchun, "What kind of an 'expert' is Fei Xiaotong after all?" *Guangming ribao,* September 8, 1957.

21. The great nationalities research project was hastily concluded in 1958 in the frenzied atmosphere of the Great Leap Forward, and most of its results never published; see China Academy of Sciences, Nationalities Research Center, ed., *Minzu yanjiu gongzuo de yuejin* (The great leap in nationalities research; Peking, 1958), especially pp. 8-24; and various articles in the journal *Minzu yanjiu* in 1958. Some of Fei's team's Yunnan finds were given scholarly analysis in *Dali Bai-zu zizhizhou lishi wenwu diaocha ziliao* (Investigation of historical relics in the Bai nationality autonomous district, Dali; Yunnan, 1958).

22. Letter to William F. Carr, October 17, 1955, quoted in Carr's "A History of the Development of Anthropology in China" (MA thesis, Columbia University, 1959), pp. 64-65.

23. Letter in *Encounter* 23:73-74 (August 1955). Dover says he had several conversations with Fei in October and November of 1955, which must be a mistake for an earlier year.

24. Kingsley Martin, "China in Uniform," *The New Statesman and Nation,* May 21, 1955, p. 710. Martin describes his friend as a literary writer and translator, but Fei's remark, "It is true, as Mr. Martin said in his article, that I've put on weight" ("Old Friends"), suggests that he was the friend.

25. W. R. Geddes, *Peasant Life in Communist China* (Society for Applied Anthropology Monograph No. 6; Lexington, Ky., 1963), p. 7.

26. *Encounter* 16:78-80 (January 1955) and 23:74-75 (August 1955).

Letters about Fei taking issue with Wittfogel are in *Encounter* 23:73–75 (August 1955); 26:60–61 (November 1955); 29:67–70 (February 1956); 51:64–65 (December 1957); 53:65–66 (February 1958). Wittfogel also wrote about Fei in "The Tragedy of a Chinese Agrarian Reformer," *New Leader* 38.11:15–18 (March 14, 1955).

8. THE HUNDRED FLOWERS AND AFTER

1. Mao Zedong, "Talk at the Chengtu Conference," translated in Stuart Schram, ed., *Chairman Mao Talks to the People* (New York, 1974), pp. 116–117.
2. Zhou Enlai, "On the Question of the Intellectuals" (January 14, 1955), *Communist China 1955–1959: Policy Documents with Analysis* (Cambridge, Mass., 1962), pp. 128–144. The sentence quoted is on p. 134.
3. Theodore Ch'en, *Thought Reform,* Chapters 11–13, seems quite good on the early stages of the Hundred Flowers period.
4. Mao Zedong, "On the Ten Major Relationships" (April 25, 1956), *Selected Works of Mao Tsetung,* Vol. V (Peking, 1977), p. 296.
5. Lyman P. Van Slyke, *Enemies and Friends* (Stanford, 1967), pp. 213, 242.
6. Lu Dingyi, "Let a Hundred Flowers Bloom, a Hundred Schools of Thought Contend!" (May 26, 1956), in *Communist China 1955–59,* pp. 151–162. The quotation is from p. 153.
7. Roderick MacFarquhar, *The Origins of the Cultural Revolution, I: Contradictions among the People, 1956–1957* (New York, 1974) is a discussion of the upper-level policy disputes connected with the Hundred Flowers period.
8. The original text has never been published, but the gist, leaked through East Europe, may be found in *The New York Times,* June 13, 1957.
9. Mao Zedong, *Miscellany of Mao Tse-tung Thought, 1949–1968* (Arlington, Va., Joint Publications Research Service no. 61269, February 1974), Part I, pp. 63–71.
10. Richard Solomon, "One Party and '100 Schools' Leadership, Lethargy, or Luan?" *Current Scene* 7.19/20:1–49 (October 1, 1969). See also his *Mao's Revolution and the Chinese Political Culture* (Berkeley, 1971).
11. *Guangming ribao,* April 24, 1957.
12. *Renmin ribao,* August 8, 1957; Qi Yanming, *Quangming ribao,* September 25, 1957; *Renmin ribao,* August 30, 1957.
13. Nanjing *Xinhua ribao,* July 29, 1957.
14. Liu Rongqu and Yu Shengchun, *Renmin ribao,* August 19, 1957.
15. Mao, *Selected Works* V, 503 (October 13, 1957).
16. Ibid., V, 432–433 (March 12, 1957).

17. Ge Yang, *Xin guancha*, August 1, 1957, p. 8; Xiao Di, *Xin guancha*, September 1, 1957, p. 35. That the article was printed in *Renmin ribao* probably indicates official approval. There was at some point "an order that all Rightists views must be published verbatim"; Mao, *Selected Works*, V, 465 (July 9, 1957). But I suspect this was in May and not the case in March.
18. Liu Rongqu and Yu Shengchun, *Renmin ribao*, August 19, 1957.
19. *Guangming ribao*, August 24, 1957.
20. *Xinhua banyuekan* 1957, 16:175; New China News Agency, Peking, July 4, 1957, trans. in *Survey of the China Mainland Press* 1574:2-3.
21. *Renmin ribao*, July 26, 1957; *Xin guancha*, August 1, 1957, pp. 3-6.
22. *Renmin ribao*, July 7 and 4, 1957, in *Xinhua banyuekan* 1957, 15:166.
23. *Guangming ribao*, June 21, 1957, trans. in *Survey of the China Mainland Press* 1566:24.
24. Nanjing *Xinhua ribao*, July 29, 1957.
25. *Guangming ribao*, August 24, 1957.
26. Liu Rongqu and Yu Shengchun, *Renmin ribao*, August 19, 1957.
27. *Renmin ribao*, July 26, 1957.
28. Min Ganghou in *Renmin ribao*, July 4, 1957, as quoted in Roderick MacFarquhar, ed., *The Hundred Flowers Campaign and the Chinese Intellectuals* (New York, 1960), pp. 167-168. Cf. *Survey of the China Mainland Press* 1571:27.
29. *Communist China*, 1955-1959, pp. 141, 157.
30. *Renmin ribao*, January 23, 1957; reprinted in *Xinhua banyuekan* 1957, 4:151-153 (February 25).
31. Wu Jingchao, "Shehuixue zai xin Zhongguo hai you diwei?" (Is there still a place for sociology in new China?), *Xin jianshe* 1957, 1:61 (January 3). Wu later admitted that the article was meant to test the situation and that he had not asked for the Party's direction "as he should have"; Guan Feng, *Xin jianshe* 1957, 10:30-32 (October 3).
32. See *People's China* 1957, 3:13-17 (March); and 4:26-30 (April).
33. *Renmin ribao*, August 30, 1957, trans. in *Survey of the China Mainland Press* 1613:21.
34. *Xin jianshe* 1957, 7:40-47 (July 3).
35. *Guangming ribao*, June 9, 1957, trans. in *Survey of the China Mainland Press* 1562:6-7. Fei's role in this document was revealed by Qian Jiaju in *Renmin ribao*, July 15, 1957, reprinted in *Xinhua banyuekan* 1957, 16:175, and trans. in *Survey of the China Mainland Press* 1581:11-12; by Fei in 1957Jl13; and elsewhere.
36. *Renmin ribao*, April 21 and 22, 1957; trans. in *Union Research Service* 7, 289-291.

37. *Wen hui bao,* May 30, 1957; Yan Xinzhe had taught and written on sociology in the 1930s and 1940s.
38. Sun Benwen, "On the nature and content of contemporary bourgeois sociological theory," *Xueshu yuekan* 1957, 4:27-36 (April 10). Perhaps there was some flexibility in his statement that, if the study of various aspects of socialist society were to develop, it would be a new discipline and not sociology.
39. For the conspiracy to restore bourgeois sociology see: *Renmin ribao,* August 30, 1957, trans. in *Survey of the China Mainland Press* 1613:21-24; *Guangming ribao,* August 30, 1957; Sun Dingguo, *Xin jianshe* 1957, 9:1-5 (September 3), trans. in *Extracts from China Mainland Magazines* (U.S. Consulate General, Hong Kong) 116:6-15; and Wu Jiang, *Xuexi* 1957, 18:15-18 (September 18). The list of names is from *Renmin ribao* and *Guangming ribao,* August 30, 1957.
40. *Renmin ribao,* August 30, 1957, trans. in *Survey of the China Mainland Press* 1913:21-22.
41. Kaneko Mitsuru, "Chūgoku sha-gaku-kai [i.e., shakaigaku] no kinkyō" (The current state of Chinese sociology), *Shakaigaku hyōron* 31 (Vol. 8, No. 3):107-108 (May 1958). One presumes the interview must have been very early in July, before the Anti-Rightist Movement had really gotten under way.
42. Society for Applied Anthropology Monograph No. 6; (Lexington, Ky., 1963).
43. *Renmin ribao,* July 26, 1957.
44. Huang Wanlun, *Zhexue yanjiu,* April 1958, p. 1. In London in 1969, I was unable to find this correspondence in Routledge's files.
45. But the 1936 figures (6 bushels, at 67 lb. a bushel and 1.1 lb. a catty, comes to 365 catties) would seem to have been for husked rice, at least according to Fei's later indications (*NDNC:*5; *Earthbound:*71; *XTCJ:*80), in which case the rise in productivity, while still appreciable, is not as great as Fei indicates. Geddes's estimate of 718 catties per *mu* (unhusked) is impossibly high as he himself indicates (p. 9) and at odds with the figure of 560 he gives elsewhere (p. 38); his comparisons with Fei's 1936 figures are muddled, not only by the husked/unhusked problem, but also by taking Fei's *Peasant Life* "bushel" as 55 lb. instead of 67.
46. Fei gave figures for an average family budget as follows. The agricultural cooperative distributed in addition to 380 catties of grain 35.5 yuan to each person, or 142 yuan for a family of four. Such a family, Fei estimated, would spend annually another 35 yuan for food, 40 yuan for fuel, 20 yuan for social expenses, 60-65 yuan for clothes for adults, plus 60 yuan for miscellaneous daily expenses and some more for children's clothes, house repairs, and tools, totaling about 250 yuan a year; which is

to say they needed 80 yuan, or 20 yuan per person additional income from outside agriculture. (I cannot explain why 250 minus 142 leaves 80.)
47. *Guangming ribao,* September 5, 1957, trans. in *Survey of the China Mainland Press* 1613:30.
48. Mao, *Selected Works* V, 351 (January 1957).
49. *Renmin ribao* and *Guangming ribao,* June 11, 1957.
50. *Renmin ribao,* June 18, 1957.
51. See, for example, *Guangming ribao,* June 21, 1957, trans. in *Survey of the China Mainland Press* 1566:24: New China News Agency, Peking, June 30, 1957, in *Survey of the China Mainland Press* 1571:14, and New China News Agency, Peking, July 2, 1957, in *Survey of the China Mainland Press* 1566:43.
52. *Dagong bao,* June 20, 1957.
53. For example, at June 18 and 19 Democratic League meetings (*Renmin ribao,* June 20, 1957, in *Xinhua banyuekan* 1957, 14:69–70).
54. *Renmin ribao,* June 26, 1957, trans. in *Survey of the China Mainland Press* 1571:8.
55. *Renmin ribao,* July 6, 1957, in *Xinhua banyuekan* 1957, 15:179, trans. in *Survey of the China Mainland Press* 1575:15–17.
56. Although Pan Guangdan, presumably trying to protect his old friend, left Fei's name out in listing Luo's clique; New China News Agency, Peking, July 5, 1957, trans. in *Survey of the China Mainland Press* 1571:34.
57. Min Ganghou, *Renmin ribao,* July 4, 1957; trans. in *Survey of the China Mainland Press* 1571:27–29.
58. *Renmin ribao,* July 6 and 5, 1957, in *Xinhua banyuekan* 1957, 15:166, and trans. in *Survey of the China Mainland Press* 1571:35–37.
59. *Xinhua banyuekan* 1957, 15:54–57.
60. *Xinhua banyuekan* 1957, 16:57–59.
61. Yang Dongchun, National People's Congress July 12, *Xinhua banyuekan* 1957, 17:106–108.
62. *Xinhua banyuekan* 1957, 17:51–52.
63. For example by Hu Sheng, *Xinhua banyuekan* 1957, 18:89–92, who said Fei's *Xiangtu chongjian* served landlord interests.
64. *Renmin ribao,* July 15 to 25, in *Xinhua banyuekan* 1957, 16:175–180. See also *Guangming ribao* July 8, 1957, for an interview with the scientist Lü Zhenyu, in which he criticizes the social science proposal.
65. *Renmin ribao,* July 26, 1957.
66. *Renmin ribao,* August 17, 1957.
67. *Renmin ribao,* August 11, in *Xinhua banyuekan* 1957, 17:150.
68. *Guangming ribao,* August 24, 1957; and Xia Kangnong in *Xin Guancha,* August 1. Lin Yaohua's August 2 article in *Renmin ribao* was from an Institute wall poster.

69. Nanjing *Xinhua ribao,* July 29, 1957.
70. The Academy of Sciences meetings August 29 to September 5 and September 18 to 23; they were amply covered in the press, some of which coverage can be found in *Xinhua banyuekan* 1957, 20:81–86.
71. *Fandui zichan jieji shehui kexue fubi, di er ji* (Oppose the restoration of bourgeois social science, 2nd collection; Peking, 1958).
72. *Guangmin ribao,* September 28, 1957.
73. Liu Shui Sheng (pseud.), "Life in a Chinese University," *Atlantic Monthly,* December 1959, p. 90.
74. A. Doak Barnett, *Cadres, Bureaucracy, and Political Power in Communist China* (New York and London, 1967), p. 34.
75. Some 36 of the most important anti-Fei articles were reprinted in Hong Kong in about 1972 in a convenient volume entitled *Fei Xiaotong pipan ziliao huibian* (Collected materials in criticism of Fei Xiaotong, n.p., n.d.). I had previously gathered a larger number, mostly from the files of the Union Research Institute in Hong Kong. Four articles have now been translated by James P. McGough in *Fei Hsiao-t'ung: The Dilemma of a Chinese Intellectual* (White Plains, 1979): Zhou Shulian, Li Futong, and Zhang Siqian, "Exposing 'Yangzi village revisited'," from *Xin guancha,* August 1, 1957; Zhao Weibang, "The reactionary nature of the functionalist social anthropology imported by Fei Xiaotong and others," from *Sichuan daxue xuebao* 1958, 3/4 (February 1959); Li Da, "A critique of Fei Xiaotong's compradore sociology," from *Zhexue yanjiu,* October 1957; and Lin Yaohua, "The sinister and ugly Fei Xiaotong," from *Renmin ribao,* August 2, 1957 (also translated in *Current Background* 475: 6–9).
76. In addition to the Academy of Sciences speeches cited above, there are: Huang Wanlun, *Fei Xiaotong "nongcun diaocha" de fandong benzhi* (The reactionary nature of Fei Xiaotong's "rural investigations"; Shanghai, 1958); Li Da, *Fei Xiaotong de maiban shehuixue pipan* (A critique of Fei Xiaotong's compradore sociology; Shanghai, 1958); Sun Dingguo, *Fencui zichan jieji youpai huifu zichan jieji shehuixue de zhengzhi yinmou* (Smash the bourgeois rightists' political conspiracy to restore bourgeois sociology; Shanghai, 1958); and a couple other such titles listed in *Quanguo zong shumu 1958,* pp. 22–23, 47. I have seen only the first, which is virtually identical to a magazine article (*Zhexue yanjiu,* April 1958). Li Da's book, too, bears the same title as a very long article he published in *Zhexue yanjiu* in October 1957, and the other books are perhaps also reprinted from periodicals.
77. Huang Wanlun, *Xuexi* 1957, 18:12 (September 18); cf. trans. in *Extracts from China Mainland Magazines* 119:1.
78. Yu Shengchun, *Guangming ribao,* September 8, 1957.

79. Lin Yaohua, *Renmin ribao*, August 2, 1957, trans. in *Current Background* 475:6-9.
80. New China News Agency, Peking, June 1, 1957, in *Survey of the China Mainland Press* 1544:13.
81. Huang Wanlun, *Xuexi*, September 18, 1957, trans. in *Extracts from China Mainland Magazines* 119:1-17.
82. Huang Wanlun, *Zhexue yanjiu*, August 1958.
83. Li Da, *Zhexue yanjiu*, October 15, 1957.
84. See, in particular, the report of a meeting in Kunming, in *Renmin ribao*, August 30, 1957.
85. Xu Jiarui, *Yunnan ribao*, August 8, 1957.
86. He Ming, *Guangming ribao*, August 10, 1957.
87. *Yunnan ribao*, September 5, 1957.
88. Qi Yanming, *Guangming ribao*, September 25, 1957.
89. Sun Dingguo, *Zhexue yanjiu*, October 15, 1957, p. 18.
90. Fan Wenlan, *Renmin ribao*, September 30, 1957.
91. For example: Wang Kang, "On the reactionary nature of bourgeois sociology," *Xin jianshe* 1957, 8:18-23 (August 3): Li Da, "A critique of Fei Xiaotong's compradore sociology," *Zhexue yanjiu* 1957, 5:1-14 (October 15); Li Chengxi, "Why is bourgeois sociology reactionary?," *Xueshu yuekan* 1958, 1:18-23 (January 10); Dong Jie, "Does bourgeois sociology have 'useful parts' which can be 'absorbed'," *Xueshu yuekan* 1958, 2:88-91 (February 10).
92. For example, the Chinese translation of a Russian book on "Some characteristics of contemporary reactionary bourgeois sociology" is summarized by Bai Lin in *Xuexi* 13:27 (August 3, 1957).
93. Hu Sheng, *Zhexue yanjiu*, October 1958.
94. Zhao Weibang, *Sichuan daxue xuebao*, February 1959.
95. Hu Sheng, *Zhexue yanjiu*, October 1958; Li Chengxi, *Xueshu yuekan*, January 1958; Xia Yulong et al., *Xueshu yuekan*, January 1958; etc.
96. He Zhiping, *Renmin ribao*, October 16, 1957; Li Da, *Zhexue yanjiu*, October 15, 1957; Tao Delin, *Xuexi*, February 1958.
97. Cf. 22.5% increase in net per capita income (from 657 to 825 catties of husked rice equivalent) for 1936 to 1956 given by Zhou Shulian et al. in *Xin guancha*, August 1, 1957, p. 9; 36.5% increase (from 624 to 852 catties) in Huang Wanlun, *Zhexue yanjiu*, April 1958, p. 3; and 63.4% (from 61.2 to 100 yuan, which was considerably above national average of 78.9 yuan) in Huang Wanlun, *Xuexi*, September 18, 1957, trans. in *Extracts from China Mainland Magazines* 119.6.
98. These various criticisms of Fei's article on Kaixiangong are from the three articles cited in the preceding note.
99. Mao, *Selected Works*, V, 505. Italics mine. The version in the unofficial

Red Guard collection *Mao Zedong sixiang wansui!* (I, 136–137) is slightly different. In particular, Mao is quoted there as going on to say, "That's what I talked with him about in early June. So it's good to have some rightist friends, to have contact with rightists in order to understand their psychological state." Did Mao then consider Fei a friend, and have talks with him from time to time? For a translation of this passage, see *Chinese Law and Government* 9.3:49 (fall 1976).

100. Mao, *Selected Works*, V, 343–346.
101. Mao, *Miscellany*, p. 78.
102. *Xiandai Hanyu cidian* (1977), a large dictionary of some 50,000 or so entries, does not include *shehuixue*.
103. Wong Siu-lun has discussed this with great sensitivity and insight in "Social Enquiries in the People's Republic of China," *Sociology* 9.3:459–476 (September 1975); there is also L. C. Young, "Mass Sociology: the Chinese Style," *The American Sociologist* 9:117–25 (August 1974); and Ambrose Yeo-chi King and Wong Tse-sang, "Social Investigations in Communist China: the Emergence of Maoist Sociology," *Journal of Social and Political Affairs* 1.3:257–72 (July 1976).
104. Franz Schurmann, interviewing refugees in Hong Kong, was struck by their ability to analyze their experiences rewardingly for a sociologist; *Ideology and Organization in Communist China* (Berkeley, 1968), p. 48.
105. Michel Oksenberg describes in detail an example, based on refugee interviews, in "Methods of Communication within the Chinese Bureaucracy," *China Quarterly* 57:1–39 (1974), at pp. 24–27.
106. Mao wrote in 1956: "If you are to win over the peasants and rely on them, you must conduct investigations in the rural areas. The method is to investigate one or more villages and spend a few weeks there to get a clear idea of the class forces, the economic situation, living conditions and so on, in the countryside. The principal leaders, such as the general secretary of the Party, should themselves undertake this work and get to know one or two villages; they should try to find the time, for it is well worth the effort. Though there are plenty of sparrows, it is not necessary to dissect every one of them; to dissect one or two is enough." (*Selected Works*, V, 26–27).
107. *The New York Times,* June 6, 1978.
108. *Renmin ribao,* December 5, 1959.
109. For some published accounts, see "Interview"; 1974My; Jonathan Mirsky, "China after Nixon," *Annals of the American Academy of Political and Social Science* 402:84–106 (1972); and Liu Xiaoxiao in *Ming bao yuekan* 84:42–47 (December 1972), trans. in *Dilemma*. I am grateful to a number of people who shared with me their experiences and unpublished notes of conversations with Fei in the 1970s.

110. *Renmin ribao,* March 28, 1978.
111. Foreign Broadcast Information Service, *Daily Report—People's Republic of China,* February 15, 1979, p. E9.
112. Ibid., May 17, 1979, pp. L19–20; May 18, 1979, pp. L10–11.
113. *Beijing Review,* March 30, 1979, pp. 29–30.
114. *Renmin ribao,* February 25, 26, 28, and March 9, 1978. His name also appeared in *Renmin ribao,* for example, for attending a memorial service on the anniversary of Sun Yat-sen's death (March 13, 1978), being present at a May Day meeting on nationalities unity (May 2, 1978), sending a wreath to the funeral of Qi Yanming (November 3, 1978), and being part of a high-level delegation to celebrate the 20th anniversary of the Ningxia Hui Autonomous Region (October 25, 1978). There is, no doubt, significance to the publication of a photograph of Fei and Mao beaming at each other at a 1956 Political Consultative Conference meeting (*Beijing Review,* January 19, 1979); several other pictures of Fei may be found in early 1979 issues of *China Reconstructs* and *China Pictorial.*
115. *Renmin ribao,* February 24, 1979.
116. I met him for the first time then, but the manuscript for this book was already finished and none of the information in it comes from Fei directly; in our two-hour private talk, he refused to discuss himself or my work on him, of which he had read an earlier version.
117. It is interesting to note that recently a wall poster in a Wuhan steel mill has demanded a social science organization independent of the government (*New York Times,* December 12, 1978); such a development, however, seems most unlikely.
118. Foreign Broadcast Information Service, *Daily Report,* December 15, 1980, p. L22.
119. Ibid., February 2, 1981, pp. L9–10.
120. Ibid., August 20, 1980, p. L9.
121. *Wen hui pao,* January 4, 1980.
122. *Renmin ribao,* March 8, 1980.
123. As in, for example, Foreign Broadcast Information Service, *Daily Report,* August 20, 1980, p. L9.
124. Foreign Broadcast Information Service, *Daily Report,* March 13, 1980, p. L15; Joint Publications Research Service #7537 (March 13, 1980), p. 10; *Beijing Review,* March 21, 1980, pp. 6–7.
125. Martin K. Whyte and Burton Pasternak, "Sociology and Anthropology," in *Humanities and Social Science Research in China: Recent History and Future Prospects,* ed., Anne F. Thurston and Jason F. Parker, (New York, Social Science Research Council, 1980), pp. 140–162.
126. *Renmin ribao,* March 21, 1979; *Guangming ribao,* March 21, 1979, trans. in Joint Publications Research Service #073474, p. 41.

127. *Wen hui bao,* January 4, 1980.
128. Ibid.
129. George Baybrooke, "Recent Developments in Chinese Social Sciences, 1977-79," *China Quarterly* 79:593-607 (1979).

*Annotated Bibliography
of the Works of Fei Xiaotong*

The source for most of the information in this book about Fei's ideas has been, naturally, the writings of Fei Xiaotong himself. Where I have drawn on the works of others for background material, they are cited in the notes. There is a small but growing literature on Fei, which includes some recent works I was not able to use. Two new scholarly and thoughtful books I received too late to benefit from are both by authors in Hong Kong, where there seems to be considerable interest in this intellectually Western yet patriotic Chinese: Li Yefu, *Fei Xiaotong zhuan* (Biography of Fei Xiaotong; Hong Kong, Yi shan tushu gongying gongsi, 1976); and Siu-lan Wong, *Sociology and Socialism in Contemporary China* (London, 1979). James P. McGough, trans., *Fei Hsiao-t'ung: The Dilemma of a Chinese Intellectual* (White Plains, 1979) is a collection of articles by and about Fei, mostly from the 1950s; I have added references to these translations to my notes and bibliography. An older article is Elise Hawtin, "The 'Hundred Flowers Movement' and the Role of the Intellectual in China: Fei Hsiao-t'ung, a Case History," *Papers on China* 12:147-198 (East Asian Research Center, Harvard University, 1958). More recently there is A. R. Sanchez and S. L. Wong, "Research Note: On 'An Interview with Chinese Anthropologists," *China Quarterly* 60:775-790 (1974); and Ambrose Yeo-chi King and Wang Tse-sang, "The Development and Death of Chinese Academic Sociology," *Modern Asian Studies* 12.1:37-58 (1978). The hostile articles about Fei published in China in 1957-1958 are far too numerous to list; I have cited many in the notes to Chapter 8, and a handy sampling may be had in *Fei Xiaotong pipan ziliao huibian* (Collected materials in criticism of Fei Xiaotong; n.p., n.d., [Hong Kong, c. 1972?]). There have been occasional articles about Fei in the Hong Kong, or more rarely Taiwan, press; any I found helpful are cited in the notes. Finally, the biography of Fei in Howard L. Boorman, ed., *Biographical Dictionary of Republican China* Vol. II (New York, 1968), is basically accurate.

What follows is as complete a list of all of Fei's writings as I have been able to compile, including translations he made of works by others. The only intentional exclusions have been the dozens of articles that also appeared in book form; these have not been listed individually as articles, although where they first appeared is indicated in the annotations to the books. It must be added, however, that Fei published profusely and widely. I have searched through scores of periodicals and found items from his pen in forty or so newspapers and journals, but cannot hope to have found everything. Particularly for the war years, I know of several serials in which he published but which are not to be found now outside the People's Republic.

In the annotations, I have tried to provide a concise summary of the major theme of each work. I have accorded more space here to less important works, particularly articles, than to important books discussed at length in the text. Information is also given about translations, reprintings, and other bibliographic matters. Most items may be found in the Harvard-Yenching Library; for the remainder, locations are specified. Authors other than Fei (joint authors, or of works he just translated or edited) have been indicated, as well as the few occasions in which he used a pen name. If no name is specified, the author is understood to be Fei Xiaotong alone. I have departed, in the case of Chinese articles, from the usual practice of providing romanization of titles in addition to Chinese characters and translation. It should also be noted that, in giving page references in the text, I have used roman numerals to indicate separately paginated front matter (e.g., *GDYN*:v–xx), though the page numbers were not so written in the Chinese original.

The arrangement of this bibliography and the abbreviations used to refer to it in the text may appear complex and cumbersome at first sight, but they were designed for the reader's convenience and, once understood, will, I hope, prove easy to use. I had two goals in mind. First, I wanted the bibliography to be useful and informative in itself, so that an interested reader could browse through and get some sense of Fei's *oeuvre;* this necessitated a system of arrangement more meaningful than the English alphabet. The more important works were separated from the hundreds of briefer articles and grouped together in Bibliography A, which includes all Fei's books, pamphlets, and series of five or more articles. (The inclusion of the last is based on the fact that many, if not most, of Fei's books were originally published as series of articles in newspapers or magazines and that those two or three series which never appeared as books logically belong together with those that did.) Then, it seemed a good idea to separate articles in Chinese (put in Bibliography B) from those in English (Bibliography C); this is for the convenience of the reader who does not read Chinese but might be interested in a list of Fei's English articles. The few unpublished works I have seen, all in English, are listed together with the English articles. Thus, the bibliography is in three parts:

Bibliography

A. Books, Pamphlets, and Series of Five or More Articles
B. Articles in Chinese
C. Articles and Unpublished Materials in English

Within each part, the arrangement is chronological according to date of first publication. In the case of books of articles, the approximate date when most of the articles first appeared seemed more significant than the year when the book itself was published; thus, for example, *Neidi nongcun* (1946) is treated as dating from about 1940–1942, and *China's Gentry* (1953) from 1947–1948. For convenience, references in the text to Chinese articles are indexed in Bibliography B rather than by code number in the Index.

In the second place, this bibliography serves as the key to the coded abbreviations used in parentheses in the text to refer to Fei's works. From the form of the reference, one knows what kind of a work it is and, thus, which part of the bibliography to look in, as explained in the "Note on the Form of References" at the beginning. Thus, an abbreviation like 1943Ja1 indicates a Chinese article, which will be in Bibliography B and, since the symbol indicates the date (January 1, 1943) there should be no trouble locating it in the chronological list. "Review of Zhao" indicates an English article in Bibliography C, which is short enough for the reader to run his eye over all the abbreviated titles. Finally, *XTZG* and *Earthbound* are books in Bibliography A; in many cases the reader will know from the discussion in the text the approximate date but, if he doesn't, the alphabetical list of abbreviations below indicates the year under which each item may be found.

A. BOOKS, PAMPHLETS, AND SERIES OF FIVE OR MORE ARTICLES

CFMG 1945	*JCTX* 1936	*RWLX* 1944
CFYL 1947	*JZS* 1943	*RX&JQ* 1946
Dilemma 1979	*LBTX* 1947–1948	*SHBQ* 1935–1936
DXGZ 1949–1950	*LCNT* 1941	*SYZD* 1947
Earthbound 1945	*Machine Age* 1944	*3 Types* 1943
GDYN 1947	*MGRXG* 1947	*WHL* 1937–1938
Gentry 1947–1948	*MZ,XF,RQ* 1946	*WZYN* 1949–1950
GTBR 1935–1946	*NDNC* 1940–1942	*XDMZ* 1951
HHC 1955	*Peasant Life* 1939	*XTCJ* 1947–1948
HLY 1936	*RQ&BJ* 1943–1944	*XTZG* 1947–1948
HQ&SQ 1947		

1935–1936

SHBQ William F. Ogburn. *Shehui bianqian* 社会变迁 (Social change), Trans. Fei Xiaotong 费孝通 and Wang Tonghui 王同惠. Shanghai, Shangwu 商务, 1935. Not seen.

GTBR Fei and Wang Tonghui. "Wei diaocha yanjiu Gui-sheng tezhong buzu renzhong" 为调查研究桂省特种部族人种 (To investigate and study the minority tribal races of Guangxi), *Yuzhou xunkan* 宇宙旬刊 3.4:36–38, 3.8:23–28, 3.9:37–38, 3.11:27–33, 4.1:47–52, 4.2:32–40, and 4.3:35–40 (October 15, November 25, December 5 & 25, 1935, January 15 & 25, and February 5, 1936). At Stanford. All but one of the 19 parts were also published, under the title "Gui xing tongxun" 桂行通讯 (Reports from a trip in Guangxi), in the Beiping *Chen-bao* 晨报, October 23, November 6, December 11 & 18, 1935, and January 8, 15 & 22, 1936 ("Shehui yanjiu" 社会研究 [Social research]* Nos. 107, 109, 114, 115, 118, 119, and 120); and Tianjin *Yi-shi bao* 益世报, May 13, 20, & 27, 1936 ("Shehui yanjiu" n.s. Nos. 2, 3, 4). A series of 19 reports, 13 by Fei and 6 by Wang, written every few days over a two-month period from September 25 to November 25 during their trip to Guangxi. Full of fresh impressions and details of their day-to-day activities.

HLY Wang Tonghui. *Guangxi-sheng Xiang-xian Dongnan-xiang Hualan Yao shehui zuzhi* 广西省象县东南乡花蓝猺社会组织 (Social organization of the Hualan Yao people of Southeast xiang, Xiang county, Guangxi). Introduction by Wu Wenzao. Edited with an afterword (pp. 49–52) by Fei. Shanghai, Shangwu (Guangxi provincial government special research report), 1936. 11 & 52 pp. illus. An edition of 500 (according to notice in *Yi-shi bao*, May 19, 1937). Simultaneously published in *Yi-shi bao*, July 1, 8, 15, 22, 19, and August 5, 1936 ("Shehui yanjiu" n.s. Nos. 9, 10, 10 [i.e. 11], 12, 13, 14). An earlier version of Fei's "editor's afterword" had already appeared in *Yi-shi bao*, June 6, 1936 ("Shehui yanjiu" n.s. No. 5). Put together by Fei from his wife's notes after her death, this book gives a description of marriage, the family, kinship, life cycle, village organization, and economy of this small (700) non-Chinese tribe isolated in the mountains of China's far south.

JCTX "Jiang-cun tongxun" 江村通讯 (Reports from a Yangzi village), *Yi-shi bao,* July 10, 22, 29, August 26, and September 9, 1936 ("Shehui yanjiu" n.s. Nos. 10 [i.e. 11], 12, 13, 17, 19). In seven parts, dated July 3 to August 25, 1936. Letters from the field in Kaixiangong, while he was collecting the data used in *Peasant Life.* On why he chose to use ethnographic methods to study a peasant village in his own society; the importance of trading boats; population limitation and *tongyangxi* (girls adopted as future daughters-in-law); ill-suited aspects of the modern education system; sheep-raising and the decline in the silk industry; and cross-cousin marriage.

*For a description of this newspaper supplement see under 1933O11 below.

1937-1938

WHL Bronislaw Malinowski. *Wenhua lun* 文化论 (Theory of culture). Trans. Fei et al. Preface by Fei, with a chart of culture by Wu Wenzao. Chongqing, Shangwu (Shehuixue congkan 社会学丛刊), 1944; also, Shanghai, Shangwu, 1947; Taibei, Shangwu, 1967. 133 pp. Two-thirds of the translation first appeared in *Yi-shi bao,* February 27, March 3, and May 5, 1937 ("Shehui Yanjiu" n.s. Nos. 42, 43, 52), and the whole in *Shehuixue jie* 社会学界 10:111-206 (June 1938), with Jia Yuanyi 贾元羲 and Huang Di 黄迪 , whose names do not appear on later editions, listed as co-translators. Translated from a manuscript Malinowski gave Wu Wenzao in 1936; it was an expansion of his article on "Culture" in the *Encyclopedia of the Social Sciences* (New York, 1931), IV, 621-646, which he said he planned to publish as a book called *What is Culture?*, but which has in fact never appeared in English, so far as I know.

1939

Peasant Life *Peasant Life in China: a Field Study of Country Life in the Yangtze Valley.* Preface by Bronislaw Malinowski. London, G. Routledge, and New York, Dutton, 1939; also, London, Kegan Paul ("International Library of Sociology and Social Reconstruction," ed. Karl Mannheim), 1943 (fifth impression 1962); New York, Oxford University Press, 1946; n.p., n.d. (Taibei?, 1960s?); and New York, AMS Press, 1976. 26 & 300 pp. illus. All editions are identical except the Taiwan photo-reprint which omits Fei's name, the dedication to Wang Tonghui, the page of acknowledgments, and some illustrations, and truncates Malinowski's name to "Bronis Malin." The last regular printing was 1962, after which Routledge and Kegan Paul undertook, on Fei's written request, never again to reprint it. Only slightly revised from Fei's London PhD thesis ("Kaihsienkung"), this is the study of one village in Fei's native Wujiang county, emphasizing economic topics such as land tenure, agriculture, subsidiary occupations, marketing, finance, household expenditures, property, and inheritance, as well as family and kinship. The field work was done in July and August 1936. Summarized in Elman R. Service, *Profiles in Ethnology* (rev. ed., New York, 1971), Chapter 20. Never published in Chinese, it was translated immediately into Japanese (Japan occupied the area in November 1937) twice by translators working independently in Peking and Tokyo:

Shina no nōmin seikatsu 支那の農民生活 (Peasant life in China). Trans. Ichiki Ryō 市木亮 . Tokyo, Kyōzaisha 教材社, 1939. 22 & 385 pp. illus. Lacks appendix and index. At Berkeley.

Shina no nōmin seikatsu—Yōsukō ryūiki ni okeru den'en seikatsu no jittai chōsa 支那の農民生活-楊子江流域に於ける田園生活の實態調査 (Peasant life in China, a field study of country life in the Yangzi valley). Trans. and preface by Senba Yasuo 仙波泰雄 and Shioya Yasuo 塩谷 安夫. Tokyo, Seikatsusha 生活社, 1940 (orig. 1939). 15 & 365 pp. illus. At Yale.

1940-1942

NDNC *Neidi nongcun* 内地农村 (Villages of the interior). Shanghai, Shenghuo, 1946; also, H.K., "Mei-ming" 未名, n.d. (c. 1972). 7 & 131 pp. Articles which had all, except the 1946 preface, been published in 1940-1942. I have seen most of the original articles, whose titles need not be listed here, in *Jinri pinglun* 今日评论 3.11:170-173 (March 17, 1940), 3.14:216-218 (April 7, 1940), 3.17:265-267 (April 28, 1940), 3.23:362-364 (June 9, 1940), 4.3:40-42 (June 21, 1940), 5.6 (February 6, 1941) and 5.10 (not seen); *Dongfang zazhi* 东方杂志 37.13: 48-50 (July 1, 1940); *Dangdai pinglun* 当代评论 1.13:183-185 (September 29, 1941) and 1.20 (November 1941; not seen, answering and answered by articles by Wu Wenhui 吴文晖 in the same journal 1.10 [September 1941] and 2.3 [February 1942]). The last article in the book, arguing at length for the development of rural industry in China, had appeared, with two more pages, as the preface, dated September 1941, to Zhang Ziyi 张子毅, *Yi-cun shougongye* 易村手工业 (Handicrafts in Yi-cun; Chongqing, 1943; translated as Part II of *Earthbound China*), pp. 1-20; part had also been published as " 乡土工业的两种型式 " (Two types of rural industry), *Xin jingji* 新经济 6.7:139-142 (January 1, 1942). Not research reports, although in a sense they grow out of Fei's Yunnan investigations, these articles are more in the nature of discussions of government policies that affect rural areas in the southwest during the war; naturally he has many policy suggestions.

LCNT *Lu-cun nongtian* 禄村农田 (The paddy fields of Lu village). Chongqing, Shangwu (Shehuixue congkan), 1943. 193 pp. At Columbia. Originally published in mimeographed form by the Yunnan University Sociological Research Station in 1941 (see review by Wu Jingchao 吴景超 in *Xin Jingji* 6.9:195-198 [February 1, 1942]). Summarized in *3 Types*; translated and revised to become Part I of *Earthbound*. A full report of Fei's 1938-1939 four-month field study of a Yunnan village 70 miles west of Kunming; concentrating on the land system and agricultural economy.

1943-1944

JCS "Jizu chaoshan ji" 鸡足朝山记 (A pilgrimage to Jizu mountain), *Shenghuo dao-bao* 生活导报 16:4, 18:4, 19:4, 20:4, & 21.4 (March 6, 27, April 3, 10 & 17. 1943). A five-part series on a trip with some other Kunming scholars up a mountain near Dali in western Yunnan; partly about Buddhism, it concludes by recounting a miraculous legend connecting the mountain with the Buddha's disciple Kasyapa.

3 Types Li Youyi 李有益, Fei, and Zhang Ziyi. *Three Types of Rural Economy in Yunnan*. New York, Institute of Pacific Relations, 1943. Mimeo., 35 pp. Short summaries of Fei's *LCNT*, Zhang's *Yi-cun shougongye* (both of which are translated in full in *Earthbound*), and a work by Li about a mixed community of Chinese and Lolos.

RQ&BJ Renqing yu bangjiao–lü Mei ji yan 人情与邦交 – 旅美寄言 (Human feelings and international relations–letters from America). Kunming, Ziyou luntan 自由论坛, 1945. 6 & 72 pp. Originally published in the Kunming *Shenghuo dao-bao* and *Ziyou luntan* 自由论坛 fall 1943 to spring 1944. Articles on the U.S., written while Fei was there.

Machine Age Shi Guoheng 史国衡. *China Enters the Machine Age: A Study of Labor in Chinese War Industry*. Supplementary chapter by Tian Rukang 田汝康. Trans. and ed. Fei and Francis L.K. Hsu 许烺光. Cambridge, Mass., Harvard University Press, 1944. 24 & 206 pp. Translation of Shi's *Kun chang laogong* 昆厂劳工 (Labor in a Kunming factory; Shanghai, Shangwu, 1946). An "Editorial Note" by Elton Mayo and Dorothea Mayo indicates that Fei made the translation with their help, and speaks of Fei elaborating and expanding the last chapter; the subsequently published Chinese version has an "Afterword" by Fei (see 1946a). The book describes worker inefficiency and discontent, as found in a factory in 1940–1941 by a younger colleague from Fei's research station.

RWLX Raymond Firth. *Renwen leixing* 人文类型 (Human types). Trans. Fei. Chongqing, Shangwu (Shehui congkan), 1944. 157 pp. Seen at Columbia, which has subsequently lost it. Translation of a well-known anthropology primer, *Human Types* (first published in 1938) by Malinowski's successor at L.S.E.

1945

Earthbound Fei and Zhang Ziyi ["Chang Chih-i"]. *Earthbound China: A Study of Rural Economy in Yunnan*. Rev. Eng. ed. prepared in collaboration with Paul Cooper and Margaret Park Redfield. University of Chicago Press, 1945; also, London, Routledge and Kegan Paul (International Library of Sociology and Social Reconstruction), 1949. 319 pp. Translation, prepared by Fei in the U.S. in 1943–1944, of his own *LCNT* and Zhang's *Yi-cun shougongye* and "Yu-cun tudi he ziben" 玉村土地和资本 (Land and capital in Yu-can; "not yet published" in 1946 [*NDNC,* iii]). An introduction discusses the method of "community studies," intensive anthropological investigations of the total life in a small area, guided by theoretical generalizations which are tested and refined. The conclusion argues that the three studies and *Peasant Life* taken together demonstrate the following facts: most Chinese peasants need supplemental income from outside agriculture; the development of commerce with the outside tends to increase tenancy by destroying the kind of labor-intensive rural industry that provides employment for peasants, and promoting the kind of capital-intensive industry that further concentrates wealth and land ownership; and, finally, the solution is the development of technologically modernized, cooperative rural industries. Excerpts reprinted in D. J. Dwyer, *China Now* (Harlow, Essex, 1974), pp. 87-110.

CFMG *Chu fang Meiguo* 初訪美國 (First visit to America). Chongqing, U.S. Office of War Information, 1945; also, Shanghai, Shenghuo 生活, 1946. 182 pp. Chapters 3, 5, 10 and 12 appeared in *Zhou bao* 周报 39:12-15, 40:14-16, 41:15-17, & 42:17-19 (June 1, 8, 15, & 22, 1946); and Chapters 8-10 were summarized in 1946Je6. Essays about the United States, written mostly after he had returned to China (a few pages are from *RQ&BJ*). Trying to explain American culture to the Chinese, Fei discusses the American past, political trends, social problems of industry, Chinese-Americans, social customs, attitudes towards old people, relations between the sexes, the role of tradition, religion, and so on. Not uncritical, but basically hopeful that America is moving towards economic equality as well as political democracy.

RX&JQ Fei, Zhang Ziyi, Zhang Luoqun 张华群, and Yuan Fang 袁方. *Renxing he jiqi–Zhongguo shougongye de qiantu* 人性和机器–中国手工业的前途 (Human nature and the machine–the future of China's handicraft industries). Shanghai & Chongqing, Shenghuo (Shidai pinglun xiao congshu 时代评论小丛书), 1946. 28 pp. Appeared under Fei's name alone in *Zaisheng* 再生 105:11-13, 106:9-11, & 107:13-14 (March 25, April 1, & 8, 1946) apparently reprinted from a pamphlet published by Fei's Kunming *Shidai pinglun* 时代评论. Fei later said this piece resulted from a conversation in a Kunming teahouse about China's handicrafts industries, which he then wrote up (1947N8a). Describes the defects of Western urban industrial civilization, and argues that China should not go that way, but can't reject machines either. The answer is mechanizing village handicrafts; this is in accord with human nature.

MZ,XF,RQ *Minzhu, xianfa, renquan* 民主,宪法,人权 (Democracy, constitutions, and human rights). Preface by Pan Guangdan 潘光旦. Shanghai, Shenghuo (Qingnian zixue congshu 青年自学丛书), 1946 (5th printing 1948). 10 & 89 pp. Various chapters can be found in *Dagong bao* 大公报 April 14, 1946, pp. 2-3; *Zaisheng* 109:10-12, 123:8-11 (April 20 and July 27, 1946); *Wen cui* 文萃 22:14-15, 27:7-9, 31:6-8, & 34:18-20 (March 21, April 25, May 23, & June 13, 1946); and *Zhong Mei pinglun* 中美评论 1:22-24 (June 20, 1946).

"This is a collection of my papers on Democracy. These papers were first published in a weekly edited by myself and eventually forced to stop [*Shidai pinglun*], and then widely republished [in] at least five to six big papers in China. When it appeared as a book, it spread like in a wind. China is fully prepared to receive democratic ideas" (12/4/46 to MPR).

1947

SYZD *Shengyu zhidu* 生育制度 (The institutions for reproduction). Preface by Pan Guangdan. Shanghai, Shangwu (Shehuixue congkan), 1947. 45 & 200 pp. Preliminary versions of early chapters are 1941Ag30, 1941O15, and 1941O30. Based on Fei's course on the family at Yunnan University and Lianda. A functionalist examination of the family, comparing various courtship, marriage, child-rearing, and kinship practices in China, the modern West, and primitive peoples, with a view to determining their true functions. Fei believes that the basic function of marriage and the family is raising children, which is necessary for society. Abounds with references to Malinowski and other Western anthropologists and social and natural scientists, and Fei's own observations in China.

CFYL *Chong fang Ying-lun* 重访英论 (England revisited). Shanghai, Dagong bao (Dagong bao congshu 大公报丛书), n.d. [1947]. 92 pp. The first article was published in the *Shidai pinglun* and then in *Wen cui* 26:9-11 (April 18, 1946). The others were written from England or shortly after returning for the *Dagong bao;* e.g. Shanghai *Dagong bao,* December 15, 21, 1946, January 4, 21 & 28, March 1, 26, 27, and April 16, 1947. Articles from Fei's three-month visit to England in 1946-1947. Fei is encouraged and inspired by the example of peaceful and democratic socialist revolution ending special privilege under the new Labour Party Government.

GDYN John Edward D. Hall. *Gongdang yi nian* 工党一年 (Labour's first year). Trans. Fei and Shi Jing 史靖, Preface by Fei. Shanghai, Shenghuo, 1947. 29 & 192 pp. In the Library of Congress. The first four chapters appeared in *Xue feng banyuekan* 雪風半月刊 (Beiping). Translation mostly by Fei (Shi helped with Chapters 15-21) of *Labour's First Year* (London, 1947), a British journalist's summary of the Parliamentary debates in the 1945-1946 session. Fei's 29-page introduction admiringly explains the democratic spirit of the English political system and the moderate socialism of the Labour Government.

MGRXG *Meiguoren de xingge* 美国人的性格 (The American character). Shanghai, Shenghuo, 1947. 90 pp. Originally published in *Guancha* 观察 2.11:13-14, 19, 2.13:12-13, 2.15:9-10, 2.16:13-14, 2.17:10-12, 2.20:12-14, 2.21:14-16, & 2.22:12-14 (May 5, 24, June 7, 14, 21, July 12, 19, & 26, 1947). Based on Margaret Mead, *And Keep Your Powder Dry: An Anthropologist Looks at America* (New York, 1943;

English edition entitled *The American Character*), which Fei started to translate but ended by freely adapting for Chinese readers. On American cultural characteristics and their bases in American history and child-rearing practices.

1947-1948

XTZG Xiangtu Zhongguo 乡土中国 (Rural China). Shanghai, Guancha (Guancha congshu 观察丛书), 1948 (6th printing 1949); also, Taibei, Lüzhou 绿州, 1967 (author: "Fei Tong"); Hong Kong, Fenghuang 凤凰 (Renwen kexue congshu 人文科学丛书), n.d. (c. 1971; with *XTCJ* and 1957Je1). 106 pp. All but the last two chapters were originally published (some in slightly different form) in *Shiji pinglun* 世纪评论 2.3:15-17, 2.5, 2.7:12-14, 2.12: 13-16, 2.16:13-15, 2.18:13-15, 2.21:13-15, 3.1:10-12, 3.4:12-14, 3.6: 12-14, 3.8:14-15, 3.10:12-14, & 3.13:14-16 (July 19, August 2 & 16, September 20, October 18, November 1 & 22, 1947, January 1 & 24, February 7 & 21, March 6 & 27, 1948). Not at all like his field work reports, these essays, developed for a course on rural sociology, describe the general characteristics of village life in China and the rural bases of Chinese culture, somewhat along the lines of what Margaret Mead had tried to do for America. Most of the fourth article and a few sentences from the fifth are translated in J. Mason Gentzler, ed., *Changing China* (New York, 1977), pp. 210-214.

HQ&SQ Wu Han 吴晗, Fei, et al. *Huang-quan yu shen-quan* 皇权与绅权 (Imperial power and gentry power). Afterword by Fei. Shanghai, Guancha (Guancha congshu), 1948. 177 pp. Fei's three articles (pp. 1-38) appeared originally in *Guancha* 3.2:9-12, 3.8:11-15, & 3.18: 10-12, 7 (September 5, October 18, & December 27, 1947), and were later translated in *Gentry*:17-74; there are some differences in these three versions. Fei discusses the Chinese gentry over the centuries, the basis of their social position, their power relations with the throne, and their bias against technical knowledge.

XTCJ Xiangtu chongjian 乡土重建 (Rural recovery). Shanghai, Guancha (Guancha congshu), 1948 (4th printing 1949); also Taibei, Lüzhou, 1967 (author: "Fei Tong"); Hong Kong, Fenghuang, n.d. (c. 1971; with *XTZG* and 1957Je1). 169 pp. Essays mostly previously published in the Shanghai *Dagong bao,* February 21, April 27, June 3, September 23 and 24, October 26, November 30, 1947, January 11, February 14, March 7, 9, & 23, 1948; and one in *Zhongguo jianshe* 中国建设 6.2:32-34 (May 1, 1948). The first was originally a talk given in English ("L.S.E. Speech"); the third, fifth, seventh, and eighth articles are translated in *Gentry*:75-141; and the tenth, eleventh, twelfth, thirteenth, and fourteenth are translated in "Problems" and "Financing." On the rural economy, the economic relations between town and country, the desertion of the gentry from the countryside, and the need for landlords to give up their privileges and become productive. Fei offers proposals for improving and promoting cooperative rural industries.

Gentry *China's Gentry: Essays in Rural-Urban Relations.* Rev. and ed. Margaret Park Redfield, with six life histories of Chinese gentry families collected by Yung-teh Chow 周榮德 . Introduction by Robert Redfield. Chicago, University of Chicago Press, 1953 (paperback edition, 1968). 289 pp. illus. Pp. 17–141 are translations made by Fei in collaboration with Mrs. Redfield in Peking in the fall of 1948 of seven 1947–1948 essays: the three by Fei from *HQ&SQ* and four from *XTCJ*. Excerpts reprinted in William T. Liu, ed., *Chinese Society Under Communism: A Reader* (London & New York, 1964), pp. 47–55. On the gentry and the rural economy.

LBTX "Lu-bian tianxia" 炉边天下 (The world from fireside), *Guancha* 3.16:18–19, 3.18:18–19, 3.20:18–19, 3.22:17,19, 4.2:17–18, 4.3:18, 4.5:13–14, 5.10:14–15, 5.14:11 (December 13 & 27, 1947, January 10 & 24, March 6, 13, & 27, October 30, November 27, 1948). A series of articles on international relations, begun in late November 1947. Four months later Fei pronounced winter over, his fire out, and the series terminated; he had written ten columns, he said, two of which the editor had run as special articles (presumably 1948Ja17a and 1948Ja31; I can't account for the tenth, perhaps it had been 1948Ja31 or 1948F28). The following winter, explaining that he was badly in need of money because of the inflation, he started the series again; two articles appeared before the Communists took the Qinghua campus in December 1948. There are articles on the internal politics and foreign affairs of the United States, Great Britain, France, Italy, Greece, and China. Running through them all is the theme of American foreign policy and its harmful effects on the world. The Cold War is caused by the U.S. and serves its business interests; the Marshall Plan, too, is for the purpose of securing an economically healthy market for U.S. goods. But China is not as important to American capitalists as Europe, and a Marshall Plan for China is not to be expected.

1949–1950

DXGZ Daxue de gaizao 大学的改造 (Reform of the universities). Shanghai, Shanghai chuban gongsi 上海出版公司, 1950. 147 pp. Articles, some originally published in *Xinhua yuebao* 新华月报 1.1:201–203 (November 15, 1949; reprinted from *Guangming ribao* 光明日报 , August 18, 1949); *Xin jianshe* 新建設 1.4:14–16, 1.6:11–14, & 2.2:20–23 (October 20, November 17, 1949, & March 12, 1950). One article (pp. 52–66) was translated in *Shakai-gaku hyōron* 社会学評論 17:89–97 (1954). Articles on various changes or proposals for change in the universities in the first year or so of Communist control: curriculum reform, the role of sociology, political study, emphasis on technical education, de-emphasis of entrance examinations and competition, the use of vacations for practical work, the rationalizing of salaries and simplifying of administration, democratic decision-making, health insurance and savings schemes. Fei seems less to be offering personal suggestions than reporting (presumably for the benefit of those at other colleges) what has been done or decided at Qinghua, a major Peking university.

WZYN *Wo zhe-yi nian* 我这一年 (This year for me). Shanghai, Sanlian 三联, 1950. 76 pp. Articles, originally published in *Xinhua yuebao* 1.1:54 (November 15, 1949; from a New China News Agency release, September 7, 1949); 1.4:1003–1004 (February 1950; from *Renmin ribao* 人民日报, January 3, 1950); *Guancha* 6.2:11–12, 6.6:12–13, 6.7:13–15, 6.9:20–21, 6.12:15, 17 (November 16, 1949, January 16, February 1, March 1, April 16, 1950); and *Xuexi* 学习 2.3:20–22 (April 11, 1950). Three also appeared in other collections: "我这一年" (This year for me), in Pei Wenzhong 裴文中 et al., *Wo-de sixiang shi zenyang zhuanbian-guolai-de* 我的思想是怎样转变过来的 (How my thought was changed; Peking, 1950), pp. 71–77.

"解放以来" (Since Liberation), in Zhang Zhizhong 张治中 et al., *Zenyang gaizao* 怎样改造 (How to reform; Hong Kong, 1950), pp. 36–41.

"知识分子与政治学习" (The intellectuals and political study; retitled "超越政治" [Being above politics] in WZYN), in Fei et al., *Jiu renwu de gaizao* 旧人物的改造 (Reform of people from the old society; Canton & Hong Kong, 1950), pp. 1–7.

Articles on various aspects of thought reform for intellectuals educated in the "old society." Fei relates some personal experiences in discussing what should and should not be done. Topics include: learning that real democracy is the kind of mass support that brought the Communists to power; how to run a political study class and answer objections frequently heard from college students; studying Marxism-Leninism and actively working to change one's outlook; getting over petty bourgeois individualism and learning to cooperate to serve the people; overcoming exploitative attitudes through labor (in his case gardening); getting rid of the notion that the goal of study is to acquire a skill to live from; and the danger for those who have been progressive in the past of being self-satisfied.

1951

XDMZ *Xiongdi minzu zai Guizhou* 兄弟民族在贵州 (Fraternal nationalities in Guizhou). Shanghai, Sanlian, 1951. 90 pp. Originally serialized in *Xin guancha* 2.6:14–15, 2.7:16–17, 2.8:17–18, 2.9:10–11, 2.10:12–13, 2.11:14–17, 2.12:12–14 (March 25, April 10, 25, May 10, 25,

June 10, 25, 1951). Condensed translation as "Kweichow." What Fei learned about ethnic minorities in this southwestern province while on a six-month goodwill mission representing the new government.

1955

HHC *Hua shuo Hulunbei'er caoyuan* 话说呼伦贝尔草原 (The story of the Hulunbuir Prairie). Peking, Tongsu wenyi 通俗文艺, 1956. 44 pp. Serialized in *Xin guancha* 17:12-13, 19:27-29, 21:11-13, 22:11-13 (September 1, October 1, November 1 & 15, 1955). (My page references are to the *Xin guancha* series; I have not seen the other.) An informal discussion of nomadic life in a part of the Inner Mongolia grasslands, based on a visit in the fall of 1954. People live in tents, eat cows' milk products and sheeps' meat, and ride horses. The beginnings of cooperatives and of feeding herds with mechanically cut grass augur fixed settlements and a better life in the future.

1979

Dilemma Fei Hsiao-t'ung: The Dilemma of a Chinese Intellectual. Trans. and ed. with an introduction by James P. McGough. White Plains, M.E. Sharpe, Inc., 1979. 144 pp. Translations of 1947O15, 1957F20, 1957Je1, and 1957Jl13, together with four 1957-1958 articles against him and a report of a 1972 interview with Fei.

FMLY "Fang-Mei lüe ying" 访美掠影 (Glimpses of America), *Wen hui bao* 文汇报 (Shanghai), January 9 to February 4, 1980, daily (27 installments). On Fei's April 1979 trip to the United States. Partially translated as "Glimpses of America."

B. ARTICLES IN CHINESE

Numbers following the entries on Chinese articles refer to the principal places in the text where such articles are mentioned.

1930 "第五届华东暑期大学东吴同学会杂记" (Notes of the Suzhou University students association in the fifth session of the East China Summer School), *Dongwu niankan 1930* 东吴年刊 ("The Soochow Annual"), pp. 355-356. Signed "Tong" 通; on p. 325 Fei is identified as secretary of the group. College yearbook reminiscences of summer school; light, poetic, humorous; in classical Chinese. 10

1932 Fei Qing 费青 and Fei Xiaotong, trans., "中日战争目击记" (An eyewitness account of the Sino-Japanese War), *Zaisheng* 再生 1.7:1-26* (November 20); 1.8:1-23* (December 20); 1.9:1-26* (January 20, 1933). A translation of James Allen, *Under the Dragon Flag*

---

*Pagination is separate for each article.

(London, 1898), an English sailor's record of Chinese cowardice and incompetence, and Japanese butchery in the 1894 war. The translators' preface is an emotional call for the courage to fight for the nation.   13

1933J1 "季亭史社会学理论摘论" (A summary of Giddings's sociological theories), *Shehuixue kan* 社会学刊 4.1:1–14*
A translation of F. H. Hankins, "Franklin Henry Giddings, 1885–1931: some aspects of his sociological theory," *American Journal of Sociology* 37:349–367 (November 1931).   30

1933O1 "社会学者派克教授论中国" (The sociologist Professor Park discusses China), *Zaisheng* 2.1:1–10*. Translation of a short piece by Robert E. Park on the maturity of Chinese culture, where people's roles mesh harmoniously and it is not possible to change one part and leave the rest. In the last four pages, Fei provides a biography of Park and an introduction to his theories.   32, 36, 52–53

1933O11 "社会研究的程序" (The process of social research), Beiping *Chen bao* 晨报 ("Shehui yanjiu" 社会研究 No. 6). Not seen.

"Shehui yanjiu" (Social research) was a full page, edited by Yanjing sociology students and faculty, carried in the newspaper *Chen bao* every Wednesday from September 6, 1933, to March 18, 1936, and then in the Tianjin *Yi-shi bao* from May 6, 1936, to July 7, 1937. Harvard has a good run of the *Chen bao* and two incomplete separately bound volumes of "Shehui yanjiu" for 1933–1935. The *Yi-shi bao* was to be found nowhere in the United States, Japan, Taiwan, or Hong Kong when I began this study, but has subsequently become available from the Center for Chinese Research Materials in Washington, D.C., on a microfilm from South Korea. Author indexes for most of the issues of "Shehui yanjiu" may be found in *Chen bao* September 5, 1934 (Special No. 50); September 4, 1935 (No. 101); and *Yi-shi bao* May 5, 1937 (n.s. No. 52).

1933N15 "社会变迁研究中都市和乡村" (City and country in the study of social change), *Chen bao* ("Shehui yanjiu" No. 11). To understand social change in China it is more important to study cities, which are the source even of rural change, and their "natural communities"; follows R.E. Park, "Sociology," in *Research in the Social Sciences*, ed. Wilson Gee, (New York, 1929), pp. 3–49.   32, 37, 53, 54

1933D "派克及季亭史二家社会学学说几个根本的分歧点" (Basic differences in the sociological theories of Park and Giddings), in *Paike shehuixue lunwen ji* 派克社会学论文集 (Essays on R.E. Park's sociology. Ed. Yanjing Sociology Club;

*Pagination is separate for each article.

Beiping), pp. 185-225. At Stanford. Long, thoughtful, analytical comparison of two American sociologists; Fei tends to favor Park. 30, 46

1933D27 " 韦柏论社会科学之应用及其限制 " (The Webbs on the uses and limitations of social science), *Chen bao*, December 17, 1933, & January 10, 1934 ("Shehui yanjiu," No. 18 [i.e. 17] & 18). Translation of the last chapter of Sidney and Beatrice Webb, *Methods of Social Study* (London, 1932), on how sociology contributes to social progress but cannot supply moral values. 24, 30-31

1934F7 " 论社会组织 " (Social organization), *Chen bao* ("Shehui yanjiu," No. 22). Social organization is the sum of individuals' social roles, a part of inherited culture, adapted to the environment. When the environment changes, people no longer know their roles, and social organization disintegrates. 32-33, 52, 53

1934Mr7 " 从'社会进化'到'社会平衡' " (From "social evolution" to "social equilibrium"), *Chen bao* ("Shehui yanjiu," No. 25). The dominant concept of social theory is changing from evolution to equilibrium; today the emphasis is on functions and interrelatedness of parts of a culture, and the study of concrete groups. 38-39

1934My7 " 周族婚姻制度及社会组织一考 " (An examination of the Zhou people's marriage system and social organization), *Qinghua zhoukan* 清华周刊 41.7:22-27. At Library of Congress. The vestiges of cross-cousin marriage in the Zhou dynasty system are revealed by *Er-ya* and *Shuo-wen* definitions of relationship terms. 33

1934My16 " 宗教热忱 " (Religious ardor), *Chen bao* ("Shehui yanjiu," No. 34). Commenting on his sister's article in the *Dagong bao*, May 10, which said that China was hampered by the lack of religious ardor which motivates people to work for society. Park too thinks social building requires religious ardor. But China has Confucianism as its basic spirit and does not need illusions. 20, 53

1934Je6 "' 知我罪我 '" ('That by which I will be known or condemned'), *Chen bao* ("Shehui yanjiu," No. 37 [i.e. 38]). On how, when the environment changes and culture is no longer adapted to it, we lack clear social roles, which are the basis for common life. Those who live in an age of change, therefore, suffer great stress. The title is Confucius speaking about the *Chun-qiu*, which he wrote (Fei says) in response to social disintegration. 53

1934Je " 亲迎婚俗之研究 " (An examination of the *qin-ying* custom [the groom going to get the bride]), *Shehuixue jie* 社会学界 8:155-186. Fei's BA thesis on an old wedding custom practiced in some areas and not in others. A thorough and careful historical examination, based on numerous local gazetteers; includes maps of the geographical distribution of this practice. 33-34

1934Ag8 "霍布浩士社会发展论概论" (Outline of Hobhouse's theory of social development), *Chen bao*, August 8 & 15 ("Shehui yanjiu," No. 47 & 48). A lengthy summary of L. T. Hobhouse's writings, pointing out how his theory, unlike Spencer's, justifies social reformism. 31

1934O17 "分析中华民族人种成分的方法和尝试" (Methods and attempts to analyze the racial composition of the Chinese people), *Chen bao*, October 17 ("Shehui yanjiu," No. 56). Calling for anthropometrical field work on Chinese races, following the example of Shirokogoroff. 39–40

1935Je19 "体质研究和社会选择" (Anthropometry and social selection), *Chen bao* ("Shehui yanjiu," No. 90). Fitness is relative to what kind of job one does. Instead of eugenicists' talk about "improving" the race as a whole, what is needed is the study of physical types and then social engineering to put people in appropriate jobs. 39–40

1935Ag14 Review of R. U. Sayce, *Primitive Arts and Crafts: an Introduction to the Study of Material Culture* (Cambridge, England, 1933), *Chen bao* ("Shehui yanjiu," No. 98). Signed "Tong"; fully identified in index (in No. 101, September 4, 1935, and at front of bound volume).

1935N15 "译「甘肃土人的婚姻」序" (Preface to the translation of *Le mariage chez les T'ou-jen du Kan-sou*), *Yuzhou xunkan* 宇宙旬刊 3.7:36–38. At Stanford. Fei's preface to Wang Tonghui's translation (never published?) of Louis Schram's book (Variétés sinologiques No. 58; Shanghai, 1932) about Monguors in Gansu. Fei advocates taking the patient ethnographic field work of this foreign missionary as a model and studying local customs, a study which is also an old Chinese tradition, instead of wildly trying to transplant Western institutions. 61, 63

1936F12 "关于追悼同惠的通讯" (Letter in memory of Tonghui), *Chen bao* ("Shehui yanjiu," No. 123). The whole page is a memorial issue for Miss Wang.

1936Je24 "社会研究中的价值问题" (Value questions in social research), *Yi-shi bao* ("Shehui yanjiu," n.s. No. 8). Fei urges the social researcher not to judge customs, but simply to describe them. On the basis of a thorough understanding of the culture (which only social research can supply), criticism and value judgments can be made later. 59

1936Jl22 "社会研究能有用么?" (Can social research be useful?), *Yi-shi bao* ("Shehui yanjiu," n.s. No. 12). This depends on government administrators. If they do not make use of research, it is not the fault of the researchers. 97

1936Ag12 "写在「汶上县的私塾组织」的前面" (Foreword to 'The Organization of old-style private schools in Wenshang hsien'), *Yi-shi bao* ("Shehui yanjiu" n.s. No. 15). This work, by Liao

Taichu 廖泰初, Fei calls an example of new functionalist community research, which—unlike the shallow and vacuous sociology seen in China so far—can provide the foundation for social reform. 28, 54

1936S2 "社会研究的关键" (The crux of social research), *Yi-shi bao* ("Shehui yanjiu," n.s. No. 16). Examples from Fei's own work in the Yao Mountains and Kaixiangong are used to show how the social researcher shouldn't use a pre-established survey form, for he can't know ahead of time what will be worth pursuing.

1936O14 Liao Taichu and Fei, "论普遍与特殊" (Universals and particulars), *Yi-shi bao* ("Shehui yanjiu," n.s. No. 23). Social research should concentrate on the particular, the individual, the unexpected—most of which are products of social disintegration.

1936D2 "伦市寄言—一本刊三年的回忆" (Letter from London—1, Recollections of three years of "Shehui yanjiu"), *Yi-shi bao* ("Shehui yanjiu," n.s. No. 30). On how a small group of sociology students gradually got into real field research in China. The next step, Fei urges, should be comparative, leading to generalizations.

1937F10 "伦市寄言 —二, 关于「动变中的中国农村教育」的通讯" (Letter from London—2, on "Chinese rural education in change"), *Yi-shi bao* ("Shehui yanjiu," n.s. No. 40). Fei's comments on a manuscript by Liao Taichu, to the effect that social science should develop in the direction of providing comprehensive knowledge, based on field work, about Chinese culture. 59

1937F17 "「民族和文化接触」译本编后记" (Editor's afterword to the translation of *Race and Culture Contracts*), *Yi-shi bao* (Shehui yanjiu," n.s. No. 41). This translation (never published?) of a collection of papers (ed. E.B. Reuter; New York & London, 1934) was begun by Wang Tonghui in the belief that China's present crisis was the result of the contact of races and cultures, and finished by various friends after her death.

1937F24 "文化论 — 译者前记" (Translator's preface to Malinowski's "Theory of Culture"), *Yi-shi bao* ("Shehui yanjiu," n.s. No. 42). This is different from the preface to *WHL*, though the translation, as much as appeared here, is the same.

1937Mr10 "伦市寄言 —三, 关于实地研究" (Letter from London—3, Field work), *Yi-shi bao* (Shehui yanjiu," n.s. No. 44). Fei urges the social researcher to get away from books and into the field, approaching it not with a view to solving particular problems (which would prejudice him) but studying the whole, for the parts are interrelated. A good way to begin is by visiting each family in the community. 59

1937Mr17 Fei and Huang Di 黄迪, "理论与实地社会研究" (Theory and field work), *Yi-shi bao* ("Shehui yanjiu," n.s. No. 45).

An exchange of letters. Fei admits that field workers can't help having viewpoints and presuppositions which influence what they see and how they interpret it, but he is against going to the field with firm generalizations about society in mind. 43, 54

1937Mr24 " 再论社会变迁 " (More on social change), *Yi-shi bao* ("Shehui yanjiu" n.s. No. 46). Summary and discussion of seven articles from the journal *Africa* about methods of studying African cultural change following contact with European culture. Fei disapproves of methods that involve historical reconstruction; social research should stick to the present and avoid theorizing about the vanished past. Social change is best studied with Malinowski's three-column method of charting forces for resisting it, and the resulting situation. 55–56

1937Ap14 " 从社会变迁到人口研究 " (From social change to population research), *Yi-shi bao* ("Shehui yanjiu," n.s. No. 49). On how and why to study social change; studying Chinese social change in a way that will be both scientific and useful for social policy; and the problems population researchers should be studying. 43, 51–52

1937Ap28 " 书评 " (Book reviews), *Yi-shi bao* ("Shehui yanjiu," n.s. No. 51). Reviews of Karl Mannheim, *Ideology and Utopia*, and Ch'ao-ting Chi, *Key Economic Areas in Chinese History*.

1937Ap21 " 伦市寄言–'继替'" (Letter from London–"Succession"), *Yi-shi bao* ("Shehui yanjiu," n.s. No. 50). Summary of Park's article on "Succession, an Ecological Concept," *American Sociological Review* 1.2:171–179 (1936), stressing the idea that social organization involves a restriction of the struggle for survival; when the social order is destroyed there is a period of intense biological competition until a new order is formed. 52

1937My5 " 浣乡寄言–论马氏文化论" (Letter from the Huan [-dian-li-qiu; England, unidentified] countryside—Malinowski's theory of culture), *Yi-shi bao* ("Shehui yanjiu," n.s. No. 52). The origins of Malinowski's functionalism are in Freudian psychoanalysis, which sought functions below the surface, and in a rather English practical stress on actual facts. 53

1937My19 " 复刊周年通讯" (Communication on the first anniversary of ["Shehui yanjiu"] republication), *Yi-shi bao* ("Shehui yanjiu," n.s. No. 54). Expressing satisfaction that this publication, "our child," has been nursed through adversity and is now flourishing.

1937Jl7 " 有骨有肉的切片素描 " (Vivid description which has flesh and bones), *Yi-shi bao* ("Shehui yanjiu," n.s. No. 60). Field workers should give detailed descriptions of life such as those found in *Dream of the Red Chamber*, which Firth has praised as a vivid portrayal of kinship. 59

1938Je Raymond Firth, "中国农村社会团结性的研究——一个方法论的建议" (The study of social cohesion in Chinese villages—a methodological proposal), trans. Fei, *Shehuixue jie* 10:249-257. Written specially for this journal and not elsewhere published, according to the editor's note. Firth urges the use of anthropological techniques.

1940Ap1 "农期参差性和劳力利用" (Irregularity of the farm calendar and the utilization of labor), *Xin jingji* 新经济 3.7:162-165. On seasonal farm workers in Yunnan.

1940My19 "患土地饥饿症者" (The land-hungry), *Jinri pinglun* 今日评论 3.20:316-318. Land is not a good investment for those with capital, who usually acquire it only when borrowers default. The ones who want it are those who will work it themselves; these, however, have trouble accumulating savings as laborers, while the landed are reluctant to sell. 83, 92

1940Ag5 "消遣经济" (A leisure economy), *Zhanguo ce* 战国策 9:6-11. At Columbia. Similar to *LCNT* 108-111. The traditional habit of restricting consumption, higher wages may turn out to be a disincentive to labor; workers may prefer increased leisure to increased consumption, and work less. 130

1940S12 "娱乐？工作？" (Recreation or work?), *Zhanguo ce* 12:25-30. At Columbia. The basic difference between work and recreation is not physiological (tiring vs. restorative) or psychological (unpleasant vs. pleasant), but social (for others vs. for oneself). In dialogue form.

1940O6 "西南工业的人力基础" (Southwest industry's labor base), *Jinri pinglun* 4.14. Not seen.

1940? "农贷方式的检讨" (An examination of the method of making peasant loans), *Zhong nong yuekan* 中农月刊, issue and date not known. Not seen.

1941Ja12 "劳工的社会地位" (The social status of labor), *Jinri pinglun* 5.1:9-11. The low status of labor impairs industry's ability to attract workers. Disdain for manual work is a leftover from agricultural culture where people work in fields like animals; it is inappropriate in the case of factory work, which is supervising machines. 130-131

1941Ag30 "种族绵续的保障—生育制度的功能" (To guarantee the continuation of the race—the function of the family), *Dongfang zazhi* 东方杂志 38.17:31-39. Later revised to become Chapter 1 of *SYZD*. 99

1941O15 "双系抚育的确立—人类婚姻的意义" (A firm basis for bilateral child-raising—the significance of human marriage), *Dongfang zazhi* 38.20:27-33. Children need role models of both sexes. Revised to become Chapters 2 and 3 of *SYZD*.

1941O30 "夫妇之间 生育制度结构中的一个难题" (Between husband and wife—a difficult topic in the structure of the family), *Dongfang zazhi* 38.21:28–34. Revised to become chapters 4 and 5 of SYZD. 148

1942Jl24 "武器和社会" (Weapons and society), *Dangdai pinglun* 当代评论 2.5:73–76. At Guomindang archives, Taiwan. Expensive modern weapons are increasingly monopolized by a few states, which are thus able to enslave the have-nots; it would be better if they were in the hands of an international police force.

1942Ag10 "论神经战" (On psychological warfare), *Dangdai pinglun* 2.8:122–124. At Guomindang archives, Taiwan. Civilian morale is very important; honest factual reporting and open criticism will alleviate people's fear of the unknown and counter the enemy's psychological war.

1942D11 "论工余" (After work), *Shenghuo dao-bao* 生活导报 200 5:1–2. Modern city workers must learn how to rest after their work, which is much more stressful than work in a non-industrial society. 131

1943Ja1 "过年过日子与过度心理" (Passing New Year's, passing time, and the psychology of just enduring life), *Shenghuo dao-bao* 8:1. Harshly critical of Chinese passivity, as seen in attitudes toward time, which are contrasted to the Western way of using time to work for the future. 112

1943Ja30 "为孩子" (For the children's sake), *Shenghuo dao-bao* 11:1. Chinese society should become more youth-centered and less oriented to and controlled by the old. 113

1943F22 "人生的时序" (The stages in a man's life), *Shenghuo dao-bao* 14:1–2. On the problems caused by the different speeds of physical and social development in an individual, especially by sexual maturity coming before social maturity.

1943Mr "战后经济问题座谈会的发言" (Statement at a forum on problems of the post-war economy), *Dangdai pinglun* 3.15/16. Not seen.

1943Mr20 "狂者进取" ("The headstrong will make progress" [*Analects* 13.2]), *Shenghuo dao-bao* 17:2. Stagnant Chinese culture has failed; it lacks wild utopian ideas which stimulate people to change their world. 113

1943Ap3 "最后的一个上帝" (The last god), *Shenghuo dao-bao* 19:1. Signed "Jiang Tong" 江通. This and other articles in this weekly newspaper are marked as Fei's in his own hand on the copies he brought to Harvard in 1943 (see 1/23/44 to WCF & JKF). Gloomy fantasy about the end of the world at the hands of a power-mad dictator who with a monopoly of atomic power rules mankind; he kills all the intellectuals and then comes to need them. 180

1943Ap10 "狂馀漫笔" (Random thoughts after madness[?]), *Sheng-*

huo dao-bao 20:2. Unsigned. A short piece about longing for one's native place. 99

1943My15 "编蝇拍的老竹匠" (The old weaver of bamboo fly swatters), *Shenghuo dao-bao* 25:2. Signed "Jiang Tong." The old peasant doesn't understand why city people dislike flies; on rural ignorance —or is it a parable?

1944My7 "物伤其类－袁 [i.e. 陶] 云逵" (All creatures grieve for their own kind—Tao Yunkui), *Shenghuo dao-bao* 67.2. In memory of the former head of Yunnan University Sociology Department. 264

1944O22 [Chinese title not known] (China must not lose her last allied friend—the United States), *Ziyou luntan* 自由论坛. Summary enclosed in October 31, 1944, dispatch of William R. Langdon, American Consul General in Kunming; in WCF letter file. Fei points out that American criticisms of Chinese corruption, bribery, profiteering, cheating, and lack of national consciousness, while perhaps a bit harsh, should not be ignored out of pique.

1944D23 "美国民主精神的展望" (Hopes for the American democratic spirit), *Minzhu zhoukan* 民主周刊 (Kunming) 1.3:7–10. On U.S. political history; similar to parts of *CFMG* Chapters 2, 3, 5, 14.

1945F "历史到民间去" (History for the people), *Minzhu zhoukan* (Kunming) 1.9:9–10. A review of Wu Han 吴晗, *You sengbo dao huang quan* 由僧钵到皇权. Fei says he, and most Chinese, are ignorant of history because there are not enough readable but accurate books like this one.

1945Mr? "亡城无宝" (A fallen city has no valuables). Clipping from an unidentified newspaper enclosed in 3/16/45 to WCF with the comment, "Recently I wrote some short stories for diversion." This story is about a French nobleman who doesn't care that his valuable collection of paintings is destroyed in World War II, for he himself will soon die.

1945Mr27 "论效率" (On efficiency), *Minzhu zhoukan* (Kunming) 1.14:7–9. Harvard's Western Electric experiments showed worker efficiency depends more on morale than on physical surroundings. Factory workers under capitalism lack group spirit; they feel exploited, their work lacks meaning, they are less happy than villagers, and consequently less efficient. 133–134

1945Ag6 "平民世纪的展开" (The coming of the century of the common man), *Minzhu zhoukan* (Kunming) 2.5:4–6. Welcoming the Labour Party's victory in the British elections; the English should be proud that the common people have been able to defeat the privileged democratically and without bloodshed.

1945S16 "祸根未除" (The roots of disaster have not been pulled out), *Minzhu zhoukan* (Kunming) 2.9:4–5. The Americans are making a mistake in not removing the Japanese Emperor or the old social order; Japan will rearm in the future if an aggressive spirit is allowed to remain. 127

1945N? "我们不要作人类的罪人" (We must not become mankind's criminals). Clipping from an unidentified newspaper enclosed in 11/28/45 letter to WCF. Atomic power presents great constructive potential and also great danger; "God is giving mankind a serious test." We must prevent a civil war in China as it might spark an atomic world war. 184

1945N10 "论美国对华政策" (On U.S. policy towards China), *Minzhu zhoukan* (Kunming) 2.15:4–5. Reprinted in *Wen cui* 文萃 8.5–6 (November 27, 1945). Post-war economic problems are forcing the U.S. to choose between seeking to control foreign markets, a course which may end in war, or seeking a new world order in the interests of all nations, which would require that America's problems be solved through national economic planning. 125

1945N26 "怎样解决东北问题" (How to solve the problem in Manchuria), *Minzhu zhoukan* (Kunming) 2.17:4–5. The U.S. and U.S.S.R. had originally agreed to keep Manchuria neutral, but civil war there has been provoked by the Nationalists; and the U.S. has intervened, creating a danger of Russian response. The only solution is coalition government, neutralizing Manchuria. 184

1946a "书后" (Epilogue), in Shi Guoheng 史国衡, *Kun chang laogong* 昆厂劳工 (Labor in a Kunming factory; Shanghai, Shangwu, 1946), pp. 200–235. Dated December 18, 1944. This essay, which was written subsequently, does not appear in the English translation Fei made of Shi's book while in the United States (*Machine Age*). In order to illustrate how sociological research tests theory, Fei recounts at length the original 1940 Research Station plan for examining various social aspects of new industry in southwest China, and the problems encountered in the study. Then he summarizes the Harvard Western Electric findings on the importance, for factory efficiency, of informal worker groups. Next he discusses how the wide gap in status between workers and managers, who look down on manual labor—a gap inherited from the traditional agrarian culture—is harmful to cooperation in industry. Finally comes a critique of modern urban industry, based on Le Play and Durkheim; compared to village life, it is an environment without social order. A new, closely integrated, social organization needs to be created for modern industry. 130–134

1946b "教授生活之一章" (One chapter in a professor's life), in Guoli Xinan Lianho Daxue, *Lianda ba nian* 联大八年 (Eight years of [National Southwest] Associated University; Kunming, 1946). Not seen.

1946Ja12 Pan Guangdan 潘光旦, Wen Yiduo 闻一多, Fei Xiaotong, and Wu Han, "致马歇尔特使书" (Letter to Ambassador Marshall), *Minzhu zhoukan* (Kunming) 2.23:11–14,16. At Stanford. In 1/8/45 [i.e. 46] to WCF, Fei implies he was the principal author. The Civil War can't be ended unless the basis for democracy can be established: demobilization, end of secret police, civil liberties, multi-party elections, elimination of economic abuses, etc. 188

1946Ja21 "从倫敦会议到莫斯科会议" (From the London Conference to the Moscow Conference), *Minzhu zhoukan* (Beiping) 1:12–13. U.S. public opinion, alarmed by rumors of war, forced the American government to compromise with the Russians at Moscow; both sides made concessions and peace has been strengthened.

1946My1 "一封未拆的信" (An unopened letter), *Shanghai wenhua* 上海文化 4:24–25. Fond recollections of a woman, recently dead, who had taught Fei in primary school. 7

1946Je6a "美国人怎样办报读报" (How Americans manage and read newspapers), *Shanghai wenhua* 5:14–16. At Chicago. In praise of American journalism; China won't be able to modernize unless the quality of her newspapers improves. 200

1946Je6b "从日常生活论中美文化" (Chinese and American culture seen from the standpoint of daily life), *Shanghai wenhua* 5:19–21. A summary of *CFMG*, Chapters 8–10.

1946Jl1 "土地里长出来的文化" (A culture which has grown out of the ground), *Shanghai wenhua* 6:16–17. Chinese culture, based on farming with its limited opportunities, traditionally has valued contentment and not acquisitiveness. But now desires have been stimulated by the sight of the West, and official corruption has become far worse, which increases the difficulty of establishing modern industry and a new culture. 144–145, 157

1946Jl21 Statement on Li Gongpu's murder, *Qunzhong* 群众 11.12:22. His murder was shameless, but the struggle for democracy will soon be won.

1946Jl25 "论武器" (On weapons), *Lilun yu xianshi* 理论与现实 3.2:37–42. Modern weapons are more easily monopolized by governments than were swords and clubs, and now atomic weapons can be monopolized by just a few governments, who could enslave the rest of the world. They also threaten humanity with extinction unless war is eliminated.

1946Jl30 "美国人民將考验杜鲁门" (The American people will test Truman), *Minzhu zhoukan* (Shanghai), 39:984–987. The coming Congressional elections will be a test of support for Truman's anti-Soviet and anti-labor policies. The people don't want war, and Truman will have to move toward negotiations with the U.S.S.R. The Civil War in China hurts Truman, but it is secretly being encouraged by the State Department.

1946Ag1 "文化的物质面与精神面" (The material and spiritual aspects of culture), *Shanghai wenhua* 7:18-19. At Chicago. Signed by Fei, this article is an excerpt from his translation of Malinowski's revised article on culture, *WHL,* pp. 3-6 (corresponding roughly to pp. 621-623 of the *Encyclopedia of the Social Sciences* article). The appearance of Fei's name over Malinowski's words may indicate Fei's state of panic in late July 1946, just after the Li-Wen murders, or his unqualified acceptance of Malinowski's theory of culture; or it might be a mistake on the part of the journal editor. 46

1946N1 "'爱的教育'之重沐" (Reimmersion in "The Heart of a Boy": for Principal Wang Jiyu on the 40th Anniversary of Zhenhua Girls' School), *Shanghai wenhua* 10:28-29. Revisiting his old school and recalling Miss Wang's kind devotion to her pupils, Fei now realizes why his favorite book is the translation of Edmondo de Amicis' *Cuore* [1886; an inspirational, sentimental, and very popular Italian novel of school life]. 7

1947Mr "英国为什么也闹煤荒?" (Why does England have a coal shortage?), *Xin shijie* 新世界, pp. 1-2. Repeating much of, and then bringing up to date, Fei's article in the January 21, 1947, *Dagong bao,* which became *CFYL,* Chapter 5. On the economic problems of the coal industry, and the government's emergency measures for the crisis, which Fei calls industry's Dunkirk.

1947My3 "没有安排好的道路" (There is no fixed route), *Guancha* 观察 2.10:6-7. May Fourth thoughts on the contrast between the comfort and security of student life when Fei was in school and the hardships and uncertainties experienced by students today. On the eve of widespread student demonstrations (the article is dated April 23; the demonstrations climaxed in May), Fei expresses sympathy with the student movement. Reprinted in *Ming bao yuekan* 明报月刊 29: 18-20 (May 1968). 207

1947Je1 "美国对华政策的一种看法" (One view of America's China policy), *Zhishi yu shenghuo* 知识与生活 4:4-6. A condensed version appeared in *Guancha* 2.16:21-22 (June 14), and a summary in the *New York Times,* July 11, p. 8. American policy had been to make China part of the American sphere in the Far East: an economic market and a line of defense against the U.S.S.R. Since the failure of the Marshall mission in China, the U.S. is now turning more to Japan. The Guomindang Government is too rotten, and the U.S. will probably not push it to reform or give it big loans. 128

1947Je14 "传统在英国" (Tradition in England), *Shiji pinglun* 世纪评论 1.24:9–10. The English love tradition, which they use as an old bottle in which to put new wine—for example the present-day monarchy and quaint Parliamentary traditions do not stand in the way of real democracy. But the Chinese, by contrast, change the name on old wine and fool themselves into thinking it is different. Chinese tradition is rotten.

1947Je15 "同是在两大之国" (Also between the two great powers), *Dagong bao*, p. 2. Harmful effects of the Cold War on Greece, France, and Great Britain. 126

1947Jl1 "不应固执地去看美国外交" (U.S. foreign policy shouldn't be seen rigidly), *Zhishi yu shenghuo* 6:4–6. U.S. policy is fickle because the public, distrustful of its leaders and uninformed about conditions abroad, easily changes its mind. The Truman Doctrine has caused conflict with the U.S.S.R.; but the people don't want war, nor is the government irrevocably anti-Soviet. 127, 128

1947Jl2 "从杜鲁门主义到马歇尔主义" (From the Truman Doctrine to the Marshall Plan), *Dagong bao*, p. 2. The Marshall Plan, offering aid even to the U.S.S.R., is a reversal of the Truman Doctrine. But will the Republican Congress appropriate the funds?

1947Jl19 "消夏夜话" (An evening conversation cooling off), *Dagong bao*, p. 3. Dialogue with three friends on Wedemeyer's coming visit; Fei thinks it won't mean continued U.S. support for the Civil War, as U.S. security against the U.S.S.R. does not require an anti-Communist China. 128

1947Ag1 "美国的苦闷" (America's anguish), *Zhishi yu shenghuo* 8:4–5. While the U.S. wants peace, Truman's anti-Soviet policies create a danger of war. 125

1947Ag10 "与美国箴言报论「中国或日本」" (Discussing "China or Japan" with the *Christian Science Monitor*), *Dagong bao*, p. 2. Fei's reply to a *Monitor* editorial on the *Times'* summary of 1947Je1, about growing U.S. support for Japan. Fei suggests the best way for the U.S. to avoid war with the U.S.S.R. is not a pro-American Japan but a neutral China as a buffer. 127

1947Ag29 "工党二年" (Two years of the Labour Party), *Dagong bao* August 29, p. 3, and August 30, p. 3. Britain's economic problems could be reduced by dissolving the empire and bringing home overseas troops, instead of following an anti-Soviet policy in order to get loans from the U.S. 196

1947S1 "美国民意的动向" (Trends in U.S. public opinion), *Zhishi yu shenghuo* 10:7–9. Most Americans think war a possibility, yet they still want the United States to put its own interests first; they expect depression, yet aren't inclined to change the economic system. Economic insecurity has brought American democracy to its nadir, and this is a threat to world peace.

1947S6 "所谓家庭中心说" (The theory of "familism"), *Shiji pinglun* 2.10:14-16. Fei takes issue with the idea that the Chinese value the family more than Westerners do. Unlike the American family, the Chinese peasant family is an economic and child-rearing institution; social life, friendship, and even conversation are found largely outside it, with peers of the same sex, who are more apt to have common experiences, ideas, and values.

1947S13 "欧州仲夏夜之梦" (Europe's midsummer night's dream), *Guancha* 3.3:3-7. Soviet refusal to participate in the Marshall Plan is dividing Europe.

1947S20 Hu Shi 胡适, and Fei Xiaotong, "关于「美国人的性格」通信" (Correspondence regarding "The American Character"), *Guancha* 3.4:23. Fei's brief reply to Hu's accusation of two "big errors" about "things that everyone knows" in the article which became *MGRXG*, Chapter 8: that Churchill was half American and Lord North was a British prime minister, not a general.

1947Oa Pan Guangdan and Fei Xiaotong, "科举与社会流动" (The examination system and social mobility), *Shehui kexue* 社会科学 4.1:1-22. Translated as "Social Mobility." Quantitative historical research on the family background of a group of successful Qing dynasty examination candidates, suggesting that the examination system provided only limited opportunity for social mobility for peasants.   155, 300

1947Ob "亦谈社会调查" (More on social research), *Dushu yu chuban* 读书与出版 2.10:37-41. At Stanford. Social researchers should stop trying to trick people into revealing things, and instead be friendly and respectful. If a researcher shows he is working for the peasants' interests, and allows them to participate in the analysis, he will get reliable data.

1947O1 "中秋时节 欧美之间" (Autumn Festival: between Europe and America), *Zhishi yu shenghuo* 12:4-5. Will the Marshall Plan be high-interest loans? Will there be anti-socialist requirements attached? What will Congress do? The United States can't make up its mind.

1947O4 "如是他见" (As He Saw It), *Guancha* 3.6:24. Review of Elliot Roosevelt's book about his father at the summit conferences.

1947O15 "中国社会学的长成" (The growth of Chinese sociology), *Wenxun yuekan* 文讯月刊 7.4:8-11. Written for Japanese sociologists; the Japanese version is "中国社会学の發展," *Shakai kagaku kenkyū* 社会科学研究 1.3 (1948). Translated in *Dilemma*: 19-31. Traditional Chinese writings on society, though voluminous, are normative, and scientific sociology is a Western import. In the 1920s, socialism and social science—ideals and empirical methods, which should complement each other—unfortunately bifurcated. In the 1930s, university sociology, cut off from the masses, was little more than empty academic theorizing; social reformers gathered data uninformed by social theory; and socialists, after their revolution failed in 1927, debated social history dogmatically. Then the war forced scholars, their books gone, into villages, and community research was done by the Qinghua National Census Institute, the Yanjing-Yunnan Sociological Research Station, and the West China University Border Research Institute. This was an important advance, but further progress requires closer contact between researchers and those working for social change. 25-26

1947N1 " 英国政府的改组 " (The reorganization of the British government), *Zhishi yu shenghuo* 14:4-5. The cabinet shake-up was due to economic crisis; an analysis of the new ministers shows Attlee is attempting the difficult course of trying to maintain domestic socialism while making foreign policy concessions to the Americans in order to get loans from them. 196

1947N8a " 小康经济 " (An economy of sufficiency), *Guancha* 3.11: 8-12. Answering Wu Jingchao's criticism of *RX&JQ* (in *Jingji pinglun* 经济评论 1.20:4-7 [August 16, 1947]), Fei stresses that Wu's dream of American-style industrialization cannot be realized in China for generations. His own proposals for partly mechanized rural industry—far from being, as Wu charged, nostalgia for traditional handicrafts or hatred of machines—represented a practical way to raise peasant living standards in the immediate future. 134, 168, 201

1947N8b " 悼锡德兰·韦柏先生 " (In memory of Sidney Webb), *Dagong bao*, p. 3. An admiring account of Webb's efforts, through the Fabian Society and Labour Party, to achieve a gradual, bloodless, non-radical revolution in England. 203

1947N15 " 美国之内 " (Inside U.S.A.), *Guancha* 3.12:20. Reading John Gunther's book makes Fei think that U.S. foreign policy may be explained by the disproportionate political influence of rural Americans, who are conservative and individualistic; postwar foreign aid, which was 70% food, has benefited them rather than industry, as has the rift between Western Europe and food-exporting Eastern Europe.

1947N16 " 美苏争霸论 " (The struggle between the United States and the U.S.S.R.), *Zhishi yu shenghuo* 15:4-7. A comparison of the strength of the two powers: American democracy probably has more popular support than Russian despotism; the war left America stronger in resources; but organization is hard to judge. 126

1948Ja1a " 漫谈桑梓情谊 " (Thoughts about local sentiment),

Zhongguo jianshe 中国建設 5.4:30–32. Love for one's native place does not interfere with nationalism: on the contrary, it is a basic group feeling of solidarity on which the nation must be built. In China it has unfortunately been lost in the last 50 years, as those with higher education, such as Fei, have moved to cities, and the result has been social disintegration with self-seeking replacing local and family solidarity.   4, 157, 158

1948Ja1b " 一年来的世界大势 " (World trends in the last year), *Zhishi yu shenghuo* 17/18:4–5. A year of disillusionment: Marshall's failure in China; economic trouble in England; the failure of the Labour Government to adopt a new foreign policy and create a bridge between the United States and the U.S.S.R.; American enmity to the U.S.S.R.; the replacement of U.N. hopes with Cold War polarization. The fate of the world, Fei concludes, lies with the Americans, who lack the experience to be leaders; faced with a depression, they might resort to war.   126

1948Ja17a " 华莱士竞选的道德意味 " (The moral significance of Wallace's campaign), *Guancha* 3.21:3–5. Henry Wallace's independent campaign for the American presidency has no chance for success, and Europeans are afraid it will help Republicans, who are less favorable to the Marshall Plan. But it has a moral significance in making the public realize that both parties represent the interests of business and not the people, for both support policies in Europe designed not really to protect "freedom" and "democracy" but to protect American world markets against socialist governments.   127, 128

1948Ja17b " 与时代俱逝的鲍尔温 " (Stanley Baldwin, who died with his era), *Dagong bao*, p. 3. Gentlemanly, honest, conservative, and anti-labor, Baldwin represented the dying tradition of English capitalism.

1948Ja31 " 雄圣甘地 " (Gandhi, hero and saint), *Guancha* 3.23:4–6. Gandhi, just killed, is praised in the highest terms for his opposition to violence and his vision of a world united by morality (no mention is made of his efforts to promote cottage industries). He is said to represent the moral tradition of the Orient, which the Chinese have forgotten and which must be revived to confront and to save the violent West.   203

1948F28 " 关于日本复兴会不会威胁中国 ?" (On "Does Japan's Rehabilitation Threaten China?"), *Guancha* 4.1:21. Replying to an article by James T. C. Liu in *Guancha* 3.24, Fei is not reassured that Japan can never again invade China, militarily or economically. The United States did not change the basic social structure in Japan; and the American presence in Japan is no guarantee for China, for there is no certainty that the United States and China would be allies in a future war.   127

1948Mr1a " 关于「城」乡 问题 " (On the rural-urban problem), *Zhongguo jianshe* 5.6:30–31. In answer to an article by Jiang Qingxiang

姜庆湘 In *Zhongguo jianshe* 5.5:34-37 (Febuary 1, 1948), which had taken issue with Fei's January 11 *Dagong bao* article on achieving a moderate standard of living for the common people (*XTCZ:* 79-88; *Gentry;* 110-126). Fei had advocated restoring a healthy relationship between city and countryside through reviving rural industry; Jiang had objected that rural-urban relations had always been exploitative, and that it was the system of land rent that most needed to be changed. Now Fei says he wants to clarify his views on two points. First, by "rural industry" he meant not just old-fashioned handicrafts, but technologically modernized home and small-factory industry. Second, he was not seeking to protect the privileges of the gentry, but proposed that they give up their privileges and help villagers by bringing them modern technology.   127, 160, 208

1948Mr11 "马歇尔能复兴欧洲吗 ?" (Will the Marshall Plan effect European recovery?), *Zhishi yu shenghuo* 22:4-5. Europe's economic problems, caused by the loss of colonies, would be solved by a closer tie between the industrial West and the agricultural East. But the Marshall Plan, anti-Soviet in intent, perpetuates the division between East and West Europe, leading the West European nations to try to retain their colonies. The Marshall Plan also deepens the conflict between classes, which makes economic recovery more difficult.

1948Mr20 "关于「乡土工业」与「绅权」" (On "rural industry" and "gentry power"), *Guancha* 4.4:13-14,18. Parts are similar to *XTCJ:*157-163. Responding to criticism, Fei admits traditional industry wasn't all rural; but court-sponsored industries, and town industries probably supplied little to the countryside, which was largely self-sufficient. Rural-urban relations were basically one-sided, especially in the recent past. On the subject of gentry power, Fei complains he has been misunderstood; he is not advocating gentry supremacy or a return to the past. On government, he admits modern conditions require strong, effective government, but it should be limited by a constitution, and made responsible to the people by democratic representative institutions.   157, 159, 208

1948Ap10 "郑兆良和积铁" (Zheng Chaoliang and the metal construction toy), *Guancha* 4.7:15-16. In praise of a maverick friend who invented an erector-set type of toy for Chinese children, in order to encourage in Chinese the habit of using the hands to manipulate physical things. The longstanding Chinese reluctance to do that is an obstacle to industrialization.

1948Ap24 "再论美国大选" (More on the U.S. presidential election), *Guancha* 4.9:6-7. Discussing various possible candidates and some *Nation* articles, Fei favors Wallace.   128

1948My15 "读赫尔回忆录" (Reading Cordell Hull's memoirs), *Guancha* 4.12:6-7. The former Secretary of State's recollections, serialized in the *New York Times* and sent to Fei by a friend, prompt the thought that American foreign policy is made by the State Department, the President, the military, the Treasury Department, and other agencies, a division of power which is in part responsible for the confusion in the world situation.

1948My16 "知识分子的社会地位" (The social position of intellectuals), *Zhishi yu shenghuo* 27:6. Very short summary of a speech given at a Qinghua forum on intellectuals on April 5. A fuller version apparently was carried in *Zhanwang* 展望 2.3, an issue which is not available in the United States. Quoted in *Qunzhong* 群众 (Hong Kong) 2.28:14 (July 22, 1948). The knowledge of the intellectuals, according to Fei, has been literary, impractical, and unproductive; and people who lack the time and money to acquire it are excluded from the ruling, exploiting class. Intellectuals should learn to use their hands, while one day the common people will be able to master writing and be intellectuals. 207

1948My29 "和平之谜" (The riddle of peace), *Guancha* 4.14:3–5. On recent developments in Soviet-American relations. The U.S. government uses anti-Russian slogans to get support for the expensive Marshall Plan, the purpose of which is to enable Europe to consume American goods. Stalin, Fei believes, wants peace. 128

1948Jl3 "杜威入选与对华政策" (Dewey's nomination and China policy), *Guancha* 4.19:3–4. Dewey will call for aid to China in the campaign, but the United States won't send troops, and Congress may reduce the amount of aid. 128

1948Jl20 "论'苦撑待变'" (On hanging on and waiting for a change), *Zhong jian* 中建 (Beiping) 1.1:4–6. U.S. anti-Soviet policy, economically motivated, probably won't lead to war or to greatly increased U.S. support for the Nationalists in China. Don't be misled by election rhetoric, Fei warns; China is not another Greece in importance or in possibilities for the United States. 127

1948Jl31 "两分三裂的民主党" (The divided Democratic Party), *Guancha* 4.22:6–8. On Truman's unpopularity with many Democrats, and the possibility of a three-way race giving no party a majority in Congress, resulting in compromise politics. 128

1948Ag5a Zhang Dongsun 张东荪, Xu Deheng 许德珩, Fei Xiaotong, and 47 others, "知识分子今天的任务" (The present-day duty of the intellectuals), *Zhong jian* (Beiping) 1.2:2–8. Forum at Qinghua, July 5 and 23, 1948. Fei's remarks concern the point that in China productive knowledge has been looked down on and literacy, good only for enjoyment and government, valued. Today some intellectuals still have gentry habits of using political connections to exploit the people. Writing, education, and intellectuals must all change. 207

1948Ag5b "和难战亦不成" (Peace is difficult but war won't do either), *Zhong jian* (Beiping) 1.2:9–11. The Russian blockade of Berlin, in response to U.S. refusal to talk peace, increases the danger of war but may well succeed in forcing the United States to talks. 128

1948Ag28 "评晏阳初「开发民力建设乡村」" (On James Yen's "Develop the people's strength to build up the countryside"), *Guancha* 5.1:4–7. Fei criticizes Yen's article (in the August 14 *Dagong bao*) and the Sino-American Joint Commission on Rural Reconstruction for emphasizing literacy education, which is an old-fashioned elitist attitude; for promoting technical measures in their approach to rural reconstruction; and for opposing land reform. Illiterate peasants already know what the problem is: rent, taxes, conscription, and soldiers; but Yen and the U.S.-financed J.C.R.R. don't seek to reform the social system. 163

1948S5 "休战不是和平" (Ceasefire is not peace), *Zhong jian* (Beiping) 1.4:4–5. At Stanford. Open debate has failed to reach agreement because the two sides lack common goals and because there is no informed public opinion, the press being monopolized for propaganda. The Moscow meetings between Soviet leaders and U.S., British, and French ambassadors mark a return to secret diplomacy and power politics, which can achieve at best only a temporary and partial truce, not true peace. 200

1948S20 "外交战扩及北非" (The diplomatic war spreads to North Africa), *Zhong jian* (Beiping) 1.5:7–8. Speculation about the various powers' interests in the disposition of Italy's former colonies in North Africa.

1948O1 "城乡联系的又一面" (Another aspect of rural-urban relations), *Zhongguo jianshe* 7.1:32–35. Translated as "City and Village." City workers usually retain village ties: they have family and home there, where they can go if unemployed; they give jobs to fellow villagers, and send money home, which drains capital from industry.

1948O5 "真知识与假知识—一个社会科学工作人员的自由" (True and false knowledge: the confession of a worker in the social sciences), *Zhong jian* (Beiping) 1.6:6–7. Chinese social science, including Fei's own work, has been too academic, bookish, theoretical, dogmatic, and foreign-derived. It has not been responsible, practical, related to real social problems, and thus has been ignored by those in power.

1948O20 "论英美的武装警备政策" (On the Anglo-American policy of armed vigilance), *Zhong jian* (Beiping) 1.7:5–6. Armed vigilance is very expensive; Europe is too poor, and the United

States unwilling to shoulder the entire cost. Thus Truman has vacillated, at moments leaning towards making peace with Moscow. 128

1948N5 "读张菊生先生「刍荛之言」" (On reading Zhang Yuanji's 张元济 "My humble view"), *Zhong jian* (Beiping) 1.8:6–7. In praise of the old scholar's September 23 speech deploring the suffering caused by the Civil War. Fei suggests that one side does not care about the welfare of the people. 207, 209

1948N20 "从美国大选看美国民主" (American democracy from the perspective of the election), *Zhong jian* (Beiping), 1.9:10–12. Truman's surprise victory shows that voters are not too influenced by the capitalist-controlled press, which favored Dewey. But in many ways Wallace didn't have a fair chance, which raises the question of whether American democracy exists in more than name. 129

1948D5 "美国政治动向会变更吗?" (Will the direction of American politics change?), *Zhong jian* (Beiping) 1.10:6. We can't know what Truman's policies will be, but there is no reason to think his election means American politics are moving towards socialism.

1948D18 "英国并未忘情远东" (England has not forgotten the Far East), *Guancha* 5.17:6–7. The prospects are good for trade between England and a Communist China.

1949S8 "白皮书的剖析" (Dissecting the White Paper), *Xin jianshe* 新建设 1.1:5–6. The purpose of the U.S. State Department's White Paper, which reveals the American aim all along was to make China a colony, is (1) to explain the American failure to the Wall Street bosses, (2) to fool the American people with propaganda about seeking democracy and peace and preventing Soviet expansion, and (3) to hide the continued covert political offensive against China carried out by Philippine and Korean puppets. 218

1949O6 "中国革命人民大团结" (The great unity of the Chinese revolutionary people), *Xin jianshe* 1.3:6–9. The Political Consultative Conference strengthens the unity of the four revolutionary classes; its Common Program, suggesting that socialism won't come for a while and that capitalism is still necessary, has reassured the bourgeoisie. 218, 219

1949D6 "人民首都，人民当了主人" (The people's capital, the people are boss), *Xin jianshe* 1.7:2–3. The Second Peking Congress of Representatives of Various Circles has elected a government which is making plans for municipal services, has adopted tax measures, voted to close brothels, and set up unemployment insurance and after-work schools. 217

1949D31 "论北京的税收" (Peking's taxes), *Renmin ribao* 人民日报. Reprinted in *Xinhua yuebao* 新华月报 1.4:932–935 (February 1950). On why it was right to raise municipal taxes.

Rural subsidies for cities can now be stopped; such taxes are progressive, for welfare and constructive purposes; etc. 217, 308

1950Ja29 "中英建立外交关系与帝国主义对华新政策" (China and Great Britain establish diplomatic relations, and imperialism's new strategy toward China), *Xin jianshe* 1.11:11–12. British recognition of China is a victory for the Chinese people, but also a new imperialist tactic undertaken in league with Washington as part of an attempt to divide the socialist camp. 218

1950F26 "奠定于世界和平的基石" (Laying the foundation for world peace), *Xin jianshe* 2.1:4. The Sino-Soviet treaty guarantees world peace by deterring U.S. imperialism from war. The American charge that the U.S.S.R. has territorial designs on China is slander. 218

1950Mr16a "思想战线的一角" (One corner of the intellectual front), *Xuexi* 学习 2.1:17–19. A detailed description of how, during several very tense days, everyone at Qinghua wrote "thought summaries," using small-group criticism and self-criticism. Thought reform is a battle between old ideas and new, carried out in a spirit of mutual help. 221

1950Mr16b "从「为人民服务」引起的谈话" (A conversation about "serving the people"), *Guancha* 6.10:13–15. A discussion with students about why concentrating only on technical studies is not enough—political study is necessary if one is to serve the people.

1950My21 "理论与实际一致和课程改革" (The unity of theory and practice, and curriculum reform), *Xin jianshe* 2.7:22–24. The old universities were not altogether useless; they were strongholds of anti-imperialism, science, etc. They should not be turned into technical schools, but should teach people to use theory creatively, by means of theoretical, scientific, and general cultural studies. 225

1950Jl1 "教育者本身的教育 – 记首届全国高等教育会议" (Educating the educators—on the first session of the National Conference on Higher Education), *Xin guancha* 新观察 1.1:33–35. Partial translation as "Educating the Educators," *China Weekly Review*, July 29, 1950, p. 157. Much needs to be done on the ideological reform of teachers, and on curriculum reform, but it would be a mistake to neglect theoretical science in favor of practical technical studies.

1951Je1 "发展为少数民族服务的文艺工作" (Developing art which serves minorities), *Xin jianshe* 4.3:43–47. Minorities' art forms should be used to break down ethnic barriers and to encourage minorities to make social reforms voluntarily. We must avoid imposing our ways on them. 232

1951Je16 "克服盲从" (Overcome blind following), *Xuexi* 4.5:23. Fei now regrets that he had kept quiet his early doubts about the movie

Wu Xun zhuan 武训传 until it came under public attack. This experience shows that non-proletarian intellectuals should not follow the lead of the proletariat blindly, but should speak out their thoughts.

1951D9 "Symposium on Criticism of Reformism," Hong Kong *Dagong bao*, January 1, 1952; trans. in *Current Background* 169:23. Contains a statement of Fei's at a Peking meeting on how his past ideology was reformist, individualistic, and bourgeois.

1952Ja "关于广西壮族历史的初步推考" (Preliminary investigations into the history of the Zhuang nationality of Guangxi), *Xin jian she* 1:29–33. A scholarly discussion of possible historical and linguistic ties between the Zhuang people and other ancient and modern ethnic groups.   233

1952O "学习共同纲领中的民族政策" (Study the minorities policy of the Common Program), *Xin jianshe* 10.

1953Jl31 "打开了和平大门" (The gate to peace has been opened), *Guangming ribao* 光明日报. The armistice in Korea is a great victory, but U.S. imperialism will continue to plot, and we should prepare by intensifying thought reform.

1954Je16 "看了民族歌舞" (On seeing ethnic dances), *Xin guancha* 12:24–25. In adapting minorities' songs and dances for the stage, it is necessary for cultural worker teams of the Central Institute for Nationalities to make some changes, but these should be based on understanding and be acceptable to the minorities.

1954Jl16 "宪法偶谈" (A chance conversation about constitutions), *Xin guancha* 14:8–9. China's new draft constitution is unlike bourgeois constitutions, which, Fei now understands, only protect the interests of the bourgeoisie.   242

1954Ag21 "中华人民共和国宪法案保障了各民族发展自己语言文字的自由" (The People's Republic of China draft constitution guarantees to each nationality the freedom to develop its own writing system), *Guangming ribao*. Writing systems should be created for those national minorities who lack them and want them; they should not be compelled to use Chinese.   232

1955 "卡瓦社会概况" (Kawa social conditions), *Zhongguo minzu wenti yanjiu jikan* 中国民族问题研究集刊 (Collected studies on China's nationalities problem), second collection. Not seen (referred to in 1956Ag:7n2). The Kawa are a minority group in Yunnan province.

1956Ap27 "发动群众通风报信来做好考古工作" (Encourage the masses to report archaeological finds), *Wenwu cankao ziliao* 文物参考资料 4:23–25. The masses should be taught to preserve and report archaeological finds.   234

1956My10 "开展少数民族地区和与少数民族历史有关的地区的考古工作" (Develop archaeology in minority areas and areas relevant to the history of national minorities), *Kaogu tongxun* 考古通讯 3:1–10. Speech to an archaeological work conference, February 21, 1956. Minority historical studies, on which Fei has been working, involve many interesting and significant questions; it would be a help if archaeologists would cooperate and do some work in the southwest in particular. 234

1956My "什么是民族区域自治" (What is local autonomy for nationalities?), in Fei et al., *Shenma shi minzu quyu zizhi* (What is local autonomy for nationalities?; Hong Kong, 1956), pp. 1–4. Rather simplistic ("... since exercising regional autonomy, the minority nationalities love more ardently the nation, the Chinese Communist Party, and Chairman Mao."). 232

1956Jl16 "全国人民代表大会会后记" (After the meeting of the National People's Congress), *Xin guancha* 14:3–4. Fei says he had often felt that China was democratic more in form than in content, but was encouraged by the critical and substantive discussion at this recent congress. There should be more contact between representatives and those they are supposed to represent. 243, 260

1956Jl26 "为西湖不平" (Unfair to West Lake), *Renmin ribao*. Fei complains about the ugly tombs and monuments around this famous lake near Hangzhou. 242

1956Jl27 "开展少数民族地区调查研究工作" (Develop investigation and research work in minority nationalities areas), *Guangming ribao*. The Nationalities Committee of the National People's Congress has organized a project to investigate the social history of various nationalities. This will help in determining what concrete steps towards will deepen our knowledge of social development, and provide an opportunity for intellectuals to put their skills to practical use. 234, 235
will deepen our knowledge of social development, and provide an opportunity for intellectuals to put their skills to practical use.

1956Ag Fei and Lin Yaohua 林耀华, "当前民族工作提给民族学的几个任务" (Tasks which current nationalities work raises for ethnology), *Kexue tongxun* 科学通讯 8:1–17. The first three parts (constituting the bulk of this long article, minus only footnotes, preface, Part 4 on religion, and concluding remarks) appeared also in *Renmin ribao*, August 10, 14, 16, 1956; and were translated in *Current Background* 430:11–30 (December 10, 1956). There is an incomplete German translation of Part 2 in *Wissenschaft und Fortschritt* 8.4:129–131 (1958). Nationalities work needs ethnological research: (1) to determine which groups are really nationalities; (2) to collect data on different nationalities' stages of social development, which is in reality quite complex; (3) to study the culture and ways of life peculiar to each people, something which is partly independent of social stage; and (4) to assemble information on their religious beliefs. 235

1956O16 " 为西湖一文补笔 " (Additional notes on West Lake), *Xin guancha* 20:28–29. 1956Jl26 had set off a controversy. Of course, Fei says, historical relics shouldn't be destroyed, but many monuments there have no historical significance, and we certainly shouldn't ruin the scenery with new buildings. 242

1957F8 " 云南大理历史文物的初步察访 " (Initial inspection of historical objects from Dali, Yunnan), *Kaogu tongxun* 3:1–7 (May 10); originally published in *Yunnan ribao* 云南日报, February 8 & 9, 1957, in slightly different form. On a trip to Yunnan in the latter half of 1956, a minorities social history research team found neolithic implements, possible archaeological sites, tombstones, stone inscriptions, sculptures, and old documents. Many things are being lost or destroyed because people don't realize their value. Archaeological work is needed. 236

1957F20 " 关于社会学说几句话 " (A few words about sociology), *Wen hui bao* 文汇报. Summarized in *Zhexue yanjiu* 哲学研究 3:148–149 (June 15, 1957); and more briefly in *Xuexi* 9.9 (May 3, 1957); the latter summary was translated in *Extracts from China Mainland Publications* 92:14–15 (July 29, 1957). Translated in *Dilemma*: 32–38. The new society has new problems which need to be studied, and old sociology students and teachers have the necessary skills. Fei proposes a sociological research institute or social research institute in the Academy of Sciences, though he says he is personally content to do research on minorities. 250–251

1957Mr24 " 知识分子的早春天气 " (The early spring weather of the intellectuals), *Renmin ribao*. Reprinted in *Xinhua banyuekan* 新华半月刊 8:109–112 (April 25, 1957). Intellectuals in institutes of higher education have enjoyed much better conditions since Zhou Enlai's January 1956 speech. What they need most now is to raise their professional level through research, conferences, and going abroad; the major obstacle to this at present is not lack of time or equipment but lack of strong leadership in research—direction in choosing topics, relating research to teaching, cooperation with others, organizing forums, etc. The desire to do research is not selfish but aimed towards better teaching. Free discussion is important in advancing the intellectuals' thought reform, but they have been reticent and their leaders have dragged their feet; thus the political activism of intellectuals has not been fully developed. 244–246, 354, 355

1957Ap3 "人口问题研究搞些什么?" (What is demographic research all about?), *Xin jianshe* 4:4-5. A list of topics on which Fei thinks population research should be done.

1957Ap10 "社会学的对象和内容决定于他的任务" (The subject and content of sociology are determined by its tasks), *Xin jianshe* 7:45-46 (July 3, 1957). Statement made at a forum on April 10. Socialist society has a number of problems that need to be studied and, although the old sociology was based on the wrong premises, it had methods and data that would be useful in making a new sociology. It is too early to re-establish sociology departments; for the moment we should do research on concrete problems. 252

1957Ap " 科学研究和教学工作是不是有矛盾?" (Is there a contradiction between scientific research and teaching?), *Zhengming* 争鸣, April 1947 [No. 6], pp. 10-13. Scientific research can strengthen the researcher's grasp of theory and improve his teaching. There is no contradiction between research and teaching. 247

1957My " 关于社会科学的问题 " (On the problem of the social sciences), *Zhengming*, May 1957 [No. 7]. Not seen. Extracts published in *Fandui ziben jieji shehui kexue fubi* 反对资产阶级社会科学复辟 (Oppose the restoration of bourgeois social science), II (Peking, 1958), 764-765. Developing a new social science requires figuring out what can be used from bourgeois social science so that the old social scientists can be of service. 252

1957My31 "' 早春 ' 前后 " (Before and after "Early Spring"), *Guangming ribao*. 1957Mr24, which has caused much comment, was written after talking to intellectuals in the southwest but not sent off until Mao's "Contradictions" speech. Critics have said that there is nothing wrong with the weather, it has been spring since Liberation, the trouble is with the intellectuals; but Fei says he thinks there are contradictions between intellectuals and the Party, and shortcomings on both sides which need to be worked on. 244, 246-247

1957Je1 " 重访江村 " (Yangzi village [Kaixiangong] revisited), *Xin guancha* 11:3-7 (June 1, 1957) and 12:11-14 (June 16, 1957). A projected third part was never published. The gist of his findings, as reported to Suzhou officials, was summarized in " 费孝通在开弦弓「下马看花」" (Fei Xiaotong "dismounts to look at flowers" in Kaixiangong), *Renmin ribao*, June 1, 1957; this news article was translated in W. R. Geddes, *Peasant Life in Communist China* (Society for Applied Anthropology Monograph No. 6; Lexington, Ky., 1963), pp. 65-66; it was also summarized in a New China News Agency release, Peking, June 1, 1957, which was printed in *Survey of China Mainland Press* 1544:13 (June 5, 1957). The original two articles have been reprinted with *XTZG* and *XTCJ* in *Xiangtu Zhongguo, Xiangtu chongjian, Chong fang jiang-cun* (Hong Kong, Fenghuang, n.d. [c. 1971]). Translated in full in *Dilemma:* 39–74. Revisiting Kaixiangong for 20 days, after 21 years, Fei found that socialism had improved people's lives, but there were still problems. Agricultural productivity was up but sideline industries, particularly silk, were off, with the result that average per capita income was about the same as in 1936. There were some complaints of food shortages, however, which Fei thought could be attributed to the fact that people were consuming more and not saving for emergencies; they had lost their old habits of frugality due in part to one-sided propanganda which emphasized only the benefits and not the problems of socialism. 254–259, 270–272, 273

1957Je10 " 一则以喜，一则以忧 " (Partly happy, partly worried), *Guangming ribao*. Statement at a Democratic League Central Committee meeting, June 10. Summarized in *Renmin ribao*, June 11, 1957. Fei says people should continue to speak out—freedom of speech must be preserved—but it would be better if the atmosphere weren't so tense.

1957Je17 " 费孝通检查自己的立场 " (Fei Xiaotong examines his own point of view), *Renmin ribao*, June 18, 1957. Summarizing the statement he made at a June 17 meeting.

1957Jl13 " 向人民伏罪 " (I admit my guilt to the people), *Renmin ribao*, July 14, 1957. Reprinted in *Xinhua banyuekan* 18:57–59 (September 25, 1957). Translated in *Current Background* 470:10–14 (July 26, 1957), and also in *Dilemma:*75–84. Speech to National People's Congress, July 13, 1957. Fei confesses that, during the Hundred Flowers period, working together with rightists Zhang Bojun and Luo Longji, he had tried to stir up anti-Party, anti-socialist sentiment among intellectuals; he had tried to weaken ideological re-education by stressing intellectuals' professional duties; he had demanded the restoration of bourgeois social science; etc. "Had the Party not clubbed me awake in time, I don't know what monstrous crimes I would still be committing." 260–261, 266–267

1962Mr9 [Chinese title not known] (Fei Xiaotong's visit to his relatives), *Wen hui bao* (Hong Kong). Translated in *Selections from China Mainland Press* 2722:15–18 (April 19, 1962). Original not seen. Visiting his 84-year-old father in Suzhou, Fei finds the area prosperous and the old man ebullient, writing poetry and memoirs; the aged are happy and well-off today. 277

1974My Interview with Zhao Haosheng 赵浩生 (Howard Chao), *Dagong bao* (Hong Kong), July 14–30, 1974. Also in *Huaqiao ribao* 华侨日报 (New York), August 10, 14, 17, 1974. Partial Japanese translation in *Asahi shimbun* 朝日新聞, July 10, 1974. Partial English translation in *China News Analysis* 980:4–6 (November 15, 1974). Fei explains to a foreign visitor how his ideas have been changed as a result of experiencing 20 years of revolution and contact with workers, peasants, and soldiers.

1979Jl15 " 重访金秀瑶山 " (The Yao mountains of Jinxiu revisited), *Minzu tuanjie* 民族团结 1979, 1:25–29. Reprinted in *Xinhua yuebao* 1979, 8:209–213. Like "Yao Revisit," on how much life has improved for the Yaos.

1980Ja10a " 关于我国民族的识别问题 " (On the problem of distinguishing our country's nationalities), *Zhongguo shehui kexue* 中国社会科学 1980, 1:147–162. Translated as "Ethnic Identification."

1980Ja10b "' 非洲的种族，译后记 " (Translator's afterword to [C. G. Seligman's] *Races of Africa*), *Dushu* 读书 1980, 1:109–112. A finished translation of this 1930 classic by Malinowski's teacher was lost in the Cultural Revolution, and Fei had to do it all over again in 1978–1979.

1979S " 赴美访学观感点滴 " (Scattered impressions from a study tour of the United States), in Chinese Academy of Social Sciences Delegation, *Fang-Mei guangan* (Impressions of America; C.A.S.S. internal publication), pp. 34–49. On whom Fei met and what he learned about American sociology and anthropology on his spring 1979 trip.

1980Nl " 我从事社会学五十年 " (My 50 years as a sociologist), *Zhongguo qingnian bao* 中国青年报 . Written in answer to the youth newspaper's question, "Under what conditions did you resolve to devote yourself to your present career?"

C. ARTICLES IN ENGLISH AND UNPUBLISHED MATERIALS

"Relationship System" "The Problem of Chinese Relationship System," *Monumenta Serica* 2:125–148 (1936–1937). Analysis of relationship terms should be based on what people actually say and not (like Chen and Shryock and others) on the written language. Spoken systems vary widely from place to place; Fei gives his own (Wujiang) and five others recorded from native informants.

"Kaihsienkung" "Kaihsienkung: Economic Life in a Chinese Village," PhD thesis in Anthropology, London School of Economics and Political Science, June 1, 1938. 325 pp. Basically the same, except for the first and last chapters, as *Peasant Life*.

"Review of Feng" Review of H. Y. Feng, *The Chinese Kinship System* (Philadelphia, 1937), *Man* 38:135 (August 1938).

9/10/38 to BM One letter to Bronislaw Malinowski, 1938. At Yale University, in the Malinowski papers, Box 9. In quoting from these and others of

Fei's English letters, I have sometimes made silent corrections of spelling or punctuation.

"Review of *Wuxing Economy*" Review of China Institute of Economic and Statistical Research, *A Study of the Rural Economy of Wuxing, Chekiang* (Shanghai, 1939), *Nankai Social and Economic Quarterly* 11:178–180 (January 1940).

"Agr. Labor" "Agricultural Labor in a Yunnan Village," *Nankai Social and Economic Quarterly* 12:146–168 (January 1941). An early research report on Fei's study of Lu-cun, discussing in detail the demand for labor, its decreasing supply due to the war, and the leisure class.

–/–/– to WCF Twenty-three letters to Wilma C. Fairbank (including one to John K. and Wilma Fairbank), 1943–1948. In Mr. and Mrs. Fairbank's possession, Cambridge, Massachusetts. (There are also copies of four letters to others.)

–/–/– to WLH, in IPR– Ten letters to William Holland, 1943–1948. At Columbia University, in the Institute of Pacific Relations archives, Boxes 68, 98, 330. There are also copies of three letters to others. An excerpt from one letter has been published in Marion J. Levy and Kuo-heng Shih, *The Rise of the Modern Chinese Business Class* (New York, 1949), pp. 58–59.

"Harris Lecture" "Some Social Problems of Free China," in Harley F. MacNair, ed., *Voices from Unoccupied China* (Chicago, 1944), pp. 46–64. Paper read before the Harris Foundation Conference, University of Chicago, August 6, 1943 (not 1944, as Fei has it in "Peasantry":17). The war has brought to Yunnan villages a labor shortage, increased prosperity, and urban refugees with new ideas. These social changes cause a number of problems.

"International Proposal" "A Proposal for Co-operation Between the United States and China in Social Science Research," c. October-November 1943. 3 pp. Enclosed in 11/4/43 to WCF. Fei proposes field work in China by American researchers using Chinese assistants.

"Chicago Talk" "Development of Sociological Research in War-time China: A report of the work of the Yenching-Yunnan Station for Sociological Research read before the Social Research Society, University of Chicago," c. November 1943. 20 pp. Enclosed in 11/22/43 to WCF. On community field studies; a condensed version of this appears in *Earthbound*, "Foreword" and "Introduction."

–/–/– to MPR Forty-six letters to Margaret Park Redfield (including a few to Robert Redfield), 1944–1949. Formerly in Mrs. Redfield's possession, Wallingford, Vermont.

"Symposium Memo" "Memorandum on a Symposium on Social Change in War-time China," c. 1944. 2 pp. Enclosed in William R. Langdon (Consul

General, Kunming) dispatch No. 110 to the Secretary of State, November 11, 1944, Department of State Records in the National Archives. Fei proposes commissioning papers from a number of Chinese scholars, to be translated into English and published in the United States.

"Review of Zhao" Review of Zhao Chaogou 赵超构, Yan'an yi yue 延安一月 (One month in Yan'an; Chongqing, 1944), Pacific Affairs 18.4:391–393 (December 1945).

"Peasantry" "Peasantry and Gentry: An Interpretation of Chinese Social Structure and its Changes," American Journal of Sociology 52.1:1–17 (July 1946). Reprinted as Peasantry and Gentry.... New York, International Secretariat, Institute of Pacific Relations, n.d. 17 pp. Reprinted in R. Bendix and S. M. Lipset, eds., Class, Status, and Power: A Reader in Social Stratification (Glencoe, 1953), pp. 631–650. Reprinted in abridged form in Yehudi A. Cohen, Social Structure and Personality: A Casebook (New York, 1961), pp. 24–35. Written in 1945 for a State Department-funded symposium (6/19/45 to MPR; 9/3/45 to MPR: 4). The ways of life of the two social classes are contrasted. Peasants tolerated their exploitation by the gentry because the gentry protected them against the Central Government. Social mobility between peasantry and gentry was very limited. Now the intrusion of Western industrial power has given rise to new classes and undermined the importance of the gentry.

"L.S.E. Speech" "Social Change in Modern China," lecture given at the London School of Economics, January 30, 1947. Mimeo. 10 pp. Translation published in Dagong bao, February 21, 1947, and reprinted in XTCJ, 1–15. Brief excerpt in Gentry, 142. Traditional China's ideology of contentment was well adapted to the agrarian economy of scarcity; but social integration was at the cost of technical stagnation. Now China must modernize, and old values are no longer appropriate. The West, however, lacks social integration (factory workers have no sense of the significance of their work), and does not present a good model; China should find her own way.

"Social Unity" "Social Unity and Culture Diversity," 1947? 12 pp. Maurice Freedman of the London School of Economics gave me copies of this and "L.S.E. Speech." Cultural differences in China are less between regions than between social classes. Chinese agriculture requires a large population during the busy season, but the availability of unemployed labor at other times reduces the incentive to develop labor-saving devices and so causes technical stagnation.

"Gentry Draft" Fei and Quentin Pan, "The Chinese Gentry: A Study of Chinese Social Structure," 1947. 15 pp. Enclosed in 8/10/47 to WLH, in IPR 330. Draft of the first chapter of a proposed book. On the origins of the gentry, "a class of people who chiefly derive their income from land, possess leisure to develop various literary and cultural pursuits, and enjoy their fruits, and win their way to the very apex of the social pyramid. They secure their power and influence . . . mostly through their own literary achievement" (p. 1). There is also reference in a letter to an earlier 60-page draft left with Raymond Firth in London, but I don't know what became of this (6/30/47 to WLH, in IPR 330).

"Silk" "Is Silk the Answer?" Source not located (a Chinese Industrial Cooperative Movement magazine?), 1947? Two-page clipping in the possession of Wilma Fairbank. To raise peasant income the Chinese Industrial Cooperative Movement should concentrate on reviving rural industries, particularly silk. Fei suggests the C.I.C. solicit foreign investment and take over the silk factory at Kaixiangong.

"Social Mobility" Pan Guangdan and Fei, "City and Village: The Inequality of Opportunity," in Johanna M. Menzel, ed., *The Chinese Civil Service: Career Open to Talent?* (Boston, 1963), pp. 9–21. Translation of 1947Oa.

"Problems" "Problems of Rural Industrialization," *China Economist* 1.4: 102–109 (April 26, 1948). Translation of three *Dagong bao* articles (March 7, 9, & 23, 1948) reprinted in *XTCJ*, 99–124.

"Financing" "Financing Rural Industrialization," *China Economist* 2.5:108–113 (August 1, 1948). Translation of two articles in *XTCJ*, 125–143.

"City and Village" "Relations between City and Village in China," *China Economist* 3.138–139, 149 (November 15, 1948). Translation of 1948O1.

"New Peking" "New Peking—The People's Capital," *People's China* 1.3:9–11 (February 1, 1950). A thumbnail history of the city and how today, for the first time, municipal government is "in the people's hand."

"Kweichow" "The Minority People in Kweichow," *China Monthly Review*, December 1951, pp. 289–294, and January 1952, pp. 55–63. Reprinted as "Minority Groups in Kweichow," *Current Background* 150:1–16 (January 10, 1952). Condensed translation of *XDMZ*.

"Multi-national" "China's Multi-national Family," *China Reconstructs* 3:23–25, 28–29 (May–June 1952). Reprinted as "China's Minority Nationalities," *Far Eastern Economic Review*, July 17, 1952, pp. 89–91. A brief survey of China's minority peoples, how they were oppressed in the past, liberated by the People's Liberation Army, and are now making progress towards equality, democratic self-rule, economic growth, and improved health and education.

[Note: English translations made by the U.S. Consulate General in Hong Kong for some of Fei's 1950s articles are noted under the Chinese articles, in particular 1956Ag and 1957Jl13.]

"Free" "Free and Equal Family," *People's China* 10:16–20 (May 16, 1955). Summarized in a New China News Agency release, Peking, May 15, 1955, which was printed in *Survey of China Mainland Press* 1048:31–32 (May 14–16, 1955). Similar to the last: China's many national minorities, previously all oppressed, are now developing economically and in other ways. Here, however, Fei also stresses overcoming "big-Han chauvinism" and not interfering with minority customs.

"Encounter Letter" Letter, *Encounter* 29:67-69 (February 1956). Chinese translation as "费孝通教授给英国'评比'杂志的一封信," *Guangming ribao*, October 7, 1955 (which is thus, oddly, earlier than the October 25, 1955 date on the English version). Fei's response to a minor controversy in *Encounter* (January, August, & November, 1955), set off by Karl Wittfogel's review of *Gentry* suggesting that Fei must be unhappy with the Communists' treatment of the peasants. Fei here replies that his ideas have changed since he wrote the *Gentry* articles and that Wittfogel is maliciously trying to sow dissension between the Chinese and American peoples.

"Names" "Chinese Names," *People's China* 23:37-38 (December 1, 1955). Surnames come first, etc.—on that level.

"Old Friends" "Old Friends and a New Understanding," *People's China* 11:12-17 (June 1, 1956). For a Chinese translation, see "老朋友之间的新认识," *Guangming ribao*, June 12, 1956; reprinted in Ma Yinchu 马寅初 et al., *Ba zhishi xian gei zuguo* 把知识献给祖国 (Giving knowledge to the motherland; Hong Kong, 1956), pp. 23-36. Continuing the discussion in *"Encounter* Letter," Fei insists he is happy with his new life and that he has changed some of his old ideas—voluntarily, for one's thoughts cannot be coerced.

"Ways" Fei and Lin Yaohua, "Ways of Life Among China's Minorities," *China Reconstructs*, April 1957, pp. 18-22. Reprinted in John Gittings, ed., *A Chinese View of China* (New York, 1973), pp. 133-137. Similar to Part 2 of 1956Ag.

12/27/63 to Routledge One letter to Mr. John G. Carter, Routledge & Kegan Paul, London. In Routledge's files.

"Interview" Gene Cooper, "An Interview with Chinese Anthropologists," *Current Anthropology* 14.4:480-482 (October 1973). Includes transcript of Fei's remarks to an American delegation in March 1972, and translation of letter dated October 11, 1972, from Fei, Wu Wenzao, and Lin Yaohua, commenting on Cooper's account of the interview. Fei said that his recent two and a half years of physical labor had enabled him to get over his earlier disdain for peasants, but there still was no place in China for professional sociology or anthropology.

"Szechuan" "Szechuan: Calamity and Recovery," *China Reconstructs*, January 1979, pp. 59-63. On the strife and chaos suffered by the province from 1966 to 1976 due to Lin Biao and the Gang of Four. Based on Fei's one-month visit in the summer of 1978 with a Chinese People's Political Consultative Conference delegation.

"Yao Revisit" "Revisiting the Mountains of the Yao People," *China Recon-*

structs, May 1979, pp. 44–48, and June 1979, pp. 30–33, 61. Revisiting the Dayao Mountains of Guangxi 43 years after he was there with Wang Tonghui, Fei is "utterly astonished by the changes that had taken place."

"Ethnic Identification" "Ethnic Identification in China," *Social Sciences in China* 1980, 1:94–107 (March). Translation of 1980Ja10a, omitting one section on the emendations which should be made to Stalin's criteria for distinguishing nationalities.

"Glimpses of America," *Datamation* 26:234–240 (May 1980). Subtitled "An eminent Chinese sociologist attributes the great changes in the U.S. in the past 35 years to the high level of electronic technology." Selections from *FMLY,* translated by Martin Whyte.

"Toward a People's Anthropology," *Human Organization* 39.2:115–120 (Summer 1980). Address to the Society for Applied Anthropology, on being presented its Malinowski Award, Denver, March 21, 1980. (I am told there is also a collection of Fei's articles on national minorities being published under this title.)

Glossary

The following list gives Chinese characters for all Chinese and Japanese names, terms, and titles mentioned in the text and in the notes, with the exceptions of Fei Xiaotong's works, which are in the Bibliography, and well-known names of provinces, cities, and major historical figures. Book and article titles are listed under the authors' names.

Ai Siqi 艾思奇
Ajia rekishi jiten アジア歴史辞典
Ba Jin 巴金
bagong 拔贡
bai hua qi fang, bai jia zhengming 百花齐放,百家争鸣
Bai Lin 白林
Ban Yao 板瑶
baojia 保甲
Bing Xin. See Xie Wanying
Bo wen zazhi 波文杂志

Canxue Guan 蚕学馆
Cao Yu 曹禺
Chen Da, *Lang ji shi-nian* 陈达,浪跡十年
Chen Guofu 陈果夫
Chen Hansheng 陈翰生
Chen Lifu 陈立夫
Chen Qitian (Yilin), *Zuijin sa-nian Zhongguo jiaoyu shi* 陈启天(翊林),最近卅年中国教育史
Chen Zhenhan 陈振汉
cheng 城
Chenggong 呈贡
Chenggong xianzhi 呈贡县志
chi ren de lijiao 吃人的礼教

Chu Anping 储安平

Da-Qing jinshen quanshu 大清缙绅全书
Dacheng Yao mountains 大橙瑶山
Dagong bao 大公报
Dali Bai-zu zizhizhou lishi wenwu diaocha ziliao 大理白族自治州历史文物调查资料
dan 石
dang tianxia 党天下
Dangdai pinglun 当代评论
Dangdai Zhongguo mingren lu 当代中国名人录
Dantu 丹徒
Deng Chumin 邓初民
Ding county 定县
Dong Jie 董杰
Dongfang zazhi 东方杂志
Dongwu Daxue 东吴大学
Dongwu niankan 东吴年刊
dou 斗
Duli pinglun 独立评论
Duzhi 笃志

Er-ya 尔雅

Fan Wenlan 范文澜
Fan Yanqiao, Wujiang-xian xiangtu zhi 范烟桥 吴江县乡土志
Fandui zichan jieji shehui kexue fubi 反对资产阶级社会科学复辟
Fang Xianting (H.D. Fong) 方显庭
Fei Chengwu 费成武
Fei Dasheng 费达生 "复兴丝业的先声"
Fei Huo 费霍
Fei Pu'an 费朴安
Fei Qing 费青
Fei Xiaotong pipan ziliao huibian 费孝通批判资料汇编
Fei Zhendong, Ho-shu Dong-Indu gaikuang 费振东 荷属东印度概况
Fei Zonghui 费宗惠
Feixiang 肥乡
Feng Youlan 冯友兰
Funü zazhi 妇女杂志

Gao Shukang, Zhongguo shougongye gailun 高叔康 中国手工业概论
Gao Xianggao 高向果

Ge Yang 戈扬
Geliao 革獠
Gendai Chūgoku jinmei jiten 现代中国人名辞典

gong 工
Gu Bao 谷苞
Gu Hongming 辜鸿铭
Gu Jiegang 顾颉刚
Guan Feng 关锋
Guan Linzheng 关麟征
Guancha 观察
Guangming ribao 光明日报
Gui Youguang 归有光
Guo Moruo 郭沫若
Guoji maoyi dao-bao 国际贸易导报

Han 汉
Han Dezhang 韩德章
He Da 何达, "我的老师费孝通先生"
He Ganzhi, *Zhongguo qimeng yundong shi* 何幹之, 中国启蒙运动史
He Lian (Franklin Ho) 何廉
He Ming 何明
He Zhiping 贺致平
Hou Wailu 侯外卢
Hu Lin, *Yi-er-yi de hiuyi* 胡麟, 一二一的回忆

Hu Qiaomu 胡乔木
Hu Qingjun 胡庆钧, "费孝通及其研究工作"
Hu Sheng 胡绳
Hu Shi 胡适
Huabei Gongye Gaizao She 华北工业改造社
Hualan Yao 花蓝瑶
Huang Mingzheng 黄明正
Huang-Qing jing-shi wen-bian 皇清经世文编
Huang Sha 黄沙
Huang Wanlun, Fei Xiaotong "nongcun diaocha" de fandong benzhi 黄万伦, 费孝通'农业调查'的反动本质
Hushuguan 浒墅关

jia 家
Jian Bozan 翦伯赞
Jiang-cun (Kiangts'un) 江村
Jiang Qingxiang 姜庆湘
Jiangsu-sheng Nongmin Yinhang 江苏省农民银行
Jiangsu Shengli Nüzi Canye Xuexiao 江苏省立女子蚕业学校
Jiangxia 江夏

jin 斤
Jin Yuelin 金岳霖
jing-shi 经世
Jingji pinglun 经济评论

jiu 舅
juren 举人

Kaixiangong 开弦弓
Kaixiangong Shengsi Jingzhi Yunxiao Youxian Hezuoshe 开弦弓生丝精制运销有限合作社

Kaneko Mitsuru 金子载 中国社学会の近况

kaoju 考据
Kawa 卡瓦
Kindai Chūgoku kenkyū 近代中国研究
Kuige (Queike) 魁阁

Lao She 老舍
li 礼
Li Anzhe 李安宅
Li Changfu, *Fen-sheng dizhi—Jiangsu* 李长傅，分省地志—江苏
Li Chengxi 李成蹊

Li Da, *Fei Xiaotong de maiban shehuixue pipan* 李达，费孝通的买办社会学批判
Li Futong 李孚同
Li Gongpu 李公朴
Li Ji (Li Chi) 李济
Li Jinghan 李景汉，"中国社会调查运动"

Li Yefu, *Fei Xiaotong zhuan* 李业富，费孝通传
Li Youyi 李有义
Li Zonghuang 李宗黄
Lianda (Xinan Lianhe Daxue) 联大（西南联合大学）
Liang Qichao 梁启超
Liang Shuming 梁漱溟

Liang Shuming & Zhou Xinmin, *Li Wen bei hai zhenxiang* 周新民，李闻被害真相
Lilun yu xianshi 理论与现实
Lin Yaohua (Lin Yueh-hua) 林耀华
Liu Dajun (D. K. Lieu) 刘大钧
Liu Rongqu 刘荣焌
Liu Xiaoxiao, *Ming bao yuekan* 刘潇潇，明报月刊

Liu Yuren 刘育仁
Long Guanhai, Shehuixue yu shehui wenti lun cong, Shehui diaocha gai shu 龙冠海,社会学与社会问题论丛,社会调查概述
Long Yun 龙云
Lu-cun 禄村
Lu Dingyi 陆定一
Lü Zhenyu 吕振羽
Lufeng 禄丰
Luo Changpei 罗常培
Luo Longji 罗隆基
Luo Zhenyu 罗振玉

Mai Qianzeng 麦倩曾
Mei Yiqi 梅贻琦
Meng Yin 孟吟
Miao 苗
Miao Yuntai 缪云台
Min bao 民报
Min Ganghou 闵刚侯
mingfen 名分
Minzhu zhoukan 民主周刊
Minzu tuanjie 民族团结
Minzu yanjiu 民族研究
Minzu yanjiu gongzuo de yuejin 民族研究工作的跃进

minzuxue 民族学
mu (mow) 亩
Muramatsu Yūji, Kindai Kōnan no so-san 村松祐次,近代江南の租桟

Nankai 南开
Nongxue bao 农学报
Nü can 女蚕

Pan Dakui 潘大逵
Pan Guangdan (Quentin Pan) 潘光旦
Pang Xinmin 庞新民 广西瑶山调查杂记
Peng Pai 彭湃
Peng Zhen 彭真

Qi Yanming 齐燕铭
Qian Duansheng 钱端升
Qian Jiaju 千家驹
Qian Weichang 钱伟长
Qian Zhongshu 钱钟书
Qiao Qiming 乔启明
qin-ying 亲迎
Qinghe 清河
Qinghua (Tsinghua) 清华
Qinghua tongxue lu 清华同学录
Qinghua xiaoyou tongxun 清华校友通讯

Qinghua zhoukan 清华周刊
Qu Tongzu (Ch'ü T'ung-tsu) 瞿同祖
Quanguo Zhongwen jikan lianhe mulu 全国中文期刊联合目录
Quanguo zong shumu 全国总书目
Qunzhong 群众

Ren Guorong 任国荣 瑶山两月观察记
Renmin nianjian 人民年鉴
Renmin ribao 人民日报
Renmin shouce 人民手册

Shakaigaku hyōron 社会学評論
Shanzi 山子
She 畲
shehui diaocha 社会调查
"Shehui yanjiu" 社会研究
shehui zhuyi 社会主义
shehuixue 社会学
Shehuixue jie 社会学界
Shehuixue kan 社会学刊

Shen bao nianjian 申报年鉴
Shen Peixian 沈佩弦, 吴江历年高小毕业生调查报告
Shenghuo dao-bao 生活导报
Shenghuo shudian 生活书店
shengyuan 生员
shequ yanjiu 社区研究
shi 市
Shi Guoheng, *Kun chang laogong* 史国衡, 昆厂劳工
Shi Jing 史靖
Shi yu wen 时与文
Shidai pinglun 时代评论
Shiji pinglun 世纪评论
Shuo-wen 说文
si 私
Sichuan daxue xuebao 四川大学学报
Sili Yanjing daxue yilan 私立燕京大学一览

Su Kejin 苏克勤
Su Nong 苏农
Su Xuelin 苏雪林

Sun Benwen, *Dangdai Zhongguo shehuixue* 孙本文当代中国社会学

Sun Dingguo, *Fencui zichan jieji youpai huifu zichan jieji shehuixue de zhengzhi yinmou* 孙定国 粉碎资产阶级右派恢复资产阶级社会学的政治阴谋

Suzhou Cansang Zhuanmen Xuexiao 苏州蚕桑专门学校

Suzhou Nüzi Canye Jiangxisuo 苏州女子蚕业讲习所

Tang Deming 汤德明 "小商品生产的梦呓"

Tang Dingyu 汤定宇

Tao Delin 陶德麟

Tao Menghe (L. K. Tao) 陶孟和

Tao Xisheng 陶希圣

Tao Yunkui 陶云逵

tewu 特务

Tian Rukang, *Mangshi bianmin de bai* 田汝康, 芒市边民的摆

tianxia yi jia 天下一家

Tōkyō Kōtō Sanshi Gakkō 東京高等蚕丝学校

Tongli-zhen 同里镇

tongyangxi 童养媳

waihang 外行

Wan Dianwu 万典武

Wang Deqian 王德乾

Wang Ganyu 王赣愚

Wang Jiyu 王季玉

Wang Jizhao 王季昭

Wang Kang 王康

Wang Peizheng 王佩铮

Wang Tonghui 王同惠

Wang Wuke 王武科

Wen cui 文萃

Wen hui bao 文汇报

Wen Yiduo 闻一多

"Women duiyu dangqian wujia wenti de yijian" 我们对于当前物价问题的意见

Wu Han 吴晗

Wu Han wenji 吴晗文集

Wu Jiang 吴江

Wu Jingchao 吴景超 "加增中国农民收入的途径" "中国手工业的前途" "社会学在新中国还有地位"

Wu Qiyuan 伍启元

Wu Wenzao 吴文藻

Wujiang 吴江

wuwei 无为
Xia Kangnong 夏康农
xia xiang 下乡
Xia Yulong 夏禹龙
Xiandai Hanyu cidian 现代汉语词典
Xiang county 象县
"Xiangcun jianshe" 乡村建设
Xiangcun jianshe shiyan 乡村建设试验
xiangtu zhi 乡土志
Xiao Di 萧荻
xiao jiazu 小家族
xiaoqian 消遣
Xie Wanying (Bing Xin) 谢婉莹（冰心）
Xin guancha 新观察
Xin jianshe 新建设
Xin jiaoyu 新教育
Xin jingji 新经济
Xin lu 新路
Xin Zhongguo renwu zhi 新中国人物志
Xinhai geming Jiangsu diqu shiliao 辛亥革命江苏地区史料
Xinhua banyuekan 新华半月刊
Xinhua ribao (Nanjing) 新华日报

Xu Dantu xianzhi 续丹徒县志
Xu Jiarui 徐嘉瑞
Xu Jiming 徐季明
Xu Langguang (Francis L. K. Hsu) 许烺光
Xu Shilian (Leonard Shih-lien Hsu) 许仕廉
Xueshu yuekan 学术月刊
Xuexi 学习
xundao 训导
yamen 衙门
Yan Fu 严复
Yan Jingyao 严景耀
Yan Xinzhe 言心哲
Yan Yangchu (James Yen) 晏阳初
Yang Dongchun 杨东莼
Yang Dunyi (Cuiqing, Sumin), Hanzi muyin shi, Zhuidao za yong, Man-yi hua Xia shimo ji 杨敦颐（粹卿甦民），汉字母音释，追悼杂咏，满夷猾夏始末记
Yang Jikang (Jiang) 杨季康（绛）
Yang Jiwei 杨季威
Yang Kaidao (Cato Young), Noncun lingxiu 杨开道，农村领袖

Yang Niulan (Xilun) 杨纽兰（锡纶）
Yang Qingkun (C. K. Yang) 杨庆堃
Yang Tianji (Qianli) 杨天骥（千里）
Yang Xiren 杨锡仁
Yanjing (Yenching) 燕京
Yao 瑶 (formerly 猺)
Yi (Lolo) 彝
Yi-cun 易村
Yi-li 仪礼
Yi-shi bao 益世报
Yin Haiguang 殷海光
Yin Liangying, Zhongguo canye shi 尹浪莹 中国蚕业史
yougong 优贡
Yu-cun 玉村
Yu gong 禹贡
Yu Shengchun 余胜椿
Yuan Fang 袁方
Yue 越
Yue Sibing, Zhongguo cansi 乐嗣炳, 中国蚕丝
Yunnan ribao 云南日报
Yunnan-sheng nongcun diaocha 云南省农村调查

Zaisheng 再生
zanmen 咱们
Zhang Bojun 章伯钧
Zhang Dongsun 张东逊
Zhang Jian 张謇
Zhang Junmai (Carsun Chang) 张君劢
Zhang Siqian 张思骞
Zhang Xiruo 张奚若
Zhang Zhidong, Quan xue pian 张之洞 劝学篇
Zhang Ziyi (Zhiyi) (Chang Chih-i) Yi-cun shougongye 张子毅（之毅）易村手工业
Zhang Zongjiong 张宗颖
Zhao Chengxin 赵承信 "社会调查与社区研究"
Zhao Weibang 赵卫邦
zhen 镇
Zhenhua 振华
Zheng Bijiang 郑辟疆
Zheng Dekun (Cheng Te-k'un) 郑德坤
Zhenze 震泽
Zhexue yanjiu 哲学研究
zhizu 知足
zhizu chang-le 知足常乐
Zhishi yu shenghuo 知识与生活

Zhong 仲
Zhong jian 中建
Zhongguo ge xiao dangpai xiankuang 中国各小党派现况
Zhongguo jianshe 中国建设
Zhongguo jindai nongye shi ziliao 中国近代农业史资料
Zhongguo jindai jingji-shi tongji ziliao xuanji 中国近代经济史统计资料选辑
Zhongshan daxue, Yuyan lishi xue yanjiusuo zhoukan 中山大学语言历史学研究所周刊
Zhongyang Minzu Xueyuan 中央民族学院
Zhongyang yanjiuyuan, Lishi yuyan yanjiusuo jikan 中央研究院,历史语言研究所集刊
Zhou bao 周报
Zhou Baoshan 周宝山
Zhou Shulian 周叔莲
Zhu Youyu (Y. Y. Tsu) 朱友渔
Zhuang 僮(壮)
Ziyou luntan 自由论坛
Zou Jingheng 邹景衡
Zouping 邹平
zu 族
Zuijin guan shen lüli huilu 最近官绅履历汇录
Zuo Zongtang 左宗棠

INDEX

Academy of Sciences, 253, 261–262, 277
Academy of Social Sciences, 279–280, 282, 283, 284
Agriculture, 75, 80–81; yields, 58, 83, 255, 298; technology, 92, 165–166; farm size, 114, 165–166; labor requirements, 164, 341
Ai Siqi, 221
Allen, James, 335–336
Amicis, Edmondo de, 346
Anthropology, 15, 37–46 passim, 55; and complex societies, 89, 93–94; and imperialism, 63, 87–89, 269; in China, 278, 285, 365
Anthropometrics, 39–40, 46, 62, 64
Anti-Rightist Movement, 258–269, 276–277. *See also* Criticism of Fei in 1957
Archeology, 234
Attlee, Clement, 345
Awards (to Fei), 282, 285

Ba zhishi xian gei zuguo, 365
Ba Jin, 16
Bachofen, 15
Bai Lin, 319
Baldwin, Stanley, 350
Beard, Charles, 121, 199
Beauclair, Inez de, 312
Benedict, Ruth, 144
Bing Xin (Xie Wanying), 16, 29, 260
Birth limitation. *See* Population and birth limitation
British Boxer Indemnity Fund, 40, 80, 110–111

British Council, 193
Buck, John L., 27, 58, 92, 139
Buck, Pearl, 92
Bucklin, J.S., 27
Buddhism, 17–18, 328
Budgets, peasant, 86–87, 163, 255–256, 270–272
Burgess, J.S., 27, 28
Bushel, size of Fei's, 298–299

Canada, Fei's visits to, 282
Cao Yu, 106
Capitalism, 130, 133, 201, 256, 285
Carr, William F., 313
CC Clique, 181
Central Institute of Nationalities (Zhongyang Minzu Xueyuan), 229, 247, 253–254, 261–264, 270, 277, 278, 283
Cephalic index. *See* Anthropometrics
Chang Chih-i. *See* Zhang Ziyi
Chang, Carsun (Zhang Junmai), 43, 62, 182
Chang, Tse-i (Tzu-i). *See* Zhang Ziyi
Chao, Howard (Zhao Haosheng), 360
Chen Zhenhan, 261
Chen bao, 336
Chen Da, 16, 27, 37, 109, 139, 250, 251, 253, 301
Chen Hansheng, 92, 283, 305
Chenggong (Yunnan), 98, 100, 138
Chi Ch'ao-ting, 340
"Chicago Talk," 90, 92, 93, 362
Chicago, University of, 107–109
China and the West compared, 118;

China and the West *(continued)*
  attitudes to old age, 112–113, 116–117; display of emotions, 120; social relations, 146–147; wartime morale, 181–182
China Enters the Machine Age, 102, 107, 130–131, 301, 329
China Reconstructs, 280
China Weekly Review, 139
China's Gentry (Gentry), 152–161, 237, 265, 304, 333
Chinese-Americans, 122, 124, 285
Chinese characteristics: habitual morality, 52, 145–146; contentment and non-acquisitiveness, 75, 83, 118, 119, 130, 145, 157, 256, 345; desire for leisure, 82, 119, 130, 153; passivity, 112; traditionalism, 112–113, 116–117, 145–146; lack of ideals, 113, 122; jealousy, 120; selfishness, 120, 122, 147; contempt for manual labor, 130, 160; concern for "face," 146, 160; unemotionality, 148–149
Chinese People's Political Consultative Conference, 214, 267, 277, 280, 354
Chinese Sociological Society, 26, 253, 280, 282–283
Chong fang Ying-lun (CFYL), 194–197, 201, 331
Christianity, 4, 7–8, 10–15, 20, 61, 65, 80, 121–122
Chu Anping, 258–259
Chu fang Meiguo (CFMG), 111, 115, 132–134, 148, 310, 330
Cities: and countryside, Fei's feelings about, 18–19, 52, 59–60, 118–119, 121, 150; as an object of study, 32, 36; economic relations with countryside, 83–84, 158–159, 161; and social disintegration, 133–135, 200–201; and examination system, 155, 158; and towns, types of, 159; urban sojourners, 353. *See also* Industry, urban
Class differences, rural, and Fei's work, 77, 81–83, 87–88, 94–96, 146, 157, 271, 286. *See also* Gentry; Land tenure; Village leaders
Communists, Fei's early attitude to, 96, 189, 204, 206–211, 216
Community studies *(shequ yanjiu):* Park and Wu Wenzao on, 36; Fei's idea of, 58–59, 89–90; Shirokogoroff on, 79; Fei's among the earliest, 93
Comte, Auguste, 268
Confucianism, 69; Fei's kind words for, 135, 143, 145, 157, 158, 337. *See also* Traditional Chinese culture, Fei's attitude to
Constitutions, 198–200, 242
Cooley, Charles H., 144
Cooper, Gene, 365
Cooper, Paul, 107
Cooperatives, 169; Kaixiangong silk, 71–72, 256, 265; agricultural, 254–255, 257, 265
Cosmopolitanism. *See* Patriotism and cosmopolitanism, Fei's
Credit, rural, 74, 77, 84, 96, 305
Crime, 35, 39, 201, 285
Criticisms of Fei before 1949, 170, 208
Criticisms of Fei in 1957, 258–263, 286; personal attacks, 263–264; of his pre-1949 writings, 87, 96, 264–265, 273; of his early 1950s activities, 265–266; regarding minorities, 232–233, 266; of his 1956-1957 work with intellectuals, 266–267; of plotting to restore bourgeois sociology, 268–273
Cross-cousin marriage, 35, 75, 326
Cultural lag, 52, 131, 151
Cultural Revolution, 277, 284, 286
Culture, 38, 44–54 passim, 149–150; influence of environment on, 52–54, 120, 144, 337

Dagong bao, 140, 193–194
Daxue de gaizao (DXGZ), 220–221, 223–225, 227, 333
Democracy: China's need for, 114, 146, 175, 188, 197, 202; Anglo-American, admired, 114, 121, 198–200, 265, 330–331, 347; Anglo-American, criticized, 128–129, 216–217; in the People's Republic, 216–217, 224, 243, 248, 274
Democratic movement (Kunming, 1945–1946), 184–191, 198
Democratic League, 178–179, 182–183, 188–191, 204–205, 215, 240, 243–

244, 248, 252, 258-261, 266-267, 277, 280
Democratic Socialist Party, 62, 182-183
Dong Jie, 315
Dongfang zazhi, 60
Dongwu Daxue. *See* Suzhou University
Dover, Cedric, 236
Dream of the Red Chamber (Story of the Stone), 16, 340
Durkheim, Emile, 133, 143-144, 201

"Early Spring (1957 Mr 24)," 244-246, 358, 359
Earthbound China, 80-85, 91, 95-96, 102, 107, 163, 164-165, 193, 329
Economic analyses, Fei's, 85-87, 96, 162-164, 298-299
Economist, 125
Education: foreign influences on Chinese universities, 11-12, 25-28, 223; village schools, 78, 326; peasant literacy, 149-150, 152, 272, 353; post-1949 universities, 223-225, 247, 267, 283
Ellis, Havelock, 15
Embree, John, 94
Encounter, 1950s controversy about Fei, 237-238, 365
England: Fei's first visit to (1936-1938), 40-46; Fei's relations with English, 110-111, 125; culture, 118, 158, 347; Fei's second visit to (1946-1947), 192-197; politics, 194-197, 203, 216-217, 243; foreign relations of, 127, 196, 218; Fei's 1981 visit to, 282
Er-ya, 33
Eugenics, 40
Evolution. *See* Social change
Examination system, 155
Experts Bureau, 243-244, 261

Fabianism, 203
Fairbank, John, 192, 265
Fairbank, Wilma C., 102, 106, 110, 117, 192, 265, 301, 302, 362
Family. *See* Marriage and the family
Fan Wenlan, 319
"Fang-Mei lüe-ying" (*FMLY*), 284-285, 335
Fang Xianting (H.D. Fong), 27, 305

Fei Chengwu, 292
Fei Dasheng (sister), 5, 20, 68-73, 170, 192, 254-255, 305
Fei Huo (brother), 5
Fei Pu'an (father), 2, 3-4. 5-6, 17, 20, 219, 277
Fei Qing (brother), 5, 13, 41, 62, 182, 188, 210, 215
Fei Xiaotong pipan ziliao huibian, 318
Fei Zhendong (brother), 4-5
Fei Zhonghui (daughter), 98
Feng Youlan, 16, 226
Feng, H.Y., 361
Fiction, Fei's, 342, 343
Financial sources, Fei's, 80, 101, 106-111, 142, 304
Firth, Raymond, 15, 41-43, 46, 193, 269, 329, 340, 341, 364
Fong, H.D. (Fang Xianting), 27, 305
Foreign economic impact on China, 78, 84-85, 92, 169
Foreign visitors to Fei (after 1949), 236-237, 278-280, 283
France, 127
Frazer, Sir James George, 15, 45
"Free and Equal Family," 231-232
Freedman, Maurice, 94
Freud, Sigmund, 15, 50, 340
Fudan University, 283
Functionalism, 41, 44-45; Fei's, 38, 46-56, 75-77, 88, 95, 150; Communist critique of, 87, 269

Gamble, Sidney, 27
Gandhi, Mohandas, 167, 203, 350
Gang of Four, 282
Gao Xianggao, 295
Ge Yang, 315
Geddes, W.R., 236-237, 254
Gentry, 18, 88, 153-160, 304, 351; Fei's views on, criticized, 208, 264-265. *See also* Class differences, rural; Intellectuals; Land tenure
"Gentry Draft," 153, 304, 363
Germany, 41, 198
Ghosts, 116-117
Giddings, F.H., 15, 27, 30, 31, 38, 46, 336
"Glimpses of America," 284-285, 366
Gongdang yi nian (GDYN), 197-198, 310, 331

Government: impact of, on villages, 78; traditional restraints on, 156–157; need for strong, 151–152, 199, 205, 208; danger of strong, 169, 202. *See also* Democracy; Nationalist Government; Village leaders
Greece, 127–128
GTBR. *See* "Wei diaocha yanjiu Guisheng tezhong buzu renzhong"
Gu Bao, 103, 283
Gu Jiegang, 34
Guan Feng, 315
Guan Linzheng, 187
Guancha, 141–142
Guangming ribao, 244, 248, 259
Guangxi, 62–68, 280
Gui Youguang, 295
Guizhou, 229–231, 233
Gunther, John, 349
Guo Moruo, 262
Guomindang. *See* Nationalist Government

Hall, J.E.D., 197, 331
Han Dezhang, 168
Handicrafts. *See* Rural industry
"Harris Lecture," 99, 301, 362
Harris, Marvin, 299
Harvard University, 107, 108, 115–116, 131, 192
Hawthorne (Western Electric) studies, 132, 343, 344
Hayes, C.J.H., 284
He Da, 300
He Ming, 319
He Zhiping, 319
Historical research, Fei's, 33–36, 152–153; on minorities, 233, 235–236. *See also* Written materials, Fei's distrust of
Hobhouse, L.T., 15, 31, 38, 41, 54
Hsu, Francis L.K. (Xu Langguang), 41, 103, 108, 301, 329
Hsu, Leonard (Xu Shilian), 28, 29
Hu Qiaomu, 279–280
Hu Qingjun, 103, 251, 283, 300
Hu Sheng, 310, 314, 319
Hu Shi, 303, 348
Hua shuo Hulunbei'er caoyuan (HHC), 231–232, 334
Hualan Yao shehui zuzhi (Guangxi-sheng Xiang-xian Dongnan-xiang) (HLY), 62, 65–68, 88, 90–91, 326
Huang Di, 327, 339–340
Huang Sha, 248, 261
Huang Wanlun, 316, 318, 319
Huang-quan yu shen-quan (HQ&SQ), 152–153, 160, 301, 304, 332
Hull, Cordell, 351
Hulumbuir Steppe, 231
Hundred Flowers period, 239–242, 258; Fei and minorities research, 233–238; Fei and intellectuals, 242–249, 266–267; Fei and sociology, 249–254, 283; Fei and Kaixiangong, 254–257, 270–272

Ichiki Ryō, 327
Imperialism. *See* Anthropology: and imperialism; Foreign economic impact on China
Individual and society, 43, 46, 49, 50–51, 53, 146–147, 200–201; individualism of Chinese intellectuals criticized, 219–220. *See also* Social belonging, importance of, to Fei
Industry, urban, 344; prospects of, for China, 115, 164; and Chinese rural habits, 129–131; problems of, in West, 121, 131–135
Inflation, 99, 113, 142, 180, 182, 285
Inheritance, 78, 82
Institute of Nationalities Studies (Ethnology), 282, 283
Institute of Pacific Relations (IPR), 106–108, 193, 304
Institute of Sociology, 283
Intellectuals: character of, 160, 218–220, 352–353; needed for rural reform, 170, 172, 304–305; and the Nationalist Government, 177–178; and the Communists (1940s), 204–205; in China in 1950s, 217, 237–238; Fei and (1957), 244–246, 266–268, 274. *See also* Gentry
International relations, Fei's articles on, 125–129, 196–197, 218
Internationalism. *See* Patriotism and cosmopolitanism, Fei's
"Interview with Chinese Anthropologists," 278, 365
Italy, 127

Index

Japan, 127, 128, 343-344, 347, 350; Fei's visit to, 280, 282
Jefferson, Thomas, 121
Jia Yuanyi, 327
Jiang Qingxiang, 304, 310, 350-351
"Jiang-cun tongxun" *(JCTX)*, 68, 73, 89, 326
Jin ping mei, 285
Jin Yuelin, 109, 226
Jiu renwu de gaizao, 334
"Jizu chaoshan ji" *(JCS),* 99, 328
Journey to the West (Xiyouji), 19
Juvenile delinquency, 283

Kaixiangong, 68-79, 83-93, 161-163, 254-259, 264-265, 270-272, 359-360
Kaneko Mitsuru, 316
Kawa nationality, 356
Kinship terms, 33, 35
Korea, 356
Kroeber, Alfred L., 15
Kuige. *See* Research Station, Fei's, Yunnan
Kulp, D.H., 27, 93, 297, 303
Kunming, Yunnan, 79-80, 97-100, 138-140; factories, 130-131; political atmosphere in 1945-1946, 176-178, 184-191, 204
Kuomintang (KMT). *See* Nationalist Government

Laborers: Yunnan, 95-96, 99; rural, 162
Land tenure, 161-162; Yunnan, 58, 81-82, 84; Kaixiangong, 74, 83, 85
Landlords, 74, 77, 96, 159, 161-163, 202-203, 264-265
Lao She, 106
Lao-zi, 16, 52
Laski, Sir Harold, 42, 195, 203
Latent functions, 76
Le Play, Pierre, 133, 201
Leong, Y.K., 41
Levy, Marion, 300
Li Anzhe, 16, 283
Li Chengxi, 319
Li Da, 260, 303, 318, 319
Li Futong, 318
Li Gongpu, 189
Li Ji, 16

Li Jinghan, 27, 58, 250-254, 261, 283
Li Youyi (Li Yu-i), 80, 102, 283, 301, 328
Li Zonghuang, 187
Lianda (Xinan Lianhe Daxue), 97, 139, 177, 184-187, 190. 307, 344
Liang Shuming, 16, 36, 60, 150, 199
Liao Taichu, 338-339
Liberation, 214-216
Liberty, 200-201
Lieu, D.K. (Liu Dajun), 27
Lin Yaohua, 14, 59, 109, 235, 238, 264-265, 283, 317-318, 357, 365
Lin Yutang, 139
Lineages (clans), 74, 82, 154
Linton, Ralph, 107, 108
Liu Rongqu, 314, 315
Liu Xiaoxiao, 320
Liu, James T.C., 350
Lolo nationality, 230
London School of Economics, 40-42, 135, 180, 193, 195, 363
Long Yun, 177-178
Lowie, Robert H., 15
"Lu-bian tianxia" *(LBTX),* 125-129, 142, 333
Lu-cun (Yunnan village), 80, 88, 91, 92, 95-96. 118, 147, 162-163, 164, 171, 362
Lu-cun nongtian (LCNT), 80-84, 88-89, 107, 311, 328
Lü Zhenyu, 317
Luce, Clare Booth, 114
Luo Changpei, 226
Luo Longji, 183, 248, 258-260, 266-268
Lynd, Robert and Helen, 93
"L.S.E. Speech," 135, 363
L.S.E. *See* London School of Economics

Machine Age. See China Enters the Machine Age
Maine, Sir Henry, 15, 144
Malinowski, Bronislaw, 15, 23, 35, 40-46, 47, 49, 53, 55, 57, 75, 78, 87, 88, 91, 96, 144, 149-150, 193, 265, 284, 285, 327, 339, 340, 346, 361
Malone, C.B., 27
Malthus, Thomas, 51
Manchuria, 344

Mannheim, Karl, 42, 340
Mao Zedong, and Fei, 214, 273-274, 321
Marriage and the family, 35, 47-51, 99; Zhou dynasty, 33; *qinying,* 33-35; cross-cousin marriage, 35, 75; *tongyangxi,* 51, 326; Yaos, 65-66; Chinese peasant, 74-76, 148-149, 348; Chinese and Western compared, 147-149; current sociological investigations of, 283
Marshall Plan, 125-127, 347-348
Marshall, General George, 188
Martin, Kingsley, 236
Marxism, Fei's attitude to, 26, 38, 43, 54, 57, 88, 209, 310, 311; Marxist analysis of minorities social history, 234-235
May Seventh Cadre School, 278
Mayo, Dorothea, 107, 110, 131, 329
Mayo, Elton, 107, 110, 131-133, 329
McGough, James P., 318, 335
McKenzie, R.D., 296
Mead, Margaret, 124, 143, 331-332
Meiguoren de xingge (MGRXG), 123-135, 149, 331-332
Meng Yin (wife), 98, 192, 286
Miao nationality, 230-231
Miao Yuntai, 101, 108
Military: soldiers, 39-40; weapons, 342, 344; psychological war, 342
Min Ganghou, 314, 317
Minority nationalities, 60, 62, 228-229, 286; Guangxi Yaos (1930s), 63-66, 365-366; Guizhou ethnic groups (1950), 229-231; Mongols (1954), 230-232; relations with Han majority, 66, 230-233; social history research, 233-236, 277, 279, 357, 358; art forms, 232, 355, 356; Fei's work with, criticized, 266
Minzhu zhoukan, 184, 188-189
Minzhu, xianfa, renquan (MX, XF, RQ), 198-200, 242, 310, 330-331
Mirsky, Jonathan, 320
Moneylenders. *See* Credit, rural
Mongolian nomads, 231-232
Moon, P.T., 284
Morgan, L.H., 15, 35, 47, 234
Muramatsu Yūji, 289

Nation, 121, 125, 127

National People's Congress, 235, 242-243, 248, 260-262, 267, 277, 280, 357
Nationalism. *See* Patriotism and cosmopolitanism, Fei's
Nationalist (Guomindang) Government, Fei's criticism of: rural policies, 62-63, 96-97, 305; population policy, 163-164; inflation, corruption, and oppression, 113-114, 180-182, 188, 198; Civil War, 184, 188; American support of, 123, 128-129
Nationalist (Guomindang) Government, Fei's relations with, 108, 163, 180-182, 184-193
Nationalities Affairs Commission, 229
Nationalities Research Society, 280
Neidi nongcun (NDNC), 82-83, 92-93, 98, 161-166, 168, 170, 305
New Republic, 121
New Statesman, 125
New York Times, 141

Objectivity in social research, 59, 88
Office of War Information (OWI), 109, 111
Ogburn, W.F., 30, 31, 38, 51-52, 61, 107, 325
"Old Friends and a New Understanding," 222, 237-238, 365
Oldfield, W.H., 296

Pan Dakui, 185
Pan Guangdan (Quentin Pan), 15, 16, 27, 34, 37, 153, 155, 183-184, 188-190, 192, 198, 228, 238, 246, 251, 253, 262, 277, 304, 317, 330, 345, 348, 363
Pang Xinmin, 296
Park, Robert E., xiii, 15, 23, 27, 30, 31-33, 35-36, 46, 52, 93, 106, 144, 336-337
Parsons, Talcott, 107
Patriotism and cosmopolitanism, Fei's, 8-9, 13, 14, 20-21, 110-112, 196-197, 210
Payne, Robert, 97, 178, 190, 307
Peaceful revolution, Fei's hopes for, 159, 194, 199, 203-204

Peasant Life in China, 73-79, 86, 88-89, 91, 95-96, 254, 264, 270-272, 277, 290, 298, 327
"Peasantry and Gentry," ("Peasantry"), 152, 304, 362-363
Peking Congress of Representatives of Various Circles (1949), 217, 243, 354
Peking University, 11, 26, 248
Picul, size of Fei's, 298-299
Poland and Hungary, 1956 events in, 246, 267
Population and birth limitation, 48, 51, 65, 75, 163, 283, 295, 359
Potter, Jack, 299
Press: in the U.S., 128-129, 345; freedom of, 198, 200; Fei's 1940s use of, 39-42, 181, 184; Fei's 1957 use of, 247-248, 259, 274
Progress. *See* Social change

Qi Yanming, 314, 319, 321
Qian Duansheng, 185, 226
Qian Jiaju, 315
Qian Weichang, 259, 265
Qian Zhongshu, 10
Qiao Qiming, 27
Qinghua University, 37-40, 139, 192, 209, 221, 223-225, 228, 248, 259
Quantitative data, Fei's use of, 31, 36, 85-87
Queike. *See* Research Station, Fei's, Yunnan

Race. *See* Anthropometrics
Radcliffe-Brown, A.R., 15, 41, 94
Rawski, Evelyn, 69
Redfield, Margaret Park, 106, 110, 129, 152, 193, 210, 215, 304, 333, 362
Redfield, Robert, 91, 93, 106-108, 129, 144, 210, 303, 333
Reformism, social, 30-31, 55-56, 69-70, 96-97, 203-204
"Relationship System," 35, 361
Religion, 17, 20, 122, 337
Ren Guorong, 296
Renging yu bangjiao (RQ&BJ), 113-119, 181-182, 328
Renmin ribao, 282
Renxing he jiqi (RX&JQ), 132-135, 160, 164, 283, 330, 349

Research Station, Fei's, Yunnan ("Kuige"), 80, 92, 97-103, 106, 108, 129-130, 138, 193, 283, 302
Reuter, E.B., 339
"Review of Zhao," 206-207
Richards, Audrey I., 41
Rightist label, Fei's, 277, 282, 286
Rivers, W.R.H., 15
Robinson, Joan, 236
Rockefeller Foundation, 80, 108, 111
Romantic love, 148-149
Roosevelt, Eliot, 348
Roosevelt, Franklin D., 125, 194
Roser, Harold C., Jr., 190-191
Routledge and Kegan Paul, 254, 277, 365
Rural economy (1940s), 160-161, 305
Rural industry: in Kaixiangong, 71-74; in Yunnan, 80, 84; decline of, 77-78, 84, 92; sources of Fei's ideas on, 93; peasant economic need for, 163; Fei's proposals for reviving, 166-173, 351, 363, 364; and England, 196; political argument for, 202; criticisms of Fei's views on, 171, 208, 221-222, 237, 265; in post-1949 China, 172; in Kaixiangong in 1957, 255-257, 271
Rural reconstruction movement, 36-37, 70, 92, 206, 353

Salter, Leonard A., Jr., 107
Sayce, R.U., 338
Schram, Louis, 61, 63, 338
Seligman, C.G., 284
Senba Yasuo, 328
Sericulture, 68-74, 92, 250, 255, 265, 363-364
Shehui bianqian (SHBQ), 31, 51, 325
"Shehui yanjiu," 336, 340
Shehuixue jie, 28-29
Shehuixue kan, 26
Shenghuo dao-bao, 108, 140, 181, 342
Shenghuo Shudian, 310
Shengyu zhidu (SYZD), 15-16, 35, 47-51, 148, 331
Shi Guoheng (Shih Kuo-heng), 102-103, 107-108, 130-131, 301, 310, 329, 344
Shi Jing, 197, 331
Shidai pinglun, 140-141, 186, 188, 198, 331
Shiji pinglun, 141-142

Shioya Yasuo, 328
Shirokogoroff, S.M., 23, 34, 37-39, 42, 46, 63-64, 79
Shuo-wen, 33
Smith, Adam, 144
Snow, Edgar, 206
Social belonging, importance of sense of, to Fei, 20, 133, 152, 195, 216, 350. *See also* Individual and society
Social change, 31, 35, 36, 45, 38-39, 44-45, 47, 51-53, 91-92, 151-152, 340
Social equilibrium and harmony, 38, 52, 54, 75-77, 150, 337
Social erosion, xv, 1, 157-158
Social investigation, Communist, 270, 276
Social mobility, 155
Social planning, need for, 151
Social relations, Chinese and Western, compared, 146-147
Social research, China's need for, 37, 40, 54-55, 72-73, 96-97, 234, 251-252, 283
Social roles (*mingfen*), 32-33, 46, 53, 337
Social surveys, Fei's distrust of, 58, 92, 94
Socialism: British, admired, 194-197; dangers of, for China, 169, 201-202. *See also* Cooperatives
Society for Applied Anthropology, 285
Sociology in China: traditional antecedants, 25, 32-33; early development, 23, 25-28, 36, 57; at Yanjing, 28-30; in 1930s and 1940s, 94, 269, 348-349; Fei's hopes for after 1949, 210-211, 227; early 1950s elimination of, 226-228, 252, 265; 1957 revival of, 249-254, 268, 358, 359; Communist critique of, 268-269; political vulnerability of, 275, 281; 1979 revival, 280, 282-283, 286; in universities, 283
Sociology Work Committee, 253
Sombart, Werner, 130
"Some Social Problems of Free China" (Harris Lecture), 99, 297, 362
Soochow University. *See* Suzhou University
Sorokim, Pitirim, 107
Southwest Associated University. *See* Lianda
Spectator, 125
Spencer, Herbert, 31, 38, 46, 54, 268

Spengler, Oswald, 118, 144
Story of the Stone (Dream of the Red Chamber), 16, 340
Stuart, John Leighton, 11, 61
Students, Fei's, 92, 94, 101-103, 108, 248, 251, 283
Su Kejia, 247
Su Xuelin, 10
Sun Benwen, 253
Sun Dingguo, 316-319
Sun Yat-sen, 77
Survivals, 35, 44, 53
Suzhou, 6-9, 18, 119, 154, 192
Suzhou (Soochow) University (Dongwu Daxue), 7-10, 182
"Szechuan," 280

Tang Dingyu, 302
Tao Delin, 319
Tao Menghe (L.K. Tao), 27, 41, 106, 253
Tao Yunkui, 264, 343
Tawney, R.H., 42, 83, 92, 118, 130
Taylor, George, 107, 109
Taylor, J.B., 27, 305
Technical knowledge: peasant, 150; gentry, 160; for rural industry, 168-170
Theory, and fieldwork, 90
Thought reform, 218-223, 259; Fei's own, 222-223, 237
Three Types of Rural Economy in Yunnan (3 Types), 102, 301, 328
Tian Rukang (T'ien Ju-k'ang), 102, 130-131, 193, 283, 301, 329
Time, 141
Tongli-zhen, 2-3
Tongyangxi, 51, 326
Tönnies, Ferdinand, 143
"Toward a People's Anthropology," 285, 366
Traditional Chinese culture, Fei's attitude to, 16-17, 20, 25, 32-35, 52-54, 115, 119, 143, 150, 347. *See also* Confucianism
Truman, Harry, 126, 345, 352
Tsinghua University. *See* Qinghua University
Tsu, Y.Y. (Zhu Youyu), 26
TVA, 123, 158
Tylor, Edward, 35

Index

United States: educational influences on China, 11-12, 25-28; Fei's visit to (1943-1944), 106-119, 180-181; Fei's relations with Americans, 107-112, 129, 190-191, 265; Fei's 1979 visit to, 280, 282, 284, 361; Fei's 1980, 1981 visits to, 282. *See also* Financial sources, Fei's

United States, Fei's view of American: religion, 20, 121-122, 285; wartime conditions, 133-115; women, 114, 148, 285; culture, 117-118, 120, 124, 284-285; politics, 121-125, 128-129, 194, 196, 198-200, 216-217, 285, 354; factories and unions, 121, 124, 131; race relations, 122, 124, 285; support for Nationalists, 123, 128-129, 185, 188; foreign policy, 125-129, 196, 218, 343-355; press, 126, 128-129, 345; travel and communications, 284; social science, 285, 286

Universities, post-1949 reform of, 223-225, 265, 355

U.S. Consulate General, Kunming, 190-192

U.S. State Department, 106, 107, 109, 111, 304

U.S.S.R., 188; Fei's remarks on (1940s), 125-126, 128, 134, 151-152, 194, 345, 349, 352, 353, 355; Fei's 1950s comments on, 218, 248

Village leaders, 77-78, 146, 156-157; Kaixiangong, 87-88

Village studies. *See* Community studies

Villages: types of, 90; connections with the outside, 89-90

Waley, Arthur, 193
Wallace, Henry, 128-129, 350
Wan Dianwu, 304, 310
Wang Deqian, 295
Wang Ganyu, 252
Wang Jiyu, 7, 346
Wang Jizhao, 7
Wang Kang, 319
Wang Peizheng, 34
Wang Tonghui (wife), 61-68, 98, 264, 325-326, 338-339
Wang Wuke, 80

Wang, Y.C., xv-xvi
Wayland, J.W., 284
Webb, Sidney and Beatrice, 24, 30-31, 38, 203, 337, 349
Weber, Max, 130
Wedemeyer, A.C., General, 347
"Wei diaocha yanjiu Gui-sheng tezhong buzu renzhong" *(GTBR)*, 62-66, 325-326
Wells, H.G., 284
Wen hui bao, 244, 248, 250, 284
Wen Yiduo, 188-191, 345
Wenhua lun (WHL), 41, 44, 327, 339
West Lake, 242
Westermarck, Edvard, 15
Western intellectual influences on Fei, 14-16, 24
Westernization for China, Fei's attitude to, 54, 115-116, 118, 134-135, 199-200, 223, 363
Whitehead, T. North, 15, 107, 131-132
Wilkinson, J.R., 4
Wittfogel, Karl, 108, 237-238, 365
Wo zhe-yi nian (WZYN), 216-223, 334
Wo-de sixiang shi zenyang zhuanbian-guolai-de, 334
Women, 82, 110, 114, 148
Written materials, Fei's distrust of, 35-36, 57, 92-94, 153
Wu Han, 188, 207, 304, 332, 343, 345
Wu Jiang, 316
Wu Jingchao, 47, 78, 115, 200-201, 250, 251, 253, 261, 297, 305, 349
Wu Qiyuan, 185
Wu Wenhui, 328
Wu Wenzao, 16, 29-31, 34, 36, 40-41, 59, 61, 67, 80, 100, 228, 238, 251, 253, 277, 283, 296, 365
Wu Xun zhuan, 355-356
Wujiang (Jiangsu province), 2-4, 5, 6. *See also* Kaixiangong
Wuxing, Zhejiang, 362

Xia Kangnong, 260, 317
Xia Yulong, 319
Xiangtu chongjian (XTCJ), 93, 135, 152-161, 163, 166-169, 199-200, 202-203, 208, 211, 264-265, 304, 317, 334
Xiangtu Zhongguo (XTZG), 118, 141, 142-152, 332

Xiao Di, 315
Xie Wanying (Bing Xin), 16, 29, 260
Xin guancha, 244, 247-248, 254, 261
Xin jianshe, 215, 251
Xiongdi minzu zai Guizhou (XDMZ), 230-231, 334
Xu Deheng, 352
Xu Jiarui, 319
Xu Jiming, 305

Yan Fu, 25
Yan Xinzhe, 283
Yan Yangchu (James Yen), 60, 163, 192, 353
Yang Dongchun, 317
Yang Dunyi (grandfather), 2-3, 7
Yang Jikang (Jiang), 10
Yang Jiwei, 80
Yang Kaidao, 29
Yang Niulan (mother), 4, 7
Yang Tianji (cousin), 3
Yang Xiren (cousin), 3
Yang, C.K. (Yang Qingkun), 13-14, 29, 59, 109
Yanjing (Yenching) University, 10-14, 23, 28-32, 41, 61, 80, 111
Yanjing-Yunnan Station for Sociological Research. *See* Research Station, Fei's, Yunnan
Yao nationality, 63-66, 92, 95, 280, 283
Yen, James (Yan Yangchu), 60, 163, 192, 353
Yi nationality, 230
Yi-cun, 84, 171
Yi-shi bao, 89, 336
Yin Haiguang, 308
Yu Shengchun, 313-315, 318
Yu-cun, 84
Yuan Fang, 103, 251, 283, 330

Yunnan, 79-90; Fei's 1956-1957 trip to, 235-236, 267, 358
Yunnan University, 80, 97, 100, 106, 138-140, 190, 264
Yunnan-sheng nongcun diaocha, 58

Zaisheng, 62, 182
Zenyang gaizao, 334
Zhang Bojun, 258-260, 266-268
Zhang Dongsun, 199, 214, 352
Zhang Junmai (Carsun Chang), 43, 62, 182
Zhang Luoqun, 283, 330
Zhang Siqian, 318
Zhang Xiruo, 177, 190
Zhang Yuanji, 354
Zhang Zhidong, 69
Zhang Zhongjiong, 80
Zhang Ziyi (Zhiyi) (Chang Chih-i, Tse-i Chang), 80, 84, 102, 108, 167, 251, 283, 301, 328, 330
Zhao Chaogou, 363
Zhao Chengxin, 253
Zhao Haosheng (Howard Chao), 360
Zhao Weibang, 318, 319
Zheng Bijiang, 70
Zheng Chaoliang, 351
Zheng Dekun, 296
Zhenhua Girls' School, 7, 192
Zhong jian, 141
Zhou dynasty, 33
Zhou Baoshan, 87, 264
Zhou Enlai, 1956 speech on intellectuals, 239-240, 244-245, 249, 267
Zhou Shulian, 318, 319
Zhu Youyu (Y.Y. Tsu), 26
Zhuang nationality (Guangxi), 223
Ziyou luntan, 140, 184
Zou Jingheng, 292

Harvard East Asian Monographs

1. Liang Fang-chung, *The Single-Whip Method of Taxation in China*
2. Harold C. Hinton, *The Grain Tribute System of China, 1845–1911*
3. Ellsworth C. Carlson, *The Kaiping Mines, 1877–1912*
4. Chao Kuo-chün, *Agrarian Policies of Mainland China: A Documentary Study, 1949–1956*
5. Edgar Snow, *Random Notes on Red China, 1936–1945*
6. Edwin George Beal, Jr., *The Origin of Likin, 1835–1864*
7. Chao Kuo-chün, *Economic Planning and Organization in Mainland China: A Documentary Study, 1949–1957*
8. John K. Fairbank, *Ch'ing Documents: An Introductory Syllabus*
9. Helen Yin and Yi-chang Yin, *Economic Statistics of Mainland China, 1949–1957*
10. Wolfgang Franke, *The Reform and Abolition of the Traditional Chinese Examination System*
11. Albert Feuerwerker and S. Cheng, *Chinese Communist Studies of Modern Chinese History*
12. C. John Stanley, *Late Ch'ing Finance: Hu Kuang-yung as an Innovator*
13. S. M. Meng, *The Tsungli Yamen: Its Organization and Functions*
14. Ssu-yü Teng, *Historiography of the Taiping Rebellion*
15. Chun-Jo Liu, *Controversies in Modern Chinese Intellectual History: An Analytic Bibliography of Periodical Articles, Mainly of the May Fourth and Post-May Fourth Era*
16. Edward J. M. Rhoads, *The Chinese Red Army, 1927–1963: An Annotated Bibliography*
17. Andrew J. Nathan, *A History of the China International Famine Relief Commission*
18. Frank H. H. King (ed.) and Prescott Clarke, *A Research Guide to China-Coast Newspapers, 1822–1911*
19. Ellis Joffe, *Party and Army: Professionalism and Political Control in the Chinese Officer Corps, 1949–1964*
20. Toshio G. Tsukahira, *Feudal Control in Tokugawa Japan: The Sankin Kōtai System*

21. Kwang-Ching Liu, ed., *American Missionaries in China: Papers from Harvard Seminars*
22. George Moseley, *A Sino-Soviet Cultural Frontier: The Ili Kazakh Autonomous Chou*
23. Carl F. Nathan, *Plague Prevention and Politics in Manchuria, 1910–1931*
24. Adrian Arthur Bennett, *John Fryer: The Introduction of Western Science and Technology into Nineteenth-Century China*
25. Donald J. Friedman, *The Road from Isolation: The Campaign of the American Committee for Non-Participation in Japanese Aggression, 1938–1941*
26. Edward Le Fevour, *Western Enterprise in Late Ch'ing China: A Selective Survey of Jardine, Matheson and Company's Operations, 1842–1895*
27. Charles Neuhauser, *Third World Politics: China and the Afro-Asian People's Solidarity Organization, 1957–1967*
28. Kungtu C. Sun, assisted by Ralph W. Huenemann, *The Economic Development of Manchuria in the First Half of the Twentieth Century*
29. Shahid Javed Burki, *A Study of Chinese Communes, 1965*
30. John Carter Vincent, *The Extraterritorial System in China: Final Phase*
31. Madeleine Chi, *China Diplomacy, 1914–1918*
32. Clifton Jackson Phillips, *Protestant America and the Pagan World: The First Half Century of the American Board of Commissioners for Foreign Missions, 1810–1860*
33. James Pusey, *Wu Han: Attacking the Present through the Past*
34. Ying-wan Cheng, *Postal Communication in China and Its Modernization, 1860–1896*
35. Tuvia Blumenthal, *Saving in Postwar Japan*
36. Peter Frost, *The Bakumatsu Currency Crisis*
37. Stephen C. Lockwood, *Augustine Heard and Company, 1858–1862*
38. Robert R. Campbell, *James Duncan Campbell: A Memoir by His Son*
39. Jerome Alan Cohen, ed., *The Dynamics of China's Foreign Relations*
40. V. V. Vishnyakova-Akimova, *Two Years in Revolutionary China, 1925–1927*, tr. Steven I. Levine
41. Meron Medzini, *French Policy in Japan during the Closing Years of the Tokugawa Regime*
42. *The Cultural Revolution in the Provinces*
43. Sidney A. Forsythe, *An American Missionary Community in China, 1895–1905*
44. Benjamin I. Schwartz, ed., *Reflections on the May Fourth Movement: A Symposium*
45. Ching Young Choe, *The Rule of the Taewŏn'gun, 1864–1873: Restoration in Yi Korea*

46. W. P. J. Hall, *A Bibliographical Guide to Japanese Research on the Chinese Economy, 1958–1970*
47. Jack J. Gerson, *Horatio Nelson Lay and Sino-British Relations, 1854–1864*
48. Paul Richard Bohr, *Famine and the Missionary: Timothy Richard as Relief Administrator and Advocate of National Reform*
49. Endymion Wilkinson, *The History of Imperial China: A Research Guide*
50. Britten Dean, *China and Great Britain: The Diplomacy of Commerical Relations, 1860–1864*
51. Ellsworth C. Carlson, *The Foochow Missionaries, 1847–1880*
52. Yeh-chien Wang, *An Estimate of the Land-Tax Collection in China, 1753 and 1908*
53. Richard M. Pfeffer, *Understanding Business Contracts in China, 1949–1963*
54. Han-sheng Chuan and Richard Kraus, *Mid-Ch'ing Rice Markets and Trade, An Essay in Price History*
55. Ranbir Vohra, *Lao She and the Chinese Revolution*
56. Liang-lin Hsiao, *China's Foreign Trade Statistics, 1864–1949*
57. Lee-hsia Hsu Ting, *Government Control of the Press in Modern China, 1900–1949*
58. Edward W. Wagner, *The Literati Purges: Political Conflict in Early Yi Korea*
59. Joungwon A. Kim, *Divided Korea: The Politics of Development, 1945–1972*
60. Noriko Kamachi, John K. Fairbank, and Chūzō Ichiko, *Japanese Studies of Modern China Since 1953: A Bibliographical Guide to Historical and Social-Science Research on the Nineteenth and Twentieth Centuries, Supplementary Volume for 1953–1969*
61. Donald A. Gibbs and Yun-chen Li, *A Bibliography of Studies and Translations of Modern Chinese Literature, 1918–1942*
62. Robert H. Silin, *Leadership and Values: The Organization of Large-Scale Taiwanese Enterprises*
63. David Pong, *A Critical Guide to the Kwangtung Provincial Archives Deposited at the Public Record Office of London*
64. Fred W. Drake, *China Charts the World: Hsu Chi-yü and His Geography of 1848*
65. William A. Brown and Urgunge Onon, translators and annotators, *History of the Mongolian People's Republic*
66. Edward L. Farmer, *Early Ming Government: The Evolution of Dual Capitals*
67. Ralph C. Croizier, *Koxinga and Chinese Nationalism: History, Myth, and the Hero*
68. William J. Tyler, tr., *The Psychological World of Natsumi Sōseki*, by Doi Takeo

69. Eric Widmer, *The Russian Ecclesiastical Mission in Peking during the Eighteenth Century*
70. Charlton M. Lewis, *Prologue to the Chinese Revolution: The Transformation of Ideas and Institutions in Hunan Province, 1891-1907*
71. Preston Torbert, *The Ch'ing Imperial Household Department: A Study of its Organization and Principal Functions, 1662-1796*
72. Paul A. Cohen and John E. Schrecker, eds., *Reform in Nineteenth-Century China*
73. Jon Sigurdson, *Rural Industrialization in China*
74. Kang Chao, *The Development of Cotton Textile Production in China*
75. Valentin Rabe, *The Home Base of American China Missions, 1880-1920*
76. Sarasin Viraphol, *Tribute and Profit: Sino-Siamese Trade, 1652-1853*
77. Ch'i-ch'ing Hsiao, *The Military Establishment of the Yuan Dynasty*
78. Meishi Tsai, *Contemporary Chinese Novels and Short Stories, 1949-1974: An Annotated Bibliography*
79. Wellington K. K. Chan, *Merchants, Mandarins, and Modern Enterprise in Late Ch'ing China*
80. Endymion Wilkinson, *Landlord and Labor in Late Imperial China: Case Studies from Shandong by Jing Su and Luo Lun*
81. Barry Keenan, *The Dewey Experiment in China: Educational Reform and Political Power in the Early Republic*
82. George A. Hayden, *Crime and Punishment in Medieval Chinese Drama: Three Judge Pao Plays*
83. Sang-Chul Suh, *Growth and Structural Changes in the Korean Economy, 1910-1940*
84. J. W. Dower, *Empire and Aftermath: Yoshida Shigeru and the Japanese Experience, 1878-1954*
85. Martin Collcutt, *Five Mountains: The Rinzai Zen Monastic Institution in Medieval Japan*

STUDIES IN THE MODERNIZATION OF THE REPUBLIC OF KOREA: 1945-1975

86. Kwang Suk Kim and Michael Roemer, *Growth and Structural Transformation*
87. Anne O. Krueger, *The Developmental Role of the Foreign Sector and Aid*
88. Edwin S. Mills and Byung-Nak Song, *Urbanization and Urban Problems*
89. Sung Hwan Ban, Pal Yong Moon, and Dwight H. Perkins, *Rural Development*

90. Noel F. McGinn, Donald R. Snodgrass, Yung Bong Kim, Shin-Bok Kim, and Quee-Young Kim, *Education and Development in Korea*
91. Leroy P. Jones and Il SaKong, *Government, Business, and Entrepreneurship in Economic Development: The Korean Case*
92. Edward S. Mason, Mahn Je Kim, Dwight H. Perkins, Kwang Suk Kim, David C. Cole et al., *The Economic and Social Modernization of the Republic of Korea*
93. Robert Repetto, Tai Hwan Kwon, Son-Ung Kim, Dae Young Kim, John E. Sloboda, and Peter J. Donaldson, *Economic Development, Population Policy, and Demographic Transition in the Republic of Korea*
94. Parks M. Coble, *The Shanghai Capitalists and the Nationalist Government, 1927-1937*
95. Noriko Kamachi, *Reform in China: Huang Tsun-hsien and the Japanese Model*
96. Richard Wich, *Sino-Soviet Crisis Politics: A Study of Political Change and Communication*
97. Lillian M. Li, *China's Silk Trade: Traditional Industry in the Modern World, 1842-1937*
98. R. David Arkush, *Fei Xiaotong and Sociology in Revolutionary China*
99. Kenneth Alan Grossberg, *Japan's Renaissance: The Politics of the Muromachi Bakufu*